Teacher Implementation Guide

W9-ANJ-023

MATH TRAILBLAZERS™
A Mathematical Journey Using Science and Language Arts

A TIMS® Curriculum from the
University of Illinois at Chicago

KENDALL/HUNT PUBLISHING COMPANY
4050 Westmark Drive   Dubuque, Iowa 52002

Teacher Implementation Guide

A TIMS® Curriculum from the
University of Illinois
at Chicago

MATH TRAILBLAZERS™
A Mathematical Journey Using Science and Language Arts

Dedication
This book is dedicated to the children and teachers who let us see the magic in their classrooms and to our families who wholeheartedly supported us while we searched for ways to make it happen. The TIMS Project

UIC The University of Illinois
at Chicago

This material is based on work supported by the National Science Foundation under grant No. MDR 9050226 and the University of Illinois at Chicago. Any opinions, findings, and conclusions or recommendations expressed in this publication are those of the authors and do not necessarily reflect the views of the granting agencies.

10 9 8 7 6 5 4 3 2

Teacher Implementation Guide

Acknowledgments

GRADE
5

TIMS Elementary Mathematics Curriculum Project

Director and Co-Principal Investigator
Philip Wagreich

Co-Principal Investigator
Howard Goldberg

Associate Director
Joan L. Bieler

TIMS Senior Curriculum Developers
Janet Simpson Beissinger   Astrida E. Cirulis
Marty Gartzman   Howard Goldberg
Carol Inzerillo   Andy Isaacs
Catherine Randall Kelso   Leona Peters
Philip Wagreich

TIMS Curriculum Developers
Janice C. Banasiak   Lynne Beauprez
Andy Carter   Lindy M. Chambers
Kathryn Chval   Diane R. Czerwinski
Jenny Knight   Sandy Niemiera
Janice Ozima   Polly Tangora
Paul Trafton

Research Consultant
Andy Isaacs

Mathematics Education Consultant
Paul Trafton

Editors
Jay Becker   Lynelle Morgenthaler

Designer/Production Coordinator
Sarah Nelson

Production Staff
Glenda L. Genio-Terrado   Mini Joseph
Sarah Nelson   Biruté Petrauskas

Illustrator
Kris Dresen

National Advisory Committee

- Carl Berger, Director, Instructional Technology, University of Michigan, Ann Arbor, Michigan
- Tom Berger, Professor of Mathematics Education, Colby College, Waterville, Maine
- Hugh Burkhardt, Project Director, Balanced Assessment for the Mathematics Curriculum, University of California, Berkeley and Shell Centre for Mathematical Education, University of Nottingham, England
- Donald Chambers, Director of Dissemination, National Center for Research in Mathematical Sciences Education, University of Wisconsin at Madison, Madison, Wisconsin
- Naomi Fisher, Co-Director, Mathematicians and Education Reform Network, University of Illinois at Chicago, Chicago, Illinois
- Glenda Lappan, Professor of Mathematics, Michigan State University, East Lansing, Michigan
- Mary Lindquist, Callaway Professor of Mathematics Education, Columbus College, Columbus, Georgia
- Eugene Maier, President, Math Learning Center, Portland, Oregon
- Lourdes Monteagudo, Director, Teachers' Academy for Mathematics and Science, Chicago, Illinois
- Elizabeth Phillips, Specialist in the Department of Mathematics, Michigan State University, East Lansing, Michigan
- Thomas Post, Professor of Mathematics Education, University of Minnesota, Minneapolis, Minnesota

Additional TIMS Elementary Mathematics Curriculum Project Staff

Research and Outreach Staff

Janet Simpson Beissinger	Birch Burghardt	Andy Carter
Astrida E. Cirulis	Barbara Crum	Marty Gartzman
Jerry Overmyer	Michelle Perry	Maria Varelas

Teacher Contributors

Jean Clement	Ann Watson Cohn	Catherine Hamilton
Donna Holt	Mary Pat Larocca	Beth Savage

Copyeditor

Anne Roby

Institute for Mathematics and Science Education Support Staff

David Browdy	Jocelyn Buchanan	Philomina Cox
Shanila Dada	Robert Denton	Rajiv Desai
Nadine Dombrowski	Delores Flores	Helen Gary
Lucy Gong	Byron S. Gudiel	Miriam Gutierrez
Judy Kim	Frannie Los Bañes	Cassandra Lucas
Alex Mak	Christie Manisto	Kim Meyer
Jerry Overmyer	Enrique Puente	Laura Ratcliffe
Monica Rodriguez	Leah Rosenstein	Ellen Rydell
Vishal Sheth	Dorothy Sholeen-Modrzyk	
Patty Stevenson	Ami Thaker	Greg Waddoups
Louise Wall	Marie Walz	Mikka Whiteaker

Video and Photographic Documentation

Joan L. Bieler	Henrique Cirne-Lima	Paul A. Wussow

Contributing Writers, Artists, and Consultants

Mary Lou Andacht	Steven Bloom	Elizabeth Cape
Pam Conrad	Barbara A. Frase	Julie Hall
Karen Harrington	Vida Ivancevic	Bob Kann
Betty Romanek	Carol Saller	Bonnie Saunders

Field Test Schools and Teachers

Hans Christian Andersen Elementary School, Chicago, Illinois
Principal: Marie Iska

Alicia Acevedo

Daniel Boone School, Chicago, Illinois
Principal: Paul Zavitkovsky

Sybil Bennin	Ruta Buntinas	Myung Chi
Susan Dietz	Norma Duarte	Paula Hyman
Sandra Kantz	Juliet Kasha	Mila Kell
Julia Kline	Barbara Mandel	Deanna Mendieta
Janice Ozima	Vlada Polin	Lizette Rhone
Dixie Rouleau	Mariah Seton	Cecilia Somma
Jenny Soro	Cheryl Strong	Margaret Therriault-Jenkins
Lauretta Williams	Constance Winschel-Cook	
Elina Yelishevich	Argentina Yousif	

John C. Burroughs School, Chicago, Illinois
Principal: Richard Morris

Paul Durkin	Michelle Sanborn

Drexel School, Cicero, Illinois
Principal: Cliff Pluister

Deborah Fantozzi	Jeanette Ibarra	Kristin Wilderman

Elmwood School, Elmwood Park, Illinois
Principal: Doug Lia

Joanne Hoffmann	Mary Anne Kirsch	Linda Norris
Marlene Ryan		

Gavin Central School, Ingleside, Illinois
Principal: Theresa Dunkin

Nannette Borzewski	Judith Dahl	Betty Denk
Carrie Frebault	Jennifer McCracken	Jodi Minsky
Peggy Owczarski	Pat Scully	Barbara Smejkal
Dawn Smith		

Hammerschmidt Elementary School, Lombard, Illinois
Principal: James Adams

Shelly Humphreys

Emma Stark Hampton Elementary School, Detroit, Michigan
Principal: Chrystal Tibbs

Margaret Erle	Janet Flessa	Therese Sadlier
Clare Whitaker	Michelle Williams	

Abraham Lincoln School, Oak Park, Illinois
Principal: Carol Dudzik

Sandra Adams	Marilyn Blenz	Nell Bloyd
Peggy Callahan	Susan Casagrande	Cheryl Cohen
Catherine Hamilton	James Harrington	Karen Heffner
Donna Holt	Paula Hughes	Frank LoCoco
Susan McNish	Miraflor Metropoulos	Joyce Moore
Karl Radnitzer	Jane Samuelson	Jarvia Thomas
Shirley Warner	Kathleen Wiedow	Lynne Zillman

James McCosh School, Chicago, Illinois
Principal: Barbara Eason-Watkins

Louise Dearman	Leah Fulton	Shelley Hefner
Inez Jacobson	Dorothy Turner	Jacquelyne White

John Mills School, Elmwood Park, Illinois
Principal: Patricia Duggan

Deanna Crum	Lisa Loffredo	Cathy McGovern
Bonnie Mize		

Mt. Hope Elementary School, Lansing, Michigan
Principal: Betty Nichols

Corin Bennett	Deidre Bennett	Sue Fillingham
Della Gregory	Geneva Martin	Deborah Muth
Sue Usiak	Dawn Vanzee	Terri Weinlander

Piedmont Elementary School, Charleston, West Virginia

Principal: Steve Knighton

Beth Brown	Brigid Haney	Catherine Hastings
Eva Jones	Louise Tabor	

Pilsen Community Academy, Chicago, Illinois
Principal: Ana Espinoza

Jennifer Chadwick	Judy Rappin	Juliet Rempa

William H. Ray School, Chicago, Illinois
Principal: Cydney Fields

Bill Salvato	Marie Schilling

St. Ambrose School, Chicago, Illinois
Principal: Sr. Dolores Lytle

Dorothy Rivers

James Shields School, Chicago, Illinois
Principal: Rita Gardner

Julie Cartwright	Iris Delgado	Bob Kaszynski
Wilhelmina McGee	Terry McInerney	Maranielly Vazquez

Spring Hill School, Roselle, Illinois
Principal: Sally Pryor

David R. Vilmin

Westwood Primary School, Phoenix, Arizona

Principal: Martha Braly

Denise Ahart	Denise Arnold	Shelley Carson
Merrillyn Curtis	Antoinette DiCarlo	Ginny Fields
Alphine Glenn	Nancy Herbert	Jane Hoyle
Nancy Hunt	Cecilia Kelly	Cindy Lauersdorf
Candace Manger	Diane Nonack	Kathie Pabst
Lori Perry	Denise Pizzi	Maureen Riordan
Anita Rothman	JoAnn Salem	Timothy Salem
Kathy Schaeffer	Ken Schofield	Sheri Starke
Susie Sweeney	Jamie Tinkelman	Jackie Williams
Nan Williams		

Edward H. White School, Chicago, Illinois

Principal: Yvonne Womack

Judy Hobson	Harrison Jackson	Kathleen Pidrak

Edith Wolford Elementary School, Colorado Springs, Colorado

Principal: Gary Langenhuizen

Sherrie Antes	Karen Combs	Jeremy Cramer
Carol Eames	Kelly Garnhart	

Foreword

MATH TRAILBLAZERS is the product of more than seven years of concerted effort by the TIMS (Teaching Integrated Mathematics and Science) Project team. It has its roots in the pioneering work of Howard Goldberg, who conceived the idea of a quantitative approach to elementary science in the mid-1970s. His vision and productivity have been an underlying current of creativity throughout this entire project.

Over the past 15 years, the TIMS Project has worked with children, teachers, and administrators to improve the quality of mathematics and science curriculum and instruction in the Chicago area and nationwide. In 1990, the TIMS Project was awarded a grant by the National Science Foundation to develop a new elementary mathematics curriculum to meet the needs of children who will be entering the world of work in the 21st century.

The primary goal of this curriculum has been to create an educational experience that results in children who enjoy mathematics, who are comfortable and flexible mathematical thinkers, and who see the connections between the mathematics they learn in school and the thinking they do in everyday life. One of our principal beliefs is that children can succeed in mathematics and that if more is expected of them, more will be achieved. This curriculum incorporates the best of traditional mathematics while widening the horizons of mathematical thinking.

We hope you will enjoy teaching this curriculum. The collective wisdom from the hundreds of pilot and field test teachers who have used TIMS materials over the five years of development has been a crucial component of this project. The dedication and insight we saw in our teacher-collaborators is something which constantly encouraged and inspired us. The extensive input we received from them significantly reshaped our view of the curriculum and is deeply embedded in this first edition.

Creating a kindergarten through fifth-grade curriculum is an enormous undertaking, considerably larger than we had ever imagined in 1990. I have been continually amazed by the dedication, selflessness, and talent of the project staff. The success of the project is due to their enormous efforts; they did what had to be done, often beyond the call of duty, because of their personal belief in our mission. In particular, I thank two staff members who have been with me from the beginning: Marty Gartzman for his creativity, vision, and ability to see the next step; and Joan Bieler for being the voice of reason, for doing all that was necessary to make it really happen, and for dealing with the human side of the project.

I would like to thank the National Science Foundation for having the vision to see that a catalyst was needed to ensure that mathematics education reform would really happen. In particular, Midge Cozzens, the Director of the NSF Division of Elementary, Secondary, and Informal Education, has been a strong advocate for all the NSF-funded comprehensive curriculum projects. We also are indebted to the support, understanding, and input of our program officers: Tom Berger, Joe Adney, Jim Sandefur, Eric Robinson, and Spud Bradley.

The work of the TIMS Project would have been impossible without the moral and financial support of the University of Illinois at Chicago. Chancellor (now

President) James Stukel, Interim Chancellor David Broski, Vice Chancellor for Research John Wanat, Deans Jay Levine and Sid Simpson, and Department Heads John Wood, Henri Gillet, and Uday Sukhatme have all been instrumental in supporting the project as well as the broader program of the UIC Institute for Mathematics and Science Education.

I would also like to thank our publisher, Kendall/Hunt Publishing Company, whose faith in our vision has been extraordinary. Their unusual approach to publishing is that one can be successful while publishing materials that shift the traditional teaching paradigm.

In a special way, I thank my wife Lorraine Owles and our son Alexander, whose love inspired me and whose support kept me going. Only an extraordinary woman like Lorraine could understand a husband who was physically present, but whose mind was preoccupied with ways to engage students in thinking about "using patterns to make predictions."

Philip Wagreich

Philip Wagreich
Director
Institute for Mathematics and Science Education

Teacher Implementation Guide

Table of Contents

GRADE 5

Introduction

The *Introduction* outlines the various sections of this document and explains how to get the most out of them.

A teacher and a student explore equivalent fractions.

Introduction

Part I | ## What Is the Teacher Implementation Guide?

The Teacher Implementation Guide (TIG) is the reference manual for MATH TRAILBLAZERS. The TIG, combined with the Unit Resource Guide (URG), provides teachers and schools with a comprehensive set of resources to assist in the implementation of the curriculum. The URG is the teacher's "working guide," providing information and instructions related to the planning and teaching of units and individual lessons—it is intended to be used on a day-to-day basis. The TIG supplements the URG by addressing larger issues related to the curriculum. Information in the TIG can be roughly categorized into three groups: general background about MATH TRAILBLAZERS; specific information about the program; and deep background about important math/science concepts. The TIG is a valuable resource for use in long-range planning regarding math instruction, curriculum, related implementation issues, and staff development.

Below are brief descriptions of sections found in the TIG:

- **Foundations of MATH TRAILBLAZERS**
  The underlying philosophy of the program is described.

- **Components and Features Guide**
  MATH TRAILBLAZERS is a multicomponent program. Grades 1–5 include three books for students (the Student Guide, Discovery Assignment Book, and Adventure Book) and two volumes for teachers (the TIG and the URG). The Components and Features Guide is a road map to help you understand the purposes of the various components and where to find key information. Examples of important features taken from actual student and teacher pages are illustrated.

- **Unit Summaries**
  Unit summaries include a narrative description of the content for each unit and a list of important math concepts covered in the individual units. This provides a snapshot view of the curriculum for your grade.

- **Connections with the NCTM *Standards***
  MATH TRAILBLAZERS was developed to reflect the goals and approaches outlined in the *Curriculum and Evaluation Standards* of the National Council of Teachers of Mathematics. The TIG includes detailed information, using text and tables, about how the program aligns with the *Standards.*

- **Scope and Sequence**
  The curriculum's scope and sequence is presented in the TIG. The Scope and Sequence is organized to correspond with the nine content standards of the NCTM *Standards,* providing additional detailed information about MATH TRAILBLAZERS' alignment with the *Standards.* Two scope and sequence charts—one for the unit lessons and one for the *Daily Practice and Problems*—are provided.

- **Summary of Approaches to Math Facts and Whole-Number Operations**
  The MATH TRAILBLAZERS program for presenting the math facts and whole-number operations is summarized in the TIG. Background information about our approach and expectations for grades are outlined.

- **DPP and HP Guide**

  An essential component of *Math Trailblazers* is a carefully designed sequence of short problems in grades 1–5, called the *Daily Practice and Problems* (DPP). In third grade, a component called *Daily Home Practice* (DHP) is introduced. This component provides additional practice with skills and concepts. In fourth and fifth grade it is called *Home Practice* (HP).

- **Assessment in *Math Trailblazers* (Assessment Guide)**

  Math Trailblazers includes a comprehensive program of student assessment. The philosophy and components of the assessment program are described in the TIG. Assessment materials from the curriculum are used to illustrate key ideas. Specific suggestions for implementing the assessment program are included.

- **TIMS Tutors: Background Information for Teachers**

  The TIG includes a series of 13 documents called *TIMS Tutors.* The tutors provide extensive information on a wide variety of topics in pedagogy, mathematics, and science. The tutors serve as a source of deep background information for teachers and others. Some tutors, such as the tutor on *Math Facts,* supply specific information needed by teachers to plan particular portions of the *Math Trailblazers* program. Other tutors, such as the tutor on mass, focus on math/science content. Still others, such as the tutor on portfolios, address pedagogical concerns.

- **Manipulatives List**

  A listing of the manipulatives required for program implementation is included in the TIG.

- **Literature List**

  Math Trailblazers incorporates the use of commercially available trade books in many lessons. A listing of these trade books is included in the TIG.

- **Games List**

  Games are often used in *Math Trailblazers* to engage students in practicing basic arithmetic and other math concepts. Once introduced, these games can be used throughout the year for ongoing practice. A complete listing of the games for your grade and a description of the games are provided.

- **Software List**

  Math Trailblazers does not *require* the use of computers. We do, instead, suggest the use of some software programs that could supplement the curriculum. A listing of these programs and some suggested uses for them are provided.

- **Suggestions for Working with Parents**

  When adopting a math program that is new and different, such as *Math Trailblazers,* it is important to keep parents informed and educated about the program. Some hints for working with parents regarding *Math Trailblazers* are outlined in the TIG. A brochure about the program, in English and Spanish, is provided.

Part II How to Use the Teacher Implementation Guide

Use of the TIG will differ depending upon your purpose. Suggestions for using the TIG for different purposes are described below.

If you are a teacher considering whether to use *MATH TRAILBLAZERS:*

The TIG provides much useful information for adoption committees or individual teachers who are considering *MATH TRAILBLAZERS.* General information about the program, such as the philosophy, alignment with the NCTM *Standards,* scope and sequence, the unit summaries, and plan for math facts and whole number operations will probably be most important for this group. The *Components and Features Guide* will help reviewers understand the purposes of the different student and teacher books. Other specific information, such as the *Assessment Guide,* may also be useful for potential users of the curriculum.

If you are a teacher who is about to use *MATH TRAILBLAZERS* for the first time:

There is too much information in the TIG and the Unit Resource Guide for any teacher to digest all at once. To make effective use of the TIG, it is best to select portions of the manual to examine at different points in the curriculum implementation. Prior to using *MATH TRAILBLAZERS,* it would be useful to glance at the Foundations section of the TIG in order to get a sense of our overall philosophy. However, you will probably want to spend more time reviewing the sections that provide specific information about using the curriculum. This information will help you get started and plan for the year.

You should carefully review the *Components and Features Guide* so that you see the big picture of the program's components and features. This information will eventually become "second nature" to you as you gain experience with the curriculum, but it will be helpful at first to at least see what is included in the program. We suggest that you review the *Unit Summaries* so that you get a feel for what is covered over the course of the year and can plan ahead. It will be easier to make instructional decisions at any given moment if you know what is planned for later lessons. The *Assessment in MATH TRAILBLAZERS* and the *DPP and HP Guide* are essential and should be read prior to beginning the curriculum. Among the *TIMS Tutors,* we suggest that you first review *Math Facts.* It outlines our philosophy and plan for introducing the math facts. The manipulatives and literature list are useful tools if you are ordering manipulatives or if you want to see what has been included in any manipulative kits your school has ordered. The section on working with parents will also be useful to read prior to using the curriculum. Use the rest of the TIG as the need arises. Review the descriptions of the TIG's contents given above and make a mental note of what is here. Then, keep the TIG handy for future reference.

If you are a teacher who is already using MATH TRAILBLAZERS:

During your first several years of using MATH TRAILBLAZERS, you will likely refer to the TIG on a regular and ongoing basis. You will find the TIMS Tutors par-

ticularly valuable in helping you better understand the content and approaches of key parts of the curriculum. There are numerous "pointers" in the Unit Resource Guide that refer you to individual tutors. The scope and sequence supplements the unit summaries in terms of providing detailed information about when specific concepts are covered. The *Games List* and *Software List* should be reviewed periodically to help you in lesson planning. If there is background information that you don't find in the Unit Resource Guides, there is a good chance you will find it in the TIG.

If you are a school administrator in a school that is using MATH TRAILBLAZERS:

Principals and other school administrators are likely, at some point, to be queried by parents or even the media about the school's math program. It is therefore useful to have some familiarity with the program's philosophy and at least a general view of the program's content. The *Foundations of MATH TRAILBLAZERS* section of the TIG is a good start for this. The sections that outline the curriculum's alignment with the NCTM *Standards* provide useful information about the national recommendations that underlie MATH TRAILBLAZERS. We also strongly recommend that administrators read the section on working with parents. Parental support is important for any program. The TIG section on working with parents provides suggestions and resources for communicating the goals of the curriculum to parents. Administrators may also want to review the section that outlines our approaches to teaching math facts and whole number operations; most potential parental concerns are likely to address that topic.

If you are planning staff development sessions about MATH TRAILBLAZERS:

Implementation of MATH TRAILBLAZERS will be much more effective if it is accompanied by a good staff development program. A week-long orientation to MATH TRAILBLAZERS is made available to schools through Kendall/Hunt Publishing Company. We recommend that schools supplement this with additional staff development, preferably to support teachers *at least* through the initial year of implementation. Several sections of the TIG—especially the *TIMS Tutors, Assessment in MATH TRAILBLAZERS, Foundations of MATH TRAILBLAZERS*, and the portions that outline the curriculum's alignment with the NCTM *Standards*—are ready-made to be used within the context of a staff development program. For specific suggestions about developing local staff development efforts related to MATH TRAILBLAZERS, contact the TIMS Project at (312) 996-2448.

Foundations of *MATH TRAILBLAZERS*™

The *Foundations of MATH TRAILBLAZERS* describes the philosophy behind *MATH TRAILBLAZERS* and discusses the curriculum's key features.

Students work together to solve problems.

Foundations of *MATH TRAILBLAZERS*™

MATH TRAILBLAZERS is an elementary mathematics curriculum for schools that want their math programs to reflect the goals and ideas of the National Council of Teachers of Mathematics *Standards.* With funding from the National Science Foundation and over six years of development and testing, the TIMS (Teaching Integrated Mathematics and Science) Project at the University of Illinois at Chicago has created a comprehensive program that embodies the *Standards.*

MATH TRAILBLAZERS is based on the belief that mathematics is best learned in real-world contexts that make sense to children; that all students deserve a richer and more challenging curriculum; and that a balanced and practical approach to mathematics learning is what students need and what teachers want.

Following are explanations of some important features of *MATH TRAILBLAZERS:*

- **Alignment with Reform Recommendations**
  Recognition of the inadequacies of our nation's mathematics and science education has led to numerous recommendations for reform.

  Three reports from the National Council of Teachers of Mathematics (NCTM)—the *Curriculum and Evaluation Standards for School Mathematics* (1989), the *Professional Standards for Teaching Mathematics* (1991), and the *Assessment Standards for School Mathematics* (1995)— express a broad-based consensus about how to reform mathematics education. These documents recommend that:

    - The mathematics curriculum should be conceptually oriented;

    - Students should be actively involved;

    - Instruction should stress thinking, reasoning, and applying;

    - Calculators and computers have appropriate uses beginning in the earliest grades;

    - A broad range of content needs to be included and assessed.

  Shortly after the publication of the NCTM *Standards,* the National Science Foundation (NSF) recognized that comprehensive reform curricula were essential if schools were to be expected to adopt the reform vision of mathematics teaching and learning reflected in the *Standards.* The NSF decided to support a handful of projects to develop such programs and selected the TIMS Project at the University of Illinois at Chicago as one of the participants. The result of more than six years of NSF-supported work is the *MATH TRAILBLAZERS* curriculum, which has been designed with the specific goal of attempting to assist you in creating a vibrant, *Standards*-based classroom.

  More specific connections between *MATH TRAILBLAZERS* and the NCTM *Standards* are discussed in *Scope and Sequence & the NCTM Standards* (Section 5).

- **High Expectations and Equity**
  Experience in schools has shown that children can handle more difficult mathematics and science than is often assumed. Accordingly, we introduce challenging content in every grade: computation, measurement, data collection, statistics, geometry, ratio, probability, graphing, simple algebra, estimation, mental arithmetic, and patterns and relationships.

  Contexts for this demanding content begin with students' lives. Lessons are grounded in everyday situations, so abstractions build on experience. By presenting mathematics in rich contexts, the curriculum helps students make connections between real situations, words, pictures, data, graphs, and symbols. The curriculum also validates students' current understandings while new understandings develop. Students can solve problems in ways they understand while being encouraged to connect those ways to more abstract and powerful methods.

- **Problem Solving**
  A fundamental principle of *MATH TRAILBLAZERS* is that mathematics is best learned through active involvement in solving real problems. Questions a student can answer immediately may be worthwhile exercises, but *problems,* by definition, are difficult.

  This emphasis on problem solving is probably best described by the NCTM *Standards,* which states, "Problem solving is not a distinct topic but a process that should permeate the entire program and provide the context in which concepts and skills can be learned." (NCTM, 1989, p. 23) Throughout the curriculum, students apply the mathematics they know and construct new mathematics as needed. Students' skills, procedures, and concepts emerge and develop as they solve complex problems.

- **Connections to Science and Language Arts**
  Real-world problems are naturally interdisciplinary, so that any problem-solving curriculum should integrate topics that are traditionally separated. Accordingly, we have integrated mathematics with many disciplines, especially science and language arts.

Connections to Science

MATH TRAILBLAZERS is a full mathematics program that incorporates many important scientific ideas.

Traditionally, school science has focused on the results of science. Students learn about plate tectonics, the atomic theory of matter, the solar system, the environment, and so on. Knowing basic facts of science is seen as part of being educated, today more than ever. However, the facts of science, important and interesting as they are, do not alone comprise a comprehensive and balanced science curriculum.

Science has two aspects: results and method. The results of scientific inquiry have enriched human life the world over. More marvelous than the results of science, however, is the method that has established those results.

Without the method, the results would never have been achieved. MATH TRAILBLAZERS aims to teach students the method of science through scientific investigation of everyday phenomena. During these investigations, students learn both mathematics and science.

The method scientists use is powerful, flexible, and quantitative. The TIMS Project has organized this method in a way that is simple enough for elementary school children to use. Students use the TIMS Laboratory Method in a rich variety of mathematical investigations. In these investigations, students develop and apply important mathematical skills and concepts in meaningful situations. Their understanding of fundamental scientific concepts is also enhanced through the use of quantitative tools.

Investigations begin with discussions of experimental situations, variables, and procedures. Then, students draw pictures in which they indicate the experimental procedures and identify key variables. Next, students gather data and organize it in data tables. Then, they graph their data. By analyzing their data or studying their graphs, students are able to see patterns in the data. These patterns show that there is a relationship between the variables. The relationship can be used to make predictions about future data. The last phase of the experiment is an in-depth analysis of the experimental results, structured as a series of exploratory questions. Some questions ask students to make predictions and then to verify them. Other questions probe students' understanding of underlying concepts and explore the role of controlled variables. As students advance through the curriculum, the questions progress from simple to complex, building eventually to problems that require proportional reasoning, multiple-step logic, and algebra.

The TIMS Laboratory Method initiates children into the authentic practice of science. Identifying variables, drawing pictures, measuring, organizing data in tables, graphing data, and looking for and using patterns are a major part of many scientists' work. This is a major goal of science: to discover and use relationships between variables—usually expressed in some mathematical form—in order to understand and make predictions about the world.

The science content in MATH TRAILBLAZERS focuses on a small set of simple variables that are fundamental to both math and science: length, area, volume, mass, and time. Understanding these basic variables is an essential step to achieving scientific understanding of more complex concepts. Measurement is presented in meaningful, experimental situations.

Emphasizing the scientific method and fundamental science concepts helps students develop an understanding of how scientists and mathematicians think. These habits of mind will be important in all aspects of life in the 21st century. See the TIMS Tutor: *The TIMS Laboratory Method* for more discussion of these ideas.

Connections to Language Arts

Reading, writing, and talking belong in mathematics class, not only because real mathematicians and scientists read, write, and talk mathematics and science constantly, but also because these activities help students learn. All three sets of NCTM *Standards* (1989, 1991, 1995) emphasize the importance of communication and discourse if students are to achieve at high levels.

In school mathematics, results should be accepted not merely because someone in authority says so, but rather because persuasive arguments can be made for them. A result and a reason are often easier to remember than the result alone. By discussing the mathematics they are doing, students increase their understanding of that mathematics. They also extend their ability to discuss mathematics and so to participate in a community of mathematicians. Talking and writing about mathematics, accordingly, are part of every lesson. Journal and discussion prompts are standard features in the teacher's guide for each lesson.

Reading is also built into this curriculum. Many lessons, especially in the primary grades, use trade books to launch or extend mathematical investigations. The curriculum also includes many original stories, called Adventure Books, that show applications of concepts being studied or sketch episodes from the history of mathematics and science. Literature is used to portray mathematics as a human endeavor, so that students come to think of mathematicians and scientists as people like themselves. Mathematics embedded in a narrative structure is also easier to understand, remember, and discuss. And, of course, everyone loves a good story. In addition, students regularly write about their mathematical investigations, even in the early grades. See the TIMS Tutor: *Journals* for more information.

- **Collaborative Work**
  Scientists, mathematicians, and most others who solve complex problems in business and industry have always worked in groups. The reasons for this are not hard to understand: Most interesting problems are too difficult for one person working alone. Explaining one's work to another person can help clarify one's own thinking. Another person's perspective can suggest a new approach to an unsolved problem. Ideas that have been tested through public scrutiny are more trustworthy than private notions.

  All these are reasons for collaborative work in schools as well. But there are other reasons, too. Students can learn both by receiving and by giving explanations. The communication that goes with group work provides practice in verbal and symbolic communication skills. In group discussion, a basic assumption is that mathematics and science ought to make sense—something, unfortunately, that many students cease to believe after only a few years of schooling. Social skills, especially cooperation and tolerance, increase, and the classroom community becomes more oriented towards learning and academic achievement.

Lesson guides include hints or suggestions for use of collaborative groups.

• **Assessment**

There are three major purposes for assessment: (1) Helping teachers learn about students' thinking and knowledge; this information can then be used to guide instruction. (2) Communicating the goals of instruction to students and parents. (3) Informing students and parents about progress toward these goals and suggesting directions for further efforts.

Assessment in MATH TRAILBLAZERS reflects the breadth and balance of the curriculum. Numerous opportunities for both formal and informal assessment of student learning are integrated into the program. Many of the assessment activities are incorporated into the daily lessons; others are included in formal assessment units. Assessment activities include a mix of short, medium-length, and extended activities. Some are hands-on investigations; others are paper-and-pencil tasks. In all cases, assessment activities are designed to be worthwhile educational experiences.

In grades 1 and 2, there is a strong balance throughout the year between informal assessment activities and paper-and-pencil assessment. Two units, one near the beginning of the year and one near the end, are assessment units. The early unit helps teachers gain insight into the entry-level skills of their students, thereby helping teachers design appropriate instruction; the later unit helps provide a concrete measure of student progress. Both assessment units have been designed specifically to help teachers gauge student progress towards the key goals of the curriculum. A paper-and-pencil end-of-year test is also provided to help teachers and schools with program evaluation efforts.

Between the formal assessment units in grades 1 and 2 are many specially designed assessment tasks and numerous identified opportunities to observe and listen to students, thus helping teachers keep abreast of the developing conceptual understandings of their students. These assessments are specific to the content of the unit. Many provide good material for placement into student portfolios. Every unit also includes an *Assessment Record Sheet*, an organizational tool for helping teachers keep an anecdotal record of student progress towards the key ideas of the unit.

In grades 3 through 5, there are assessment units at three points in the year: early in the year, at the end of the first semester, and at the end of the year. In the early assessment units, the teacher can assess students' knowledge of a wide variety of concepts and skills to determine their level of knowledge as they enter a grade. The activities from these units can be placed in the child's portfolio and used as a benchmark for comparison with later assessment units. The later units are designed to help teachers gauge student progress on key ideas. Assessment units include a range of activities: a long (three- to five-day) activity, usually a laboratory experiment; a "mid-level" problem-solving activity; and short tasks. Student progress with the math facts is assessed formally on a regular basis as part of the *Daily Practice and Problems.*

Many formal assessment activities and numerous other identified assessment opportunities have been carefully integrated into the grades 3 through 5 program. Teachers will find an abundance of formal and informal ways to assess student progress throughout the year. As in grades 1 and 2, an *Assessment Record Sheet* is included with each unit to help teachers keep an anecdotal record of student progress towards the key ideas of the unit.

Because most lessons in this curriculum involve multiple mathematical skills and topics, assessing student progress requires varied tools that examine the various dimensions of a given activity. Among the tools provided in grades 3–5 is a scoring rubric—an analytic scoring guide—for evaluating student progress. The *TIMS Multidimensional Rubric* addresses three dimensions of mathematical learning: understanding mathematical content; solving problems; and communicating. Using these three dimensions broadens the focus of assessment from the traditional emphasis on rote procedures to a more complete view of mathematics learning. The rubric outlines criteria for excellence and provides an explicit indication of what we value in mathematics.

One of the goals of the curriculum is for students to be able to assess their own work in mathematics. An adaptation of the scoring rubric, the *TIMS Student Rubric,* informs students about the criteria for success by setting goals for the three dimensions described above. Using the *Student Rubric* encourages a new approach to learning mathematics by helping students reflect upon mathematics as they do it and reminding them to review and analyze their work. (For a detailed discussion of assessment in *MATH TRAILBLAZERS,* refer to *Assessment in MATH TRAILBLAZERS* (Section 8), and the TIMS Tutor: *Portfolios.*)

- **Developed with Extensive Teacher Input**
  A critical component of the six-year development process for *MATH TRAILBLAZERS* was the prepublication use of the materials in classrooms with thousands of students. More than 150 teachers used draft versions of the curriculum materials and provided extensive feedback that was incorporated into this first edition. The teachers came from schools representing a wide diversity of geographic, socioeconomic, and racial/ethnic composition. The result is a curriculum that reflects the needs and wisdom of classroom teachers.

  Throughout the development process, teachers provided feedback on many issues, ranging from the appropriateness of the content and reading levels to the safety of the manipulatives and equipment to the quality and accuracy of the artwork. This input helped create a balanced program that is appropriate for your students and that represents genders and racial/ethnic groups in traditional and nontraditional roles.

- **More Time Studying Math**
  One cannot reasonably expect to cover all the concepts in a traditional program, add many new topics, and utilize an approach that emphasizes problem solving, communication, reasoning, and connections in the same amount of time that is used to teach a traditional math curriculum. In developing *MATH TRAILBLAZERS,* we have attempted to achieve some efficiencies, such as building review into new concepts and making use of effective strategies to ease the learning of math facts and procedures. However, we make no appeal to magic with *MATH TRAILBLAZERS.* Implementing a comprehensive, "reform" mathematics curriculum will require more time than a traditional program. It simply cannot be implemented in the 30 to 45 minutes that is currently allotted for math

instruction in most schools. **We assume that one hour every day will be devoted to teaching mathematics.**

In some schools, finding an hour per day for math instruction may require a restructuring of the daily school schedule. Please note, however, that because MATH TRAILBLAZERS includes extensive connections with science and language arts, *some* time spent with MATH TRAILBLAZERS can be incorporated within science or language arts time. Thus, it may be possible to allot the one hour per day of mathematics instruction by simply scheduling math and science instruction back to back or including literature connections and journal writing in language arts.

Hard work on the part of students and more time spent engaged in mathematical problem solving are important ingredients for success in mathematics—no matter what program you are using. Because students using MATH TRAILBLAZERS will be actively involved in applying mathematics in meaningful contexts, our experience is that students will be highly motivated to spend this extra time studying mathematics.

- **Staff Development and Broad School Support: Essential Ingredients**
  During our six years of developing and field-testing MATH TRAILBLAZERS, we learned conclusively that implementing a *Standards*-based mathematics program will go much more smoothly if it is accompanied by a solid support system for teachers. Ideally, this includes a professional development program, in-school support, and the means to address a variety of concerns as they arise.

  Kendall/Hunt Publishing Company recognizes the need for professional development. A one-week introductory workshop for teachers and schools that are using MATH TRAILBLAZERS is available through Kendall/Hunt Publishing Company. We recommend that initial implementation of the curriculum be supported by an additional staff development program that supplements the Kendall/Hunt workshops, preferably a program that extends at least through the first year of implementation. This not only will provide valuable information and support for teachers, it also will provide a structured time for teachers to reflect upon and discuss the teaching of mathematics. This alone can dramatically improve the initial implementation of a reform mathematics program such as MATH TRAILBLAZERS. For specific suggestions about designing local staff development efforts related to MATH TRAILBLAZERS, contact the TIMS Project at (312) 996-2448.

  Overall implementation of MATH TRAILBLAZERS will also be much easier in a school that considers how it will broadly support the new program. Necessary tools such as manipulatives, overhead projectors, and transparency masters need to be provided in adequate quantities. Institutional considerations, such as classroom schedules that allot necessary time for instruction and even provide time for teachers to meet and plan together, need to be implemented. In-classroom support from resource teachers is extremely helpful. Storage and check-out systems for shared manipulatives need to be in place. Ways to engender parental support for the program, including possible ways to involve some parents in providing classroom assistance to interested teachers during math time, should be developed.

  Administrators need to maintain a long-term perspective on program implementation, recognizing that it will take some time before teachers and students are in "full gear" with the program—and they need to communicate this clearly to teachers. In short, schools need to examine their current situations and make necessary modifications to develop a school environment that supports the kind of teaching and learning that characterizes MATH TRAILBLAZERS.

- **A Balanced Approach**
We believe that a reform mathematics program should take a balanced and moderate approach. MATH TRAILBLAZERS is balanced in many different ways. Whole-class instruction, small-group activities, and individual work each have a place. New mathematical content is included, but traditional topics are not neglected. Children construct their own knowledge in rich problem-solving situations, but they are not expected to reinvent 5000 years of mathematics on their own. Concepts, procedures, and facts are important, but these are introduced thoughtfully to engender the positive attitudes, beliefs, and self-image that are also important in the long run. Hands-on activities of varied length and depth, as well as a variety of paper-and-pencil tasks, all have their place. The program's rich variety of assessment activities has been designed to reflect this broad balance.

Either-or rhetoric has too often short-circuited real progress in education: problem solving vs. back-to-basics, conceptual understanding vs. procedural skill, paper-and-pencil computation vs. calculators. MATH TRAILBLAZERS is based on the view that these are false dichotomies. Students must solve problems, but of course they need basic skills to do so. Both concepts and procedures are important, and neglecting one will undermine the other. There is a place in the curriculum both for paper-and-pencil algorithms and for calculators, and for mental arithmetic and estimation. The careful balance in MATH TRAILBLAZERS allows teachers and schools to move forward with a reform mathematics curriculum while maintaining the strengths of their current teaching practices.

Components and Features Guide

The *Components and Features Guide* presents reduced-size curriculum pages and descriptive boxes which cover each element of MATH TRAILBLAZERS.

Students use Activity, Lab, and Game Pages, which are provided in the student books.

Components of *MATH TRAILBLAZERS*™

Components and Features Guide

Teacher Materials

UNIT RESOURCE GUIDE (URG)

- comprehensive guide providing essential background information and materials for day-to-day planning, instruction, and assessment
- black and white
- nonconsumable
- contains: Parent Letters
  Assessment Pages
  Transparency and
  Blackline Masters
  Generic Pages

TEACHER IMPLEMENTATION GUIDE (TIG)

- reference guide for teachers, containing program philosophy, overview, and in-depth reference documents, including a section on assessment
- black and white
- nonconsumable

Student Materials

STUDENT GUIDE (SG)

- core material for students
- four-color
- soft cover, consumable: grades 1, 2
- hard cover, nonconsumable: grades 3, 4, 5

DISCOVERY ASSIGNMENT BOOK (DAB)

- student pages that complement the Student Guide
- soft cover, black and white
- consumable
- double- and single-sided

ADVENTURE BOOK (AB)

- collections of illustrated stories focused on math and science concepts
- available in four-color Big Adventure Book and consumable black-and-white books at grades 1, 2
- available in soft cover, four-color, nonconsumable format in grades 3, 4, 5

The following pages offer a "walk through" of the Unit Resource Guide, Discovery Assignment Book, Student Guide, and Adventure Book.

Unit Resource Guide
Letter Home (Parent Letter)

The *Letter Home* is designed to go out under the teacher's signature and explain what students will study and how their families can help. Spanish versions of letters are also provided and can be found at the end of the Unit Resource Guide File.

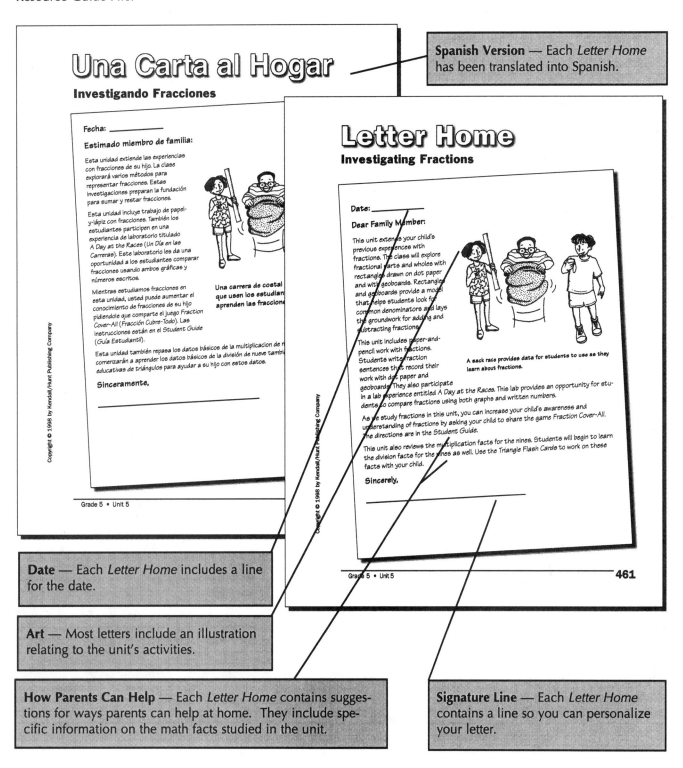

Spanish Version — Each *Letter Home* has been translated into Spanish.

Una Carta al Hogar
Investigando Fracciones

Fecha: _____

Estimado miembro de familia:

Esta unidad extiende las experiencias con fracciones de su hijo. La clase explorará varios métodos para representar fracciones. Estas investigaciones preparan la fundación para sumar y restar fracciones.

Esta unidad incluye trabajo de papel-y-lápiz con fracciones. También los estudiantes participen en una experiencia de laboratorio titulado A Day at the Races (Un Día en las Carreras). Este laboratorio les da una oportunidad a los estudiantes comparar fracciones usando ambos gráficas y números escritos.

Mientras estudiamos fracciones en esta unidad, usted puede aumentar el conocimiento de fracciones de su hijo pidiendole que comparte el juego Fraction Cover-All (Fracción Cubre-Todo). Las instrucciones están en el Student Guide (Guía Estudiantil).

Esta unidad también repasa los datos básicos de la multiplicación de n comenzarán a aprender los datos básicos de la división de nueve tambié educativas de triángulos para ayudar a su hijo con estos datos.

Sinceramente,

Una carrera de costal que usen los estudian aprenden las fraccion

Copyright © 1998 by Kendall/Hunt Publishing Company

Grade 5 • Unit 5

Letter Home
Investigating Fractions

Date: _____

Dear Family Member:

This unit extends your child's previous experiences with fractions. The class will explore fractional parts and wholes with rectangles drawn on dot paper and with geoboards. Rectangles and geoboards provide a model that helps students look for common denominators and lays the groundwork for adding and subtracting fractions.

This unit includes paper-and-pencil work with fractions. Students write fraction sentences that record their work with dot paper and geoboards. They also participate in a lab experience entitled A Day at the Races. This lab provides an opportunity for students to compare fractions using both graphs and written numbers.

As we study fractions in this unit, you can increase your child's awareness and understanding of fractions by asking your child to share the game Fraction Cover-All. The directions are in the Student Guide.

This unit also reviews the multiplication facts for the nines. Students will begin to learn the division facts for the nines as well. Use the Triangle Flash Cards to work on these facts with your child.

Sincerely,

A sack race provides data for students to use as they learn about fractions.

Copyright © 1998 by Kendall/Hunt Publishing Company

Grade 5 • Unit 5   461

Date — Each *Letter Home* includes a line for the date.

Art — Most letters include an illustration relating to the unit's activities.

How Parents Can Help — Each *Letter Home* contains suggestions for ways parents can help at home. They include specific information on the math facts studied in the unit.

Signature Line — Each *Letter Home* contains a line so you can personalize your letter.

Unit Resource Guide
Unit Outline

The *Unit Outline* indicates the number of lessons, what they are about, what you will need to do them, how much time they will take, and other materials you may want to introduce.

Estimated Class Sessions — The number of 60-minute class sessions needed to complete the unit.

Look Ahead — Suggestions to help you prepare for upcoming lessons.

Ongoing Activities — In-class and homework items to be completed throughout the unit.

Sessions — The number of 60-minute class sessions needed to complete the lesson.

Lesson Description — Indicates the type of lesson (Activity, Adventure Book, Assessment, Game, or Lab) and outlines its contents.

Materials List — Describes the type and/or amounts of manipulatives, lab equipment, and other materials you will need for each lesson.

Daily Practice and Problems Letters — These letters indicate the suggested DPP items for each lesson.

Connections — The material in *MATH TRAILBLAZERS* lessons often can be related to books, magazine articles, computer programs, and multimedia presentations. When a Connection is recommended for use with a specific lesson, it is included in the Lesson Guide.

Component Icon — Tells you where to find student materials for each lesson.

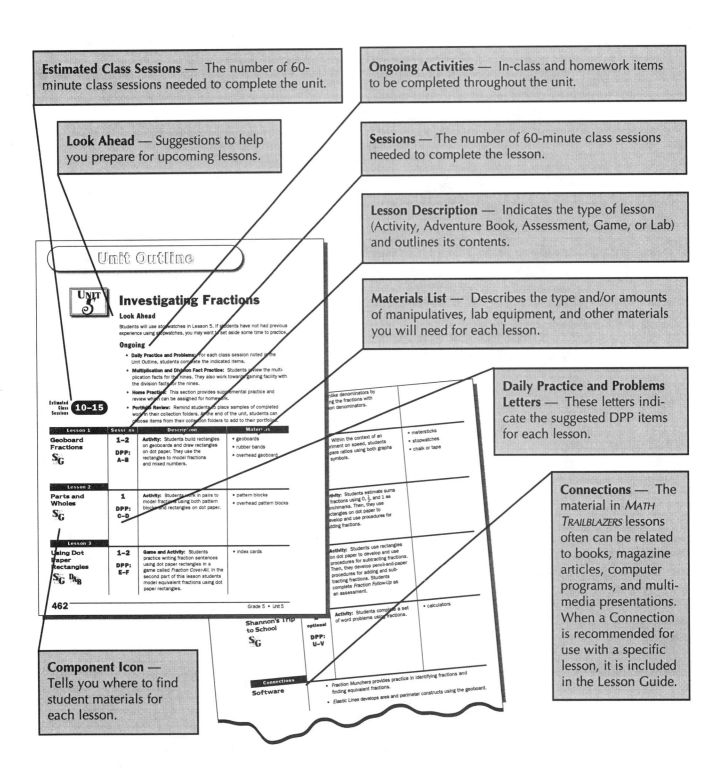

Unit Resource Guide
Background

The *Background* explains what students will learn in the unit and places the material in the larger context of the *Math Trailblazers* curriculum.

Resources — Pointers to additional information on the ideas covered in the unit are sometimes included.

Ideas to Guide Assessment — A list that orients teachers to important skills, behavior, and knowledge they can assess in the unit.

Resources

- Behr, M. J., and T. R. Post. "Teaching Rational Number and Decimal Concepts." In *Teaching Mathematics in Grades K–8: Research Based Methods.* Allyn and Bacon, Boston, 1992.
- Caldwell, J. H. "Communicating about Fractions with Pattern Blocks." In *Teaching Children Mathematics,* 2 (3), National Council of Teachers of Mathematics, Reston, VA, November 1995.
- Cramer, K., and T. R. Post. "Making Connections: A Case for Proportionality." In *Arithmetic Teacher,* 40 (6), National Council of Teachers of Mathematics, Reston, VA, February 1993.
- Curcio, F. R., and N. S. Bezuk. *Understanding Rational Numbers and Proportions.* National Council of Teachers of Mathematics, Reston, VA, 1994.
- Kouba, et al. "Result of the Fourth NAEP Assessment of Mathematics: Number, Operations, and Word Problems" in *Arithmetic Teacher,* 35 (8), April 1988.
- *Curriculum and Evaluation Standards for School Mathematics.* The National Council of Teachers of Mathematics, Reston, VA, 1989.
- Mack, N. K. "Learning Fractions with Understanding: Building on Informal Knowledge." In *Journal for Research in Mathematics Education,* 21 (1), National Council of Teachers of Mathematics, Reston, VA, January 1990.
- Post, T. R., et al. "Order and Equivalence of Rational Numbers: A Cognitive Analysis." In *Journal for Research in Mathematics Education,* 16 (1), National Council of Teachers of Mathematics, Reston, VA, January 1985.
- Suydam, Marilyn. "Manipulatives, Materials, and Achievement" in *Arithmetic Teacher,* 33 (6), February 1986.
- Trafton, Paul, and Shulte, Albert P. (editors) *New Directions for Elementary School Mathematics, 1989 Yearbook.* National Council of Teachers of Mathematics, Reston, VA, 1989.

Ideas to Guide Assessment

- Are students able to represent fractions using rectangles on geoboards or dot paper?
- Are students able to compare fractions?
- Can students collect, organize, graph, and analyze data?
- Are students able to draw proper line graphs?
- Are students able to write ratios as fractions?
- Are students able to measure length in yards and feet?
- Are students able to add fractions?
- Are students able to subtract fractions?
- Can students solve the related multiplication and division facts with the nines?

467

Background

 ## Investigating Fractions

This unit makes connections between two important strands in the curriculum: the study of fractions and the use of data to solve problems. Students review and extend their knowledge of fraction concepts to include models for finding common denominators. Using these models, they develop procedures for comparing, adding, and subtracting fractions with unlike denominators. In the lab *A Day at the Races,* students apply fraction concepts as they practice their skills collecting, displaying, and analyzing data. In this lab, they compare speeds using graphs and ratios expressed as fractions.

Modeling Fractions

The work in the first lessons of this unit builds on concepts and procedures studied in Unit 3 *Fractions and Ratios* using a different part-whole model for representing fractions. In this unit students learn to build rectangles on geoboards and draw rectangles on dot paper to represent fractions. See Figure 1.

Figure 1: *A rectangle on a geoboard divided into fourths and a rectangle on dot paper modeling ¾*

Through this work students continue to work on two fundamental concepts that are needed to understand part-whole fractions: knowing what the whole is and understanding what a part is in relation to the whole. In this unit we use an area model: area is the variable that must be equally allocated among the parts of the whole. This is illustrated in Figure 2, which shows two different ways to divide a 3 × 4 rectangle into fourths. In the rectangle on the left, all four of the fractional parts are congruent. In the other rectangle, there are two different shapes for the fractional parts; all of the parts are fourths, however, because each part has an area of 3 square units. The area model for fractions is explored in this unit with geoboards, dot paper, and pattern blocks and these models are linked with symbols (¾) and words (one-fourth).

Figure 2: *Dividing a 3 × 4 rectangle into fourths*

464

Grade 5 • Unit 5

Unit Resource Guide
Assessment Record Sheet

The *Assessment Record Sheet* is a form used to record informal observations of students' progress.

Ideas to Guide Assessment — This list is composed of some of the Ideas to Guide Assessment from the *Background.* These items focus on the skills, behavior, and knowledge you should look for as you observe students working on activities in the unit.

Optional Assessments — Additional lines are provided for you to assess other related content.

Assessment Icons — Each of the Ideas to Guide Assessment are numbered and labeled with an icon (e.g., **A1** – **A7**).

Assessment Record Sheet

A1 Are students able to compare fractions?
A2 Are students able to draw proper line graphs?
A3 Are students able to write ratios as fractions?
A4 Are students able to measure length in yards and feet?
A5 Are students able to add and subtract fractions?
A6 Can students solve the related multiplication and division facts with the nines?
A7 _____

Name	A1	A2	A3	A4	A5	A6	A7	Comments
1.								
2.								
3.								
4.								
5.								
6.								
7.								
8.								
9.								
10.								
11.								
12.								
13.								

468

Grade 5 • Unit 5

Unit Resource Guide
Daily Practice and Problems

The *Daily Practice and Problems* (DPP) is a series of short exercises designed to provide continuing review of math concepts, skills, and facts. Each set of DPP includes a Teacher's Guide, which provides specific information on the study and assessment of the math facts in the current unit.

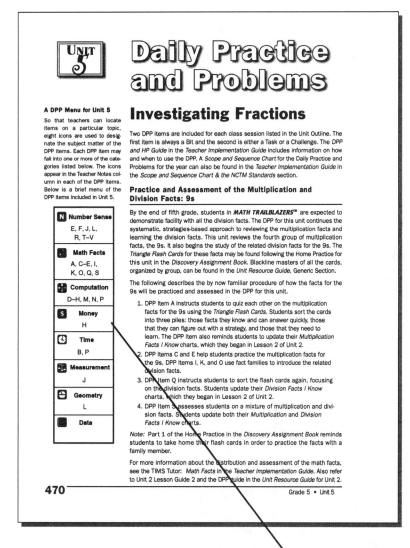

The *Daily Practice and Problems* may be used in class for practice and review, as assessment, or for homework. Notes for teachers provide the answers as well as suggestions for using the items.

Eight icons indicate the subject matter of each problem:

N **Number Sense** (estimating, partitioning numbers, skip counting, etc.);

Math Facts (practice with addition, subtraction, multiplication, and division facts);

Computation (problems which may be solved using paper-and-pencil methods, estimation, mental math, or calculators);

$ **Money** (counting change, combining various coins, and estimating total cost);

Time (telling time, solving problems involving elapsed time);

Measurement (measuring length, area, mass, volume, time, and temperature);

Geometry (work with shapes, measurement, coordinates, and other geometric topics); and

Data (collecting, organizing, graphing, and analyzing data).

DPP Menu — Sorts DPP items into categories for easy reference.

UNIT 5 — Daily Practice and Problems

Students may solve the items individually, in groups, or as a class.
The items may also be assigned for homework.

Student Questions

A Multiplication Facts: 9s

With a partner, use your *Triangle Flash Cards* to quiz each other on the multiplication facts for the 9s. One partner covers the corner containing the highest number with his or her thumb. This number will be the answer to a multiplication fact or the product. The second person multiplies the two uncovered numbers. These two numbers are the factors.

Separate the facts into three piles: those facts you know and can answer quickly, those that you can figure out with a strategy, and those that you need to learn. Practice any facts for the 9s that are in the last two piles. Make a list of these facts so that you can practice them at home.

Circle all the facts you know and can answer quickly on your *Multiplication Facts I Know* chart.

Teacher Notes

TIMS Bit

The *Triangle Flash Cards: 9s* can be found in the *Discovery Assignment Book* following the Home Practice. Blackline masters of all the flash cards, organized by group, are in the Generic Section of the *Unit Resource Guide*. Part 1 of the Home Practice reminds students to take home the list of 9s they need to study as well as their flash cards.

The *Multiplication Facts I Know* chart was distributed in the *Unit Resource Guide* for Unit 2 Lesson 2. See the Lesson Guide for more information.

Later DPP items will introduce students to the division facts for the 9s. Inform students when the quiz on these facts will be given. This quiz, which assesses students on multiplication and division facts for the 9s, appears in DPP Item S.

Student Portion

Teacher Portion

On the teacher note for an item, you will usually find one or more icons which indicate the subject matter of the item.

Each DPP item is marked by a letter which is referred to on the *Unit Outline*.

For each class session noted in a *Unit Outline*, there are two Daily Practice and Problems items. The first of these is always a TIMS Bit and the second is either a TIMS Task or a TIMS Challenge. Each item has been assigned a time/difficulty designation in its teacher's note as described below.

B All Aboard!

The Sydney train in Australia takes 8 minutes to travel between each station. It stays at each station for 3 minutes. There are 4 stations in between Canterbury and Parramatta. At what time will the train arrive in Parramatta if it left Canterbury at 5:22 P.M.? (*Hint:* Make a drawing.)

TIMS Task

$5 \times 8 = 40$ minutes of travel time

$4 \times 3 = 12$ minutes at the four stations in between Parramatta and Canterbury

52 minutes after 5:22 P.M. is 6:14 P.M.

TIMS Tasks — More difficult or longer problems which sometimes ask students to use previously learned concepts in new contexts.

C Order of Operations

A. $20 \div 5 \times 9 =$ B. $18 - 3 \times 3 =$

C. $3 + 9 \times 3 =$ D. $(6 + 3) \times 8 =$

TIMS Bit

A. 36
B. 9
C. 30
D. 72

TIMS Bits — Short items providing quick review or focused practice of a specific topic or skill.

D How Many Answers?

Leaving the numbers in the order given, use operations $(+, -, \times, \div)$ and parentheses to get as many different answers as you can. You may use an operation more than once.

Example: 2   4   6

$2 + 4 \times 6 = 26$

$(2 + 4) \times 6 = 36$

$(2 + 4) \div 6 = 1$

A. 25   5   10

B. 30   6   2

Only whole numbers are allowed at each step. For example, $2 \div 4 + 6$ is not allowed, since $2 \div 4 = \frac{1}{2}$.

TIMS Challenge

A. Some possibilities are:
$25 \div 5 \times 10 = 50$;
$(25 + 5) \div 10 = 3$;
$(25 - 5) \div 10 = 2$

B. Some possibilities are:
$30 \div 6 + 2 = 7$;
$30 \times 6 \div 2 = 90$;
$(30 - 6) \times 2 = 48$;
$30 - 6 \times 2 = 18$;
$30 + 6 - 2 = 34$

TIMS Challenges — Opportunities for students to extend their math skills.

Unit Resource Guide
Lesson Guide

The *Lesson Guide* is a "how-to" manual explaining what you need and what is involved in each lesson.

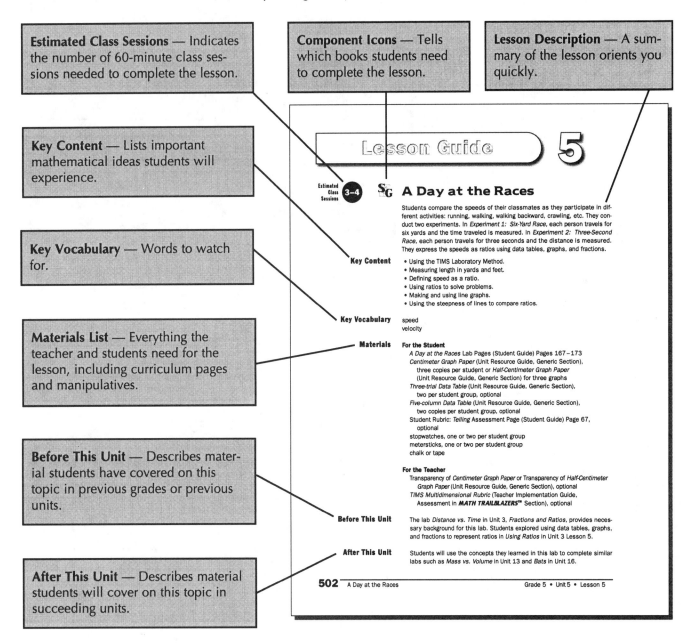

Estimated Class Sessions — Indicates the number of 60-minute class sessions needed to complete the lesson.

Component Icons — Tells which books students need to complete the lesson.

Lesson Description — A summary of the lesson orients you quickly.

Key Content — Lists important mathematical ideas students will experience.

Key Vocabulary — Words to watch for.

Materials List — Everything the teacher and students need for the lesson, including curriculum pages and manipulatives.

Before This Unit — Describes material students have covered on this topic in previous grades or previous units.

After This Unit — Describes material students will cover on this topic in succeeding units.

Lesson Guide — 5

Estimated Class Sessions **3–4**   **S‑G**   **A Day at the Races**

Students compare the speeds of their classmates as they participate in different activities: running, walking, walking backward, crawling, etc. They conduct two experiments. In *Experiment 1: Six-Yard Race*, each person travels for six yards and the time traveled is measured. In *Experiment 2: Three-Second Race*, each person travels for three seconds and the distance is measured. They express the speeds as ratios using data tables, graphs, and fractions.

Key Content
- Using the TIMS Laboratory Method.
- Measuring length in yards and feet.
- Defining speed as a ratio.
- Using ratios to solve problems.
- Making and using line graphs.
- Using the steepness of lines to compare ratios.

Key Vocabulary   speed
velocity

Materials   **For the Student**
A Day at the Races Lab Pages (Student Guide) Pages 167–173
Centimeter Graph Paper (Unit Resource Guide, Generic Section),
   three copies per student or *Half-Centimeter Graph Paper*
   (Unit Resource Guide, Generic Section) for three graphs
Three-trial Data Table (Unit Resource Guide, Generic Section),
   two per student group, optional
Five-column Data Table (Unit Resource Guide, Generic Section),
   two copies per student group, optional
Student Rubric: *Telling* Assessment Page (Student Guide) Page 67,
   optional
stopwatches, one or two per student group
metersticks, one or two per student group
chalk or tape

For the Teacher
Transparency of *Centimeter Graph Paper* or Transparency of *Half-Centimeter
   Graph Paper* (Unit Resource Guide, Generic Section), optional
TIMS Multidimensional Rubric (Teacher Implementation Guide,
   Assessment in *MATH TRAILBLAZERS*™ Section), optional

Before This Unit   The lab *Distance vs. Time* in Unit 3, *Fractions and Ratios*, provides necessary background for this lab. Students explored using data tables, graphs, and fractions to represent ratios in *Using Ratios* in Unit 3 Lesson 5.

After This Unit   Students will use the concepts they learned in this lab to complete similar labs such as *Mass vs. Volume* in Unit 13 and *Bats* in Unit 16.

502   A Day at the Races   Grade 5 • Unit 5 • Lesson 5

Student Guide - Page 167

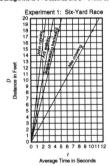

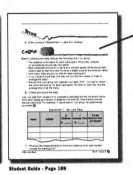

Student Guide - Page 168   **Student Guide - Page 169**

Grade 5 • Unit 5 • Lesson 5   A Day at the Races   **503**

Before the Lab/Activity — Covers what teachers need to prepare for the lesson ahead of time.

Developing the Lab/Activity — Describes what students will do in each activity.

Reduced-Size Student Pages — Most student pages are reproduced in the Lesson Guide.

Samples of Student Work — Work by actual students from the same grade levels as those in your class give you the opportunity to compare your students' work to other students' work.

Discussion Questions — Italicized questions designed to use in class.

At this point, encourage students to study the data in the tables. Ask, *"Who moved fastest? Who moved slowest? How can you tell?"*

Graphing the data as described in the *Student Guide* will give students another tool to compare speeds (Question 8). Question 7 asks for the values for distance and time as each student crosses the starting line. Since the stopwatch reads 0 seconds when each student crosses the starting line at 0 feet, this point makes sense for each participant. Remind students that when they graphed distance and time for students walking at a constant speed in the lab *Distance vs. Time* in Unit 3, the data points formed a straight line. As long as students move at a steady pace in this lab, we can assume that the data fall on a straight line. So, one point is plotted for each student's data and connected by a straight line from time t = 0 seconds and D = 0 feet. See Figure 27.

Experiment 1: Six-Yard Race

D / Distance in Feet vs. *t* / Average Time in Seconds

Figure 27: *Students can use the lines to compare speeds.*

Content Note

Graphing Speeds. When graphing lines to represent speeds, time is customarily graphed on the horizontal axis and distance is graphed on the vertical axis. This way the slopes or steepness of the lines can be used to compare speeds—the greater the slope, the greater the speed.

Questions 9–10 in the Explore section for Experiment 1 discuss the variables in the experiment. Time, distance, speed, and the activity chosen by each student (e.g., running) are all important variables. Time and distance are measured in the experiment and these two variables determine speed. Questions 11–12 ask students to compare

508 A Day at the Races   Grade 5 • Unit 5 • Lesson 5

Part 2. Experiment 1: Six-Yard Race

For each experiment, students will follow the four steps of the TIMS Laboratory Method: Draw, Collect, Graph, and Explore. The questions at the end of the lab will help students compare speeds when neither the time nor the distance is held constant. They can work in groups of four or five so they can collect data to compare four or five speeds.

The *Student Guide* describes the experimental setup which is shown in the picture in Figure 24. Students within each group should choose some faster activities such as running and walking forward and some slower activities such as crawling and walking backward so that the differences in the times will be relatively large.

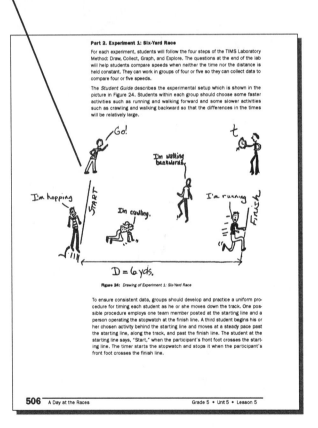

Figure 24: *Drawing of Experiment 1: Six-Yard Race*

To ensure consistent data, groups should develop and practice a uniform procedure for timing each student as he or she moves down the track. One possible procedure employs one team member posted at the starting line and a person operating the stopwatch at the finish line. A third student begins his or her chosen activity behind the starting line and moves at a steady pace past the starting line, along the track, and past the finish line. The student at the starting line says, "Start," when the participant's front foot crosses the starting line. The timer starts the stopwatch and stops it when the participant's front foot crosses the finish line.

506 A Day at the Races   Grade 5 • Unit 5 • Lesson 5

Content Notes — Specific content information relating to lesson activities.

---

26   Components of *Math Trailblazers*   Fifth Grade

Question 17 asks who traveled the fastest in the Three-Second Race. Since the time (the denominator) was held fixed in this experiment, the distances in the numerators can be compared; the greater the distance the greater the speed. Using the graph, the speed shown by the steepest line is the greatest speed.

Question 18 asks students to compare the speed for an activity in Experiment 1 to the speed for the same activity in Experiment 2. For example, John's speed running in the Six-Yard Race can be compared to Nila's speed running in the Three-Second Race. Using the sample data for both experiments, a sample data table is shown in Figure 31.

Comparing Speeds

Name	Activity	D Distance in feet	t Average Time in seconds	S in ft/s Speed in Feet per Second
John	Running	18	2.33	18 ft/2.33 s
Nila	Running	30	3	30 ft/3 s

Figure 31: Comparing speeds as fractions with unlike denominators and numerators

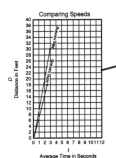

Comparing Speeds

Figure 32: Using a graph to compare speeds

Since there is no common numerator or denominator, students must choose a different strategy to compare the ratios. One solution is to graph the data as shown in the graph in Figure 32. The steeper line represents the greater speed. The graph tells us that Nila ran faster.

In Questions 19–20 students use the data to make predictions. To answer Question 19A, students can use their graphs from Experiment 1 to estimate how long it took them to travel 9 feet. For example, using the sample data in Figure 27, Nila took a little more than 5 seconds to crawl 9 feet while John only took a little more than 1 second to run 9 feet. To answer Question 19B, students will need another strategy if the point for 36 feet is not on the graph. For example, they can reason that since John took 2.33 seconds to run 18 feet, he would take twice as long or 4.66 seconds to run 36 feet.

Homework Ideas

Assign the Homework section in the *Student Guide* at the end of the lab.

Assign some or all of the word problems in Lesson 8.

Connections — How to connect the lesson to children's literature, computer programs, and other content areas such as science and social studies.

Graphs and Tables — Shows sample graphs and data tables.

Homework Ideas — Suggested homework assignments or other activities.

Assessment Ideas — How to evaluate your students' skills and their understanding of concepts.

At a Glance — A brief outline of the activities in each lesson.

Journal Prompts — Suggested prompts for writing which can be assigned to students in class or for homework.

TIMS Tips — Practical suggestions to help you get the most out of each lesson.

Assessment Ideas

To determine grades for this lab, assign points to one or more of the sections of the lab. You might choose to examine how students create data tables to organize their information. Observe students as they create the data tables in this activity. Make sure that students appropriately label the column heads, appropriately label their units, and that they title each table. See the *Assessment in MATH TRAILBLAZERS* section in the *Teacher Implementation Guide* for more suggestions for grading labs.

Use Question 18 to assess students' abilities to draw a graph and use it to solve problems. In this case, they can use the graph to compare speeds. You may want to use the *Telling Rubric* to score students' work on this problem.

Use Questions 19–20 to assess students' abilities to solve a problem and communicate their solutions. Encourage them to use the Student Rubric: *Telling* as they write their solutions. Then, using the rubric as a guide make comments and give students an opportunity to revise their work. You can score their responses using the Communicating dimension of the *TIMS Multidimensional Rubric* in the *Assessment in MATH TRAILBLAZERS* section of the *Teacher Implementation Guide*.

Include students' completed labs in their collection folders.

At a Glance

Part 1. Speed and Velocity

Students read and discuss Questions 1–4 on *A Day at the Races* Lab Pages in the *Student Guide*. These pages develop the context of the lab and help students define the variables in the lab.

Part 2. Experiment 1: Six-Yard Race

1. Students follow the directions in the *Student Guide* and set up Experiment 1. They lay out a 6-yard track.
2. Students draw pictures of the experimental setup. (Question 5)
3. Students time each other with stopwatches as they travel down the six-yard track. Each student uses a different activity (running, walking, etc.). They organize and record their data. (Question 6)
4. Students graph the data. (Question 8)
5. Students answer questions about Experiment 1 in the Explore section of the *Student Guide*. (Questions 9–12)

Part 3. Experiment 2: Three-Second Race

1. Students follow the directions in the *Student Guide* and set up Experiment 2. They draw a picture of the lab setup. (Question 13)
2. Students time each other with a stopwatch as they travel down a track. Each student uses a different activity (running, walking, etc.) from the one they used in Experiment 1. They measure the distance each person travels after three seconds. They organize and record their data. (Question 14)
3. Students graph their data. (Question 15)
4. Students answer questions about Experiment 2 in the Explore section of the *Student Guide*. (Questions 16–20)
5. Assign the Homework section in the *Student Guide*.

Unit Resource Guide
The Lesson Guide for the Adventure Book

The *Lesson Guide* is a "how-to" manual explaining what you need and what is involved in each lesson.

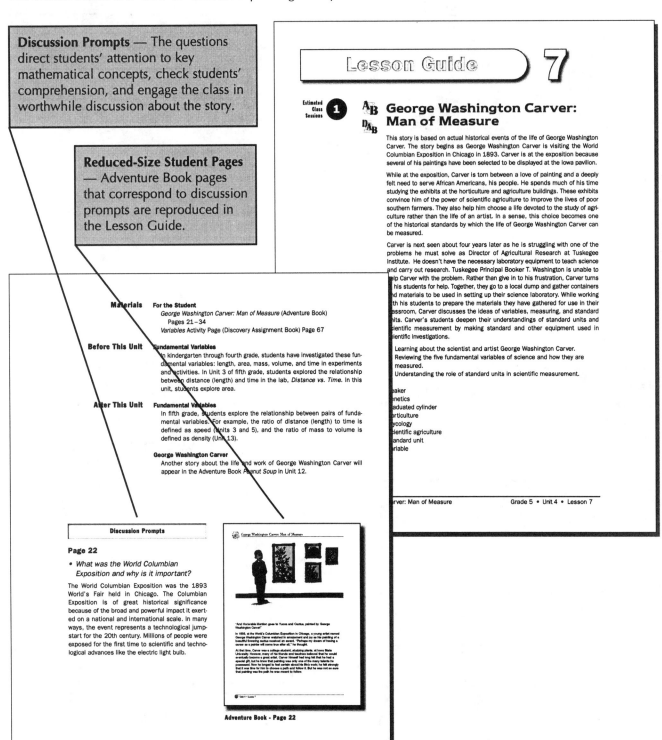

Discussion Prompts — The questions direct students' attention to key mathematical concepts, check students' comprehension, and engage the class in worthwhile discussion about the story.

Reduced-Size Student Pages — Adventure Book pages that correspond to discussion prompts are reproduced in the Lesson Guide.

Lesson Guide 7

Estimated Class Sessions 1

George Washington Carver: Man of Measure

This story is based on actual historical events of the life of George Washington Carver. The story begins as George Washington Carver is visiting the World Columbian Exposition in Chicago in 1893. Carver is at the exposition because several of his paintings have been selected to be displayed at the Iowa pavilion.

While at the exposition, Carver is torn between a love of painting and a deeply felt need to serve African Americans, his people. He spends much of his time studying the exhibits at the horticulture and agriculture buildings. These exhibits convince him of the power of scientific agriculture to improve the lives of poor southern farmers. They also help him choose a life devoted to the study of agriculture rather than the life of an artist. In a sense, this choice becomes one of the historical standards by which the life of George Washington Carver can be measured.

Carver is next seen about four years later as he is struggling with one of the problems he must solve as Director of Agricultural Research at Tuskegee Institute. He doesn't have the necessary laboratory equipment to teach science and carry out research. Tuskegee Principal Booker T. Washington is unable to help Carver with the problem. Rather than give in to his frustration, Carver turns to his students for help. Together, they go to a local dump and gather containers and materials to be used in setting up their science laboratory. While working with his students to prepare the materials they have gathered for use in their classroom, Carver discusses the ideas of variables, measuring, and standard units. Carver's students deepen their understandings of standard units and scientific measurement by making standard and other equipment used in scientific investigations.

Learning about the scientist and artist George Washington Carver.

Reviewing the five fundamental variables of science and how they are measured.

Understanding the role of standard units in scientific measurement.

beaker
genetics
graduated cylinder
horticulture
mycology
scientific agriculture
standard unit
variable

Materials

For the Student
George Washington Carver: Man of Measure (Adventure Book)
Pages 21–34
Variables Activity Page (Discovery Assignment Book) Page 67

Before This Unit

Fundamental Variables
In kindergarten through fourth grade, students have investigated these fundamental variables: length, area, mass, volume, and time in experiments and activities. In Unit 3 of fifth grade, students explored the relationship between distance (length) and time in the lab, *Distance vs. Time*. In this unit, students explore area.

After This Unit

Fundamental Variables
In fifth grade, students explore the relationship between pairs of fundamental variables. For example, the ratio of distance (length) to time is defined as speed (Units 3 and 5), and the ratio of mass to volume is defined as density (Unit 13).

George Washington Carver
Another story about the life and work of George Washington Carver will appear in the Adventure Book *Peanut Soup* in Unit 12.

Carver: Man of Measure   Grade 5 • Unit 4 • Lesson 7

Discussion Prompts

Page 22

• *What was the World Columbian Exposition and why is it important?*

The World Columbian Exposition was the 1893 World's Fair held in Chicago. The Columbian Exposition is of great historical significance because of the broad and powerful impact it exerted on a national and international scale. In many ways, the event represents a technological jumpstart for the 20th century. Millions of people were exposed for the first time to scientific and technological advances like the electric light bulb.

Adventure Book - Page 22

Unit Resource Guide

Student Pages

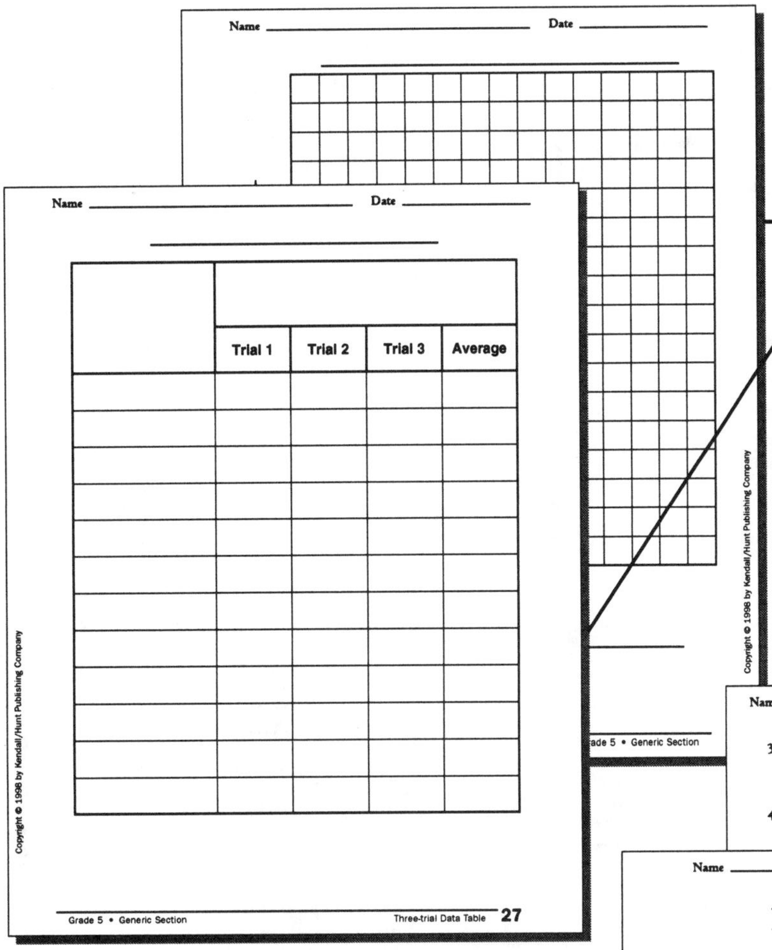

Name ______ Date ______

	Trial 1	Trial 2	Trial 3	Average

Copyright © 1998 by Kendall/Hunt Publishing Company

Grade 5 • Generic Section Three-trial Data Table 27

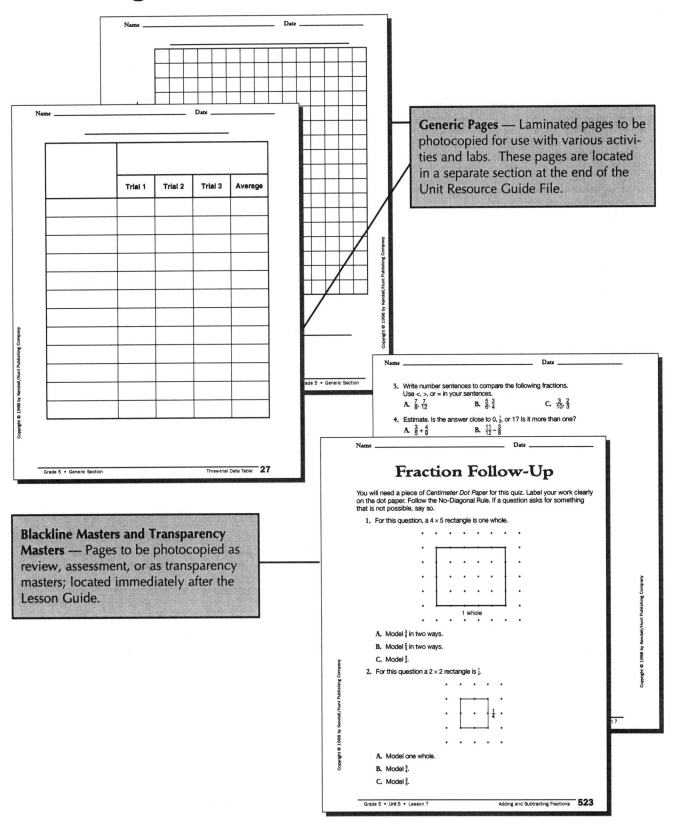

Generic Pages — Laminated pages to be photocopied for use with various activities and labs. These pages are located in a separate section at the end of the Unit Resource Guide File.

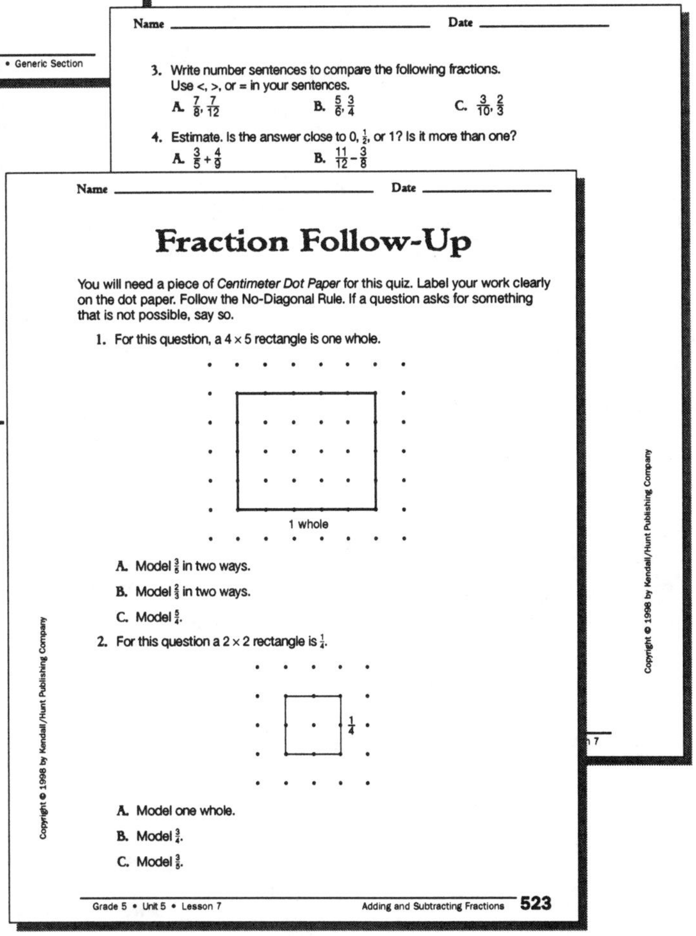

Name ______ Date ______

3. Write number sentences to compare the following fractions. Use <, >, or = in your sentences.
   A. $\frac{7}{8}, \frac{7}{12}$ B. $\frac{5}{6}, \frac{3}{4}$ C. $\frac{3}{10}, \frac{2}{3}$
4. Estimate. Is the answer close to 0, $\frac{1}{2}$, or 1? Is it more than one?
   A. $\frac{3}{5} + \frac{4}{9}$ B. $\frac{11}{12} - \frac{3}{8}$

Name ______ Date ______

Fraction Follow-Up

You will need a piece of *Centimeter Dot Paper* for this quiz. Label your work clearly on the dot paper. Follow the No-Diagonal Rule. If a question asks for something that is not possible, say so.

1. For this question, a 4 × 5 rectangle is one whole.

   1 whole

   A. Model $\frac{3}{5}$ in two ways.
   B. Model $\frac{2}{3}$ in two ways.
   C. Model $\frac{5}{4}$.
2. For this question a 2 × 2 rectangle is $\frac{1}{4}$.

   $\frac{1}{4}$

   A. Model one whole.
   B. Model $\frac{3}{4}$.
   C. Model $\frac{3}{8}$.

Copyright © 1998 by Kendall/Hunt Publishing Company

Grade 5 • Unit 5 • Lesson 7 Adding and Subtracting Fractions 523

Blackline Masters and Transparency Masters — Pages to be photocopied as review, assessment, or as transparency masters; located immediately after the Lesson Guide.

Unit Resource Guide
Answer Key

The *Answer Key* provides the solutions to problems in each unit.

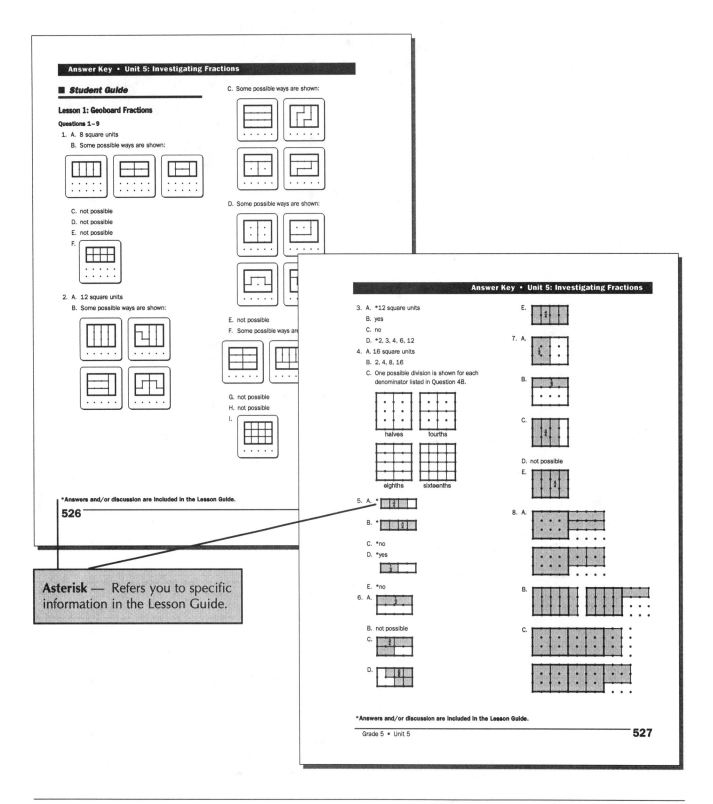

Asterisk — Refers you to specific information in the Lesson Guide.

Student Guide

The *Student Guide* contains most nonconsumable student materials, including activities, labs, and games.

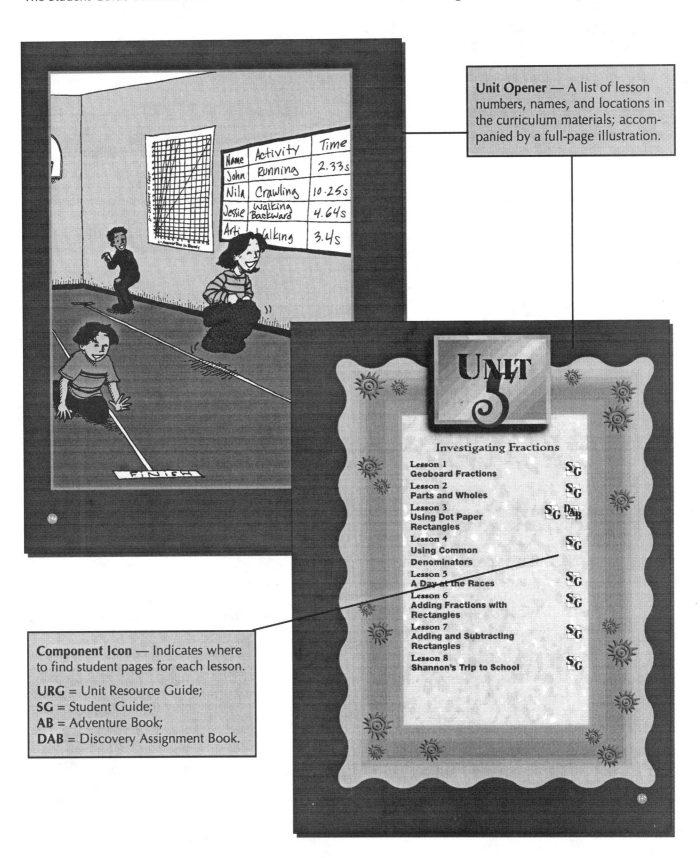

Unit Opener — A list of lesson numbers, names, and locations in the curriculum materials; accompanied by a full-page illustration.

Component Icon — Indicates where to find student pages for each lesson.

URG = Unit Resource Guide;
SG = Student Guide;
AB = Adventure Book;
DAB = Discovery Assignment Book.

A Day at the Races

On Olympic Day at Bessie Coleman School, students participated in many events including the Sack Race and the Backward Race. Roberto and Edward entered the Sack Race. Alexis and Jackie entered the Backward Race.

Contestants in the sack race took turns hopping along the track in a large cloth sack. They hopped for three seconds. Then, the racing judge measured the distance each person hopped. Roberto hopped 24 feet and Edward hopped 27 feet.

Discuss

1. A. Who moved along the track faster, Edward or Roberto? How do you know?
    B. What variables are involved in the Sack Race?
    C. What variables did students measure?
    D. Which variable was the same for all the participants in the Sack Race?

The Backward Race was different. In this race, contestants tried to run or walk backward in a straight line for six yards. Alexis took 4 seconds to travel the 6 yards from the starting line to the finish line. Jackie crossed the finish line after 2.5 seconds.

2. A. Who tra
    B. What va
    C. What va
    D. Which v

A Day at the Races

Draw

5. Draw a picture of Experiment 1. Label the variables.

Collect

Before collecting the data, discuss the following with your group:
- The distance is the same for each participant. What other variables (or procedures) should stay the same?
- Each participant should try to travel at a constant speed. Where should each person start so that he or she moves at a steady pace for the whole six yards?
- How many trials should you time for each participant?
- If you conduct more than one trial, will you find the median or mean to average the data?
- Decide how your group will organize your data. (*Hint:* You need to record the name and activity for each participant, the time for each trial, and the average time of all the trials.)

6. Collect and record the data.

Use your data from Question 6 to complete a data table like the one shown below. Write each speed as a fraction of distance over time ($\frac{D}{t}$). Note that the units are feet per second ($\frac{ft}{s}$). For example, if Jackie were in your group, her speed would be written $\frac{18\,ft}{2.5\,s}$.

Experiment 1: Six-Yard Race

Name	Activity	D Distance in _____	t Average Time in _____	S in ft/s Speed in Feet per Second

7. What are the measurements for time and distance when each student crosses the starting line?

A Day at the Races   Unit 5 • Lesson 5

B. Plot the data points in the table for each person and connect each point to the point for *t* = 0 seconds and *D* = 0 feet.
C. Who went faster? How do you know?

19. Use your data and graph from Experiment 1: Six-Yard Race to answer the following:
    A. How long did it take you to go 9 feet?
    B. If you could travel at the same speed for 36 feet, how long would it take?

20. Use your data and graph from Experiment 2: Three-Second Race to answer the following:
    A. How far did you travel in 1.5 seconds?
    B. How far would you have gone in 6 seconds at the same speed?

Homework

1. Jessie traveled 22 ft in the Three-Second Race and David traveled 25 ft in the Three-Second Race. Who traveled at the greater speed?
2. Irma ran and Nicholas jumped in the Six-Yard Race. Irma's speed was $\frac{6\,yds}{2.3\,s}$ and Nicholas's speed was $\frac{6\,yds}{2.7\,s}$. Who traveled faster?
3. If Manny ran 2 meters and Michael ran 4 meters, could you tell who was traveling faster? Explain.
4. If Lee Yah traveled for 4 hours and Blanca traveled for 3 hours, could you tell who was traveling faster? Explain.
5. Shannon runs 9 meters in 5 seconds. Felicia runs 6 meters in 4 seconds. Who traveled at the faster speed? Show how you know. (*Hint:* Write each speed as a ratio written as a fraction. Then, compare fractions.)
6. A car moves at a constant speed of 20 meters per second. How far will it travel in 5 seconds?
7. Lin can ride 2 blocks in 5 minutes on her bicycle. How long will it take her to ride 6 blocks if she travels at the same speed?
8. Romesh walked 2 miles in a half-hour. Nila walked 4 miles in 40 minutes. Who walked faster? Show how you know.

A Day at the Races   Unit 5 • Lesson 5

Discovery Assignment Book

The *Discovery Assignment Book* contains consumable student materials for activities, labs, and homework.

The *Home Practice* is a series of problems designed to be sent home with students to supplement homework assignments.

Each *Home Practice* is divided into several parts. Each part can be assigned separately.

Name _____ Date _____

Unit 5: Home Practice

Part 1. *Triangle Flash Cards: 9s*
Study for the quiz on the multiplication and division facts for the nines. Take home your *Triangle Flash Cards: 9s* and your list of facts you need to study.

Ask a family member to choose one flash card at a time. To quiz you on a multiplication fact, he or she should cover the corner containing the highest number. Multiply the two uncovered numbers.

To quiz you on a division fact, your family member can cover one of the smaller numbers. One of the smaller numbers is circled. The other has a square around it. Use the two uncovered numbers to solve a division fact.

Ask your family member to mix up the multiplication and division facts. He or she should sometimes cover the highest number, sometimes cover the circled number, and sometimes cover the number in the square.

Your teacher will tell you when the quiz on the 9s will be.

Part 2. Order of Operations
Solve the following problems using the order of operations.

A. $33 - 8 \times 3 =$ B. $35 \div 7 - 3 =$ C. $150 + 9 \times 6 =$

D. $45 \div 9 \times 4 =$ E. $100 + 200 \div 10 =$ F. $(6 + 3) \times 100 =$

G. $200 - (2 \times 70) =$ H. $60 \times 60 \div 40 =$ I. $(80 + 80) \div 40 =$

Unit 5 71

Name _____ Date _____

Part 3. Ratios
Leo made this graph. It shows the number of blocks and their total centimeters. Use the graph to answer the following questions. Explain how you solved each problem. If you find more than one way to solve, describe each method.

Leo's Blocks

1. Write the ratio of length to the number of blocks as a fraction.

2. Find the length of four blocks.

3. How many blocks will measure six centimeters?

4. Find the length of 40 blocks.

5. Find the length of 60 blocks.

Unit 5

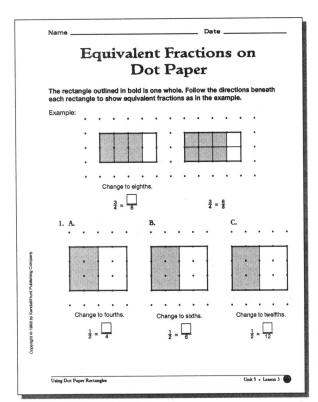

Equivalent Fractions on Dot Paper

The rectangle outlined in bold is one whole. Follow the directions beneath each rectangle to show equivalent fractions as in the example.

Example:

Change to eighths.

$\frac{3}{4} = \frac{\square}{8}$ $\frac{3}{4} = \frac{6}{8}$

1. A.   B.   C.

Change to fourths.   Change to sixths.   Change to twelfths.

$\frac{1}{2} = \frac{\square}{4}$ $\frac{1}{2} = \frac{\square}{6}$ $\frac{1}{2} = \frac{\square}{12}$

Using Dot Paper Rectangles   Unit 5 • Lesson 3

Homework — Occasionally homework appears in the Discovery Assignment Book.

Name and Date Lines — Since the Discovery Assignment Book is consumable, a name and date line has been provided.

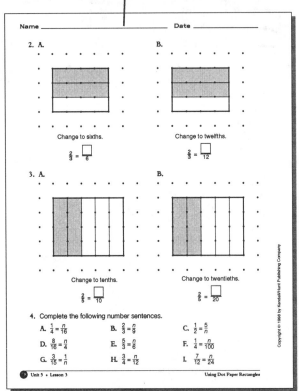

Name _____   Date _____

2. A.   B.

Change to sixths.   Change to twelfths.

$\frac{2}{3} = \frac{\square}{6}$ $\frac{2}{3} = \frac{\square}{12}$

3. A.   B.

Change to tenths.   Change to twentieths.

$\frac{2}{5} = \frac{\square}{10}$ $\frac{2}{5} = \frac{\square}{20}$

4. Complete the following number sentences.

A. $\frac{1}{4} = \frac{n}{16}$ B. $\frac{2}{3} = \frac{n}{9}$ C. $\frac{1}{2} = \frac{5}{n}$

D. $\frac{8}{16} = \frac{n}{4}$ E. $\frac{5}{3} = \frac{n}{6}$ F. $\frac{1}{4} = \frac{n}{100}$

G. $\frac{3}{15} = \frac{1}{n}$ H. $\frac{3}{4} = \frac{n}{12}$ I. $\frac{7}{12} = \frac{n}{24}$

Unit 5 • Lesson 3   Using Dot Paper Rectangles

Adventure Book

Illustrated stories which present mathematics and science concepts.

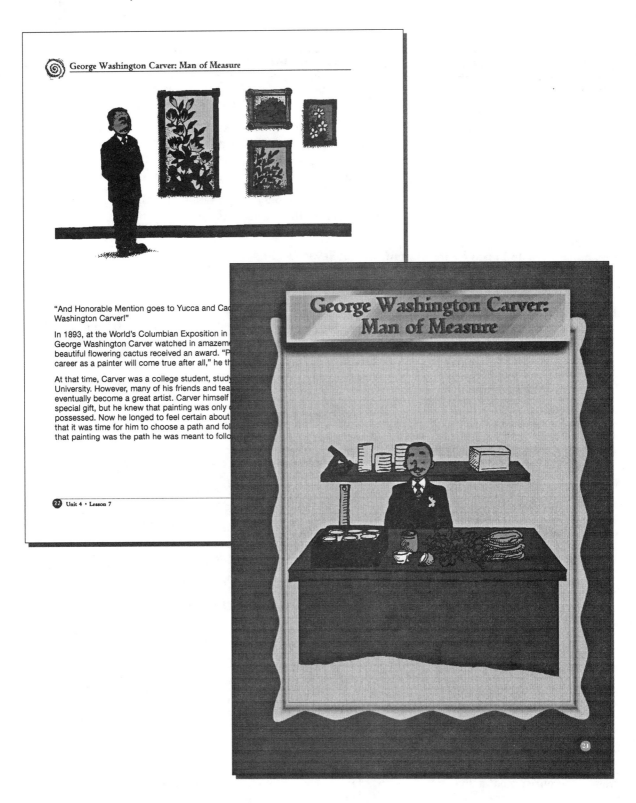

George Washington Carver: Man of Measure

"And Honorable Mention goes to Yucca and Cac[...]
Washington Carver!"

In 1893, at the World's Columbian Exposition in [...]
George Washington Carver watched in amazeme[...]
beautiful flowering cactus received an award. "P[...]
career as a painter will come true after all," he th[...]

At that time, Carver was a college student, study[...]
University. However, many of his friends and tea[...]
eventually become a great artist. Carver himself [...]
special gift, but he knew that painting was only [...]
possessed. Now he longed to feel certain about [...]
that it was time for him to choose a path and foll[...]
that painting was the path he was meant to follo[...]

22 Unit 4 • Lesson 7

George Washington Carver: Man of Measure

Quick Reference Guide

WHAT I WANT TO KNOW	WHERE TO FIND IT
What does this lesson cover?	Unit Resource Guide - Unit Outline Unit Resource Guide - Lesson Guide
What are the "big ideas" in this lesson or the entire unit?	Unit Resource Guide - Lesson Guide - Key Content Unit Resource Guide - Unit Outline Unit Resource Guide - Background Teacher Implementation Guide - Unit Summaries*
What do I need to prepare for this lesson?	Unit Resource Guide - Unit Outline - Look Ahead Unit Resource Guide - Lesson Guide - Before the Activity Unit Resource Guide - Lesson Guide - Materials List
What manipulatives do I need for this lesson?	Unit Resource Guide - Unit Outline Unit Resource Guide - Unit Outline - Look Ahead Unit Resource Guide - Lesson Guide - Materials List
What have students covered on this topic in previous grades or previous units?	Unit Resource Guide - Lesson Guide - Before This Unit Teacher Implementation Guide - Scope and Sequence* Teacher Implementation Guide - Unit Summaries*
What will students cover on this topic in later units?	Unit Resource Guide - Lesson Guide - After This Unit Teacher Implementation Guide - Scope and Sequence* Teacher Implementation Guide - Unit Summaries*
How do I teach this lesson?	Unit Resource Guide - Lesson Guide
Where is a quick summary of each lesson to help teach the lesson?	Unit Resource Guide - Lesson Guide - At a Glance
How long will it take to do this lesson (or the entire unit)?	Unit Resource Guide - Unit Outline Unit Resource Guide - Lesson Guide
How do I deal with potential trouble spots?	Unit Resource Guide - Lesson Guide - TIMS Tips Teacher Implementation Guide - TIMS Tutors Unit Resource Guide - Lesson Guide - Content Notes
How do I organize my class to do this lesson?	Unit Resource Guide - Lesson Guide
Where are the Blackline and Transparency Masters?	Unit Resource Guide - Letter Home Unit Resource Guide - Lesson Guide Unit Resource Guide File - Generic Section
Where are Journal Prompts?	Unit Resource Guide - Lesson Guide
Where are the remediation activities?	Unit Resource Guide - Daily Practice and Problems Unit Resource Guide File - Addition and Subtraction Math Fact Review section
Where is the skill practice and review?	Unit Resource Guide - Daily Practice and Problems Discovery Assignment Book - Home Practice
Where are the enrichment activities?	Unit Resource Guide - Lesson Guide - Extensions Unit Resource Guide - Daily Practice and Problems - Challenges

* The Scope and Sequence and Unit Summaries are also located in the Quick Start in the Unit Resource Guide File.

WHAT I WANT TO KNOW	WHERE TO FIND IT
What information is available for parents?	Teacher Implementation Guide - Parents and MATH TRAILBLAZERS - Parent Brochure (English and Spanish) Unit Resource Guide - Letter Home Unit Resource Guide File - Letter Home/Spanish Unit Resource Guide - Unit 2 - Information for Parents: Math Facts Philosophy
What should I assign as homework?	Unit Resource Guide - Lesson Guide - Homework Ideas Discovery Assignment Book - Home Practice
How do I assess students' progress?	Unit Resource Guide - Unit Background - Ideas to Guide Assessment Unit Resource Guide - Daily Practice and Problems - Fact Quizzes Unit Resource Guide - Assessment Record Sheets Unit Resource Guide - Assessment Units Unit Resource Guide - Assessment Lessons Unit Resource Guide - Lesson Guide - Assessment Pages Unit Resource Guide - Lesson Guide - Assessment Ideas Unit Resource Guide - Lesson Guide - Journal Prompts Teacher Implementation Guide - Assessment in MATH TRAILBLAZERS Teacher Implementation Guide - Assessment in MATH TRAILBLAZERS - Individual Assessment Record Sheet
Where do I find connections to literature, computer software, and other content areas such as social studies and science?	Unit Resource Guide - Unit Outline Unit Resource Guide - Lesson Guide - Connections Teacher Implementation Guide - Literature List Teacher Implementation Guide - Software List
How do I find background information about concepts underlying each activity?	Unit Resource Guide - Unit Background Unit Resource Guide - Lesson Guide - Content Notes Teacher Implementation Guide - TIMS Tutors
How does this activity or unit fit into the "big picture" for my grade?	Unit Resource Guide - Unit Background Unit Resource Guide - Lesson Guide - Before This Unit Unit Resource Guide - Lesson Guide - After This Unit Teacher Implementation Guide - Unit Summaries* Teacher Implementation Guide - Scope and Sequence*
What will my students do this year?	Teacher Implementation Guide - Unit Summaries* Teacher Implementation Guide - Scope and Sequence*
What manipulatives do I need for the entire year?	Teacher Implementation Guide - Manipulatives List
Where is the scope and sequence?	Teacher Implementation Guide - Scope and Sequence*
Does this curriculum match my district's objectives?	Teacher Implementation Guide - Scope and Sequence and the NCTM *Standards* Teacher Implementation Guide - Unit Summaries* Unit Resource Guide - Background - Ideas to Guide Assessment

* The Scope and Sequence and Unit Summaries are also located in the Quick Start in the Unit Resource Guide File.

Unit Summaries

The *Unit Summaries* section presents brief descriptions and lists of featured concepts. It provides a quick reference to locate concepts and activities.

Students solve a problem using money.

Unit Summaries

Below are descriptions of the fifth-grade units in the *MATH TRAILBLAZERS™* curriculum. The descriptions provide a brief summary and a list of the concepts that are featured. This list may be used as a quick reference to the concepts and activities involved in each unit. The unit summaries reflect the scope, sequence, and tone of the fifth-grade curriculum. The fundamental assumption of all the units is that math concepts and skills are best acquired through active involvement in problem solving. Thus, problem-solving activities are pervasive. Mathematics content—measurement, graphing, computation, logical reasoning, fractions, data analysis, geometry, and estimation—is included within problems in each unit. The TIMS Laboratory Method, used in laboratory experiments throughout the curriculum, incorporates experiences with some of the important tools in investigation and experimentation: drawing a picture, measuring, collecting and organizing data, constructing a graph, and posing and answering questions about the data.

Units also include:

- Suggestions for journal writing;

- Recommended homework assignments for most lessons;

- Parent letters that discuss the important ideas within the unit and provide suggestions for home activities that support lessons in school;

- Assessment, both through formal instruments and through the informal observations that a discourse-based curriculum makes possible.

Many units also include Adventure Books and recommendations for using related trade books and children's literature. A recommended software list also accompanies most units. Many of the units in the first semester include activities which review materials from fourth grade so students new to the curriculum will have the necessary skills and concepts for fifth grade.

Home Practice

The Home Practice (HP) in the *Discovery Assignment Book* consists of short problems that can be assigned as homework or assessment throughout the unit. The HP includes skill practice and problems which are related to the current unit or previous units. Problems can be solved in many ways with a variety of tools including: calculators, data tables and charts, graphs, manipulatives, and paper-and-pencil strategies.

Daily Practice and Problems

The Daily Practice and Problems (DPP) is a vital component of the curriculum and can be found at the beginning of each unit in the *Unit Resource Guide*. These short exercises provide ongoing practice, review, and study of a variety of topics. These include basic facts, computation, time, money, number sense, data, measurement, and geometry. Many word problems are included. Two DPP items are provided for each class session. TIMS Bits are short items that provide quick reviews of a topic or focused practice on a specific skill. TIMS Tasks and TIMS Challenges are problems that ask students to use previously learned concepts in a new context or to extend those concepts in a challenging new situation. The content includes:

- estimation
- basic fact practice
- number sense
- using data tables
- logic

- counting and numeration
- computation
- geometry
- problem solving
- division fact strategies

- time
- money
- measurement
- using graphs

Unit 1 | Populations and Samples

Unit Summary

This unit is designed to help you start the year off right by establishing a positive classroom atmosphere, introducing critical mathematics, and gathering baseline assessment data about your students' mathematical abilities. Students begin the unit with a lab called *Eyelets*. This lab sets a cooperative atmosphere and reviews concepts used in earlier grades. Two activities from fourth grade are also included which review finding the median and collecting, organizing, and graphing data in bar graphs. Throughout the unit, students translate between graphs and real-world events. The *Searching the Forest* lab, which will help you gather baseline data on students' mathematical abilities, focuses on populations and samples. The Adventure Book, *A Matter of Survival,* also explores these concepts. The DPP for this unit will allow you to assess students' facility with the addition and subtraction facts.

Concept Focus

- numerical and categorical variables
- addition and subtraction fact review
- interpreting graphs
- finding the probability of an event
- Adventure Book: populations and samples
- solving problems in more than one way
- choosing appropriate methods to solve problems

- TIMS Laboratory Method
- averages: medians and modes
- bar graphs
- populations and samples

Unit 2 | Big Numbers

Unit Summary

This unit focuses on place value, big numbers, estimation, and computation. It also provides opportunities to gather baseline data on students' mathematical abilities in these areas. Students complete a variety of activities that involve reading and writing big numbers, using convenient numbers to estimate products, multiplying using paper and pencil, and reading scientific notation. Activities from the fourth grade are included so students can use base-ten pieces to review place value and addition and subtraction as needed. An Adventure Book, *Sand Reckoning,* tells the story of Archimedes and his estimate for the number of grains of sand needed to fill the universe. A short assessment problem, *Stack Up,* is also included to provide baseline data on students' abilities to solve multistep problems and communicate their solution strategies. The Student Rubrics: *Telling* and *Solving* are reintroduced and students begin collection folders to make portfolios. The yearlong review of the multiplication facts and the study of the division facts begin in this unit.

Students use fact families to review the multiplication facts for the fives and tens and to develop strategies for learning the related division facts.

Concept Focus

- paper-and-pencil multiplication
- multiplication with ending zeros
- addition and subtraction review
- measuring length in centimeters
- using data to solve problems
- communicating solution strategies
- multiplication and division facts: 5s and 10s
- convenient numbers for computations
- Student Rubrics: *Telling* and *Solving*

- place value
- big numbers
- estimation
- scientific notation
- portfolios
- place value review

Unit 3

Fractions and Ratios

Unit Summary

In this unit, students build a strong conceptual foundation for work with fractions and ratios. They review fraction concepts with pattern blocks and use the concepts to develop skills and procedures such as finding equivalent fractions, ordering fractions, writing mixed numbers for improper fractions, and writing improper fractions for mixed numbers. Students also explore ratios using data tables, graphs, and symbols. This unit includes the lab *Distance vs. Time.* In this lab, speed is defined as the ratio of distance moved to time taken. Students use this definition as they apply their knowledge of fractions and ratios. The Student Rubric: *Knowing* is reintroduced. The DPP for this unit reviews the multiplication facts for the twos and threes and uses fact families to introduce the division facts for the twos and threes.

Concept Focus

- ratios
- mixed numbers
- Student Rubric: *Knowing*
- modeling fractions with pattern blocks
- writing number sentences using fractions
- measuring time with a stopwatch
- point graphs
- using data to solve problems
- multiplication and division facts: 2s and 3s

- improper fractions
- TIMS Laboratory Method
- comparing fractions
- ordering fractions
- equivalent fractions
- measuring length in yards
- best-fit lines
- speed

Unit 4

Division and Data

Unit Summary

This unit extends and applies students' knowledge of several topics: division, measuring area, averages (means and medians), and accuracy in measurement and estimation. Division is explored first by modeling with the base-ten pieces, then by a paper-and-pencil method called the "forgiving" method. Students explore area and use it as a basis for making estimates. They check the accuracy of their estimates using 10% as a benchmark. For the first time in fifth grade, students use the mean to average a set of data. This unit also includes the lab *Spreading Out*. This lab draws upon many of the concepts in the unit including area, 10% as a standard for error analysis, and averages. As part of the lab, students decide when it is appropriate to use a bar graph and when it is appropriate to use a point graph. The Adventure Book: *George Washington Carver: Man of Measure* explores many of the variables involved in math and science. This unit also marks the midpoint of the semester. A midterm test is included that assesses many of the concepts and skills studied thus far. The DPP for this unit reviews the multiplication facts for the square numbers and introduces the division facts for the square numbers.

Concept Focus

- area
- modeling division with base-ten pieces
- choosing appropriate graphs
- manipulated, responding, and fixed variables
- interpreting remainders
- estimation
- 10% as a standard for estimation
- averages: medians and means
- Adventure Book: variables in math and science
- multiplication and division facts: square numbers

- TIMS Laboratory Method
- paper-and-pencil division
- ratios
- estimating quotients
- point graphs
- best-fit lines
- midterm test
- order of operations

Unit 5   Investigating Fractions

Unit Summary

This unit makes connections between two important strands in the curriculum: the study of fractions and the use of data to solve problems. Students review and expand their knowledge of fraction concepts to include models for finding common denominators. Students use rectangles on dot paper, geoboards, and pattern blocks as their primary fraction models. They then use these models to develop procedures for comparing, adding, and subtracting fractions with unlike denominators. These concepts are further explored in the lab *A Day at the Races*. In this lab, students use the TIMS Laboratory Method and their knowledge of fractions to compare speeds by comparing ratios. The DPP for this unit reviews the multiplication facts for the nines and introduces the division facts for the nines.

Concept Focus

- representing fractions with models
- fractions and ratios
- numerators and denominators
- unit whole
- fractional parts of wholes

- comparing fractions
- adding fractions using models
- subtracting fractions using models
- TIMS Laboratory Method
- measuring length

- equivalent fractions
- common denominators
- communicating solution strategies
- multiplication and division facts: 9s
- speed and velocity
- point graphs
- best-fit lines
- Student Rubric: *Telling*

Unit 6   Geometry

Unit Summary

In this unit, students investigate patterns and concepts in geometry. They draw triangles and other plane figures and discover properties of the shapes. Students discover the relationship between the number of sides of a polygon and the sum of the angles. Then, they describe and classify shapes. Tessellations are explored using quilt designs. This unit contains a short assessment, *Making Shapes,* in which students draw shapes when given specific properties and measurements. To complete the assessment, they use the *Telling* Rubric as a guide for their writing as they explain the strategies they used to draw the shapes. The DPP for this unit reviews the last six multiplication facts (4×6, 4×7, 4×8, 6×7, 6×8, and 7×8) and introduces the 12 related division facts.

Concept Focus

- acute, obtuse, right, and straight angles
- congruence
- naming polygons
- properties of triangles and polygons
- measuring angles with a protractor
- drawing angles and shapes
- communicating solution strategies
- multiplication and division facts: last six facts
- similarity
- tessellations
- sums of angles in polygons
- triangulation
- classifying shapes
- Student Rubric: *Telling*

Unit 7   Decimals and Probability

Unit Summary

A major goal of this unit is to help students understand that often a quantity can be expressed as a fraction, decimal, and a percent. Students use two models to help them make connections between fractions and decimal symbols: centiwheels (circles divided into hundredths) and squares divided into tenths, hundredths, and thousandths. Students work with these grids to reinforce place value concepts, compare decimals, round decimals, and model addition and subtraction of decimals. They use an area model to learn to place decimals in products of decimal multiplication problems. Students use their knowledge of decimals to explore probabilities. They complete a lab, *Flipping Two Coins,* in which they explore the results of coin flipping experiments. The lab is related to a real-life story with the Adventure Book, *Unlikely Heroes.* The DPP for this unit reviews all the multiplication and division facts.

Concept Focus

- reading and writing decimals
- rounding decimals
- decimal place value
- comparing decimals
- adding decimals
- subtracting decimals
- multiplying decimals
- placing decimals in products
- using fractions to write probabilities
- probabilities of flipping coins
- using decimals to write probabilities
- law of large numbers
- Adventure Book: probability
- TIMS Laboratory Method
- bar graphs
- predictions from graphs
- relationships between fractions, decimals, and percents
- multiplication and division facts

Unit 8 Applications: An Assessment Unit

Unit Summary

This unit expands and applies concepts and skills learned in the first seven units. Students are assessed on these concepts and skills as they work on the activities and labs. They demonstrate their knowledge by solving problems that arise in several contexts that have strong connections to science and social studies. Students review labs completed in the first half of the year in preparation for completing the assessment lab, *Comparing the Lives of Animals and Soap Bubbles.* As part of the lab, students apply their knowledge of percents and interpret graphs. They also read the Adventure Book, *Florence Kelley,* which describes the work of a social reformer in the late 1900s who— through data collection—was able to contribute to the passage of child labor laws in Illinois. This Adventure Book sets the stage for an assessment activity called *Florence Kelley's Report* in which students interpret Florence Kelley's data as she reported it to the governor. This unit also includes the *Mid-Year Test* and a portfolio review session. The DPP for this unit tests all the multiplication and division facts.

Concept Focus

- experiment review
- estimating products of decimals
- interpreting graphs
- point and bar graphs
- portfolio review
- TIMS Laboratory Method
- binning data
- percents
- Adventure Book: child labor
- Student Rubric: *Telling*
- communicating solution strategies
- Student Rubric: *Knowing*
- mid-year test
- multiplication and division facts

Unit 9 Connections to Division

Unit Summary

This unit focuses on division and its applications as well as its connections to other areas of mathematics. Students begin by exploring the relationship between fractions and division in order to learn strategies for finding decimal equivalents for fractions. They extend paper-and-pencil division (the forgiving method) to two-digit divisors. Extending the forgiving method in a context provides a setting for interpreting remainders in meaningful ways. In the context of checking division by using multiplication, this unit includes an optional activity which introduces a different multiplication method: lattice multiplication. The lattice method is connected to the compact and all-partials algorithms. Students also use calculators to divide larger numbers and devise strategies to find whole number remainders with calculators. To conclude the unit, students again connect fractions and division by employing calculator strategies to add and subtract fractions. The DPP for this unit reviews the division facts for the fives and tens.

Concept Focus

- fractions and division
- decimal equivalents for fractions
- paper-and-pencil division
- interpreting remainders
- calculator strategies for adding and subtracting fractions
- checking division with multiplication
- paper-and-pencil multiplication
- calculator strategies for dividing
- repeating decimals
- division facts: 5s and 10s

Unit 10

Maps and Coordinates

Unit Summary

This unit starts with a discussion of negative numbers within several real-world contexts, including measuring temperature and tracking money in a bank account. Then, positive and negative numbers are applied to the task of making coordinate maps. The activity, *Mr. O*, continues students' investigation of coordinates begun in first grade. An Adventure Book *Wherefore Art Thou, Romeo?* emphasizes the importance of the positive and negative signs in coordinate pairs. Students develop their spatial visualization skills and understanding of geometric concepts by investigating the results of flips and slides on shapes in the coordinate plane. The DPP for this unit reviews the division facts for the twos and the squares.

Concept Focus

- negative numbers
- signed numbers
- four quadrants
- plotting points
- reading maps
- using the scale on a map
- division facts: 2s and squares
- Cartesian coordinates
- coordinate pairs
- slides and flips
- Student Rubric: *Knowing*
- Adventure Book: coordinates
- tessellations

Unit 11

Number Patterns, Primes, and Fractions

Unit Summary

In this unit students investigate some of the underlying structures of arithmetic, often referred to as number theory. They play a game in which they must find all the factors of the numbers from one to forty. They identify prime and composite numbers using a hundreds chart and a process developed by Eratosthenes, a famous Greek mathematician. They then examine and describe patterns in the chart. Students complete an assessment activity, *A Further Look at Patterns and Primes,* using the same process on a different chart. In a different activity, students investigate patterns in square numbers. In the latter part of the unit, students use common factors and common multiples to rename, compare, and reduce fractions. The DPP for this unit reviews the division facts for the threes and nines.

Concept Focus

- factors
- Sieve of Eratosthenes
- exponents
- prime factorization
- common denominators
- comparing fractions
- adding and subtracting fractions
- number patterns
- division facts: 3s and 9s

- primes
- composites
- factor trees
- square numbers
- reducing fractions to lowest terms
- point graphs
- communicating mathematically
- Student Rubric: *Telling*

Unit 12   Using Fractions

Unit Summary

In this unit, students continue their study of fractions by using pattern blocks and other models to represent fractions in different ways. This helps students generalize concepts and procedures which they can then apply in new situations. For example, they use pattern blocks to model addition of mixed numbers and multiplication of fractions in order to develop pencil-and-paper methods for these operations. Students also use pattern blocks to solve an assessment problem, *Pattern Block Candy.* They read an Adventure Book, *Peanut Soup,* which uses the context of the work of George Washington Carver to explore the use of fractions in a real-life setting. The unit concludes with a *Midterm Test,* which assesses concepts and skills studied in this and previous units. The DPP for this unit reviews the 12 division facts related to the last six multiplication facts (4×6, 4×7, 4×8, 6×7, 6×8, and 7×8).

Concept Focus

- using patterns to build number sense
- multiplying fractions and whole numbers
- multiplying fractions by fractions
- estimating the product of fractions
- using fractions in everyday situations
- communicating mathematically
- division facts: $24 \div 6$, $24 \div 4$, $28 \div 7$, $28 \div 4$, $32 \div 8$, $32 \div 4$, $42 \div 7$, $42 \div 6$, $48 \div 8$, $48 \div 6$, $56 \div 7$, $56 \div 8$

- renaming mixed numbers
- adding mixed numbers
- Student Rubric: *Solving*
- Adventure Book: fractions
- midterm test

Unit 13 | Ratio and Proportion

Unit Summary

The goal of this unit is to use the previously studied concepts of ratio and proportion as a foundation for developing more formal concepts and procedures for solving problems that involve proportional reasoning. Students first review the use of words, tables, graphs, and symbols to express ratios. Then, they learn that a proportion is a statement that two ratios are equivalent and develop strategies for solving proportional reasoning problems. Students apply proportional reasoning to the study of density in the activity *Sink and Float* and the lab *Mass vs. Volume*. The DPP for this unit reviews the division facts for the twos, fives, tens, and the square numbers.

Concept Focus

- ratios
- variables in proportion
- volume
- TIMS Laboratory Method
- division facts: 2s, 5s, 10s, square numbers
- using ratios and proportions to solve problems
- proportions
- mass
- density
- point graphs
- best-fit lines

Unit 14 | Using Circles

Unit Summary

In this unit, students apply many previously learned skills and concepts, and they explore the geometry of circles. They investigate the relationship between the circumference and the diameter of a circle, first informally, then more formally as they complete a laboratory investigation, *Circumference vs. Diameter.* In this lab they use data tables and graphs to find an accurate approximation for the ratio circumference to diameter *(C/D),* or pi (π). Then, they use this ratio to find a formula for the circumference of a circle. Students also learn to use a compass and a ruler to copy and construct circles and other shapes. As they work through each activity, they use geometric terms as needed to name parts of the circle. Finally, they interpret and construct circle graphs. The DPP for this unit reviews the threes, nines, and the 12 division facts related to the last six multiplication facts (4×6, 4×7, 4×8, 6×7, 6×8, and 7×8).

Concept Focus

- circumference
- chords, arcs, and radii
- circle graphs
- pi (π)
- point graphs
- relationship between circumference and diameter
- division facts: 3s, 9s, 24 ÷ 6, 24 ÷ 4, 28 ÷ 7, 28 ÷ 4, 32 ÷ 8, 32 ÷ 4, 42 ÷ 7, 42 ÷ 6, 48 ÷ 8, 48 ÷ 6, 56 ÷ 7, 56 ÷ 8
- diameter
- constructing circles and figures
- generating formulas
- TIMS Laboratory Method
- best-fit lines

Unit 15 | **Developing Formulas with Geometry**

Unit Summary

In this final unit on geometry, students build on previous knowledge to develop and use formulas for the area and perimeter of a rectangle and the area of a triangle. They first review strategies for finding the area of a rectangle, then develop the formula. To develop the formula for the area of a triangle, students build right triangles using geoboards and dot paper. They use different strategies for finding the area of the triangles, then record their measurements in a table. Using patterns in the table, they create a formula for the area of right triangles. Then, using similar strategies, they extend the formula to all triangles. The formula for the perimeter of a rectangle is developed through the observation that opposite sides of a rectangle are equal in length. The DPP for this unit reviews all the division facts.

Concept Focus

- right triangles
- acute triangles
- squares
- perimeter
- area of rectangles
- perimeter of rectangles
- division facts
- obtuse triangles
- rectangles
- area
- geometry formulas
- area of triangles
- formulas

Unit 16 | **Bringing It All Together: An Assessment Unit**

Unit Summary

This unit is designed to review, extend, and assess the concepts students have studied throughout the year. Students revisit each of the labs they have completed during the year in preparation for completing an assessment lab. The assessment lab is based on the Adventure Book *Bats!* in which a family helps a scientist estimate the number of bats in a cave. In the lab *How Many Bats in a Cave?* students use beans in a container to model the sampling procedures used in the story. Using a similar procedure and proportional reasoning, students estimate the number of beans in their containers. They also complete an open-ended assessment problem, *Grass Act,* in which they again use sampling to estimate the number of blades of grass in a given area. Finally, students take an *End-of-Year Test,* which assesses concepts from Units 13–15. The unit ends with a review of students' portfolios. The DPP for this unit reviews and assesses all the division facts.

Concept Focus

- experiment review
- populations and samples
- point graphs
- communicating solution strategies
- using data to solve problems
- end-of-year test
- Adventure Book: estimating animal populations
- TIMS Laboratory Method
- ratios and proportions
- best-fit lines
- Student Rubric: *Solving*
- portfolio review
- division facts

The *Scope and Sequence & the NCTM Standards* section provides descriptions and tables which show how MATH TRAILBLAZERS relates to the National Council of Teachers of Mathematics *Standards*.

Students share their data by recording it on a class data table.

Standards Narrative
Scope and Sequence & the NCTM *Standards*

The NCTM *Standards* and MATH TRAILBLAZERS complement each other: the *Standards* provides a vision of what mathematics instruction in schools should be and the curriculum turns that vision into reality. The NCTM *Standards* includes 13 curriculum standards. This section outlines how MATH TRAILBLAZERS complements these standards.

Standard 1: Problem Solving

A strong emphasis on problem solving is evident in the NCTM recommendations. The problem solving described in the *Standards* is not just an important part of instruction—it is to be the organizing principle for the mathematics curriculum.

Therefore, throughout MATH TRAILBLAZERS, students are immersed in complex problem situations in which they both apply the mathematics they know and construct new mathematics as required. Skills, procedures, and concepts are developed as students work on the problems. For example, in the third-grade laboratory experiment, *The Better "Picker Upper,"* students explore the absorbency of various brands of paper towels by dropping water on each brand and comparing the areas of the spots. As the students work through this complex problem, they learn about area (by tracing the spots on grid paper and counting square centimeters to find the areas), fractions (as they piece parts of square centimeters together to make whole square centimeters), averaging (as they aggregate the results of several trials), and graphing (as they display and interpret their data in graphs). Students also make and test predictions and generalize their results. All this mathematics grows out of one problem: "Which is the more absorbent towel?"

Putting problems first is a different and difficult way to organize a mathematics curriculum. If the focus is on problems, then careful design, meticulous planning, and continual assessment are required to ensure the timely development of skills and concepts. Despite the difficulties, the benefits are clear: students not only master skills and concepts, but can apply them flexibly to solve problems.

Standard 2: Communication

This standard calls for students to have frequent opportunities to communicate: "Students [should] relate physical materials, pictures, and diagrams to mathematical ideas." (NCTM, 1989, p. 26) It is a common experience for people to understand an idea truly when they try to explain it to others. Such communication and representations are integral to MATH TRAILBLAZERS. In many activities, students handle manipulatives, draw pictures, make graphs, and grapple with mathematical ideas. Many of the activities are collaborative exercises involving groups of students who work together to obtain, analyze, and generalize their results.

Just as people explain how they solve problems on the job, students who use the labs and activities talk about their mathematics. Students discuss, compare, contrast, and write about their problem-solving methods in both small-group and whole-class settings. This "publication" of students' mathematical thinking gives students access to a broader range of solution strategies and helps them become more reflective about mathematics.

Standard 3: Reasoning

This standard requires that reasoning permeate the curriculum. Students constantly explain their thinking and justify their solutions, first in small groups and then to the class as a whole. Sometimes they explain their thoughts verbally and other times in writing or by using pictures and other tools. Students are always encouraged to find solutions in more than one way and to compare and contrast various solution methods. Thus, meaning and understanding are emphasized, and students find that mathematics makes sense.

One example of an important area of mathematical reasoning that receives particular attention in MATH TRAILBLAZERS, especially in grades 3 through 5, is proportional reasoning. This kind of reasoning is carefully developed over time through a sequence of real-life problems which can be solved with manipulatives, patterns, graphs, or symbols. Students choose the strategies and tools which make sense to them. Using these tools helps students create visual images of this important mathematical concept, which historically has largely been taught symbolically or procedurally and has been a difficult concept for many students to grasp.

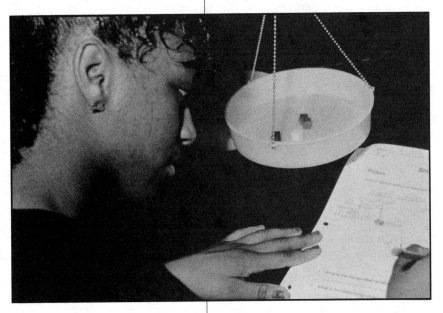

Standard 4: Connections

The fourth standard calls for connections within mathematics, between mathematics and other parts of the school curriculum, and between mathematics and daily life.

Integration of subject matter is a major focus of MATH TRAILBLAZERS. Mathematics arises naturally in science, language, history, and daily life. MATH TRAILBLAZERS does not artificially merge disparate ideas from distinct disciplines, but rather builds up the underlying unity between disciplines that we see in the real world. The basic measurement variables that are covered extensively in the curriculum—length, area, volume, mass, and time—are fundamental not only to mathematics but also to science and in daily life. The TIMS Laboratory Method effectively incorporates the method of science into the mathematics curriculum as a problem-solving tool.

The Adventure Books and Literature Connections integrate reading with the mathematics curriculum. Some Adventure Books recount the history of science and mathematics; others show how the concepts and procedures students are learning apply to the work of real scientists or to everyday life. Students are continually required to communicate their mathematical thinking orally and in writing. MATH TRAILBLAZERS is committed to the ideal of "writing across the curriculum."

Connections within mathematics are equally important. Like most real-world problems, activities in MATH TRAILBLAZERS generally involve a combination of mathematical topics. A single laboratory experiment, for example, might involve arithmetic, data collection, estimation, geometry, probability, and algebraic concepts—each covered at an appropriate level for students.

Curriculum Standards 5–13

The K–4 and 5–8 sections of the *Standards* each list nine more standards. These two sets of standards are not identical, but they cover much of the same ground. Estimation, numeration, computation, measurement, geometry, statistics and probability, fractions, patterns and functions, and algebra are all addressed at both the K–4 level and the 5–8 level. These content standards define a broad curriculum where problem solving, communication, reasoning, and connections are integral, not ancillary, issues.

Most activities in MATH TRAILBLAZERS address more than one of the content standards. Consider, for example, *The Bouncing Ball*, a fourth-grade laboratory experiment in which students investigate the relationship between the drop height and the bounce height of a tennis ball. The investigation begins with a question: "What is the relationship between how far a ball drops and how high it bounces?" Through class discussion, the variables are identified and named (D, the drop height and B, the bounce height) and experimental procedures are devised. A picture records this information. Next, the students drop the tennis balls repeatedly, measuring drop height and bounce height each time, and recording the data in a table. As the data are being gathered, the students monitor the numbers to see if they are consistent and make sense and examine the data table to see if a pattern can be discerned. Next, the students graph their data. As they work, students are asked to understand how the data table and the graph relate to the physical system, what the relationship between drop height and bounce height is, and how that relationship is evident in the table and graph. Then, students make some predictions and verify those predictions. Finally, students are asked to generalize: "What would the graph look like for a super ball?" "What would happen if the experiment were repeated on a carpeted floor?"

This single experiment involves algebra, measurement, statistics, number sense, estimation, graphing, patterns and functions, and mathematical reasoning. All these topics, moreover, relate to a single concrete context that unites them. By weaving so many themes into one complex whole, that whole becomes more meaningful and the mathematics more powerful.

Not every standard is addressed in every activity, but most activities address many standards, and all standards are addressed in many activities. MATH TRAILBLAZERS is a comprehensive and demanding curriculum that includes geometry, statistics and probability, measurement, algebra, estimation, fractions, numeration, and computation—just what the *Standards* require.

Developing a *Standards*-Based Classroom

The *Professional Standards for Teaching Mathematics* (NCTM, 1991) specify what classroom teachers, supervisors, teacher educators, and policy makers should do to improve mathematics instruction. Much of this discussion concerns four key areas: tasks, discourse, environment, and analysis. Teachers should decide what tasks to set for students; they should foster discourse about mathematics; they should establish a classroom environment conducive to high achievement and positive attitudes; and they should engage in analysis of students' thinking and their own teaching. While accomplishing these things depends more on teachers' expertise than on curricula, materials that embody the NCTM *Standards* can make the work easier.

Tasks. MATH TRAILBLAZERS provides a logical sequence of well-conceived tasks. Professional mathematicians and scientists helped develop the curriculum so that lessons focus on significant concepts and skills. Teachers and mathematics educators also helped write the curriculum, so that tasks are engaging, practical, and developmentally appropriate. Lessons are designed to develop both skills and concepts, to encourage students to make connections within mathematics and between mathematics and other subjects, to portray mathematics as a human endeavor, and to promote communication and problem-solving skills.

Discourse. Discourse is supported by many features of MATH TRAILBLAZERS. Tasks in the curriculum have enough depth for significant discourse to be possible. An emphasis on multiple solutions to problems encourages students to talk about their own thinking. The Student Guide often displays and discusses multiple solutions to problems. Journal and discussion prompts in the student and teacher materials stimulate and focus classroom discussions. Adventure books and children's literature connect language arts to mathematics and science, helping students understand that people really do talk about mathematics and science. The wide range of tools and technology in MATH TRAILBLAZERS—manipulatives, calculators, pictures, tables, graphs, and symbols—enhance discourse by broadening the means of communication beyond what is traditional. Lessons in cooperative group format also provide multiple opportunities for discussion.

Environment. Creating a classroom environment conducive to the development of each student's mathematical power is necessary for the *Standards* to come alive. This involves arranging space, time, and materials in ways that maximize student learning. MATH TRAILBLAZERS' diverse range of activities— activities of varied length, activities for groups and individuals, hands-on and paper-and-pencil investigations, activities that encourage multiple solution paths, the heavy use of manipulatives and other visual tools—all help teachers develop a classroom that builds mathematical understandings and skills for a wide range of students.

Analysis. John Dewey expressed a conviction that underlies MATH TRAILBLAZERS: "An experience is not a true experience until it is reflective." This applies both to students reflecting on their mathematical experiences and to teachers reflecting on their teaching. The curriculum's activities and assessment program provide teachers with many opportunities to assess student progress. Teachers using the curriculum will know more about their students' mathematical abilities than they ever have before. The extensive background information provided in the unit guides and in the Teacher Implementation Guide provides accessible ways for teachers to gain additional insight into how students learn mathematics. This enhanced knowledge motivates the teaching of

Alignment with the NCTM Assessment Standards for School Mathematics is discussed in Section 8 Assessment in MATH TRAILBLAZERS.

subsequent lessons. MATH TRAILBLAZERS will help you become more attuned both to your students and to your own teaching.

MATH TRAILBLAZERS: A Standards-Based Curriculum

Five student goals are mentioned in the NCTM *Standards:* (1) Students should learn to value mathematics. (2) Students should become confident in their ability to do mathematics. (3) Students should become mathematical problem-solvers. (4) Students should learn to communicate mathematically. (5) Students should learn to reason mathematically.

To reach these goals, the NCTM calls for curricula to be conceptually oriented, to involve students actively, to emphasize development of students' mathematical thinking and reasoning abilities, to emphasize applications, to include a broad range of content, and to make appropriate and ongoing use of calculators and computers.

These are admirable goals and high expectations. No curriculum can finally and fully attain such goals and fulfill such expectations—not only will there always be improvements to be made, but in the end much depends upon individual teachers and students. Yet a curriculum that has been developed specifically aligned with the *Standards* can help. The goals and characteristics described above are all hallmarks of MATH TRAILBLAZERS.

The best test of conformity with the *Standards*, however, is to observe students using the curriculum. Are they actively involved, grappling with significant concepts while learning and applying basic skills, thinking and reasoning, and using a broad range of tools to solve a broad range of realistic problems? We think you will find that MATH TRAILBLAZERS more than meets this test.

References

An Agenda for Action: Recommendations for School Mathematics of the 1980s. Reston, Va.: National Council of Teachers of Mathematics, 1980.

Assessment Standards for School Mathematics. Reston, Va.: National Council of Teachers of Mathematics, 1995.

Curriculum and Evaluation Standards for School Mathematics. Reston, Va.: National Council of Teachers of Mathematics, 1989.

Essential Mathematics for the 21st Century: The Position of the National Council of Supervisors of Mathematics. Minneapolis: National Council of Supervisors of Mathematics, 1988.

National Council of Supervisors of Mathematics. "Position Paper on Basic Skills." *Arithmetic Teacher,* 25(1), 1977, pp. 18–22.

Professional Standards for Teaching Mathematics. Reston, Va.: National Council of Teachers of Mathematics, 1991.

Standards Matrix

Scope and Sequence & the NCTM *Standards*

The Standards Matrix, which begins on the following page, illustrates how *MATH TRAILBLAZERS* relates to the National Council of Teachers of Mathematics *Standards.* Bullets are used to denote process standards; diamonds are used for content standards. The number of bullets or diamonds for each standard indicates the level of emphasis on that standard in each unit.

Grade 5, Units 1–8

	Standard												
	1. Problem Solving	2. Communication	3. Reasoning	4. Connections	5. Number and Number Relationships	6. Number Systems and Number Theory	7. Computation and Estimation	8. Patterns and Functions	9. Algebra	10. Statistics	11. Probability	12. Geometry	13. Measurement
Unit 1: Populations and Samples	••	•••	••	•••	♦♦		♦	♦♦♦	♦	♦♦♦	♦		
Unit 2: Big Numbers	•••	•••	•••	•••	♦♦♦	♦♦♦	♦♦♦	♦♦		♦			♦
Unit 3: Fractions and Ratios	•••	••	•••	•••	♦♦♦	♦♦	♦♦♦	♦	♦	♦♦			♦
Unit 4: Division and Data	•••	••	•••	•••	♦♦♦	♦	♦♦♦	♦	♦	♦♦♦		♦♦♦	♦♦♦
Unit 5: Investigating Fractions	•••	•••	•••	•••	♦♦♦	♦♦♦	♦♦♦	♦	♦♦	♦♦♦			♦♦
Unit 6: Geometry	•••	•••	•••	•••			♦	♦♦	♦			♦♦♦	♦♦♦
Unit 7: Decimals and Probability	••	••	•••	•••	♦♦♦	♦♦♦	♦♦♦	♦		♦♦♦	♦♦♦	♦	♦
Unit 8: Applications: An Assessment Unit	•••	•••	•••	•••	♦	♦	♦♦	♦♦♦	♦	♦♦♦			♦

Grade 5, Units 9–16

	Standard												
	1. Problem Solving	2. Communication	3. Reasoning	4. Connections	5. Number and Number Relationships	6. Number Systems and Number Theory	7. Computation and Estimation	8. Patterns and Functions	9. Algebra	10. Statistics	11. Probability	12. Geometry	13. Measurement
Unit 9: Connections to Division	••	••	•••	•••	♦♦♦	♦♦♦	♦♦♦	♦					♦
Unit 10: Maps and Coordinates	•••	•••	•••	•••	♦♦♦	♦♦	♦	♦	♦♦			♦♦♦	♦♦
Unit 11: Number Patterns, Primes, and Fractions	••	•••	•••	••	♦♦	♦♦♦	♦♦♦	♦♦♦	♦				
Unit 12: Using Fractions	•••	•••	•••	•••			♦♦♦	♦		♦♦		♦	
Unit 13: Ratio and Proportion	•••	••	•••	•••	♦♦		♦♦	♦♦♦	♦♦♦	♦♦♦			♦♦♦
Unit 14: Using Circles	•••	•••	•••	•••	♦♦		♦♦	♦	♦♦	♦♦♦		♦♦♦	♦♦♦
Unit 15: Developing Formulas with Geometry	•••	•••	•••	••			♦♦	♦	♦♦♦			♦♦♦	♦♦♦
Unit 16: Bringing It All Together: An Assessment Unit	•••	•••	•••	•••	♦		♦♦	♦♦	♦	♦♦♦	♦		♦

• KEY ♦

Process Standards (Numbers 1–4)

•••, ••, • The number of bullets indicates the relative importance of the standard as an organizational theme in the unit.

Content Standards (Numbers 5–13)

♦♦♦, ♦♦, ♦ The number of diamonds indicates the relative prominence of the standard in the mathematical content included in the unit.

Scope and Sequence

Scope and Sequence & the NCTM *Standards*

Scope and Sequence Chart for Lessons

MATH TRAILBLAZERS has been developed to meet the NCTM *Curriculum and Evaluation Standards for School Mathematics.* The scope and sequence chart on the following pages indicates how each unit aligns with the *Standards.* **The first four NCTM Standards—problem solving, communication, reasoning, and connections—are pervasive in every *MATH TRAILBLAZERS* unit and are therefore not included as distinct entries in the tables.** The remaining nine standards from the NCTM document for Grades 5–8 are listed across the top. By reading the chart horizontally, you will be able to see the integration of the various standards within a given unit. By reading the chart vertically, you will be able to track the development of a specific standard throughout the fifth grade curriculum. The entries in each column reflect the content of the lessons, but not the content of the Home Practice or the Daily Practice and Problems.

The scope and sequence for the fifth grade Daily Practice and Problems follows the Scope and Sequence for the lessons.

Scope and Sequence Chart for the Daily Practice and Problems

MATH TRAILBLAZERS has been developed to meet the NCTM *Curriculum and Evaluation Standards* for School Mathematics. Every unit includes a series of Daily Practice and Problems (DPP). The scope and sequence chart on the following pages indicates how the DPP aligns with the *Standards.* The nine content standards from the NCTM document for Grades 5–8 are listed across the top of the table. By reading the chart horizontally, you will be able to track the development of a specific standard throughout the fifth grade DPP. Each DPP item, which is defined by a letter, has been correlated with one or more of the standards. The appropriate letters are indicated in parentheses following each entry. Thus, the scope and sequence can also serve as a content map for the individual DPP items.

The scope and sequence for the fifth grade lessons precedes the Scope and Sequence for the *Daily Practice and Problems.* For more information about the *Daily Practice and Problems,* see the DPP and HP Guide (Section 7) in the *Teacher Implementation Guide.*

Scope & Sequence Chart for Unit Lessons

	Number and Number Relationships	Number Systems and Number Theory	Computation and Estimation	Patterns and Functions
Unit 1: Populations and Samples **Lessons** (The scope and sequence for the Daily Practice and Problems follows Unit 16 of this section.)	Investigating the concept of averages. Using a median to represent a set of data. Identifying the mode. Gathering, organizing, graphing, and analyzing data by using variables, making data tables, and drawing bar graphs. Translating between graphs and real world events. Making and interpreting bar graphs.		Solving multistep word problems. Choosing appropriate methods and tools (calculators, pencil and paper, or mental math) to calculate. Choosing to find an estimate or an exact answer.	Gathering, organizing, graphing, and analyzing data by using variables, making data tables, and drawing bar graphs. Making and interpreting bar graphs.

Gathering, organizing, graphing, and analyzing data by using variables, making data tables, and drawing bar graphs. Translating between graphs and real world events. Making and interpreting bar graphs.	Collecting, organizing, graphing, and analyzing data. Naming values of variables. Describing a classroom of students using numerical variables. Translating between graphs and real world events. Making and interpreting bar graphs. Sampling a population. Predicting population characteristics from samples. Investigating the concept of averages. Using a median to represent a set of data. Identifying the mode.	Finding the probability of an event based on collected data.		

Grade 5 • Quick Start

**Unit 2:
Big Numbers**

Lessons

(The scope and sequence for the Daily Practice and Problems follows Unit 16 of this section.)

Using known multiplication facts to learn division facts.

Understanding multiplication using the base-ten pieces.

Understanding grouping and regrouping in base ten.

Understanding the meaning of each column in a multidigit number.

Reading and understanding the magnitude of large numbers.

Reading, writing, and using scientific notation.

Using estimation to place numbers on a number line.

Modeling adding and subtracting with base-ten pieces.

Finding numbers convenient for estimating.

Reviewing terminology, patterns, and conventions used in reading and writing large numbers.

Translating between different representations of quantities (concrete, pictorial, symbolic).

Understanding grouping and regrouping in base ten.

Understanding the meaning of each column in a multidigit number.

Understanding the base-ten structure of our number system.

Reading, writing, and using scientific notation.

Using estimation to place numbers on a number line.

Using known multiplication facts to learn division facts.

Understanding multiplication using the base-ten pieces.

Using estimation to place numbers on a number line.

Modeling adding and subtracting with the base-ten pieces.

Estimating with base-ten pieces.

Multiplying numbers with ending zeros.

Self-assessing the multiplication and division facts.

Using efficient strategies to find the answers to multiplication facts.

Using paper-and-pencil methods for multiplication.

Using estimation to solve multiplication problems.

Finding numbers convenient for estimating.

Using known multiplication facts to learn division facts.

Understanding multiplication using base-ten pieces.

Reviewing terminology, patterns, and conventions used in reading and writing large numbers.

Translating between different representations of quantities (concrete, pictorial, symbolic).

Investigating patterns used in representing large and small numbers in a place value system.

Multiplying numbers with ending zeros.

Estimating with base-ten pieces.

Using patterns in data to solve problems.

Grade 5 • Quick Start

Algebra	Statistics	Probability	Geometry	Measurement
Using patterns in data to solve problems.	Using patterns in data to solve problems.			Measuring length in centimeters.

Grade 5 • Quick Start

Scope & Sequence Chart for Unit Lessons

	Number and Number Relationships	Number Systems and Number Theory	Computation and Estimation	Patterns and Functions
Unit 3: Fractions and Ratios **Lessons** (The scope and sequence for the Daily Practice and Problems follows Unit 16 of this section.)	Representing fractions using manipulatives and symbols. Finding a fraction for a given quantity when a unit whole is given. Writing improper fractions as mixed numbers. Writing mixed numbers as improper fractions. Using words, pictures, tables, graphs, and fractions to express ratios. Defining speed as a ratio. Making and using line graphs. Finding equivalent fractions.	Ordering fractions using benchmarks. Ordering fractions with common denominators. Defining speed as a ratio. Writing improper fractions as mixed numbers. Writing mixed numbers as improper fractions. Finding equivalent fractions. Finding equal ratios.	Finding equivalent fractions. Finding equal ratios. Using ratios to solve problems. Writing improper fractions as mixed numbers. Writing mixed numbers as improper fractions. Solving multistep problems. Choosing to find an estimate or an exact answer. Writing number sentences using fractions. Using data to solve problems.	Understanding equivalent fractions. Using words, pictures, tables, graphs, and fractions to express ratios. Making and using line graphs.

Algebra	Statistics	Probability	Geometry	Measurement
Using words, pictures, tables, graphs, and fractions to express ratios.	Making and using line graphs.			Measuring length in yards.
Making and using line graphs.	Collecting, organizing, graphing, and analyzing data.			Measuring time with a stopwatch.
Using ratios to solve problems.	Drawing best-fit lines.			Defining speed as a ratio.
Drawing best-fit lines.	Using data to solve problems.			
	Using medians to represent sets of data.			

Grade 5 • Quick Start

Scope & Sequence Chart for Unit Lessons

	Number and Number Relationships	Number Systems and Number Theory	Computation and Estimation	Patterns and Functions
Unit 4: Division and Data **Lessons** (The scope and sequence for the Daily Practice and Problems follows Unit 16 of this section.)	Understanding the concept of division. Estimating quotients. Interpreting remainders. Comparing the mean and the median as measures of average. Order of operations. Making and using line graphs. Using ratios to solve problems.	Modeling division with base-ten pieces. Using ratios to solve problems.	Using multiplication facts to find the area of a geometric figure. Understanding the oncept of division. Modeling division with base-ten pieces. Using paper-and-pencil methods to divide (1-digit divisors). Dividing numbers that end in zeros. Estimating quotients. Interpreting remainders. Estimating 10% of a number. Using 10% as a standard for error analysis. Computing the mean. Using means and medians to average data. Using ratios to solve problems.	Using patterns in data tables and graphs to make predictions. Making and using line graphs.

Grade 5 • Quick Start

Algebra	Statistics	Probability	Geometry	Measurement
Using patterns in data tables and graphs to make predictions.	Collecting, organizing, graphing, and analyzing data.		Strategies to find the area of a geometric figure.	Strategies to find the area of a geometric figure.
Making and using line graphs.	Identifying the manipulated, responding, and fixed variables in an experiment.		Using multiplication facts to find the area of a geometric figure.	Measuring the area of irregular shapes.
Drawing best-fit lines.	Choosing an appropriate graph to display data.		Counting square centimeters to estimate the area of a figure with curved sides.	Understanding the role of standard units in scientific measurement.
Using ratios to solve problems.	Reviewing five fundamental variables of science and how they are measured.		Generalizing the area of a rectangle as length times width.	Using multiplication facts to find the area of a geometric figure.
Order of operations.	Making and using line graphs.		Measuring the area of irregular shapes.	Counting square centimeters to estimate the area of a figure with curved sides.
	Drawing best-fit lines.			Generalizing the area of a rectangle as length times width.
	Using patterns in data tables and graphs to make predictions.			Using 10% as a standard for error analysis.
	Using 10% as a standard for error analysis.			
	Using means and medians to average data.			
	Comparing the mean and the median as measures of average.			

Grade 5 • Quick Start

Scope & Sequence Chart for Unit Lessons

	Number and Number Relationships	Number Systems and Number Theory	Computation and Estimation	Patterns and Functions
Unit 5: Investigating Fractions **Lessons** (The scope and sequence for the Daily Practice and Problems follows Unit 16 of this section.)	Defining the numerator and the denominator. Modeling mixed numbers and improper fractions. Modeling fractions with manipulatives and pictures. Identifying the unit whole when a fractional part is given. Using models to add and subtract fractions with unlike denominators. Using rectangles to subtract with unlike denominators. Defining speed as a ratio. Making and using line graphs. Writing equivalent fractions.	Defining the numerator and the denominator. Comparing fractions. Identifying the unit whole when a fractional part is given. Defining speed as a ratio. Writing equivalent fractions. Finding common denominators. Using models to add and subtract fractions with unlike denominators. Using rectangles to subtract unlike denominators.	Writing number sentences using fractions. Writing equivalent fractions. Finding common denominators. Using models to add and subtract fractions with unlike denominators. Using symbols to add and subtract fractions with unlike denominators. Solving word problems. Using ratios to solve problems.	Comparing fractions. Making and using point graphs. Using the steepness of a line to compare ratios.

Grade 5 • Quick Start

Algebra	Statistics	Probability	Geometry	Measurement
Using ratios to solve problems.	Collecting, organizing, graphing, and analyzing data.			Measuring length in yards and feet.
Making and using point graphs.	Making and using line graphs.			Measuring time with a stopwatch.
Using the steepness of a line to compare ratios.	Using the steepness of a line to compare ratios.			Defining speed as a ratio.
Using graphs to solve problems.	Using graphs to solve problems.			Comparing speeds.

Grade 5 • Quick Start

Scope & Sequence Chart for Unit Lessons

	Number and Number Relationships	Number Systems and Number Theory	Computation and Estimation	Patterns and Functions
Unit 6: Geometry **Lessons** (The scope and sequence for the Daily Practice and Problems follows Unit 16 of this section.)			Investigating the sum of the angles in a triangle. Investigating the sum of the angles in a quadrilateral. Discovering that the sum of the lengths of any two sides of a triangle is greater than the length of the third side.	Finding patterns in the sum of angles in polygons. Discovering that the sum of the lengths of any two sides of a triangle is greater than the length of the third side. Discovering that three lengths determine a unique triangle. Discovering that two lengths and the included angle determine exactly one triangle. Investigating tessellations.

Grade 5 • Quick Start

Algebra	Statistics	Probability	Geometry	Measurement
Finding patterns in the sum of angles in polygons.			Reviewing the concept of an angle.	Estimating angle measures using benchmarks.
			Identifying acute, obtuse, right, and straight angles.	Measuring angles with a protractor.
			Estimating angles using benchmarks.	Discovering that the sum of the lengths of any two sides of a triangle is greater than the length of the third side.
			Drawing angles of determined degrees.	
			Investigating the properties of polygons.	
			Naming common polygons.	Constructing polygons with specific measurements (lengths of sides and/or angle measures).
			Investigating the sum of angles in a triangle and a quadrilateral.	
			Triangulating polygons.	Investigating the sum of angles in a triangle and a quadrilateral.
			Finding patterns in the sum of angles in polygons.	
			Discovering that the sum of the lengths of any two sides of a triangle is greater than the length of the third side.	
			Exploring congruence and similarity.	
			Discovering that three lengths determine a unique triangle.	
			Discovering that two lengths and the included angle determine exactly one triangle.	
			Investigating tessellations.	
			Describing and classifying two-dimensional geometric shapes.	
			Constructing polygons with specific measurements.	

Grade 5 • Quick Start

Scope & Sequence Chart for Unit Lessons

	Number and Number Relationships	**Number Systems and Number Theory**	**Computation and Estimation**	**Patterns and Functions**
Unit 7: Decimals and Probability **Lessons** (The scope and sequence for the Daily Practice and Problems follows Unit 16 of this section.)	Using the area model to explore translations between fractions, decimals, and percents. Using fractions, decimals, and percents to represent the same quantity. Using decimal representations to compare fractions that have unlike denominators. Reviewing the role of the decimal point. Exploring area models for tenths, hundredths, and thousandths. Rounding decimals. Reading and writing decimals. Comparing and ordering decimals. Placing decimal points in products. Making and interpreting bar graphs. Estimating sums, differences, and products involving decimals. Expressing probabilities as fractions and percents.	Comparing and ordering decimals. Using place value to align decimals in addition and subtraction problems. Expressing probabilities as fractions and percents. Using the area model of multiplication to multiply decimals.	Using place value to align decimals in addition and subtraction problems. Adding and subtracting decimals using paper and pencil. Using the area model of multiplication to multiply decimals. Multiplying decimals using paper and pencil. Estimating sums, differences, and products involving decimals.	Using the area model to explore translations between fractions, decimals, and percents. Making and interpreting bar graphs.

Algebra	Statistics	Probability	Geometry	Measurement
Making and interpreting bar graphs.	Collecting, organizing, graphing, and analyzing data.	Understanding that random events are predictable "over the long run."	Finding the area of rectangles.	Finding the area of rectangles.
	Collecting and organizing data from a random process.	Linking qualitative and quantitative characteristics of probabilities.	Using the area model of multiplication to multiply decimals.	Estimating area.
	Making and interpreting bar graphs.	Exploring situations which have outcomes that are not equally likely.		Finding area by counting square centimeters.
	Understanding that random events are predictable "over the long run."	Analyzing fair and unfair games.		
	Analyzing fair and unfair games.	Listing all the ways 0, 1, and 2 heads can show when 2 coins are flipped.		
	Using probability to predict.	Computing probabilities for all possible outcomes when 2 coins are flipped.		
		Understanding that as the number of trials increases, the results of coin flipping more closely resemble the probabilities.		
		Computing probabilities of having 0, 1, and 2 boys in a 2-child family.		
		Using probability to predict.		
		Comparing probabilities with real-world data.		
		Exploring probabilities involved in flipping a coin.		

Grade 5 • Quick Start

Scope & Sequence Chart for Unit Lessons

	Number and Number Relationships	Number Systems and Number Theory	Computation and Estimation	Patterns and Functions
Unit 8: Applications: An Assessment Unit **Lessons** (The scope and sequence for the Daily Practice and Problems follows Unit 16 of this section.)	Using percents. Estimating the product of two decimals. Changing fractions to decimals to percents. Making and interpreting bar graphs. Translating between graphs and real-world events.	Using percents. Changing fractions to decimals to percents.	Estimating the product of two decimals. Changing fractions to decimals to percents. Solving multistep word problems. Using percents. Choosing to find an estimate or an exact answer.	Translating between graphs and real-world events. Grouping data in bins to see patterns. Using patterns in tables and graphs to make generalizations about data. Making and interpreting bar graphs. Comparing and contrasting the following elements of different experiments: measurement procedures, number of trials, problems solved, types of graphs, and variables.

Grade 5 • Quick Start

Algebra	Statistics	Probability	Geometry	Measurement
Making and interpreting bar graphs. Translating between graphs and real-world events.	Collecting, organizing, and analyzing data. Comparing and contrasting the following elements of different experiments: measurement procedures, number of trials, problems solved, types of graphs, and variables. Collecting and organizing demographic data. Grouping data in bins to see patterns. Making a bar graph using binned data. Translating between graphs and real-world events. Using patterns in tables and graphs to make generalizations about data.			Comparing and contrasting the following elements of different experiments: measurement procedures, number of trials, problems solved, types of graphs, and variables. Measuring time with a stopwatch.

Grade 5 • Quick Start

Scope & Sequence Chart for Unit Lessons

	Number and Number Relationships	Number Systems and Number Theory	Computation and Estimation	Patterns and Functions
Unit 9: Connections to Division **Lessons** (The scope and sequence for the Daily Practice and Problems follows Unit 16 of this section.)	Interpreting fractions as division. Finding decimal equivalents (or decimal approximations) for fractions using models. Finding decimal equivalents (or decimal approximations) for fractions using a calculator. Identifying repeating decimals on a calculator. Interpreting a remainder in a division problem. Expressing a quotient as a mixed number.	Interpreting fractions as division. Finding decimal equivalents (or decimal approximations) for fractions using models. Finding decimal equivalents (or decimal approximations) for fractions using a calculator. Identifying repeating decimals on a calculator. Interpreting a remainder in a division problem. Expressing a quotient as a mixed number. Checking work using Quotient × Divisor + Remainder = Dividend. Finding a whole number remainder using a calculator. Adding and subtracting fractions using calculators.	Finding decimal equivalents (or decimal approximations) for fractions using models. Finding decimal equivalents (or decimal approximations) for fractions using a calculator. Using paper-and-pencil methods to divide (2-digit divisors). Checking work using Quotient × Divisor + Remainder = Dividend. Using estimation to choose more accurate numbers in partial products. Lattice multiplication. Exploring different methods of paper-and-pencil multiplication. Using a calculator to divide larger numbers. Using a calculator to divide money. Finding a whole number remainder using a calculator. Adding and subtracting fractions using common denominators. Adding and subtracting fractions using calculators.	Interpreting fractions as division. Identifying repeating decimals on a calculator.

Grade 5 • Quick Start

Algebra	Statistics	Probability	Geometry	Measurement

Grade 5 • Quick Start

Scope & Sequence Chart for Unit Lessons

	Number and Number Relationships	Number Systems and Number Theory	Computation and Estimation	Patterns and Functions
Unit 10: Maps and Coordinates **Lessons** (The scope and sequence for the Daily Practice and Problems follows Unit 16 of this section.)	Developing an understanding of the coordinate system. Understanding the importance of order in ordered pairs. Understanding the importance of the sign of a number in a coordinate pair. Finding coordinates of an object relative to the origin. Plotting coordinates and making a four-quadrant map. Using a four-quadrant scale map to find distances. Graphing shapes in four quadrants. Using slides to move shapes about the coordinate system. Determining the image of a slide. Using flips to move shapes about the coordinate system. Determining the image of a flip. Using a coordinate system to find locations on a map. Using the scale on a map. Using tessellations to create art. Exploring negative numbers.	Exploring negative numbers. Exploring uses of negative numbers. Developing an understanding of the coordinate system. Understanding the importance of the sign of a number in a coordinate pair. Finding coordinates of an object relative to the origin. Plotting coordinates and making a four-quadrant map. Using a four-quadrant scale map to find distances.	Using the scale on a map.	Using tessellations to create art.

Algebra	Statistics	Probability	Geometry	Measurement
Developing an understanding of the coordinate system.			Developing an understanding of the coordinate system.	Using a four-quadrant scale map to find distances.
Plotting coordinates and making a four-quadrant map.			Understanding the importance of order in ordered pairs.	Using the scale on a map.
Graphing shapes in four quadrants.			Understanding the importance of the sign of a number in a coordinate pair.	Measuring length.
Finding coordinates of an object relative to the origin.			Finding coordinates of an object relative to the origin.	
			Plotting coordinates and making a four-quadrant map.	
			Using a four-quadrant scale map to find distances.	
			Graphing shapes in four quadrants.	
			Using slides to move shapes about the coordinate system.	
			Determining the image of a slide.	
			Using flips to move shapes about the coordinate system.	
			Determining the image of a flip.	
			Using a coordinate system to find locations on a map.	
			Using the scale on a map.	
			Using tessellations to create art.	

Grade 5 • Quick Start

Scope & Sequence Chart for Unit Lessons

	Number and Number Relationships	Number Systems and Number Theory	Computation and Estimation	Patterns and Functions
Unit 11: Number Patterns, Primes, and Fractions **Lessons** (The scope and sequence for the Daily Practice and Problems follows Unit 16 of this section.)	Making a point graph that is not a straight line. Renaming numbers as the product of their prime factors using exponents.	Identifying the factors of numbers. Identifying prime and composite numbers. Finding and generalizing number patterns. Using number patterns to solve problems. Comparing fractions. Finding the prime factorization of a number using known factors, a factor tree, and calculators. Renaming numbers as the product of their prime factors using exponents. Finding common denominators. Reducing fractions to lowest terms. Identifying patterns with multiples, factors, and primes.	Finding the prime factorization of a number using known factors, a factor tree, and calculators. Renaming numbers as the product of their prime factors using exponents. Finding common denominators. Reducing fractions to lowest terms. Adding and subtracting fractions. Solving division problems whose quotients are mixed numbers. Choosing appropriate methods and tools (calculators, paper and pencil, or mental math) to calculate.	Finding and generalizing number patterns. Using number patterns to solve problems. Identifying patterns with multiples, factors, and primes.

Algebra	Statistics	Probability	Geometry	Measurement
Using variables in formulas.	Making a point graph that is not a straight line.			
Finding and generalizing number patterns.				
Making a point graph that is not a straight line.				

Grade 5 • Quick Start

Scope & Sequence Chart for Unit Lessons

	Number and Number Relationships	Number Systems and Number Theory	Computation and Estimation	Patterns and Functions
Unit 12: **Using Fractions** **Lessons** (The scope and sequence for the Daily Practice and Problems follows Unit 16 of this section.)	Using patterns to build number sense. Renaming mixed numbers. Estimating the product of two fractions. Using fractions in everyday situations.	Renaming mixed numbers. Using fractions in everyday situations.	Adding fractions. Adding mixed numbers using manipulatives. Adding mixed numbers using paper-and-pencil procedures. Renaming mixed numbers. Multiplying a fraction and a whole number. Multiplying a fraction and a fraction using paper-and-pencil procedures. Estimating the product of two fractions. Multiplying fractions using an area model and manipulatives. Using fractions in everyday situations. Choosing appropriate methods and tools (calculators, paper and pencil, or mental math) to calculate.	Using patterns to build number sense. Using patterns in tables to make predictions about data.

Grade 5 • Quick Start

Algebra	Statistics	Probability	Geometry	Measurement
Using patterns in tables to make predictions about data.	Collecting and organizing data to solve a problem. Using patterns in tables to make predictions about data.			Creating a time schedule.

Grade 5 • Quick Start

Scope & Sequence Chart for Unit Lessons

	Number and Number Relationships	Number Systems and Number Theory	Computation and Estimation	Patterns and Functions
Unit 13: Ratio and Proportion **Lessons** (The scope and sequence for the Daily Practice and Problems follows Unit 16 of this section.)	Using words, tables, graphs, and fractions to express ratios. Expressing a multiplicative relationship between variables in proportion. Using proportions to solve problems. Making and using line graphs. Defining density as the ratio of mass to volume.	Defining density as the ratio of mass to volume.	Using proportions to solve problems. Expressing a multiplicative relationship between variables in proportion. Computing density. Solving word problems. Choosing appropriate methods and tools (calculators, paper and pencil, or mental math) to calculate.	Looking for patterns in data. Using patterns in tables and graphs to make predictions about data. Using patterns in tables and graphs to make predictions about sinking and floating.

Algebra	Statistics	Probability	Geometry	Measurement
Looking for patterns in data.	Using patterns in tables and graphs to make predictions about data.			Measuring mass in grams.
Using proportions to solve problems.	Using tables and graphs to determine whether variables are in proportion.			Measuring volume in cubic centimeters.
Using patterns in tables and graphs to make predictions about data.	Using patterns in tables and graphs to make predictions about sinking and floating.			Defining density as the ratio of mass to volume.
Using tables and graphs to determine whether variables are in proportion.	Making and using line graphs.			Writing densities using gm/cc as the unit of measure.
Making and using line graphs.	Drawing best-fit lines.			
Drawing best-fit lines.	Translating between graphs and real-world events.			
Translating between graphs and real-world events.				

Grade 5 • Quick Start

Scope & Sequence Chart for Unit Lessons

	Number and Number Relationships	Number Systems and Number Theory	Computation and Estimation	Patterns and Functions
Unit 14: Using Circles **Lessons** (The scope and sequence for the Daily Practice and Problems follows Unit 16 of this section.)	Finding and expressing the relationship between the circumference and diameter of circles. Understanding π as the ratio of circumference to diameter of a circle. Changing fractions to decimals and percents.	Understanding π as the ratio of circumference to diameter of a circle.	Changing fractions to decimals and percents. Solving multistep word problems. Choosing appropriate methods and tools to calculate. Using π to find the circumference of a circle. Using ratios to solve problems.	Learning about the properties of shapes through constructions. Using π to find the circumference of a circle. Making and using line graphs.

Algebra	Statistics	Probability	Geometry	Measurement
Understanding π as the ratio of circumference to diameter of a circle.	Collecting, organizing, graphing, and analyzing data.		Naming parts of a circle.	Making a circle graph.
Using ratios to solve problems.	Reading and interpreting data from a circle graph.		Finding and expressing the relationship between the circumference and diameter of circles.	Using rulers, protractors, and compasses to draw and label circles.
Finding and expressing the relationship between the circumference and diameter of circles.	Making a circle graph.		Understanding π as the ratio of circumference to diameter of a circle.	Using a ruler, compass, and protractor to construct geometric figures.
Making and using line graphs.	Making and using line graphs.		Using rulers, protractors, and compasses to draw and label circles.	
Drawing best-fit lines.	Drawing best-fit lines.		Using a ruler, compass, and protractor to construct geometric figures.	
	Using the mean to represent a set of data.		Using geometric language to describe the steps involved in a construction.	
			Learning about the properties of shapes through constructions.	
			Using π to find the circumference of a circle.	

Grade 5 • Quick Start

Scope & Sequence Chart for Unit Lessons

	Number and Number Relationships	Number Systems and Number Theory	Computation and Estimation	Patterns and Functions
Unit 15: Developing Formulas with Geometry **Lessons** (The scope and sequence for the Daily Practice and Problems follows Unit 16 of this section.)			Using the formula for area of a rectangle: $A = l \times w$. Finding missing measures of rectangles. Using the X^2 key on the calculator. Using the formula $A = \frac{1}{2} \times b \times h$ to find the area of triangles. Solving multistep word problems. Choosing appropriate methods and tools (calculators, paper and pencil, or mental math) to calculate.	Using patterns in tables to develop formulas.

Algebra	Statistics	Probability	Geometry	Measurement
Using the formula for area of a rectangle: $A = l \times w$.			Finding the area of rectangles.	Finding the area of rectangles.
Finding missing measures of rectangles.			Finding the area of polygons.	Finding the area of polygons.
Using patterns in tables to develop formulas.			Using the formula for area of a rectangle: $A = l \times w$.	Using the formula for area of a rectangle: $A = l \times w$.
Developing a formula for finding the area of triangles.			Finding missing measures of rectangles.	Finding missing measures of rectangles.
Using the formula $A = \frac{1}{2} \times b \times h$ to find the area of triangles.			Building triangles on geoboards and dot paper.	Finding the area of triangles.
			Finding the area of triangles.	Finding the base and height of acute and obtuse triangles.
			Developing a formula for finding the area of triangles.	Finding the perimeter of various shapes.
			Finding the base and height of acute and obtuse triangles.	Using area and perimeter to draw rectangles.
			Finding the perimeter of various shapes.	
			Using area and perimeter to draw rectangles.	

Grade 5 • Quick Start

Scope & Sequence Chart for Unit Lessons

	Number and Number Relationships	Number Systems and Number Theory	Computation and Estimation	Patterns and Functions
Unit 16: Bringing It All Together: An Assessment Unit **Lessons** (The scope and sequence for the Daily Practice and Problems follows Unit 16 of this section.)	Using graphs to express ratios. Estimating numbers in the millions. Comparing ratios for equivalency. Making and using line graphs.	Comparing ratios for equivalency.	Using ratios and proportions to solve problems. Comparing ratios for equivalency. Using patterns in tables and graphs to solve problems. Estimating numbers in the millions. Computing with large numbers.	Comparing and contrasting the following elements of different experiments: measurement procedures, number of trials, problems solved, types of graphs, and variables. Using patterns in tables and graphs to solve problems. Making and using line graphs.

Algebra	Statistics	Probability	Geometry	Measurement
Making and using line graphs. Using patterns in tables and graphs to solve problems. Using ratios and proportions to solve problems. Using graphs to express ratios.	Collecting, organizing, graphing, and analyzing data. Comparing and contrasting the following elements of different experiments: measurement procedures, number of trials, problems solved, types of graphs, and variables. Using sampling to make predictions. Graphing multiple trials. Making and using line graphs. Using a best-fit line to average multiple trials. Using a capture-recapture technique to sample a population. Designing an appropriate data table. Using patterns in tables and graphs to solve problems. Finding an average.	Using a capture-recapture technique to sample a population. Using sampling to make predictions.	Measuring area.	Comparing and contrasting the following elements of different experiments: measurement procedures, number of trials, problems solved, types of graphs, and variables. Measuring area.

Grade 5 • Quick Start

Scope & Sequence Chart for the Daily Practice and Problems

	Number and Number Relationships	Number Systems and Number Theory	Computation and Estimation	Patterns and Functions
Unit 1: Populations and Samples **Daily Practice and Problems** (The scope and sequence for all Unit Lessons begins on page 9.)	Representing and interpreting data in a bar graph. (H) Finding the median value of a set of data. (M, Q)	Listing multiples of 2, 3, 4, 5, and 10. (B, I) Even and odd numbers. (B) Addition and subtraction place value games. (N, P)	Mental computation with addition and subtraction. (A, L) Assessing students' facility with the addition and subtraction facts. (C, G, K, O) Estimating by using a sample. (D) Computing cost and change. (E) Determining the value of coins. (J) Solving addition and subtraction problems using paper and pencil. (N, P, R)	Representing and interpreting data in a bar graph. (H)

Grade 5 • Quick Start

Algebra	Statistics	Probability	Geometry	Measurement
Representing and interpreting data in a bar graph. (H)	Estimating by using a sample. (D)			
	Distinguishing between numerical and categorical variables. (F, H)			
	Naming values of a variable. (F)			
	Representing and interpreting data in a bar graph. (H)			
	Using data to solve problems. (M)			
	Finding the median value of a set of data. (M, Q)			

Grade 5 • Quick Start

Scope & Sequence Chart for the Daily Practice and Problems

	Number and Number Relationships	Number Systems and Number Theory	Computation and Estimation	Patterns and Functions
Unit 2: Big Numbers **Daily Practice and Problems** (The scope and sequence for all Unit Lessons begins on page 9.)	Finding the median value of a set of data. (C, F, J) Understanding the meaning of each column in a multi-digit number. (G, H, P, R, S) Rounding numbers to the nearest hundred and thousand. (K) Ordering large numbers. (H, L) Reading scientific notation. (FF)	Division and multiplication as inverse operations. (I, M, X) Ordering large numbers. (H, L) Using a Chinese abacus: place value and multiplication. (N) Understanding the meaning of each column in a multidigit number. (G, H, P, R, S) Multiplication and place value game. (P) Reading scientific notation. (FF) Multiplication as repeated addition. (Z)	Solving addition and subtraction problems using paper and pencil. (A) Determining the value of coins. (B) Adding time: hours and minutes. (D) Computing change. (E) Solving multiplication and division story problems. (I, M, O) Exploring multiplication using the Chinese abacus. (N) Multiplication fact practice: 5s and 10s. (B, I, M, O, Q, U, W, X, AA, CC) Assessing students' facility with multiplication and division facts for 5s and 10s. (EE) All-partials method of multiplication. (R) Adding large numbers. (S) Estimating by using a sample. (T) Multiplying by multiples of 10. (U, W, X, CC, FF) Solving multiplication problems using paper and pencil. (P, R, V, DD) Estimating sums, differences, and products. (A, Y, Z, BB, DD)	Exploring patterns when multiplying by multiples of 10. (U, W, X, CC, FF)

Algebra	Statistics	Probability	Geometry	Measurement
Determining the number of nickels and dimes given the total value of a set of coins. (B)	Finding the median value of a set of data. (C, F, J)			Adding time: hours and minutes. (D)
Writing multiplication and division number sentences. (I, M, X)	Estimating by using a sample. (T)			Measuring length. (F, J)
Solving for *n* in a multiplication number sentence. (CC)				

Grade 5 • Quick Start

Scope & Sequence Chart for the Daily Practice and Problems

	Number and Number Relationships	Number Systems and Number Theory	Computation and Estimation	Patterns and Functions
Unit 3: Fractions and Ratios **Daily Practice and Problems** (The scope and sequence for all Unit Lessons begins on page 9.)	Understanding the meaning of each column in a multi-digit number. (D) Finding the median and mode of a set of data. (F) Interpreting a bar graph. (F) Identifying the whole when given a fraction and naming a fraction when given the whole. (H) Improper fractions and mixed numbers. (I) Skip counting by halves, thirds, and fifths. (J) Ordering fractions. (M, N, Q) Solving problems involving ratios. (P, R, T) Writing equal ratios. (X)	Understanding the meaning of each column in a multidigit number. (D) Skip counting by halves, thirds, and fifths. (J) Ordering fractions. (M, N, Q) Solving problems involving ratios. (P, R, T) Writing equal ratios. (X)	Self-assessment of the multiplication and division facts for the 2s and 3s. (A, S) Multiplication fact practice: 2s and 3s. (B, C) Multiplying by multiples of 10. (C) Adding large numbers. (D) Fact families: multiplication and division facts for 2s and 3s. (E, K, O) Solving multiplication, addition, and subtraction problems using paper and pencil. (G, L) Estimating sums, products, and differences. (G, L) Solving problems involving ratios. (P, R, T) Conversions: inches, feet, yards. (R) Conversions: seconds, minutes, hours, days, and weeks. (T) Subtracting time: hours and minutes. (V) Assessing students' facility with multiplication and division facts for 2s and 3s. (W)	Interpreting a bar graph. (F) Identifying and extending patterns in a data table. (X)

Grade 5 • Quick Start

Algebra	Statistics	Probability	Geometry	Measurement
Solving for an unknown in a story problem. (B)	Interpreting a bar graph. (F)			Using a stopwatch to measure time. (J)
Interpreting a bar graph. (F)	Finding the median and mode of a set of data. (F)			Estimating length. (R)
Solving problems involving ratios. (P, R, T)	Identifying and extending patterns in a data table. (X)			Conversions: inches, feet, and yards. (R)
Identifying and extending patterns in a data table. (X)				Conversions: seconds, minutes, hours, days, and weeks. (T)
				Choosing appropriate units of measure. (U)
				Subtracting time: hours and minutes. (V)

Grade 5 • Quick Start

Scope & Sequence Chart for the Daily Practice and Problems

	Number and Number Relationships	Number Systems and Number Theory	Computation and Estimation	Patterns and Functions
Unit 4: Division and Data **Daily Practice and Problems** (The scope and sequence for all Unit Lessons begins on page 9.)	Equivalent fractions. (C) Ordering fractions. (D) Estimating products and quotients. (G, Q, W, T) Reading and writing scientific notation. (L, S) Ordering large numbers. (L) Identifying the whole when given a fraction. (P) Using a line graph to write equal ratios. (X) Finding the mean and median of a set of data. (AA, DD) Solving problems involving ratios. (B, R, X) Graphing data in a point graph and drawing a best-fit line. (X)	Solving problems involving ratios. (B, R, X) Equivalent fractions. (C) Ordering fractions. (D) Ordering large numbers. (L) Reading and writing scientific notation. (L, S) Divisibility by 2, 3, and 5. (Z)	Self-assessment of the multiplication and division facts for the square numbers. (A, Y) Conversions: inches, feet, yards, miles. (B) Multiplication fact practice: square numbers. (E) Conversions: square inches, square feet, and square yards. (F) Conversions: square millimeters and square meters. (F) Solving multiplication and division problems using paper and pencil. (G, Q, W) Estimating products and quotients. (G, Q, W, T) Fact families: multiplication and division facts for square numbers. (I, K, O, U) Elapsed time: hours. (J) Computing 10% and 20%. (R, V) Solving problems involving ratios. (B, R, X) Multiplying and dividing by multiples of 10. (U) Estimating the number of objects. (V) Order of operations. (BB) Assessing facility with multiplication and division facts for the square numbers. (CC)	Graphing data in a point graph and drawing a best-fit line. (X) Using a line graph to write equal ratios. (X) Using a graph to make predictions. (X)

Grade 5 • Quick Start

Algebra	Statistics	Probability	Geometry	Measurement
Solving problems involving ratios. (B, R, X)	Using 10% as a standard for error analysis. (V)		Measuring area of rectangles and triangles. (H, M, N)	Conversions: inches, feet, yards, and miles. (B)
Graphing data in a point graph and drawing a best-fit line. (X)	Graphing data in a point graph and drawing a best-fit line. (X)			Conversions: square inches, square feet, and square yards. (F)
Using a line graph to write equal ratios. (X)	Using a graph to make predictions. (X)			Conversions: square millimeters and square meters. (F)
Using a graph to make predictions. (X)	Finding the mean and median of a set of data. (AA, DD)			Measuring area of rectangles and triangles. (H, M, N)
Order of operations. (BB)	Collecting data. (DD)			Elapsed time: hours. (J)
	Using a line graph to write equal ratios. (X)			

Grade 5 • Quick Start

Scope & Sequence Chart for the Daily Practice and Problems

	Number and Number Relationships	Number Systems and Number Theory	Computation and Estimation	Patterns and Functions
Unit 5: Investigating Fractions **Daily Practice and Problems** (The scope and sequence for all Unit Lessons begins on page 9.)	Finding the mean value of a set of data. (F) Identifying the whole given a fraction. (L) Estimating sums, differences, and products. (M, N) Ordering numbers. (N) Estimating the sums and differences of fractions. (R) Comparing fractions. (T, V) Solving problems involving ratios. (P, V)	Identifying the whole given a fraction. (L) Ordering numbers. (N) Comparing fractions. (T, V)	Finding the mean value of a set of data. (F) Self-assessment of the multiplication and division facts for the 9s. (A, Q) Elapsed time: minutes. (B) Order of operations. (C, D) Multiplication fact practice: 9s. (E) Multiplying by multiples of 10. (E) Mental computation with subtraction. (G) Computing change. (H) Fact families: multiplication and division facts for the 9s. (I , K, O) Solving addition, subtraction, multiplication, and division problems using paper and pencil. (M, N) Estimating sums, differences, and products. (M, N) Solving problems involving ratios. (P, V) Estimating the sums and differences of fractions. (R) Assessing students' facility with multiplication and division facts for the 9s. (S) Computing 10%, 50%, and 100%. (U)	

Grade 5 • Quick Start

Algebra	Statistics	Probability	Geometry	Measurement
Order of operations. (C, D)	Finding the mean value of a set of data. (F)	Listing combinations. (H)	Estimating and measuring area with nonstandard units. (J)	Elapsed time: minutes. (B)
Solving problems involving ratios. (P, V)	Using 10% as a standard for error analysis. (J)			Estimating and measuring area with nonstandard units. (J)

Grade 5 • Quick Start

Scope & Sequence Chart for the Daily Practice and Problems

	Number and Number Relationships	Number Systems and Number Theory	Computation and Estimation	Patterns and Functions
Unit 6: Geometry **Daily Practice and Problems** (The scope and sequence for all Unit Lessons begins on page 9.)	Solving problems involving ratios. (B, N) Estimating the sums and differences of fractions. (H) Estimating products and quotients. (I) Ordering fractions and mixed numbers. (L)	Ordering fractions and mixed numbers. (L)	Self-assessment of the multiplication and division facts for the last six facts (4×6, 4×7, 4×8, 6×7, 6×8, 7×8). (A, K) Solving problems involving ratios. (B, N) Order of operations. (D) Multiplication fact practice: last six facts. (E) Fact families: multiplication and division facts for the last six facts. (G) Estimating the sums and differences of fractions. (H) Solving multiplication and division problems using paper and pencil. (I) Estimating products and quotients. (I) Computing cost with 10% discount. (J) Assessment of students' facility with the last six multiplication and division facts. (O)	Representing data in a point graph and drawing a line through the data points. (B)

Grade 5 • Quick Start

Algebra	Statistics	Probability	Geometry	Measurement
Solving problems involving ratios. (B, N)	Representing data in a point graph and drawing a line through the data points. (B)		Estimating angle measurements. (C)	Estimating angle measurements. (C)
Representing data in a point graph and drawing a line through the data points. (B)			Measuring area. (F)	Measuring area. (F)
Writing number sentences. (D)			Solving problems involving the angle measurements of a triangle. (M, P)	Solving problems involving the angle measurements of a triangle. (M, P)
Solving for an unknown in a story problem. (N)				

Grade 5 • Quick Start

Scope & Sequence Chart for the Daily Practice and Problems

	Number and Number Relationships	Number Systems and Number Theory	Computation and Estimation	Patterns and Functions
Unit 7: Decimals and Probability **Daily Practice and Problems** (The scope and sequence for all Unit Lessons begins on page 9.)	Solving problems involving ratios. (D, BB) Interpreting a point graph. (D) Place value game with decimals. (F) Comparing fractions and percents. (E) Skip counting by tenths and hundredths. (I, J) Relationships between fractions, decimals, and percents. (L) Ordering fractions and decimals. (M, N, Q) Estimating sums and differences of decimals. (P) Estimating sums, differences, and quotients. (T, Z) Reading decimals. (U)	Place value game with decimals. (F) Ordering fractions and decimals. (M, N, Q) Comparing fractions and percents. (E) Skip counting by tenths and hundredths. (I, J)	Multiplication and division fact practice. (C, G, K, O, S, W, AA) Solving problems involving ratios. (D, BB) Elapsed time: hours and minutes. (H, BB) Estimating sums and differences of decimals. (P) Adding decimals. (R) Solving addition, subtraction, multiplication, and division problems using paper and pencil. (T, Z) Estimating sums, differences, and quotients. (T, Z) Multiplication with decimals. (V) Adding and subtracting fractions. (Y) Determining the value of coins. (X) Multiplying and dividing with multiples of 10. (AA)	Interpreting a point graph. (D)

Algebra	Statistics	Probability	Geometry	Measurement
Interpreting a point graph. (D)	Interpreting a point graph. (D)		Solving problems involving the angle measurements of a triangle. (A)	Solving problems involving the angle measurements of a triangle. (A)
Solving problems involving ratios. (D, BB)			Using a protractor to draw triangles with specific measurements. (B)	Using a protractor to draw triangles with specific measurements. (B)
				Elapsed time: hours and minutes. (H, BB)
				Measuring to the nearest tenth of a centimeter. (R)

Grade 5 • Quick Start

Scope & Sequence Chart for the Daily Practice and Problems

	Number and Number Relationships	Number Systems and Number Theory	Computation and Estimation	Patterns and Functions
Unit 8: Applications: An Assessment Unit **Daily Practice and Problems** (The scope and sequence for all Unit Lessons begins on page 9.)	Estimating sums, differences, and products of whole numbers and decimals. (D, O) Equivalent fractions. (E) Comparing fractions. (F) Relationships between fractions, decimals, and percents. (G, N) Skip counting by tenths. (P) Solving problems involving ratios. (R) Representing data in a point graph and drawing a line through the data points. (R)	Equivalent fractions. (E) Comparing fractions. (F) Relationships between fractions, decimals, and percents. (G, N) Skip counting by tenths. (P) Multiples of 4. (P) Place value in decimals. (P)	Self-assessment of the multiplication and division facts. (B) Multiplication and division fact practice. (C, I, K, M) Solving addition, subtraction, multiplication, and division problems using paper and pencil. (D, P) Multiplying with decimals. (D) Adding and subtracting fractions. (F, L) Estimating sums, differences, and products of whole numbers and decimals. (D, O) Assessment of students' facility with the multiplication and division facts. (Q) Solving problems involving ratios. (R)	Representing data in a point graph and drawing a line through the data points. (R)

Algebra	Statistics	Probability	Geometry	Measurement
Solving for *n* in a multiplication or division number sentence. (C, I)	Representing data in a point graph and drawing a line through the data points. (R)	Finding the probability of an event. (J)	Measuring area. (A)	Measuring area. (A)
Representing data in a point graph and drawing a line through the data points. (R)			Using a ruler and protractor to draw a quadrilateral given specific dimensions. (H)	Using a ruler and protractor to draw a quadrilateral given specific dimensions. (H)
Solving problems involving ratios. (R)				

Grade 5 • Quick Start

Scope & Sequence Chart for the Daily Practice and Problems

	Number and Number Relationships	Number Systems and Number Theory	Computation and Estimation	Patterns and Functions
Unit 9: Connections to Division **Daily Practice and Problems** (The scope and sequence for all Unit Lessons begins on page 9.)	Estimating products of decimals. (E, O) Comparing decimals. (F, I) Changing fractions to decimals. (I) Estimating quotients. (J, N) Expressing remainders as whole numbers; expressing quotients as mixed numbers and decimals. (R, T) Interpreting remainders. (R)	Comparing decimals. (F, I) Changing fractions to decimals. (I) Addition and subtraction of decimals place value games. (L, P) Expressing remainders as whole numbers; expressing quotients as mixed numbers and decimals. (R, T)	Self-assessment of the multiplication and division facts for the 5s and 10s. (A) Elapsed time: hours. (B) Computing and comparing costs. (C) Estimating products of decimals. (E, O) Division fact practice: 5s and 10s. (G, K, M, Q) Solving a word problem involving measurement, multiplication, and division. (H) Estimating quotients. (J, N) Addition and subtraction of decimals place value games (L, P) Multiplying and dividing with multiples of ten. (M, Q) Solving multiplication and division problems with pencil and paper. (N) Assessment of students' facility with the division facts: 5s and 10s. (S) Interpreting remainders. (R) Expressing remainders as whole numbers; expressing quotients as mixed numbers and decimals. (R, T)	

Grade 5 • Quick Start

Algebra	Statistics	Probability	Geometry	Measurement
Solving for *n* in a multiplication or division sentence. (K)		Listing combinations. (D)	Measuring area. (E)	Elapsed time: hours. (B)
				Measuring area. (E)
				Conversion: centimeters and meters. (H)
				Solving a word problem involving measurement, multiplication, and division. (H)

Grade 5 • Quick Start

Scope & Sequence Chart for the Daily Practice and Problems

	Number and Number Relationships	Number Systems and Number Theory	Computation and Estimation	Patterns and Functions
Unit 10: Maps and Coordinates **Daily Practice and Problems** (The scope and sequence for all Unit Lessons begins on page 9.)	Estimating sums, differences, products, and quotients. (C, D, L) Finding the difference in temperature: work with integers. (G) Finding the average of a set of data (mean and median). (H) Solving problems involving ratios. (J, K) Coordinate geometry. (P, R) Plotting points on a four-quadrant grid paper; seeing a pattern; drawing a line. (R)	Finding the difference in temperature: work with integers. (G) Even and odd numbers. (O).	Self-assessment of the division facts: 2s and squares. (A) Using a calculator to solve division problems; finding the whole number remainder. (C) Estimating sums, differences, products, and quotients. (C, D, L) Multiplication and division fact practice: 2s and square numbers. (E, I, M, Q) Finding the difference in temperature: work with integers. (G) Solving for n in a number sentence. (I) Elapsed time: hours and minutes. (J) Solving problems involving ratios. (J, K) Solving addition, subtraction, multiplication, and division problems using paper and pencil. (L) Multiplying decimals. (L) Multiplying and dividing with multiples of ten. (M, Q) Adding and subtracting fractions. (N) Assessment of students' facility with the division facts: 2s and square numbers. (S)	Plotting points on a four-quadrant grid paper; seeing a pattern; drawing a line. (R)

Algebra	Statistics	Probability	Geometry	Measurement
Solving for *n* in a number sentence. (I)	Finding the average of a set of data (mean and median). (H)	Finding the probability of an event. (O)	Using a protractor and a ruler to draw triangles given specific measurements. (F)	Writing measurements in meters using decimals. (B)
Solving problems involving ratios. (J, K)	Plotting points on a four-quadrant grid; seeing a pattern; drawing a line. (R)		Congruence and similarity. (F)	Estimating length. (B)
Plotting points on a four-quadrant grid; seeing a pattern; drawing a line. (R)	Using data to solve a logic puzzle. (T)		Coordinate geometry. (P, R)	Using a protractor and a ruler to draw triangles given specific measurements. (F)
			Finding the midpoint of a line segment. (P)	Finding the difference in temperature. (G)
				Elapsed time: hours and minutes. (J)
				Finding the midpoint of a line segment. (P)

Grade 5 • Quick Start

Scope & Sequence Chart for the Daily Practice and Problems

	Number and Number Relationships	Number Systems and Number Theory	Computation and Estimation	Patterns and Functions
Unit 11: Number Patterns, Primes, and Fractions **Daily Practice and Problems** (The scope and sequence for all Unit Lessons begins on page 9.)	Estimating products of decimals. (C) Solving problems involving ratios. (F) Writing decimals as fractions reduced to lowest terms. (H) Estimating products and quotients. (N, T) Comparing fractions. (O) Equivalent fractions. (O) Improper fractions and mixed numbers. (R) Evaluating expressions with exponents. (U)	Identifying prime numbers. (G, J) Listing the factors of a number. (G) Divisibility rules for 2, 3, and 6. (L) Comparing fractions. (O) Equivalent fractions. (O) Using factor trees to write a number as a product of its primes. (P)	Self-assessment of the division facts: 3s and 9s. (A) Elapsed time; hours to minutes. (B) Estimating products of decimals. (C) Division fact practice: 3s and 9s. (E, I, M, Q) Computing cost with 50% discount. (F) Solving problems involving ratios. (F) Solving multiplication and division problems using paper and pencil. (N, T) Multiplying decimals. (N) Estimating products and quotients. (N, T) Dividing with multiples of ten. (M, Q) Solving for *n* in a division number sentence. (Q) Adding and subtracting fractions. (R) Assessment of students' facility with the division facts: 3s and 9s. (S) Evaluating expressions with exponents. (U)	

Algebra	Statistics	Probability	Geometry	Measurement
Solving problems involving ratios. (F)	Using data to solve a logic puzzle. (V)	Finding the probability of an event. (G)	Coordinate geometry: slides and flips. (D, K)	Elapsed time; hours to minutes. (B)
Solving for *n* in a division number sentence. (Q)				

Grade 5 • Quick Start

Scope & Sequence Chart for the Daily Practice and Problems

	Number and Number Relationships	Number Systems and Number Theory	Computation and Estimation	Patterns and Functions
Unit 12: Using Fractions **Daily Practice and Problems** (The scope and sequence for all Unit Lessons begins on page 9.)	Estimating the sum of fractions and mixed numbers. (C, H) Writing quotients as mixed numbers. (F, K) Estimating sums, differences, products, and quotients. (F)	Prime numbers. (N) Square numbers. (N, P)	Self-assessment of the division facts: the last six facts. (A) Using a map scale to determine distances. (B) Estimating the sum of fractions and mixed numbers. (C, H) Conversion: feet and inches. (D) Finding the sum of mixed numbers. (H) Division fact practice: the last six facts. (E, G, I, K, M) Solving addition, subtraction, multiplication, and division problems using paper and pencil. (F) Adding, subtracting, and multiplying decimals. (F) Estimating sums, differences, products, and quotients. (F) Writing quotients as mixed numbers. (F, K) Using known division facts to mentally solve division problems with remainders. (K) Multiplying a fraction by a whole number; multiplying two fractions. (J, L) Multiplying and dividing with multiples of ten. (I, L) Assessment of students' facility with division facts: the last six facts. (O)	Using a map scale to determine distances. (B)

Algebra	Statistics	Probability	Geometry	Measurement
Solving for *n* in multiplication and division sentences. (I)			Determining if a triangle can be formed from three given lengths. (C)	Using a map scale to determine distances. (B)
			Measuring area. (D)	Determining if a triangle can be formed from three given lengths. (C)
				Measuring area. (D)
				Conversion: feet and inches. (D)

Grade 5 • Quick Start

Scope & Sequence Chart for the Daily Practice and Problems

	Number and Number Relationships	Number Systems and Number Theory	Computation and Estimation	Patterns and Functions
Unit 13: Ratio and Proportion **Daily Practice and Problems** (The scope and sequence for all Unit Lessons begins on page 9.)	Evaluating expressions with exponents. (A) Solving problems involving ratios. (G, O, T, V) Writing quotients as mixed numbers, as a whole number with a whole number remainder, and as a decimal. (H) Completing mathematical analogies. (K) Relationship between fractions, decimals, and percents. (K, N) Estimating sums, differences, products, and quotients. (R) Comparing fractions. (V)	Comparing fractions. (V)	Evaluating expressions with exponents. (A) Self-assessment of the division facts: 2s, 5s, 10s, and squares. (B) Multiplying a fraction by a whole number. (C, V) Elapsed time. (D) Division fact practice: 2s, 5s, 10s, and squares. (E, H, I, M, Q) Adding, subtracting, and multiplying fractions; adding mixed numbers. (F) Using known facts to mentally solve division problems with remainders. (H, Q) Computing ages and spans of time (in years). (J) Solving problems involving ratios. (G, O, T, V) Solving addition, subtraction, multiplication, and division problems using paper and pencil. (R) Multiplying decimals. (R) Estimating sums, differences, products, and quotients. (R) Assessment of students' facility with the division facts: 2s, 5s, 10s, and squares. (S, U)	

Grade 5 • Quick Start

Algebra	Statistics	Probability	Geometry	Measurement
Solving problems involving ratios. (G, O, T, V)		Finding the probability of an event. (P)	Finding the sum of the angles of a polygon. (K, L)	Elapsed time. (D)
				Measuring length. (G)
				Computing ages and spans of time (in years). (J)
				Naming units of measure for volume, length, and area. (K)
				Finding the sum of the angles of a polygon. (K, L)

Grade 5 • Quick Start

Scope & Sequence Chart for the Daily Practice and Problems

	Number and Number Relationships	Number Systems and Number Theory	Computation and Estimation	Patterns and Functions
Unit 14: Using Circles **Daily Practice and Problems** (The scope and sequence for all Unit Lessons begins on page 9.)	Estimating the sum of two fractions. (D) Finding the mean value of a set of data. (F) Estimating sums, differences, products, and quotients. (L) Mixed numbers and improper fractions. (T) Using factor trees to write a number as a product of its primes with exponents. (P)	Multiples of 2 and 4. (H) Using factor trees to write a number as a product of its primes with exponents. (P)	Elapsed time: minutes. (A) Self-assessment of the division facts: 3s, 9s, and last six facts. (B) Multiplying decimals mentally. (C) Estimating the sum of two fractions. (D) Division fact practice: 3s, 9s, and last six facts. (E, G, K, O, S) Finding the mean value of a set of data. (F) Using π to find the diameter or circumference of a circle. (I) Using known facts to mentally solve division problems with remainders. (S) Solving addition, subtraction, multiplication, and division problems. (L) Multiplying decimals. (L) Estimating sums, differences, products, and quotients. (L) Dividing with multiples of ten. (O) Multiplying a fraction by a whole number; multiplying fractions. (Q, R) Adding mixed numbers. (T) Assessing students' facility with the division facts. (W)	Using π to find the diameter or circumference of a circle. (I) Using patterns to complete a data table (function machine). (J, N) Describing a pattern using variables in a number sentence. (N)

Grade 5 • Quick Start

Algebra	Statistics	Probability	Geometry	Measurement
Evaluating expressions given an input number for *n*. (J)	Finding the mean value of a set of data. (F)		Using π to find the diameter or circumference of a circle. (I, M)	Elapsed time: minutes. (A)
Finding *n*, given the output number in a number sentence. (J)	Using data to solve a logic puzzle. (X)		Using a compass, ruler, and protractor to construct a circle with a central angle, chord, and radius. (U)	Using π to find the diameter or circumference of a circle. (I, M)
Describing a pattern using variables in a number sentence. (N)			Coordinate geometry: flips and slides. (V)	Using a compass and ruler to construct a circle with a central angle, chord, and radius. (U)

Grade 5 • Quick Start

Scope & Sequence Chart for the Daily Practice and Problems

	Number and Number Relationships	Number Systems and Number Theory	Computation and Estimation	Patterns and Functions
Unit 15: Developing Formulas with Geometry **Daily Practice and Problems** (The scope and sequence for all Unit Lessons begins on page 9.)	Estimating products and quotients. (D)		Multiplying decimals mentally. (A) Self-assessment of division facts. (B) Division fact practice. (C, E, I, M) Solving multiplication and division problems using paper and pencil. (D) Multiplying decimals. (D) Estimating products and quotients. (D) Order of operations. (F) Using π to find the circumference and diameter of circles. (G) Using a map scale to determine distance. (H) Determining the number of nickels and dimes given the total value of a set of coins. (L) Elapsed time. (N)	Using π to find the circumference and diameter of circles. (G) Using a map scale to determine distance. (H)

Grade 5 • Quick Start

Algebra	Statistics	Probability	Geometry	Measurement
Order of operations. (F)	Interpreting a circle graph. (K)		Using π to find the circumference and diameter of circles. (G)	Using π to find the circumference and diameter of circles. (G)
Determining the number of nickels and dimes given the total value of a set of coins. (L)			Measuring area of triangles. (J)	Using a map scale to determine distance. (H)
				Measuring area of triangles. (J)
				Elapsed time. (N)

Grade 5 • Quick Start

Scope & Sequence Chart for the Daily Practice and Problems

	Number and Number Relationships	Number Systems and Number Theory	Computation and Estimation	Patterns and Functions
Unit 16: Bringing It All Together: An Assessment Unit **Daily Practice and Problems** (The scope and sequence for all Unit Lessons begins on page 9.)	Solving problems involving ratios. (A, B, L, N, Q, T) Estimating sums, products, and quotients. (J)	Listing factors of a number. (D)	Self-assessment of the division facts. (B) Division fact practice. (E, G, I, O) Solving problems involving ratios. (A, B, L, N, Q, T) Solving problems involving density; ratio of mass and volume. (F) Solving addition, multiplication, and division problems using paper and pencil. (J) Adding and multiplying decimals. (J) Estimating sums, products, and quotients. (J) Adding mixed numbers; adding and subtracting fractions. (M) Assessment of students' facility with the division facts. (S)	Using patterns to complete a data table (function machine). (P)

Grade 5 • Quick Start

Algebra	Statistics	Probability	Geometry	Measurement
Solving problems involving ratios. (A, B, L, N, Q, T)	Interpreting data in a circle graph. (C)		Measuring perimeter. (H, R)	Measuring perimeter. (H, R)
Solving problems involving density; ratio of mass and volume. (F)			Measuring area of triangles. (K)	Measuring area of triangles. (K)
Evaluating expressions given an input number for *n*. (J)			Measuring area of rectangles. (R)	Measuring area of rectangles. (R)
Finding *n*, given the output number in a number sentence. (J)				

Grade 5 • Quick Start

Math Facts and Whole-Number Operations

The *Math Facts and Whole-Number Operations* section outlines the MATH TRAILBLAZERS approach to developing facility with the math facts and whole number operations.

Calculators are used as a tool for solving problems.

Development of Math Facts and Whole-Number Operations

Grade	Addition	Subtraction	Multiplication	Division
K	Introduce concepts through varied problems.	Introduce concepts through varied problems.	Introduce concepts through varied problems.	Introduce concepts through varied problems.
1	Introduce concepts through varied problems. Focus on strategies for learning addition facts.	Introduce concepts through varied problems. Focus on strategies for learning subtraction facts.	Introduce concepts through varied problems.	Introduce concepts through varied problems.
2	Continue concept development through varied problems. Continue use of strategies for learning addition facts. Continue use of facts in problems. Facility with addition facts expected. Introduction to multidigit addition using base-ten pieces and paper and pencil.	Continue concept development through use in varied problems. Continue use of facts in problems. Continue use of strategies for learning subtraction facts. Introduction to multidigit subtraction using base-ten pieces and paper and pencil.	Continue concept development through use in varied problems.	Continue concept development through use in varied problems.
3	Facility with multidigit addition using base-ten pieces and paper and pencil expected. Review and use of addition facts in games and activities. Practice with multidigit addition in varied contexts.	Continue use of strategies for learning subtraction facts. Facility with subtraction facts expected. Facility with multidigit subtraction using base-ten pieces and paper and pencil expected. Practice with multidigit subtraction in varied contexts.	Multiplication problem solving in context. Strategies for learning multiplication facts. Mental multiplication with multiples of ten (e.g., 6×80). Introduction to paper-and-pencil multiplication of one digit by two digits.	Continue concept development through use in varied problems.
4	Continue practice with multidigit addition in varied contexts. Diagnosis and remediation with addition facts as required.	Continue practice with multidigit subtraction in varied contexts. Diagnosis and remediation with subtraction facts as required.	Continue use of strategies for learning multiplication facts. Facility with multiplication facts expected. Continue mental multiplication with multiples of ten (e.g., 40×300). Paper-and-pencil multiplication with two-digit multipliers. Practice with multiplication in varied contexts.	Continue concept development through use in varied problems. Strategies for learning the division facts. Introduction to paper-and-pencil division with one-digit divisors.
5	Continue practice with multidigit addition in varied contexts. Diagnosis and remediation with addition facts as required.	Continue practice with multidigit subtraction in varied contexts. Diagnosis and remediation with subtraction facts as required.	Review of multiplication facts. Review of paper-and-pencil procedures. Continue practice with multiplication in varied contexts.	Continue use of strategies for learning the division facts. Facility with division facts expected. Development of paper-and-pencil procedures with two-digit divisors. Practice with division in varied contexts.

Table 1

Math Facts and Whole-Number Operations

An important goal of *Math Trailblazers* is to prepare students to compute accurately, flexibly, and appropriately in all situations. Standard topics in arithmetic—acquisition of basic math facts and facility with whole-number operations—are covered extensively. Our approaches to these topics, however, differ from traditional mathematics programs.

In this section, we briefly describe our approach to developing facility with the math facts and whole number operations. Table 1 outlines the development of these two topics in grades K–5. We also summarize several important characteristics of our approaches below. Detailed information can be obtained from two TIMS Tutors that are included later in this Teacher Implementation Guide: *Math Facts* and *Arithmetic*.

Math Facts in *Math Trailblazers*

In developing our program for the math facts, we sought a careful balance between strategies and drill. This approach is based on a large body of research and advocated by the NCTM in the *Curriculum and Evaluation Standards for School Mathematics.* The research indicates that the approach we employed leads to more effective learning and better retention of the math facts and also helps develop essential mental math skills.

Our approach to the math facts is characterized by these elements:

- *Early emphasis on problem solving.* Students first approach the basic facts as problems to be solved rather than as facts to be memorized. They invent their own strategies to solve these problems or learn appropriate strategies from others through class discussion. Children's natural strategies, especially counting strategies, are explicitly encouraged.

- *De-emphasis of rote work.* We believe that children must indeed learn their math facts, but we de-emphasize rote memorization and the frequent administration of timed tests. Both of these can produce undesirable results. Instead, our goal here is that students learn that they can find answers easily using strategies they understand.

- *Gradual and systematic introduction of facts.* Students study the facts in small groups that can be solved by a single strategy. Early on, for example, they study facts that can be solved by counting on 1, 2, or 3. Students first work on simple strategies for easy facts and then progress to more sophisticated strategies and harder facts.

- *Ongoing practice.* Work on the math facts is distributed throughout the curriculum, especially in the Daily Practice and Problems and in the games. This practice for facility, however, takes place only after students have a conceptual understanding of the operations and have achieved proficiency with strategies for solving basic fact problems. Delaying practice in this way means that less practice is required to achieve mastery.

- *Appropriate assessment.* Students are assessed on the facts through teacher observation as well as through the appropriate use of written tests and quizzes.

- *Facts are not gatekeepers.* Students are not prevented from learning more complex mathematics because they do not perform well on fact tests.

The *MATH TRAILBLAZERS* approach to the math facts is discussed more fully in the TIMS Tutor: *Math Facts.*

Whole-Number Operations in *MATH TRAILBLAZERS*

The treatment of computation in *MATH TRAILBLAZERS* proceeds in several stages. The grade levels for the stages vary with the operation—ideas of division, for example, develop long after addition—but the general pattern is similar for all the operations. Roughly speaking, the stages are:

- developing meaning for the operation,
- inventing procedures for solving problems, and
- becoming more efficient at carrying out procedures, all leading to
- developing mathematical power.

With each of the operations, we seek a balance between conceptual understanding and procedural skill. Standard methods for solving problems are not introduced until students have developed good conceptual and procedural understandings—research has shown that the too-early introduction of such procedures may short-circuit students' common sense, encouraging mechanical and uncritical behavior. As a result, instruction in some standard procedures is delayed slightly beyond the traditional time, but problems that would normally be solved by standard procedures are often introduced sooner than is customary. This forces students to use their prior knowledge to devise their own methods to solve the problems, thus promoting students' construction of their own understandings.

Even after standard methods have been analyzed and practiced, students are still encouraged to solve problems in more than one way. Flexible thinking and mathematical power are our goals, not rote facility with a handful of standard algorithms.

Overall, we have tried to create in *MATH TRAILBLAZERS* a balanced program that will promote the coordinated development of both procedural skill and conceptual understanding. This is particularly apparent in our approach to computation. More information about the development of computational facility in *MATH TRAILBLAZERS* can be found in the TIMS Tutor: *Arithmetic.*

DPP and HP Guide

The *DPP and HP Guide* explains the purpose and use of the *Daily Practice and Problems* (DPP) and *Home Practice* (HP) within the curriculum.

Students work cooperatively to solve a problem from the Daily Practice and Problems.

DPP and HP Guide

SECTION 7

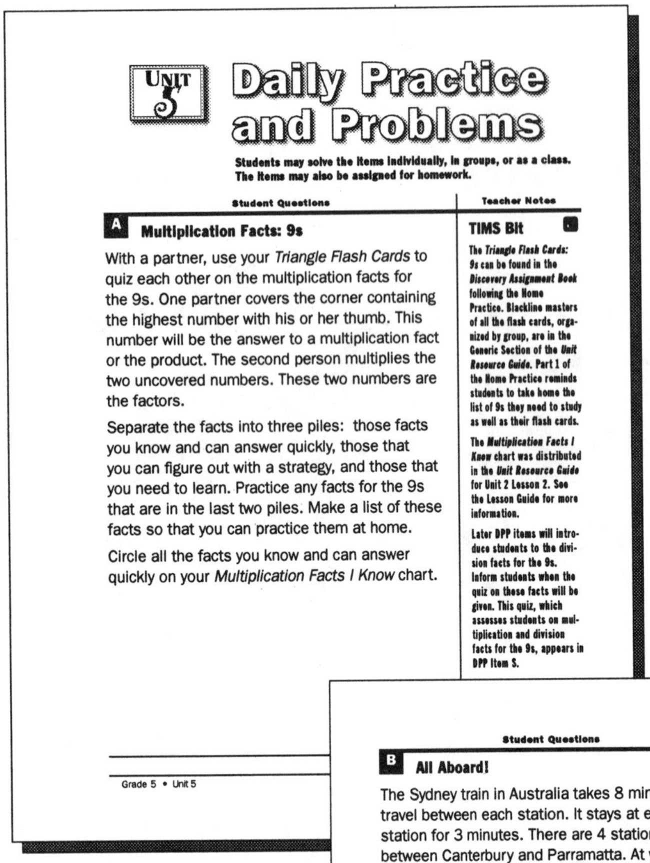

UNIT 5

Daily Practice and Problems

Students may solve the items individually, in groups, or as a class. The items may also be assigned for homework.

Student Questions	Teacher Notes
A Multiplication Facts: 9s With a partner, use your *Triangle Flash Cards* to quiz each other on the multiplication facts for the 9s. One partner covers the corner containing the highest number with his or her thumb. This number will be the answer to a multiplication fact or the product. The second person multiplies the two uncovered numbers. These two numbers are the factors. Separate the facts into three piles: those facts you know and can answer quickly, those that you can figure out with a strategy, and those that you need to learn. Practice any facts for the 9s that are in the last two piles. Make a list of these facts so that you can practice them at home. Circle all the facts you know and can answer quickly on your *Multiplication Facts I Know* chart.	**TIMS Bit** The *Triangle Flash Cards: 9s* can be found in the *Discovery Assignment Book* following the Home Practice. Blackline masters of all the flash cards, organized by group, are in the Generic Section of the *Unit Resource Guide*. Part 1 of the Home Practice reminds students to take home the list of 9s they need to study as well as their flash cards. The *Multiplication Facts I Know* chart was distributed in the *Unit Resource Guide* for Unit 2 Lesson 2. See the Lesson Guide for more information. Later DPP items will introduce students to the division facts for the 9s. Inform students when the quiz on these facts will be given. This quiz, which assesses students on multiplication and division facts for the 9s, appears in DPP Item S.

Grade 5 • Unit 5

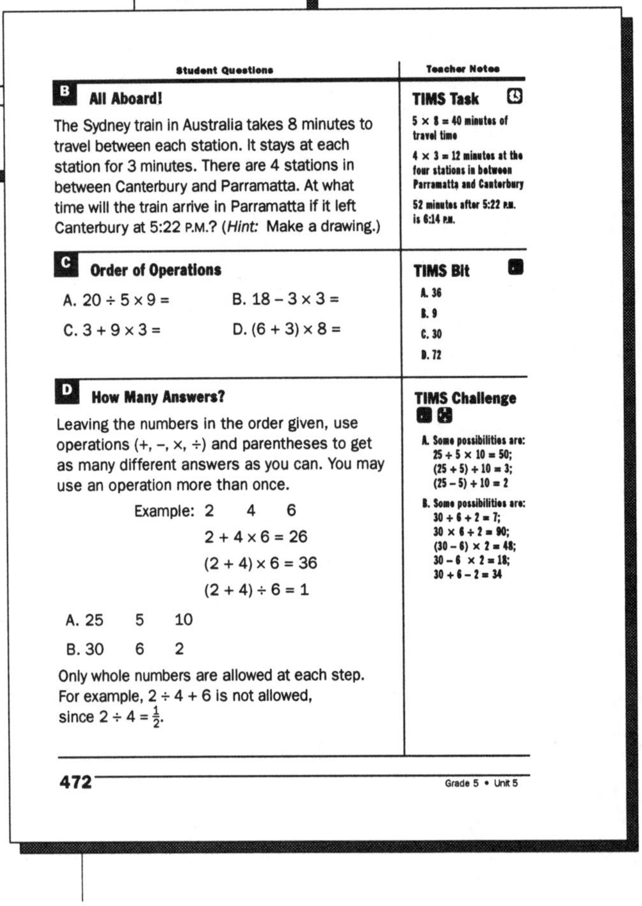

Student Questions	Teacher Notes
B All Aboard! The Sydney train in Australia takes 8 minutes to travel between each station. It stays at each station for 3 minutes. There are 4 stations in between Canterbury and Parramatta. At what time will the train arrive in Parramatta if it left Canterbury at 5:22 P.M.? (*Hint:* Make a drawing.)	**TIMS Task** 5 × 8 = 40 minutes of travel time 4 × 3 = 12 minutes at the four stations in between Parramatta and Canterbury 52 minutes after 5:22 P.M. is 6:14 P.M.
C Order of Operations A. 20 ÷ 5 × 9 = B. 18 − 3 × 3 = C. 3 + 9 × 3 = D. (6 + 3) × 8 =	**TIMS Bit** A. 36 B. 9 C. 30 D. 72
D How Many Answers? Leaving the numbers in the order given, use operations (+, −, ×, ÷) and parentheses to get as many different answers as you can. You may use an operation more than once. Example: 2 4 6 2 + 4 × 6 = 26 (2 + 4) × 6 = 36 (2 + 4) ÷ 6 = 1 A. 25 5 10 B. 30 6 2 Only whole numbers are allowed at each step. For example, 2 ÷ 4 + 6 is not allowed, since $2 \div 4 = \frac{1}{2}$.	**TIMS Challenge** A. Some possibilities are: 25 ÷ 5 × 10 = 50; (25 ÷ 5) ÷ 10 = 3; (25 − 5) ÷ 10 = 2 B. Some possibilities are: 30 ÷ 6 ÷ 2 = 7; 30 × 6 ÷ 2 = 90; (30 − 6) × 2 = 48; 30 − 6 × 2 = 18; 30 ÷ 6 − 2 = 34

472 Grade 5 • Unit 5

Figure 1: DPP pages

Daily Practice and Problems

The *Daily Practice and Problems* (DPP) is a set of short exercises which provides ongoing review, practice, and study of math concepts and skills. These exercises are found in each unit in the Unit Resource Guide immediately preceding the lesson guides. The DPP should become a routine part of daily instruction since the problems serve several important functions in the curriculum:

- They provide distributed practice in computation and a structure for systematic study of the basic math facts.
- They develop concepts and skills such as number sense, telling time, and working with money throughout the year; and
- They review topics from earlier units, presenting concepts in new contexts and linking ideas from unit to unit.

There are three types of items: Bits, Tasks, and Challenges. Bits are short and should take no more than 5 or 10 minutes to complete. They often provide practice with a skill or the basic math facts. Tasks take 10 or 15 minutes to complete and occasionally expand on a topic presented in the previous Bit. Challenges usually take longer than 15 minutes to complete and the problems are more thought-provoking. They can be used to stretch students' problem-solving skills.

Two DPP items are included for each class session listed on the Unit Outline. The first item is always a Bit and the second is either a Task or a Challenge. Each item is composed of a student question and teacher notes as shown in Figure 1.

Each set of DPP includes a Teacher's Guide, which provides specific information on the study and assessment of the math facts in the current unit.

Figure 2: DPP icons and DPP Menu on DPP page

The Teacher Notes give the answers and often discuss possible problem-solving strategies. So that teachers can locate items on a particular topic, eight icons are used to designate the subject matter of the problems. See Figure 2.

The Scope and Sequence chart for the *Daily Practice and Problems* in Section 5 of the Teacher Implementation Guide lists the topics covered in the DPP in each unit. This chart correlates the items in the DPP to the nine content standards from the National Council of Teachers of Mathematics *Curriculum and Evaluation Standards for School Mathematics.* Teachers can use this chart to track the development of a particular standard throughout fifth grade and locate items on particular topics to use for remediation, extra practice, or enrichment. For example, by looking at the *Estimation and Computation* column, teachers can follow the sequence of items providing computation and fact practice. By looking at the *Measurement* column in the same way, teachers can find all the items which deal with measuring length and area. For a specific description of the study and assessment of the math facts as organized in the DPP for all of fifth grade, see the TIMS Tutor: *Math Facts.*

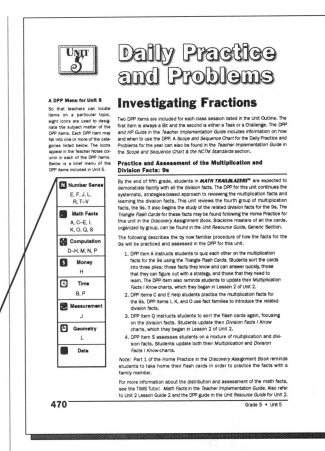

UNIT 5
Daily Practice and Problems

Investigating Fractions

A DPP Menu for Unit 5

So that teachers can locate items on a particular topic, eight icons are used to designate the subject matter of the DPP items. Each DPP item may fall into one or more of the categories listed below. The icons appear in the Teacher Notes column in each of the DPP items. Below is a brief menu of the DPP items included in Unit 5.

N	Number Sense E, F, J, L, R, T–V
	Math Facts A, C–E, I, K, O, Q, S
	Computation D–H, M, N, P
$	Money H
⏱	Time B, P
	Measurement J
	Geometry L
	Data

Two DPP items are included for each class session listed in the Unit Outline. The first item is always a Bit and the second is either a Task or a Challenge. The *DPP and HP Guide* in the *Teacher Implementation Guide* includes information on how and when to use the DPP. A *Scope and Sequence Chart* for the Daily Practice and Problems for the year can also be found in the *Teacher Implementation Guide* in the *Scope and Sequence Chart & the NCTM Standards* section.

Practice and Assessment of the Multiplication and Division Facts: 9s

By the end of fifth grade, students in *MATH TRAILBLAZERS* are expected to demonstrate facility with all the division facts. The DPP for this unit continues the systematic, strategies-based approach to reviewing the multiplication facts and learning the division facts. This unit reviews the fourth group of multiplication facts, the 9s. It also begins the study of the related division facts for the 9s. The *Triangle Flash Cards* for these facts may be found following the Home Practice for this unit in the *Discovery Assignment Book*. Blackline masters of all the cards, organized by group, can be found in the *Unit Resource Guide*, Generic Section.

The following describes the by now familiar procedure of how the facts for the 9s will be practiced and assessed in the DPP for this unit.

1. DPP item A instructs students to quiz each other on the multiplication facts for the 9s using the *Triangle Flash Cards*. Students sort the cards into three piles: those facts they know and can answer quickly, those that they can figure out with a strategy, and those that they need to learn. The DPP item also reminds students to update their *Multiplication Facts I Know* charts, which they began in Lesson 2 of Unit 2.

2. DPP items C and E help students practice the multiplication facts for the 9s. DPP Items I, K, and O use fact families to introduce the related division facts.

3. DPP Item Q instructs students to sort the flash cards again, focusing on the division facts. Students update their *Division Facts I Know* charts, which they began in Lesson 2 of Unit 2.

4. DPP Item S assesses students on a mixture of multiplication and division facts. Students update both their *Multiplication* and *Division Facts I Know* charts.

Note: Part 1 of the Home Practice in the *Discovery Assignment Book* reminds students to take home their flash cards in order to practice the facts with a family member.

For more information about the distribution and assessment of the math facts, see the TIMS Tutor: *Math Facts* in the *Teacher Implementation Guide*. Also refer to Unit 2 Lesson Guide 2 and the DPP guide in the *Unit Resource Guide* for Unit 2.

470   Grade 5 • Unit 5

Eight icons indicate the subject matter of each problem:

N **Number Sense** (estimating, partitioning numbers, skip counting, etc.);

$\begin{smallmatrix}5\\ \times 7\end{smallmatrix}$ **Math Facts** (practice with addition, subtraction, multiplication, and division facts);

Computation (problems which may be solved using paper-and-pencil methods, estimation, mental math, or calculators);

$ **Money** (counting change, combining various coins, and estimating total cost);

🕐 **Time** (telling time, solving problems involving elapsed time);

Measurement (measuring length, area, mass, volume, time, and temperature);

Geometry (work with shapes, measurement, coordinates, and other geometric topics); and

Data (collecting, organizing, graphing, and analyzing data).

How to Use the *Daily Practice and Problems*

Assign a Bit each day to present students with the review and fact practice they need. Bits are designed to be short, quick questions that need little instruction from the teacher. Students should be able to complete them independently. For many problems, it will be appropriate for students to work in pairs or groups. For other items such as fact quizzes, students should answer the questions individually. If students take more than 5 or 10 minutes to complete the problems, they are probably unfamiliar with a topic. For example, items intended to review fourth-grade topics may be new to students who are using *MATH TRAILBLAZERS* for the first time in fifth grade. If students need more instruction on the material presented in the DPP, defer the problems and the instruction until a later date, possibly during an upcoming unit which covers similar subject matter.

Choose from the Tasks and Challenges as time permits according to the interests and needs of your students. Tasks can extend a topic or provide extra practice. Challenges can be used as enrichment for those students who need less skill practice and are ready for more complex problems. Not all students will be able to complete all the Tasks and Challenges, but all should have the opportunity to try.

Teachers use the *Daily Practice and Problems* in many ways. Many problems can easily be written on the blackboard or displayed using an overhead projector. Items can also be photocopied (without the teacher portion), cut apart, and distributed to students daily or several items can be stapled together in a packet and distributed weekly. For many items (such as fact practice or mental arithmetic), it is appropriate for students to just write answers on scrap paper. For others (such as skip counting), students can respond orally. One way to establish routines is to have students use their math journals for any written responses. This will also preserve a record of their work. Teacher notes sometimes recommend conducting a discussion of students' problem-solving strategies. These discussions are an important part of the problem-solving process, but they need not be extensive since topics are revisited many times.

When to Use the *Daily Practice and Problems*

At the Beginning of Math Class. Bits and other DPP items can be used to begin class and focus students' attention on mathematics. Students immediately answer the questions and then the class can discuss the answers before they begin work on the current lesson. Alternatively, the teacher can assign the items at the beginning of a lesson and students can solve the problems as they have time during class. This is an especially effective method if students are collecting data for an experiment and have to take turns using equipment.

During Daily Routines. Bits can be used as part of morning (or afternoon) routines that also include taking the roll, calendar work, language arts practice, or geography questions. A "Problem of the Day" can also be part of the daily routine in which the teacher presents students with a Task or a Challenge which they can work on throughout the day or take home to complete for homework or as extra credit. For some Tasks and Challenges, it may be appropriate to ask students to describe their problem-solving process.

During Transition Times. Many items, especially practice with the math facts, can be used during transition times throughout the day. Possible times include when students have completed an assignment, when money or permission slips are being collected, when an activity is delayed, or when an activity ends earlier than expected.

As Homework or Assessment. Problems can also be assigned for homework or used for short assessments. See the TIMS Tutor: *Math Facts* for information on fact assessment in the DPP and the Assessment Overview in Part VI of *Assessment in MATH TRAILBLAZERS* (Section 8) for specific locations of Fact Quizzes and Fact Self-Assessment in the DPP.

Home Practice

The *Home Practice* (HP) is a series of problems designed to supplement the homework included in the lessons. The HP, like the *Daily Practice and Problems,* distributes skill practice throughout the units and reviews concepts studied in previous units. For each unit, the Discovery Assignment Book begins with two, double-sided pages of problems divided into different parts as shown in Figure 3.

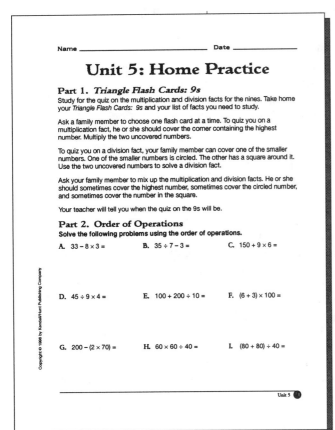

Name _____ Date _____

Unit 5: Home Practice

Part 1. *Triangle Flash Cards: 9s*

Study for the quiz on the multiplication and division facts for the nines. Take home your *Triangle Flash Cards: 9s* and your list of facts you need to study.

Ask a family member to choose one flash card at a time. To quiz you on a multiplication fact, he or she should cover the corner containing the highest number. Multiply the two uncovered numbers.

To quiz you on a division fact, your family member can cover one of the smaller numbers. One of the smaller numbers is circled. The other has a square around it. Use the two uncovered numbers to solve a division fact.

Ask your family member to mix up the multiplication and division facts. He or she should sometimes cover the highest number, sometimes cover the circled number, and sometimes cover the number in the square.

Your teacher will tell you when the quiz on the 9s will be.

Part 2. Order of Operations
Solve the following problems using the order of operations.

A. $33 - 8 \times 3 =$ B. $35 \div 7 - 3 =$ C. $150 + 9 \times 6 =$

D. $45 \div 9 \times 4 =$ E. $100 + 200 \div 10 =$ F. $(6 + 3) \times 100 =$

G. $200 - (2 \times 70) =$ H. $60 \times 60 \div 40 =$ I. $(80 + 80) \div 40 =$

Copyright © 1998 by Kendall/Hunt Publishing Company

Unit 5

Name _____ Date _____

Part 4. Fractions
You will need *Centimeter Dot Paper* to complete this part.

1. Complete each number sentence. Draw a picture on dot paper for each fraction. A 3 × 4 rectangle is one whole.

   A. $1\frac{2}{3} = \frac{n}{3}$ B. $2\frac{3}{4} = \frac{n}{4}$

   C. $1\frac{1}{6} = \frac{n}{6}$ D. $3\frac{1}{8} = \frac{n}{8}$

2. Write each mixed number as an improper fraction.

   A. $2\frac{3}{5} =$ _____   B. $3\frac{1}{4} =$ _____

   C. $3\frac{3}{10} =$ _____   D. $3\frac{5}{8} =$ _____

3. Write each improper fraction as a mixed number.

   A. $\frac{13}{6} =$ _____   B. $\frac{7}{2} =$ _____

   C. $\frac{10}{3} =$ _____   D. $\frac{14}{5} =$ _____

Part 5. Practicing the Operations

1. Solve the following problems in your head. Estimate the answers to F and G.

   A. $240 + 60 =$ _____   B. $2089 + 401 =$ _____   C. $1250 - 300 =$ _____

   D. $10,000 - 6700 =$ _____   E. $3800 + 1200 =$ _____

   F. Estimate: 89×18 G. Estimate: $1270 \div 50$

2. Use a separate sheet of paper. Solve the following problems using a paper-and-pencil method. Estimate to be sure your answers are reasonable.

   A. $473 + 1548 =$ _____   B. $28 \times 59 =$ _____

   C. $7034 \div 9 =$ _____   D. $3704 - 478 =$ _____

Copyright © 1998 by Kendall/Hunt Publishing Company

Unit 5

Figure 3: HP pages

How to Use the *Home Practice*

One way to assign the *Home Practice* is to send all parts home with students at some point during the unit. Students are responsible for completing the pages and returning them on a given day. This schedule allows for flexibility on the part of the teacher, students, and students' families. If some evenings are filled with athletic practices, meetings, family commitments, or the completion of other homework, students can choose their own times to work on the HP.

The HP is designed to be used in addition to (not as a replacement for) the unit homework. Since some parts may include content directly related to the current unit, often it is not appropriate to assign these parts during the first week of the unit. Rather, use such HP items after students have solved similar problems in class.

Another way to occasionally use the HP is for the teacher (or parents) to complete one or more parts of the assignment. The adult makes some intentional mistakes and shows how he or she solved the problems. Then, students grade the adult's work, justifying the number of points awarded to each problem.

From time to time, teachers may also want to ask students to reflect on how they completed their HP homework either in a short paragraph attached to the homework or in their math journals. Did they need help? Who helped them? Did the helper give them new strategies for solving problems? How did they organize their time?

Calculations: Paper-and-Pencil, Calculators, Mental Math, or Estimation?

The *Home Practice* provides many opportunities for practice of computational skills. Practice of paper-and-pencil calculations is emphasized throughout the HP. However, besides developing skill with paper-and-pencil computations, students also need to be able to choose when it is appropriate to use paper-and-pencil procedures, calculators, mental math, or estimation.

The following problem serves as an example:

> *The Student Council is selling 1000 pencils to make money for a school project. They have already sold 450 pencils. How many more do they have to sell?*

Students may use paper-and-pencil procedures, but subtracting across zeros is difficult and not particularly efficient. They may estimate that the student council needs to sell about 500 more, but a more exact answer is probably needed in this situation. Using a calculator is possible, but probably not necessary. Using a mental math strategy of counting up is effective and efficient. (Count up 50 from 450 to 500, then count up 500 more to 1000 to arrive at the answer of 550 pencils.) Before sending home the HP, you may want to discuss the possible strategies for particular problems and whether or not it is appropriate to use a calculator or another method of calculating. For more information on helping students choose appropriate strategies for computation, see the TIMS Tutor: *Arithmetic* in Section 9 of the Teacher Implementation Guide.

Assessment in *MATH TRAILBLAZERS*™

The *Assessment in MATH TRAILBLAZERS* section details the philosophy, goals, and components of assessment in the curriculum.

A teacher and her students assess their work on a problem.

Assessment in *Math Trailblazers*™

Part I | **Philosophy of the Assessment Program in *Math Trailblazers***

Assessment in *Math Trailblazers* is ongoing and reflects the program's content and goals. Throughout the program, assessment serves several purposes:

- It helps teachers learn about students' thinking and knowledge. This information is then used to guide instruction.

- It communicates the goals of instruction to students, parents, and others.

- It informs students, parents, and others about progress towards these goals.

The assessment program is built around two main principles: assessment should reflect the breadth and balance of the curriculum; and assessment activities should be valuable educational experiences.

Alignment with Goals

The NCTM *Standards* defines five broad goals for students: that they learn to value mathematics; that they become confident in their ability to do mathematics; that they become mathematical problem solvers; that they learn to communicate mathematically, and that they learn to reason mathematically. The term "mathematical power" is used in the *Standards* to capture the essence of these five goals. Mathematical power includes a student's ability "to explore, conjecture, and reason logically, as well as the ability to use a variety of mathematical methods effectively to solve nonroutine problems." (NCTM, 1989, p. 5) Students who possess mathematical power can apply their mathematical knowledge to a variety of situations.

Math Trailblazers is designed to develop students' mathematical power. As such, the program requires significant shifts in emphases relative to a traditional program—changes in content, learning, teaching, evaluation, and expectations. The implications with regard to student assessment are also significant. With the development of mathematical power as a primary aim of the curriculum, we can no longer focus narrowly on the assessment of only isolated skills and procedures, using single sources of information at the end of a learning cycle. Instead, assessment needs to shift toward collecting information over the course of the year from a wide variety of sources, covering a wide range of mathematical content, and incorporating the rich problem-solving situations that are characteristic of the curriculum. The NCTM's *Assessment Standards for School Mathematics* describes this as follows:

> *Possessing mathematical power includes being able and predisposed to apply mathematical understanding to new situations as well as having the confidence to do so. A comprehensive program of mathematics assessment includes opportunities for students to show what they can do with mathematics that they may not have studied formally but that they are prepared to investigate. Some assessments may be designed to determine how well students presented with an unfamiliar situation can use what they have learned previously. Other assessments may require that students learn a new mathematical concept or strategies during the assessment and use this knowledge to solve problems ... (This) not only gives students multiple opportunities to display their developing mathematical power but also increases their opportunities to learn additional mathematics.* (NCTM, 1995, pp. 11–12)

Integral with Instruction

Assessment in MATH TRAILBLAZERS is an integral part of instruction. All assessment activities are valuable educational experiences that have their own merit. By making assessment both integral to instruction and reflective of the overall mathematical content of the curriculum, we communicate what we value in mathematics. Again, the NCTM *Assessment Standards* addresses this idea:

> *Assessment that enhances mathematics learning becomes a routine part of ongoing classroom activity rather than an interruption. Assessment does not simply mark the end of a learning cycle. Rather, it is an integral part of instruction that encourages and supports further assessment.* (NCTM, 1995, p. 13)

Our assessment program is designed to give teachers frequent opportunities to assess student progress toward the primary goal of developing mathematical power. Concepts and skills are assessed in many different ways but especially as they are used within the context of solving problems. Assessments are designed to elicit more than just an answer. In solving problems, students show their thinking and give a picture of their understanding of mathematical concepts, strategies, tools, and procedures.

Integrating assessment with instruction has significant implications for the structure of the assessment program. There is no separate assessment book; assessment activities and other components of the assessment program are fully integrated into units. Furthermore, because much of the curriculum's content is revisited many times in varying contexts, students are assessed many times on many concepts. This flavors both instruction and assessment. Teachers can focus on student progress since they know that there will be other opportunities to review and assess and thus don't expect mastery at every juncture. At the same time, students' mathematical progress is not put on hold until they pass any particular assessment.

Balanced Assessment

The assessment program reflects the curriculum's instruction in another important way: it is varied and balanced. The MATH TRAILBLAZERS curriculum is balanced across several dimensions:

- Math content
  The program incorporates a broad range of mathematical content and procedures, and connections between different topics abound.

- Communication
  Students are expected to communicate their mathematical work and represent mathematical ideas in many different ways—written and oral explanations and justifications, number sentences, tables, graphs, pictures, and models are all used extensively.

- Student groupings
  Students work individually, in pairs, and in small groups.

- Length of activities
  There are short activities (5–15 minutes), tasks that take a full class period, and longer investigations.

- Amount of teacher direction
  Some activities involve substantial teacher direction; others are more student-directed.

- Varied contexts
  Mathematics is presented in a variety of contexts, such as laboratory experiments, real-life settings, word problems, and numerical problems.

Our assessment program is balanced in similar ways. A balanced assessment program gives each student an opportunity to demonstrate what he or she knows by allowing multiple approaches, covering a wide range of content, allowing access to tools when appropriate, varying the difficulty and pedagogy, and assessing within different kinds of contexts.

Using multiple sources of evidence improves the validity of judgments made about students' learning. With more than one source of information about students' progress, strengths in one source can compensate for weaknesses in others. It also helps teachers judge the consistency of students' mathematical work (NCTM, 1995, p. 19).

Promoting Student Reflection

In developing mathematical power, students come to understand that mathematics should make sense. Assessment activities in MATH TRAILBLAZERS do more than provide momentary snapshots of a student's progress. Students are often asked to revise work based upon commonly understood criteria for excellence. In grades K–2, these criteria are communicated largely by the teachers. Beginning in grade 3, the TIMS Student Rubrics provide an additional source of information to students about what is expected of them. As students become more involved in the assessment process, they become more reflective and can make constructive, critical judgments about their work and the work of others.

Part II | ## Components in Grades 1–5

Watching students grow intellectually throughout the course of the school year is one of the great satisfactions of teaching. The components of the assessment program provide teachers with the tools necessary to document students' progress over time as they acquire skills and concepts, develop their abilities to solve problems, and learn to communicate their thinking. While most components are included at all grade levels, the assessment program does vary from grade to grade based on the needs of the students.

All the materials provided to assess student learning are located in the units, either in the student materials or the Unit Resource Guide. Each unit contains assessment ideas and activities appropriate for the content and goals of the unit. This section describes the following components:

Observational Assessment
Ideas to Guide Assessment
Assessment Record Sheets
Individual Assessment Record Sheet

Written Assessments
Assessment Activity Pages
Math Journals
Assessment Ideas
Assessment Lessons
       Assessment Labs
       Open-Ended Problems
       Tests
Assessment Units
Portfolios
Fact Assessment

Observational Assessment

Teachers have always assessed student learning through informal classroom observations, thus integrating instruction and assessment. The first page of the NCTM *Assessment Standards* confirms the importance of these observations, "...much of the (assessment) information needs to be derived by teachers during the process of instruction. Teachers are the persons who are in the best position to judge the development of students' progress and, hence, must be considered the primary assessors of students." (NCTM, 1995, p. 1)

Teachers use the information gathered from classroom observations to guide instruction. While watching, questioning, and listening to students, they make moment-to-moment instructional decisions which change the direction and emphasis of the lesson. Teacher evaluation of student responses during a lesson will also affect the content of succeeding lessons.

Classroom observations can also be used to evaluate student achievement and monitor student progress. Skills such as using a graduated cylinder to measure volume, habits such as estimating regularly to check results, and behaviors such as working effectively within a group can best be assessed through observing students at work. Assessing students through observation is especially important in the primary grades because students at this age can usually communicate their thinking very well in a discussion, but often cannot fully express the same ideas on paper. Also, what we assess becomes what we value. If we only assess written work, other important behaviors such as verbal communication will be neglected. Finding a manageable way to organize and record these observations is critical to an effective assessment program.

Two tools are included in the Background of each unit to help teachers organize and document informal assessments: *Ideas to Guide Assessment* and *Assessment Record Sheets*.

Ideas to Guide Assessment

The background for each unit lists several Ideas to Guide Assessment which orient teachers to important skills, behavior, and knowledge they should assess in the unit. In grades 1–3, each of these ideas is numbered and labeled with an icon as shown in Figure 1.

In first and second grade, these icons are also placed in the At a Glance sections of the Lesson Guides to indicate which skills and concepts described in the Ideas to Guide Assessment might be assessed during that particular lesson.

Ideas to Guide Assessment

A1 Can students group and count objects by twos, fives, and tens?

A2 Given a collection of objects, can students determine how many groups of a given size and how many leftovers they can make?

A3 Can students collect, organize, and graph data as part of a scientific investigation?

Figure 1: Ideas to Guide Assessment from Grade 1, Unit 5

Figure 2 is a sample At a Glance section from Lesson 2 of Unit 5 in first grade.

The use of the icon **A1** shows that during this lesson students can be assessed on their abilities to count objects by twos, fives, and tens.

At a Glance

Part 1. Things That Come in Fives

1. Students think of objects that come in fives.
2. Students trace their hands and color in the outlines.
3. Display the tracings around the room as a guide for counting by fives and tens.

Part 2. Pennies and Nickels   **A1**

1. Students skip count to twenty by fives using *Penny Count* as a guide.
2. Show a different number of pennies on the transparency so that students can skip count by fives and ones.
3. Students estimate the number of pennies in a bag.
4. Students group the pennies into fives and leftovers.
5. Students count the pennies and discuss their counting strategies.
6. Students trade a nickel for each row of five pennies and count again.

Part 3. Pennies on Ten Frames   **A1**

1. Students group pennies into tens on the *Ten Frames* Activity Page.
2. Students count the pennies and discuss counting strategies.
3. Students trade a nickel for each complete row on the ten frames.
4. Students count by fives and ones. Collect the nickels.
5. Students trade a dime for each complete ten frame.
6. Students count by tens and ones and discover that the sum is still the same.

Figure 2: Sample At a Glance section from Grade 1, Unit 5, Lesson 2

Assessment Record Sheets

An *Assessment Record Sheet* similar to the one shown for Unit 1 of grade 5 in Figure 3 follows the background in each unit. Ideas to Guide Assessment that lend themselves to observation are listed at the top of each sheet. Additional lines are provided for teachers to include their own ideas. Each sheet has 32 rows for student names with columns for recording observations and extra space for comments. It is not necessary to record an observation about each child in each column. The grid provides a "snapshot" of the class's understanding of the main concepts, procedures, and skills covered in the unit.

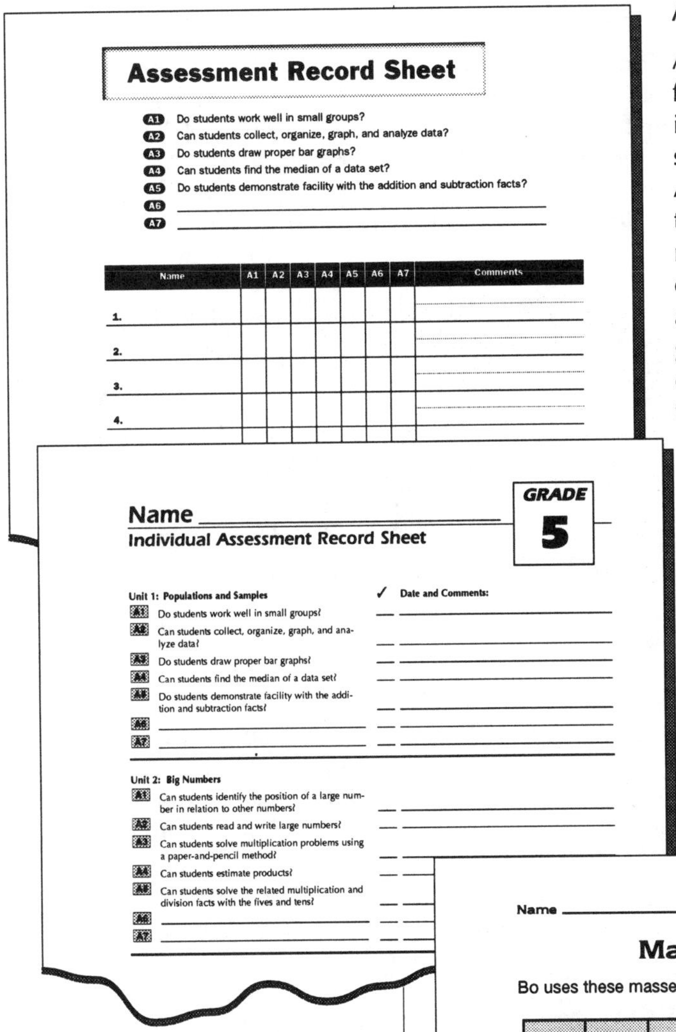

Assessment Record Sheet

A1 Do students work well in small groups?
A2 Can students collect, organize, graph, and analyze data?
A3 Do students draw proper bar graphs?
A4 Can students find the median of a data set?
A5 Do students demonstrate facility with the addition and subtraction facts?
A6 ______
A7 ______

Name	A1	A2	A3	A4	A5	A6	A7	Comments
1.								
2.								
3.								
4.								

Name ______ GRADE 5
Individual Assessment Record Sheet

Unit 1: Populations and Samples	✓	Date and Comments:
A1 Do students work well in small groups?		
A2 Can students collect, organize, graph, and analyze data?		
A3 Do students draw proper bar graphs?		
A4 Can students find the median of a data set?		
A5 Do students demonstrate facility with the addition and subtraction facts?		
A6		
A7		

Unit 2: Big Numbers		
A1 Can students identify the position of a large number in relation to other numbers?		
A2 Can students read and write large numbers?		
A3 Can students solve multiplication problems using a paper-and-pencil method?		
A4 Can students estimate products?		
A5 Can students solve the related multiplication and division facts with the fives and tens?		
A6		
A7		

Figure 3: Assessment Record Sheet *from Grade 5, Unit 1* *and* Individual Assessment Record Sheet *from Grade 5*

Grades 4 & 5

In fourth and fifth grades information from the Assessment Record Sheets can be transferred to Individual Assessment Record Sheets. The Individual Assessment Record Sheets are located at the end of Part VI of this section and are provided as an organizational tool for compiling a year-long anecdotal record for each child. Ideas to Guide Assessment for the entire year are listed together by unit along with a line for comments as shown in Figure 3.

Written Assessments

Assessment Activity Pages

Many lessons in *MATH TRAILBLAZERS* include short paper-and-pencil assessments which can be used to check skills or concepts developed in a unit. While some assessment pages can be used to assess students as they work in groups, often these pages can be used as quizzes to assess students individually. Checking student work gives both the teacher and student feedback on a student's current abilities. The assessment page *Massing an Object* from Unit 8 of second grade is shown in Figure 4 as an example. Students must combine their arithmetic skills with their measurement skills to complete the page correctly.

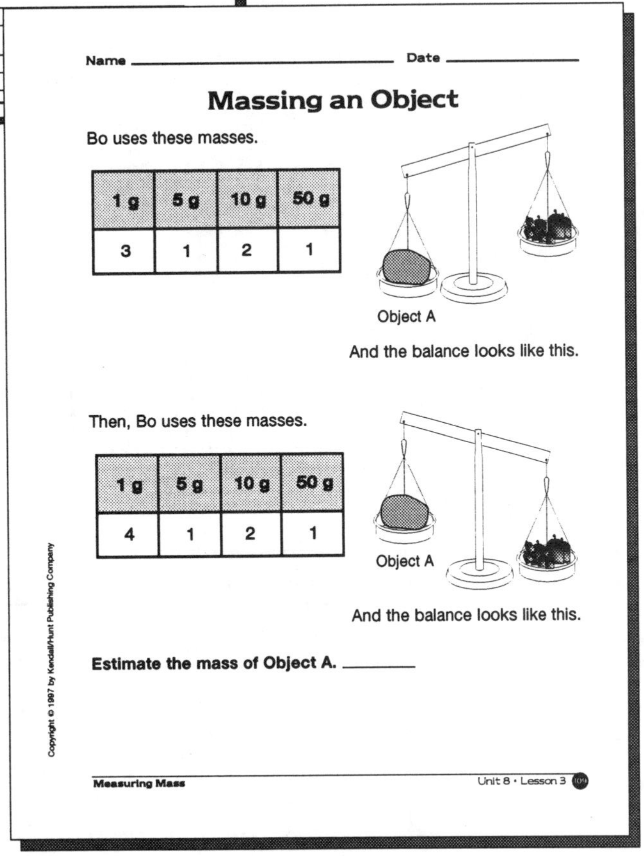

Name ______ Date ______

Massing an Object

Bo uses these masses.

1 g	5 g	10 g	50 g
3	1	2	1

And the balance looks like this.

Then, Bo uses these masses.

1 g	5 g	10 g	50 g
4	1	2	1

And the balance looks like this.

Estimate the mass of Object A. ______

Copyright © 1997 by Kendall/Hunt Publishing Company

Measuring Mass Unit 8 • Lesson 3 109

Figure 4: Assessment page from Grade 2, Unit 8

Journal Prompt

Show students a small, unopened spice jar with the mass (in grams) of the contents printed on the label. Pose this problem to the children: *How can you find the mass of the container without opening the jar? Think about how you can solve this problem.* Have students write their problem-solving strategies in their journals. ■

Figure 5: A journal prompt from Grade 2, Unit 8, Lesson 3

Math Journals

Students' entries in their math journals are a rich source of assessment information. Journal prompts, which are a regular feature in the lesson guides, are intended to elicit information about students' understanding of specific concepts, their ability to communicate this understanding in a written form, and their attitudes and feelings about mathematics. Figure 5 shows an example of a journal prompt from a lesson on measuring mass in second grade (Lesson 3, Unit 8).

Regular journal writing provides teachers and parents with a means of documenting a student's growth in mathematical thinking, attitudes, and communication skills. (For information on math journals, see the TIMS Tutor: *Journals.)* Young children often begin by drawing pictures in their journals or combining pictures with a few words. The journal entry in Figure 6 is an early effort by Jayne, a second-grader, at communicating her thoughts about a math lesson on doubling. Jayne used six circles and six squares to show two examples of doubling three. She also wrote a short paragraph about the class:

> *Today my class did some math. and we did some writ (write) some math too! I like it!*

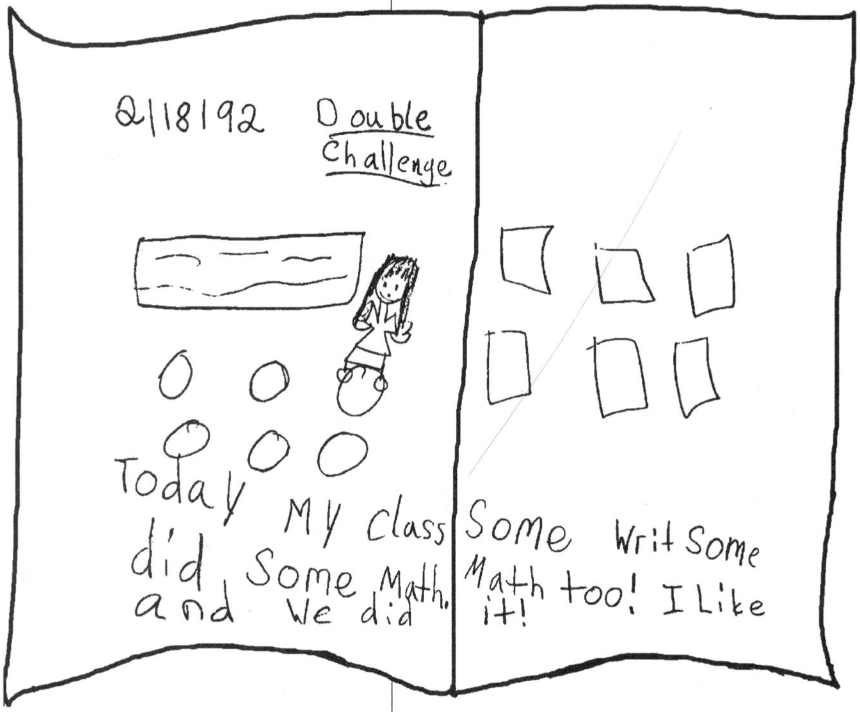

Figure 6: A second-grade journal entry

Assessment Ideas

The Assessment Ideas section of the Lesson Guide lists suggestions for assessing the content presented in the lesson. The following components are often recommended for use as an assessment: Assessment Activity Pages, journal prompts, classroom observations corresponding to the Ideas to Guide Assessment, and appropriate questions from the student pages and homework sections. The level of a student's response to these questions can also be recorded on the *Assessment Record Sheet* or in a grade book. Figure 7 shows the Assessment Ideas section for Lesson 3 of Unit 8 in second grade.

Assessment Ideas

- Use the graphs to measure students' ability to interpret data and understand the lab. Use the following criteria to assess the graphs: (1) the axes are labeled with appropriate symbols, (2) the vertical axis is scaled properly, and (3) the values for the objects are carefully plotted.
- The *Massing an Object* Assessment Page asks students to make their best estimate of the mass of an object. Their responses provide one measure of their ability to conceptualize that a mass may be between 78 and 79 grams—$78\frac{1}{2}$ grams.

Figure 7: Assessment Ideas from Grade 2, Unit 8, Lesson 3

Name _____ Date _____

Class Party

Suppose there are 25 students in your class and you have $10 for a class party. Use the prices in the table to plan a party.

Tell how you would spend the money, and explain why you would spend it that way. Use as much of the $10 as you can, but do not plan to spend more than $10. (There is no tax.) Be sure your plan works for a class of 25.

Write your plan on another piece of paper. Be sure to explain how you solved the problem and how you made your decisions.

Item	Cost
pitcher of lemonade (10 servings)	$2.50
paper cups (package of 24)	69¢
ice cream bars	30¢
oatmeal cookies (package of 16)	99¢
bag of popcorn (30 servings)	$1.09
napkins (package of 50)	49¢

Jayne

Steps

1. Lemonade $7.50
   $2.50 \times 3 = \$7.50$

2. Paper Cups $1.38
   $69 \times 2 = \$1.38$

3. Popcorn
   1.09
   $1.09 \times 1 = 1.09$

4.
   $\overset{1}{7}.50$ Lemonade
   1.38 Paper Cups
   + 1.09 Popcorn
   $\overline{\$9.97}$

4. 3¢ left over

I solved the problems the way I did because number sentences help you get the awnser

My way works because it helped me get the awnser.

The math is the same as other math because they both have driffrent ways of solving their problems and awnsering them.

Figure 8: Student's response to a third-grade problem

Assessment Lessons

Some units include specially designed assessment lessons. These lessons are generally one of three types: assessment labs, open-ended problems, or written tests composed of short items. Each type of lesson provides different kinds of information to teachers so that they can develop and document a complete picture of their students' progress toward the goals of the curriculum.

Assessment Labs. Three or four laboratory experiments in each grade have been designated as assessment labs. Teachers can use them to assess students' abilities to work with a group on an investigation that takes several days. To complete a lab successfully, students must apply many skills and concepts to a new situation. Teachers can also observe students to see if they are confident enough to tackle new ideas and to use previously learned mathematics in new contexts. Working on projects such as these—problems requiring integration and application of many concepts and skills over a period of time—more closely resembles the work of mathematicians and scientists (as well as working adults in many occupations) than any other kind of work students do in school. Suggestions for evaluating labs is included in Part III.

Open-Ended Problems. In these lessons, students are presented with a task that requires them to demonstrate their problem-solving skills individually or as they work in a group. Students are also assessed on their understanding of the mathematical content involved in the problem and their abilities to communicate their thinking strategies. They must produce a product that allows teachers to examine the process used as well as the final answer. More than a few minutes are required to solve such a problem and students will often need a whole class period to find solutions and describe their strategies. To encourage students to give full explanations and improve their writing skills, teachers can comment on students' initial responses and ask them to make revisions. Part III includes a scoring guide which can be used to score student responses to these problems.

Figure 8 shows Jayne's response to an open-ended problem written at mid-year of third grade. Jayne is the same student who wrote the journal entry shown in Figure 6. Compare her writing here with her paragraph from second grade and also with her work at the end of third grade on the *Earning Money* problem shown in Figure 18 in Part III. Comparing these three responses shows how she has developed her communication skills.

Tests. Tests designed to assess students' conceptual understanding and procedural skills also have a place in the curriculum. These tests are composed of short items which can be easily graded. There is a test in the final unit of both first and second grade. In third grade, there is a mid-year and an end-of-the-year test. In fourth and fifth grades, there is a midterm test in both the fall and spring semesters in addition to a mid-year and end-of-year test.

Assessment Units

In each grade, specific units are designated as assessment units. These units include lessons which emphasize assessment at the same time that content is reviewed and new material is introduced. Teachers can assess students' abilities to apply previously studied concepts in new contexts and their willingness to approach new mathematics.

Assessment units at the beginning of each grade provide opportunities to observe students and collect baseline data on students' mathematical knowledge. This information is used to plan instruction that meets students' needs and to begin the process of documenting students' mathematical growth over the course of the year. See the Assessment Overview in Part VI for specific information on the assessment units.

Portfolios

Portfolios are important tools for documenting students' growth throughout the year. They are collections of students' written work and teachers' anecdotal records. To provide a complete picture of a student's learning, a portfolio should include assessments which demonstrate the range of the child's abilities. Samples of student work on labs, open-ended problems, assessment activity pages, and tests can be included along with samples of students' daily work. Work from the beginning through the end of the year will show students' growth over time. Certain lessons in the assessment units are designed to assist in this process and are especially appropriate for inclusion in portfolios. Refer to the TIMS Tutor: *Portfolios* for more information about portfolios and how to use them.

Fact Assessment

In *MATH TRAILBLAZERS,* teachers assess students' knowledge of the facts through observations as they work on activities, labs, and games as well as through the appropriate use of quizzes and tests. Beginning in third grade, periodic, short quizzes in the *Daily Practice and Problems* naturally follow the study of small groups of facts organized around specific strategies. As self-assessment in third, fourth, and fifth grades, each student can record his or her progress on Facts I Know charts and determine which facts he or she needs to study. The goal of the math facts assessment program is to determine the degree to which students can find answers to fact problems quickly and accurately and whether they can retain this skill over time. For more information on teaching and assessing the math facts, see the TIMS Tutor: *Math Facts.*

Implementing the Assessment Program

Evaluating and reporting on a broad range of student achievement throughout the school year is a complex task. It is only practical if the assessment process is built into day-to-day instruction. The components of the assessment program are designed so that teachers can gather information about students as they are learning. This section outlines a plan for introducing the various components of the assessment program gradually during the first weeks of instruction and provides information on evaluating and scoring written work.

Getting Started

An assessment program that emphasizes the documentation of students' growth over time establishes a climate in which each child is valued for the knowledge and skills he or she brings to the classroom and in which each student is expected to make significant gains in mathematics. These are high expectations which also reflect reality. Students begin and end the school year with varying abilities, backgrounds, and accomplishments. Therefore, it is important to record what each student can do initially, as well as during the learning process, so that the teacher, student, and parents can fully appreciate progress throughout the year.

Begin Observational Assessments

Activities in the first two or three units of each grade provide many opportunities for observing students as they use mathematics. These observations provide a rich source of baseline information about students. For example, in Units 1 and 2 of first grade, students count objects in many contexts. By routinely observing four or five students during appropriate lessons, the teacher can make a record of those students who can count and those students who may need additional help. At the same time, all students are working on their counting skills as well as on related concepts such as comparing numbers and organizing data.

Unit 2 of third grade is also designated as an assessment unit. As part of this unit, students work on strategies in order to gain facility with the subtraction facts. Students discuss strategies, play games, work with flash cards, assess themselves using a Facts I Know chart, and investigate subtraction facts as part of a data collection activity. Observing students as they participate in each of these activities gives the teacher information about students' knowledge of the facts and, more importantly, about students' ability to use the facts to solve problems. Since students will continually use the facts in many activities as well as in the *Daily Practice and Problems,* the teacher need only record observations for a small number of students at a time. (For more information on assessment of the basic math facts, see the TIMS Tutor: *Math Facts.*)

Using Assessment Record Sheets. Before beginning assessment observations, teachers need a system for recording short, anecdotal records. Such a system should allow recording of a broad range of evidence of students' behavior, attitudes, and understanding of mathematics and should make recording and retrieving information easy and convenient. The *Assessment Record Sheets* and Ideas to Guide Assessment are designed to help organize data from observations. Teachers can develop their own shorthand to denote satisfactory progress toward a goal or proficiency with a skill or concept. The information on the *Assessment Record Sheet* can also be transferred to individual student portfolios.

Grades 4 & 5

In fourth and fifth grades, information from the Assessment Record Sheet can be transferred to Individual Assessment Record Sheets to begin a year-long anecdotal record of growth for each child. The Individual Assessment Record Sheets are located at the end of Part VI of this section. They can be copied and placed in each student's portfolio.

As part of planning for a lesson, the teacher can choose one or two behaviors, concepts, or skills to watch for during class. The Ideas to Guide Assessment for each unit and the Assessment Ideas in the Lesson Guides can facilitate this process. The teachers should choose no more than four or five students to observe in a day. Additional students can be observed in succeeding lessons or units to provide further information about individual students' progress and the improvement of the class as a whole.

Figure 9 is an example of an *Assessment Record Sheet* for Unit 1 in first grade which shows one possible scheme for recording classroom observations. Note that the teacher chose to observe students' abilities to work together as well as counting and calendar skills.

Other suggestions from teachers for organizing anecdotal records are given below:

Assessment Record Sheet

The following questions may be used to assess your students' progress.
It may be necessary to assess additional content.

- **A1** Can students count objects?
- **A2** Can students identify a small number of objects without counting?
- **A3** Are students able to tell which of two numbers is *more* or *less*?
- **A4** Can students count on from a given number?
- **A5** Can students identify days of the week in order?
- **A6** Can students work cooperatively with a partner?

Name	A1	A2	A3	A4	A5	A6	Comments
1. Susie	9/2 yes				9/6 10 15		counted a row of students 1-10 DPP item 6, #3
2. Chan	9/2 no						uses counting all
3. Roosevelt	9/2 yes						Counted blocks 1-15
4. Lee					9/1 yes		DPP item C
5. Kristen				9/3 yes		9/3 yes	Counted on from numbers less than 10 to 10, helped David
6. David				9/3 with help		9/3 yes	Counted buttons 1-10 worked well with kristen

Figure 9: Sample Assessment Record Sheet for Grade 1, Unit 1

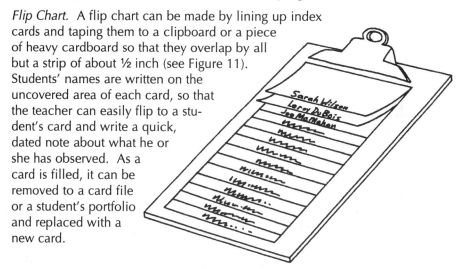

Sally Adamji	Feliz Arnez	John Boyd	Barb Crown
Willie Darno	Sarah Frank	Lee Guzman	etc.

Figure 10: Student grid

Student Grid. A teacher can make a grid which allows note-taking about all students on one piece of paper (see Figure 10). The grids include as many cells as there are students in the class, each cell labeled with a student's name. Observations are written in the cells. Like the *Assessment Record Sheet,* this provides a view of the entire class's progress.

Flip Chart. A flip chart can be made by lining up index cards and taping them to a clipboard or a piece of heavy cardboard so that they overlap by all but a strip of about ½ inch (see Figure 11). Students' names are written on the uncovered area of each card, so that the teacher can easily flip to a student's card and write a quick, dated note about what he or she has observed. As a card is filled, it can be removed to a card file or a student's portfolio and replaced with a new card.

Figure 11: Flip chart

Flip Cards. A variation of the flip chart can be made by fastening together a set of index cards—one index card labeled for each student in the class. A binder ring is placed through a hole in a corner of each card.

Self-Adhesive Notes. Some teachers prefer to write their observations about individual students on self-adhesive notes, which are then attached to a sheet of paper in the student's portfolio. These notes have the advantage of being easily transferable, so that they can be grouped and regrouped by student, subject, day, etc.

Computer Data Bases. Computer data bases are powerful tools for maintaining a record of your observations. Data bases allow you to regroup and reorganize the data in many different configurations and make it convenient for producing detailed progress reports about individual students.

Begin Math Journals

At the beginning of the year, math journals provide a safe place for students to start communicating their insights and feelings. By writing regularly in their journals, they gain the experience necessary to write more and learn to express themselves clearly. The background sections of Unit 5 of first grade and Unit 2 of second grade recommend starting math journals during those units. Journal prompts begin immediately in the first lesson of third grade. See the TIMS Tutor: *Journals* for more information on using journals to assess students.

Begin Portfolios

The TIMS Tutor: *Portfolios* recommends establishing portfolios by starting small with modest goals. This implies using portfolios to document progress in one or two specific areas such as communicating mathematically or collecting and analyzing data. One way to begin is to assign each student a collection folder so that early examples of student work can be saved. Later in the process, teachers can designate or students can select a smaller number of pieces that show evidence of growth in these areas.

It is important to choose examples of work from the beginning of the year so that a student's first efforts can be compared to later work. The earliest entries in the portfolio will most likely show results which are much less sophisticated than those that are added toward the end of the year. For example, to compare students' use of the TIMS Laboratory Method at the beginning of the year to their ability to conduct an experiment at the end of the year, include a data table and a graph from an early lab in each student's portfolio. Good choices of initial labs to collect in portfolios include the following: In first grade, first save the students' weather graph from Unit 3; in second grade, use the *Button Sizer Graph* from Unit 3, Lesson 3; and in third grade, choose student work from the lab *Kind of Bean* in Unit 1, Lesson 3, or the graph and write-up from *Spinning Differences* in Unit 2, Lesson 6. At the beginning of grade 4, include *Arm Span vs. Height* from Unit 1 Lesson 5 and *Perimeter vs. Length* from Unit 2 Lesson 2. In fifth grade, begin their portfolios with the labs *Searching the Forest* from Unit 1 Lesson 5 and *Distance vs. Time* from Unit 3 Lesson 6.

Scoring Open-Ended Problems and Evaluating Labs

In *MATH TRAILBLAZERS,* most lessons involve multiple mathematical topics, skills, and processes. Assessing student progress requires tools that allow students to respond using multiple approaches and that let teachers evaluate student communication and problem-solving strategies as well as mathematical knowledge.

Scoring Open-Ended Problems

TIMS Multidimensional Rubric. To assist teachers in evaluating student performance and in communicating progress to students and parents, we have developed a rubric—a scoring guide—for evaluating student work on open-ended problems. The *TIMS Multidimensional Rubric* addresses three dimensions of mathematical learning: (i) understanding mathematical content, (ii) solving problems, and (iii) communicating. Using these three dimensions broadens the focus of assessment from the traditional emphasis on rote procedures to a more complete view of mathematics learning. The rubric outlines our criteria for excellence and provides an explicit indication of what we value in mathematics. Examples of using the rubric to score student work are included in lesson guides beginning in grade 3. The ideas embodied in the rubric are generally applicable to younger children and can be modified for use in earlier grades. The rubric is displayed in Part V on page 159.

The three dimensions of mathematical understanding emphasized in the *TIMS Multidimensional Rubric* are described here briefly.

- *Solving Problems.* This section focuses on students' understanding of a problem and their abilities to devise a solution plan for solving it, organize information, analyze results, and reflect on the mathematical implications of the problem.

- *Understanding Mathematical Content.* This portion of the rubric examines students' comprehension of mathematical concepts and their abilities to apply procedures, rules, and facts to a given mathematical situation. This includes effective use of representations, such as written numbers, words, graphs, tables, or pictures, and the ability to make connections among different mathematical ideas.

- *Communicating.* This part of the rubric stresses students' abilities to explain their problem-solving strategies, justify their solutions, use symbols and terminology correctly, and discuss connections among mathematical topics.

The *TIMS Multidimensional Rubric* specifies criteria for assigning scores on each of the three dimensions to one piece of student work. Level 4 is the highest and is intended to represent excellence in that particular dimension. A paper might earn, for example, a 3 in Solving Problems, a 4 in Understanding Mathematical Content, and a 3 in Communicating. It is not necessary to assign a score for all three dimensions for every task. For many tasks, it may be more appropriate to give scores for only one or two dimensions.

Student Rubrics. Corresponding *Student Rubrics* for each dimension have also been developed to make the expectations of student performance clear. These rubrics provide students with goals as they solve problems, communicate their solutions, and revise their work. Students also use these rubrics as guides when assessing their own work. The student rubrics are introduced gradually in the Student Guide throughout the first semester of third, fourth, and fifth grades. They are included in assessment lessons with open-ended problems.

The *Student Rubrics* are shown in Figure 12. The *Solving* rubric corresponds to the "Solving Problems" dimension; the *Knowing* rubric corresponds to "Understanding Mathematical Content"; and the *Telling* rubric corresponds to "Communicating."

See the Assessment Overview in Part VI for the specific locations of the Student Rubrics in the fifth-grade Student Guide. Blackline Masters of the Student Rubrics are included in Part V so teachers can make transparencies or use a copier to enlarge the rubrics to make classroom posters.

Figure 12:
Student Rubrics:
Knowing
Solving
Telling

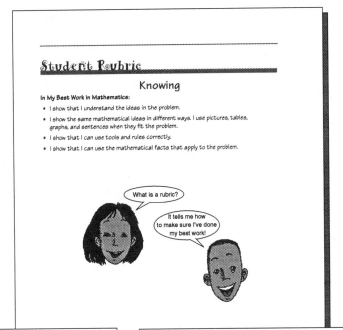

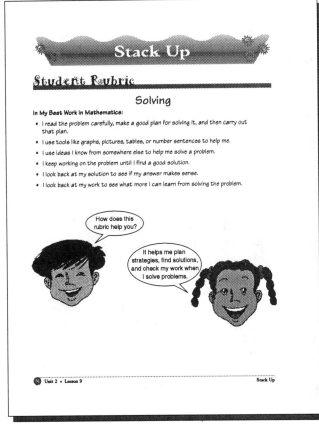

Using the Rubrics: An Early Example. Using the student rubrics to inform students of your expectations as well as using the *TIMS Multidimensional Rubric* to score student work is a process which evolves throughout the year. For example, in third grade, Lesson 6 of Unit 2 is the first assessment lesson with an open-ended problem and also the students' first exposure to the student rubrics. The problem is shown below:

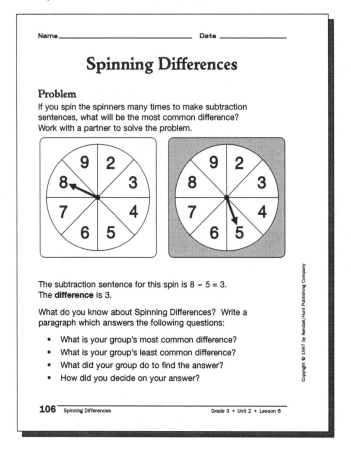

Figure 13: Assessment lesson from Lesson 6, Unit 2

To begin the lesson the class reads and discusses the problem. It is similar to the problem in an earlier lesson (Unit 2, Lesson 2—*Spinning Sums),* so students should be familiar with the procedures. They also read and discuss the *Knowing* student rubric. The teacher may ask students what tools, rules, and mathematical facts apply to the problem. She explains that she will grade their work based on the rubric.

After students understand the problem, they work in groups to plan a strategy for solving the problem and carry out their plan. Then the students write a paragraph describing their problem-solving process and their results. The teacher directs the students either to write the paragraph with their groups or write the paragraph individually. When students have completed their paragraphs, the teacher reviews their work and makes suggestions for improvement. He or she may also make transparencies of exemplary work from previous years or the lesson guide. The teacher discusses the exemplary work with the class, comparing the work to the standards set forth in the rubric. Finally, students revise their work based on the teacher's comments. A student response with teacher comments is shown in Figure 14.

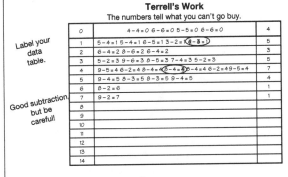

Terrell's Work
The numbers tell what you can't go buy.

Label your data table.

0	4−4 = 0 6−6 = 0 5−5 = 0 6−6 = 0	4
1	5−4 = 1 5−4 = 1 6−5 = 1 3−2 = 1 (8−3 = 1)	5
2	6−4 = 2 8−6 = 2 6−4 = 2	3
3	5−2 = 3 9−6 = 3 8−5 = 3 7−4 = 3 5−2 = 3	5
4	9−5 = 4 6−2 = 4 8−4 = 4 (8−4 = 4) 8−4 = 4 6−2 = 4 9−5 = 4	7
5	9−4 = 5 8−3 = 5 8−3 = 5 9−4 = 5	4
6	8−2 = 6	1
7	9−2 = 7	1
8		
9		
10		
11		
12		
13		
14		

Good subtraction but be careful!

Good graph. Your numbering is perfect.

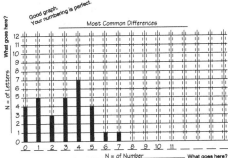

Most Common Differences

N = of Letters What goes here?

N = of Number   What goes here?

Are graph looks like a truck. Because it looked like a truck. We had the most was four. Are least common was six and seven.

Your graph does look like a truck. How did you know what was the most likely difference? Where are the highest and lowest points on your graph?

Are lowest point was at the end. Are highest point was in the middle.

Figure 14: A student response to a teacher's comments

The teacher used the Understanding Mathematical Content dimension of the *TIMS Multidimensional Rubric* to score students' work. The Lesson Guide provides questions specific to this problem to guide the teacher in the scoring. The questions provided for this problem are given below:

- Were the data table and graph appropriately labeled?

- Was the graph scaled properly?

- Were the bars correctly drawn?

- Were the subtraction sentences correct?

- Were the most common differences identified?

Because many of the criteria in the rubric overlap and because the student's data table, graph, and written paragraphs tell us about more than one component of the problem, the score for a dimension will result from the compilation of all the evidence, not necessarily from an arithmetic average of scores in each cell of the rubric. Figure 15 shows the Understanding Mathematical Content *(Knowing)* dimension of the *TIMS Multidimensional Rubric* with the teacher's notations after she scored Terrell's paper.

How would you score Terrell's work? Terrell's teacher decided that he earned a 3. He worked with his group using tools to spin the spinners 30 times, record the results in a table, and display the data in a graph. The bars are drawn correctly on the graph and the axes are scaled correctly. However, the incorrect labels on both the data table ("The numbers that tell what you can't go buy") and graph ("Most Common Differences" and "N = of Letters") indicate that he was not clear on his goal for collecting data and therefore did not completely understand the problem's concepts and applications. The incorrect labels also show major errors translating between tables, graphs, and real situations, although he did correctly identify the most common and least common differences. The correct number sentences are evidence that he knows the subtraction facts. (See the Lesson Guide for Lesson 6 in Unit 2 of Grade 3 for other examples of student work scored using the rubric.)

Understanding Mathematical Content	Level 4	Level 3	Level 2	Level 1
Understands the task's mathematical concepts, their properties and applications…	Completely	Nearly completely	Partially	Not at all
Translates between words, pictures, symbols, tables, graphs, and real situations…	Readily and without errors	With minor errors	With major errors	Not at all
Uses tools (measuring devices, graphs, tables, calculators, etc.) and procedures…	Correctly and efficiently	Correctly or with minor errors	Incorrectly	Not at all
Uses knowledge of the facts of mathematics (geometry definitions, math facts, etc.)…	Correctly	With minor errors	With major errors	Not at all

Figure 15: Scoring an open-ended problem using one dimension of the TIMS Multidimensional Rubric

Using the Rubrics: A Second Example. During the school year, students become familiar with all three of the student rubrics and use them as they solve problems. Depending on the problem, one or more of the rubrics may be used. The results of these assessments are often saved in portfolios to show students and parents progress over time. The following problem is posed to students in the final assessment unit of third grade.

Name _____ Date _____

Earning Money

Daniel, Maria, and Cora earned 5 dollars babysitting for the Farleys. Mrs. Farley gave the three sitters one 5-dollar bill.

1. If they share the money equally, how much should each babysitter get? Explain how you solved the problem.

2. What happens if you try to solve the problem on a calculator? Explain.

Write your solutions to Questions 1 and 2. Be sure to tell about all the ways you solved the problem.

Grade 3 • Unit 20 • Lesson 4

Figure 16: An open-ended problem from Grade 3, Unit 20, Lesson 4

Before students begin solving the problem, the class reads and discusses the problem. Students should understand that play money will be available to help solve the problem and that they will be asked how a calculator can be used to solve the problem. The teacher also reviews all three student rubrics and advises students that their work for this problem will be scored using all three dimensions.

Students use the tools available to them to find solutions and write about their strategies. The teacher may use samples of students' work to provide good examples for students to emulate. He or she also comments on students' first drafts and students revise their work accordingly.

Two samples of student work are shown below with scores for all three dimensions of the *TIMS Multidimensional Rubric*. The teacher was guided by additional questions in the Lesson Guide which are specific to this problem and point out elements to consider while scoring.

Marco's Work

Marco's response the first day:

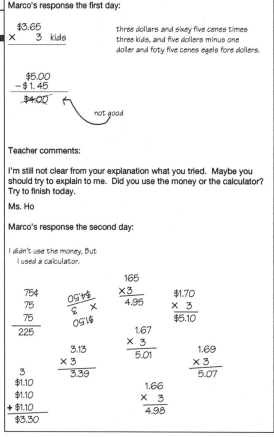

$3.65
×   3   kids

three dollars and sixey five cenes times three kids, and five dollers minus one doller and foty five cents egels fore dollers.

$5.00
− $1. 45
$4.00   *not good*

Teacher comments:

I'm still not clear from your explanation what you tried. Maybe you should try to explain to me. Did you use the money or the calculator? Try to finish today.

Ms. Ho

Marco's response the second day:

I didn't use the money, But I used a calculator.

Figure 17: Marco's work

The teacher gave Marco a 2 on problem solving. Marco chose a legitimate problem-solving strategy—guess and check—but did not use it systematically or efficiently, nor did he organize his work. His work does show evidence that he persisted in the problem-solving process, but does not show that he identified all the elements of the problem since he does not indicate that he knows that there will be money left over. He makes no connections to any previously studied math or previously solved problems.

On the understanding mathematical content dimension, the teacher gave Marco a 3 since he correctly used his knowledge of mathematics and he used appropriate tools (a calculator) and procedures (repeated addition and multiplication) to solve the problem. He did not demonstrate that he completely understood the nature of the task or show that he can translate between symbols and real situations since he did not calculate the amount of money that would be left over.

Marco received a 1 on the communicating dimension. His explanation was very short and totally unclear, with no supporting arguments. Since he did not identify which trial was successful, we are not even sure of his final answer. He used symbols to show his trials, but made no attempt to organize them. Appropriate terminology is not present.

A second sample of student work on the *Earning Money* problem is shown below:

Jayne's Work

Jayne's response the first day:

1.) Each person should get $1.66 and .2 left over. We got five dollars in change and we divided the money up between them. We got $1.66 for each person, and two cents left over.

2.) If you try on the calculator (5 ÷ 3) you would get 1.6666667. So I think it's much better to use play money or your head. The reason why you can't do it on the calculator is because the calculator will cut the coin up in half.

Teacher comments:

This is an excellent explanation! How can this problem help you solve other problems? Can you think of a way to find the remainder using your calculator?

Mrs. Vasquez

Jayne's response the second day:

1. You can check your answer by the calculator you can put $1.66 + $1.66 + $1.66 + $0.02 = $5.00.

2. This problem can help me solve other problems because it will help me divide money (if it involves money.)

3. A way to find how much is left $5.00 – $1.66 – $1.66 – $1.66 = $0.02.

Figure 18: Jayne's work

Jayne's teacher gave her a score of 4 for solving problems. She fully met the criteria in the rubric. She clearly identified the elements of the problem when she described the problem first as dividing the play money "up between them" and finding the amount left over and then as using a calculator to divide (5 ÷ 3) resulting in a repeating decimal. With prompting from the teacher, she looked for other strategies and found that she could use repeated addition and subtraction to find the remainder. All of her strategies are effective and they are presented in an organized fashion. Jayne's first conclusion that "you can't do it (find the remainder) on the calculator is because the calculator will cut the coin up in half" is insightful, although not quite correct mathematically. The use of both repeated addition and subtraction on the calculator to find the remainder shows that she made meaningful connections between the operations and that she was willing to persist in the problem-solving process.

Jayne also received a 4 in understanding mathematical content since she clearly understood the mathematical concepts of the problem. She readily translated the real situation into words when she described the process of dividing up the money and then translated words into symbols using correct addition, subtraction, and division sentences. The use of play money and a calculator is evidence that she can use tools correctly and efficiently and her calculations show that she can use the facts of mathematics correctly as well.

The teacher gave Jayne a score of 3 for the communicating dimension. Her explanations and responses were fairly complete and clear. For example, we are not entirely sure how the group shared the money. Did they trade the dollars for quarters and then the quarters for dimes, etc., or were they able to make the process more efficient in some way? Her supporting arguments are sound, but they contain a few minor gaps. Did she use repeated subtraction or repeated addition first to find the remainder? Why did she choose these operations? She used many symbols and terms correctly. However, she reported that two cents were left over and wrote it first as ".2."

Like any new tool, using the rubric efficiently will require practice. As you begin to work with the rubric, we suggest that you work closely with other teachers. For example, you might score a half-dozen papers and ask one or more colleagues to score the same set; then you can compare and discuss the results, negotiating any differences. Repeating this process over the course of the year will help establish school-wide norms for applying the rubrics.

Using Assessment Observations, Math Journals, and Portfolios. The rubrics can be combined with other components of the assessment program to provide a more complete picture of students' skills at solving open-ended problems. For example, to assess students' willingness to tackle new problems or work cooperatively in a group, teachers can observe students as they work on the problem or ask them to write in their journals about the process. For

Journal Prompt

How did your group share the work on this problem? How do you feel about working with a group in math class? ■

Figure 19: Journal prompt for Earning Money *(Grade 3 , Unit 20, Lesson 4)*

example, the journal prompt for the *Earning Money* lesson concerns students' feelings about working in groups in math class. (See Figure 19).

Considerable growth in mathematical power is often evident when several write-ups of open-ended problems from different times of the year are included in a student's portfolio. We can see growth in Jayne's problem-solving and communication skills when we look at her work on both the *Class Party* and *Earning Money* problems. (See Figure 8 in Part II and Figure 18.)

Evaluating Labs

Teachers have used the following ideas to evaluate student performance on labs:

Group Work. Students work in their groups to polish up a lab write-up and turn in one completed lab for each group or to prepare an oral report to be presented to the class. They may also include in their report how the work was distributed among the members of the group. Students can also write a paragraph in their journals describing how each of the members functioned in the group and how the process can be improved.

Using the Multidimensional Rubric. Choose one or two important questions to score using one or more dimensions of the *TIMS Multidimensional Rubric.* Often suitable questions will be suggested in the Assessment Ideas section of the Lesson Guide. These are usually open-ended questions which ask students to make predictions or solve a problem using the data collected during the experiment.

Self-Assessment. Students can grade their own labs in class. This provides a forum for discussing the most important aspects of the lab.

Using a Point System. To grade a lab, teachers can assign a given number of points to each part of the lab and grade each part based on the criteria which follow. Teachers can also choose to grade only a portion of the lab such as the picture or the graph.

1. Drawing the Picture
    - Are the procedure and the materials clearly illustrated?
    - Are the variables labeled?
2. Collecting and Recording the Data
    - Is the data organized in a table?
    - Are the columns in the data table labeled correctly?
    - Is the data reasonable?
    - Are the correct units of measure included in the data table?
    - If applicable, did students average the data (find the median or mean) correctly?

3. Graphing the Data

- Does the graph have a title?

- Are the axes scaled correctly and labeled clearly? Labeling should be consistent with the picture and the data table and should include appropriate units of measure.

- If it is a bar graph, are the bars drawn correctly?

- If it is a point graph, are the points plotted correctly?

- If the points suggest a straight line or a curve, did the student draw a best-fit line or fit a curve to the points?

- Did the students show any interpolation or extrapolation on the graph?

4. Solving the Problems

- Are the answers correct based on the data?

- Did students use appropriate tools (calculators, rulers, graphs, etc.) correctly?

- Are the answers, including the explanations, clear and complete?

Part IV   References

Assessment Standards for School Mathematics. Reston, Va.: National Council of Teachers of Mathematics, 1995.

Balanced Assessment for the Mathematics Curriculum Elementary Package. Berkeley, Calif.: Balanced Assessment Project, 1995. (In press)

Balanced Assessment for the Mathematics Curriculum Portfolio Support Package. Berkeley, Calif.: Balanced Assessment Project, 1995. (In press)

Performance Assessment in Mathematics: Approaches to Open-Ended Problems. Springfield, Ill.: Illinois State Board of Education, 1994.

Lane, Suzanne. "The Conceptual Framework for the Development of a Mathematics Performance Assessment Instrument" in *Educational Measurement: Issues and Practice.* Vol. 12, Number 2. Washington, D.C.: National Council on Measurement in Education, 1993.

Mathematics Resource Guide for Fourth- and Eighth-Grade Teachers. Montpelier, Vt.: Vermont Department of Education, 1996.

Stenmark, J.K. (Ed.) *Mathematics Assessment: Myths, Models, Good Questions, and Practical Suggestions.* Reston, Va.: National Council of Teachers of Mathematics, 1991.

This section is composed of blackline masters of the *TIMS Multidimensional Rubric* and the three Student Rubrics: *Knowing, Solving,* and *Telling.* The *Scoring Open-Ended Problems* section of Part III of the *Assessment in MATH TRAILBLAZERS* describes the rubrics and provides examples of their use in the curriculum. The *TIMS Multidimensional Rubric* is provided here so that teachers can use it as they score student work. The copies of the three student rubrics in this section can be used to make transparencies for the overhead projector or they can be enlarged to make posters for the classroom.

TIMS Multidimensional Rubric

Solving Problems	Level 4	Level 3	Level 2	Level 1
Identifies the elements of the problem and their relationships to one another	All major elements identified	Most elements identified	Some, but shows little understanding of relationships	Few or none
Uses problem-solving strategies which are...	Systematic, complete, efficient, and possibly elegant	Systematic and nearly complete, but not efficient	Incomplete or unsystematic	Not evident or inappropriate
Organizes relevant information...	Systematically and efficiently	Systematically, with minor errors	Unsystematically	Not at all
Relates the problem and solution to previously encountered mathematics and makes connections that are...	At length, elegant, and meaningful	Evident	Brief or logically unsound	Not evident
Persists in the problem solving process...	At length	Until a solution is reached	Briefly	Not at all
Looks back to examine the reasonableness of the solution and draws conclusions that are...	Insightful and comprehensive	Correct	Incorrect or logically unsound	Not present

Understanding Mathematical Content	Level 4	Level 3	Level 2	Level 1
Understands the task's mathematical concepts, their properties and applications...	Completely	Nearly completely	Partially	Not at all
Translates between words, pictures, symbols, tables, graphs, and real situations...	Readily and without errors	With minor errors	With major errors	Not at all
Uses tools (measuring devices, graphs, tables, calculators, etc.) and procedures...	Correctly and efficiently	Correctly or with minor errors	Incorrectly	Not at all
Uses knowledge of the facts of mathematics (geometry definitions, math facts, etc.)...	Correctly	With minor errors	With major errors	Not at all

Communicating	Level 4	Level 3	Level 2	Level 1
Includes response with an explanation and/or description which is...	Complete and clear	Fairly complete and clear	Perhaps ambiguous or unclear	Totally unclear or irrelevant
Presents supporting arguments which are...	Strong and sound	Logically sound, but may contain minor gaps	Incomplete or logically unsound	Not present
Uses pictures, symbols, tables, and graphs which are...	Correct and clearly relevant	Present with minor errors or somewhat irrelevant	Present with errors and/or irrelevant	Not present or completely inappropriate
Uses terminology...	Clearly and precisely	With minor errors	With major errors	Not at all

In My Best Work in Mathematics:

What is a rubric?

- I show that I understand the ideas in the problem.

- I show the same mathematical ideas in different ways. I use pictures, tables, graphs, and sentences when they fit the problem.

- I show that I can use tools and rules correctly.

- I show that I can use the mathematical facts that apply to the problem.

It tells me how to make sure I've done my best work!

In My Best Work in Mathematics:

How does this rubric help you?

- I read the problem carefully, make a good plan for solving it, and then carry out that plan.

- I use tools like graphs, pictures, tables, or number sentences to help me.

- I use ideas I know from somewhere else to help me solve a problem.

- I keep working on the problem until I find a good solution.

It helps me plan strategies, find solutions, and check my work when I solve problems.

- I look back at my solution to see if my answer makes sense.

- I look back at my work to see what more I can learn from solving the problem.

In My Best Work in Mathematics:

What does this rubric tell you?

- I show all of the steps that I used to solve the problem. I also tell what each number refers to (such as 15 boys or 6 inches).

- I explain why I solved the problem the way I did so that someone would be able to see why my method makes sense.

- If I use tools like pictures, tables, graphs, or number sentences, I explain how the tools I used fit the problem.

- I use math words and symbols correctly.
  For example, if I see "6 – 2," I solve the problem "six minus two," not "two minus six."

It helps me talk and write about math and solving problems!

The assessment overview includes short descriptions of the components in the assessment program followed by a table which lists each of the assessments in fifth grade. The table names the assessments in each unit and gives the lesson name and number, the type of assessment, and the location of the assessment within the unit.

Component Summary

Ideas to Guide Assessment: A list of important topics covered in a given unit. The Ideas to Guide Assessment help the teacher focus on important skills and behaviors that can be assessed.

Assessment Record Sheet: A tool that helps teachers record student progress on the Ideas to Guide Assessment. Information about all students in the class can be recorded on the *Assessment Record Sheet.* This provides a quick view of how both individual students and the class as a whole are progressing during the course of a unit. Student information can later be transferred to Individual Assessment Record Sheets.

Individual Assessment Record Sheet: A tool that coordinates individual students' progress with the Ideas to Guide Assessment from all sixteen units.

Assessment Ideas: Suggested ways to assess student progress during a lesson are included as Assessment Ideas in the lesson guides. Assessment ideas might highlight particular parts of an activity as appropriate for observations, direct teachers to an assessment page or activity, or suggest a journal prompt or homework questions for assessment.

Math Journals: As a part of the assessment for a lesson, students are sometimes asked to respond in their Math Journals to a specific question or prompt.

Assessment Pages: Short paper-and-pencil assessments that can be used to check skills or concepts developed in a unit. Some are designed for use in groups; others are for individual work.

Assessment Lessons: Specially designed lessons to gauge student progress. There are three basic types of assessment lessons: assessment labs, open-ended problems, and written tests composed of short items.

Assessment Labs: 2–4 laboratory experiments each year are designated as Assessment Labs. They are used to assess students' abilities to work in a group on an investigation that takes several days.

Assessment Units: Specific units in each grade that are designed to help teachers monitor student progress as part of the learning process. Units 1, 2, 8, and 16 are the Assessment Units in grade 5.

Fact Self-Assessment: As part of the *Daily Practice and Problems (DPP),* students regularly assess their knowledge of specific groups of math facts. Students categorize facts into three groups (facts I know quickly; facts I know using a strategy; facts I need to learn). They record this information on a special chart, which is updated regularly.

Fact Quiz: Periodic quizzes of small groups of math facts are given as part of the *DPP.* Facts are grouped to encourage the use of strategies in learning facts. Tests of the entire set of facts are given at mid-year and at the end of the year.

Portfolios: Collections of students' written work and teachers' anecdotal records. Portfolios are used to document students' growth over time.

URG = Unit Resource Guide   SG = Student Guide

TIG = Teacher Implementation Guide   DAB = Discovery Assignment Book

✧ = Assessment Unit

Lesson 6	**Distance vs. Time**		
	Student Rubric: Knowing Activity Page	Student Rubric	SG
	Student Rubric: Telling Activity Page	Student Rubric	SG
	TIMS Multidimensional Rubric	Scoring Guide	TIG

Unit 4	**Division and Data**		
DPP	**Item A**		
	Multiplication Facts: Square Numbers	Fact Self-Assessment	URG
	Item Y		
	Division Facts: Square Numbers	Fact Self-Assessment	URG
	Item CC		
	Quiz: Square Numbers	Multiplication/Division Fact Quiz	URG
Lesson 3	**Paper-and-Pencil Division**		
	Quiz	Assessment Activity Page	URG
Lesson 9	**Midterm Test**		
	Midterm Test	Assessment Activity Pages	URG

Unit 5	**Investigating Fractions**		
DPP	**Item A**		
	Multiplication Facts: 9s	Fact Self-Assessment	URG
	Item Q		
	Division Facts: 9s	Fact Self-Assessment	URG
	Item S		
	Quiz: 9s	Multiplication/Division Fact Quiz	URG
Lesson 5	**A Day at the Races**		
	Student Rubric: Telling Activity Page	Student Rubric	SG
	TIMS Multidimensional Rubric	Scoring Guide	TIG
Lesson 7	**Adding and Subtracting Fractions**		
	Fraction Follow-Up	Assessment Activity Pages	URG

Unit 6	**Geometry**		
DPP	**Item A**		
	Multiplication Facts: The Last Six Facts	Fact Self-Assessment	URG
	Item K		
	Division Facts: The Last Six Facts	Fact Self-Assessment	URG
	Item O		
	Quiz: The Last Six Facts	Multiplication/Division Fact Quiz	URG
Lesson 7	**Making Shapes**	Assessment Lesson	URG
	Student Rubric: Telling Activity Page	Student Rubric	SG
	Slab Orders	Assessment Activity Page	URG

Unit 7	**Decimals and Probability**		
Lesson 6	**Paper and Pencil Decimal Multiplication**		
	Decimal Quiz	Assessment Activity Page	URG

URG = Unit Resource Guide   SG = Student Guide
✧ *= Assessment Unit*   TIG = Teacher Implementation Guide   DAB = Discovery Assignment Book

URG = Unit Resource Guide   SG = Student Guide

✦ = Assessment Unit   TIG = Teacher Implementation Guide   DAB = Discovery Assignment Book

✧ = *Assessment Unit*

URG = Unit Resource Guide   SG = Student Guide
TIG = Teacher Implementation Guide   DAB = Discovery Assignment Book

Name _____

Individual Assessment Record Sheet

Unit 1: Populations and Samples

✓ **Date and Comments:**

A1 Do students work well in small groups? ___ _____

A2 Can students collect, organize, graph, and analyze data? ___ _____

A3 Do students draw proper bar graphs? ___ _____

A4 Can students find the median of a data set? ___ _____

A5 Do students demonstrate facility with the addition and subtraction facts? ___ _____

A6 _____ ___ _____

A7 _____ ___ _____

Unit 2: Big Numbers

A1 Can students identify the position of a large number in relation to other numbers? ___ _____

A2 Can students read and write large numbers? ___ _____

A3 Can students solve multiplication problems using a paper-and-pencil method? ___ _____

A4 Can students estimate products? ___ _____

A5 Can students solve the related multiplication and division facts with the fives and tens? ___ _____

A6 _____ ___ _____

A7 _____ ___ _____

Unit 3: Fractions and Ratios

A1 Are students able to find equivalent fractions? ___ _____

A2 Are students able to name fractions greater than one as mixed numbers or improper fractions? ___ _____

A3 Are students able to compare fractions? ___ _____

A4 Are students able to draw proper line graphs? ___ _____

A5 Are students able to fit a line to a set of data points when appropriate? ___ _____

A6 Are students able to measure length in yards? ___ _____

A7 Can students solve the related multiplication and division facts with the twos and threes? ___ _____

Unit 4: Division and Data

| | | ✓ | Comments: |

A1 Can students find the area of shapes?

A2 Can students use 10% as a standard for error analysis?

A3 Can students find the mean of a set of data?

A4 Can students divide using a paper-and-pencil method?

A5 Can students solve the related multiplication and division facts with the square numbers?

A6 Can students fit a best-fit line to a set of data points where appropriate?

A7

Unit 5: Investigating Fractions

A1 Are students able to compare fractions?

A2 Are students able to draw proper line graphs?

A3 Are students able to write ratios as fractions?

A4 Are students able to measure length in yards and feet?

A5 Are students able to add and subtract fractions?

A6 Can students solve the related multiplication and division facts with the nines?

A7

Unit 6: Geometry

A1 Are students able to find the degree measure of an angle?

A2 Are students able to determine whether shapes are congruent?

A3 Are students able to describe properties of various geometric shapes?

A4 Are students able to recognize regular polygons?

A5 Are students able to draw an angle with a specified degree measures?

A6 Are students able to construct shapes with given measures?

A7 Can students solve the last six multiplication facts (4×6, 4×7, 4×8, 6×7, 6×8, and 7×8) and the related division facts?

DRAFT, ©1998 Kendall/Hunt Publishing Company

Unit 7: Decimals and Probability

✓ Comments:

A1 Can students use fractions, decimals, and percents to represent the same quantity?

A2 Can students read and write decimals to thousandths?

A3 Can students compare and order decimals?

A4 Can students add and subtract decimals?

A5 Can students multiply decimals?

A6 Can students collect, graph, and analyze data?

A7 Can students use fractions and percents to give the probability of an event?

Unit 8: Applications:: An Assessment Unit

A1 Can students collect, organize, graph, and analyze data?

A2 Can students draw proper bar graphs?

A3 Can students translate between graphs and real-world events?

A4 Do students show facility with the multiplication facts and can they solve the related division facts?

A5 _____

A6 _____

A7 _____

Unit 9: Connections to Division

A1 Can students divide using a paper-and-pencil method?

A2 Can students interpret and express remainders appropriately?

A3 Can students use a calculator to solve division number sentences?

A4 Can students check division using multiplication?

A5 Can students use a calculator to add and subtract fractions?

A6 Do students demonstrate facility with the division facts for the 5s and 10s?

A7 _____

DRAFT, ©1998 Kendall/Hunt Publishing Company

Unit 10: Maps and Coordinates

A1 Can students locate an object in a room or find a location on a map using coordinates?

_____ _____

A2 Can students find negative numbers on the number line and solve problems involving negative numbers?

_____ _____

A3 Can students use a scale map to find distances?

_____ _____

A4 Can students plot ordered pairs in the four quadrants?

_____ _____

A5 Can students find the image of a figure after a flip?

_____ _____

A6 Can students find the image of a figure after a slide?

_____ _____

A7 Do students demonstrate facility with the division facts for the 2s and squares?

_____ _____

Unit 11: Number Patterns, Primes, and Fractions

A1 Can students identify the factors of a number?

_____ _____

A2 Can students rename a number as a product of its prime factors using exponents?

_____ _____

A3 Can students reduce fractions to lowest terms using common factors?

_____ _____

A4 Can students find common denominators using common multiples?

_____ _____

A5 Can students add and subtract fractions using common denominators?

_____ _____

A6 Do students demonstrate facility with the division facts for the threes and nines?

_____ _____

A7 _____

_____ _____

Unit 12: Using Fractions

A1 Can students add and subtract fractions using manipulatives and symbols?

_____ _____

A2 Can students add mixed numbers using manipulatives and symbols?

_____ _____

A3 Can students multiply fractions using manipulatives and symbols?

_____ _____

A4 Can students communicate mathematically?

_____ _____

A5 Do students demonstrate facility with the 12 division facts related to the last six facts (4×6, 4×7, 4×8, 6×7, 6×8, and 7×8)?

_____ _____

A6 _____

_____ _____

A7 _____

_____ _____

DRAFT, ©1998 Kendall/Hunt Publishing Company

Unit 13: Ratio and Proportion

✓ **Comments:**

A1 Can students write ratios as fractions and using colon notation? ____ _____

A2 Can students collect, organize, graph, and analyze data? ____ _____

A3 Can students draw proper line graphs? ____ _____

A4 Can students fit a line to a set of data points when appropriate? ____ _____

A5 Can students find the mass of an object using a two-pan balance? ____ _____

A6 Can students find the volume of an object by displacement? ____ _____

A7 Do students demonstrate facility with the division facts for the 2s, 5s, 10s, and square numbers? ____ _____

Unit 14: Using Circles

A1 Can students collect, organize, graph, and analyze data? ____ _____

A2 Can students use π to find the diameter of a circle given the circumference and vice versa? ____ _____

A3 Can students use proper mathematical terminology to help communicate mathematical ideas? ____ _____

A4 Can students use compasses and rulers to construct shapes? ____ _____

A5 Do students demonstrate facility with the division facts for the threes, nines, and the twelve division facts related to the last six facts (4×6, 4×7, 4×8, 6×7, 6×8, and 7×8)? ____ _____

A6 _____ ____ _____

A7 _____ ____ _____

Unit 15: Developing Formulas with Geometry

A1 Can students find the area of a rectangle using a formula? ____ _____

A2 Can students find the area of a triangle using a formula? ____ _____

A3 Can students find the area and perimeter of various shapes? ____ _____

A4 Can students find missing measures for rectangles? ____ _____

A5 Can students state in their own words the formulas for the area of a rectangle? ____ _____

A6 Can students state in their own words the formula for the area of a triangle? ____ _____

A7 _____ ____ _____

Unit 16: Bringing It All Together: An Assessment Unit ✓ **Comments:**

A1 Are students able to collect, organize, graph, and analyze data?

_____ _____

A2 Are students able to use data to find the solution to a problem?

_____ _____

A3 Are students able to communicate solution strategies?

_____ _____

A4 Can students use proportional reasoning to solve problems?

_____ _____

A5 Do students demonstrate facility with the division facts?

_____ _____

A6 _____

_____ _____

A7 _____

_____ _____

Additional Comments:

DRAFT, ©1998 Kendall/Hunt Publishing Company

TIMS Tutors

The *TIMS Tutors* section provides an in-depth exploration of the mathematical concepts and ideas behind MATH TRAILBLAZERS.

Students use a graduated cylinder to find the volume of small objects.

Table of Contents
TIMS Tutors

Arithmetic

TIMS Tutor

Outline

This tutor is organized as follows:

- Introduction
- Numeration and Place Value
- Basic Number Facts
- Concepts of Whole-Number Operations
- Whole-Number Computation in MATH TRAILBLAZERS
- Fractions and Decimals
- Conclusion
- References

Introduction

The last 40 years have seen many changes in elementary school mathematics. For many people, "mathematics" is synonymous with "arithmetic." But today, while reasonable people can still debate the proper content of an elementary mathematics curriculum, the pre-eminence of arithmetic in that curriculum has faded, both because of the availability of calculators and because of the realization that a curriculum focused on rote arithmetic will not meet the needs of students who will graduate from high school after the year 2010.

Much more than just arithmetic is now expected—geometry, probability, statistics, measurement, graphing, even algebra. Technology is dramatically changing the world, making it hard to imagine what our children will need to know in 20 or 40 more years, but also ensuring that many of the skills of 40 years ago will be obsolete. Despite recent advances in psychology, educational research, and curriculum design, we are far from resolving all the uncertainties of the elementary school mathematics curriculum. A few things, however, do seem to be clear:

- The school mathematics curriculum can and must be more rigorous.

- Arithmetic is only one piece, albeit an important one, of a broad mathematics curriculum.

- We need to do better at helping children connect marks on paper and the real world. Too many children and adults fail to use common sense when they are dealing with mathematical symbolism. Discussing mathematics and integrating subject matter may help students make these connections.

- As we correct for the overemphasis on skills in the traditional mathematics curriculum, we should avoid over-correcting. Problem solving requires both procedural skill and conceptual understanding. As William Brownell (1956) noted during a previous period of reform, "In objecting to the emphasis on drill prevalent not so long ago, we may have failed to point out that practice for proficiency in skills has its place too." In MATH TRAILBLAZERS, we consistently seek a balance between conceptual understanding and procedural skill.

Two short sections of the *Curriculum and Evaluation Standards for School Mathematics* summarize recommendations for changes in the content and emphases of K–8 mathematics instruction (National Council of Teachers of Mathematics, 1989, pages 20–21 and 70–71). Most of the topics and methods that are to receive "decreased attention" are part of the traditional arithmetic curriculum: complex paper-and-pencil computation, long division, written practice, and so on. While it is important to keep in mind that "decreased attention" does not mean "eliminate," one might ask—and many parents do ask—how advisable *any* shift in emphasis is, especially since American students perform fairly well on arithmetic computation compared to students in other countries, in marked contrast with their performance on higher-level skills (McKnight, Crosswhite, Dossey, Kifer, Swafford, Travers, and Cooney, 1987).

Several arguments can be made in support of the National Council of Teachers of Mathematics (NCTM) position. One is that the computational proficiency of American students comes at too high a cost. The hundreds of hours devoted to arithmetic computation in elementary school leave too little time for other important topics. The traditional rote approach to computation undermines higher-level thinking: children learn that mathematics is blindly following rules, not thinking. Worst of all, the long hours of computational drudgery teach children that mathematics is a most unpleasant business.

Another argument for shifting away from the traditional arithmetic curriculum is that technology has made paper-and-pencil calculation, if not obsolete, then at least much less important. More practical topics—probability and statistics, geometry, measurement, mental computation and estimation—deserve more attention.

A final and most important argument in favor of the changes recommended by the NCTM is that new approaches to instruction in arithmetic are more effective in helping students learn both appropriate calculation skills and how to apply those skills in solving problems. These new approaches build on students' own knowledge and intuitive methods and engage their common sense. This more meaningful approach helps students to be efficient and flexible in their computation and can reduce, though not eliminate, the amount of practice required. Thus, a greater emphasis on conceptual understanding can lead to better procedural skills and problem-solving abilities (Brown & Burton, 1978; Skemp, 1978; Hiebert, 1984; Van Lehn, 1986; Carpenter, 1986; Baroody and Ginsburg, 1986; Silver, 1986; Good, Mulryan, and McCaslin, 1992).

Numeration and Place Value

Even as the overriding emphasis in elementary mathematics shifts away from the traditional arithmetic topics, an understanding of our number system is as important as ever. This section sketches how MATH TRAILBLAZERS helps children build this understanding.

In kindergarten and grade 1, students using MATH TRAILBLAZERS practice their counting skills. They learn to count past 100 by 1s, 2s, 5s, and 10s. They count forward and backward from any given number. They group objects for counting. Students use counting to solve addition and subtraction problems. They learn to write numbers up to and beyond 100. The 100 chart is introduced and used for a variety of purposes, including solving problems and studying patterns. Students partition, or break apart, numbers in several ways (25 = 20 + 5, 25 = 10 + 10 + 5, and so on). These activities help children become familiar with the structure of the number system. Beginning in kindergarten, a ten frame is frequently used as a visual organizer. (See Figure 1.)

A final and most important argument in favor of the changes recommended by the NCTM is that new approaches to instruction in arithmetic are more effective in helping students learn both appropriate calculation skills and how to apply those skills in solving problems.

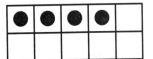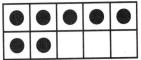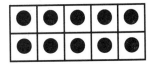

Figure 1: Sample ten frames

While formal study of place value is thus not a focus in kindergarten or grade 1, the multiple grouping and counting experiences described above provide children with a foundation for building an intuitive sense for the meaning of place value.

Work with counting continues in grade 2, especially skip counting and counting backwards. Place value is explored in the context of counting and grouping by tens. Children continue to count and group everyday objects such as buttons or peanuts. Connecting cubes are used to represent these objects and are often grouped by tens. Later, base-ten pieces are used to represent these same objects, thus linking the base-ten representations with quantities of actual objects.

Numbers well into the hundreds are explored. Counting is still used for problem solving, but more elaborate procedures may be employed. For example, a student may solve 885 – 255 by counting up, first by hundreds (355, 455, 555, 655, 755, 855) and then by tens (865, 875, 885), yielding 630 as the answer. Counting strategies for solving subtraction math facts are practiced.

More elaborate partitions of numbers are also investigated in grade 2. Particularly important are partitions in which every part is a single digit times 1, 10, 100, or 1000: 359 = 300 + 50 + 9 and so on. Attention is also given to partitioning numbers in more than one way:

$$359 = 300 + 50 + 9$$
$$= 200 + 150 + 9$$
$$= 100 + 250 + 9$$

This work with multiple partitioning is closely related to multidigit addition and subtraction. One way to think about addition and subtraction—indeed, one way to think about much of elementary mathematics—is as procedures for renaming numbers in more convenient forms. For example, 563 + 13 is a number that we usually rename as 576. 875 ÷ 25 is another number, renamable as 35 when it suits our purposes.

In grade 3, more formal study of place value takes place. Students work in varied contexts that involve numbers through the thousands. For example, students draw an outline of a coat to determine how many square centimeters of material would be required to make the coat. The use of contexts such as that example encourages students to associate quantities of actual objects with representations of the quantities using base-ten pieces and with the numerals that represent them. Most of this work is closely connected with investigations of addition and subtraction of multidigit numbers. Indeed, a good reason for studying computational algorithms is that they provide a context for learning about place value.

In grade 4, big numbers up to the millions are studied and used in various contexts. Continued efforts are made to connect the numbers with actual quantities. For example, the class creates its own base-ten pieces for large numbers—pieces we call super skinnies (10,000), super flats (100,000) and megabits (1,000,000). (See Figure 2.)

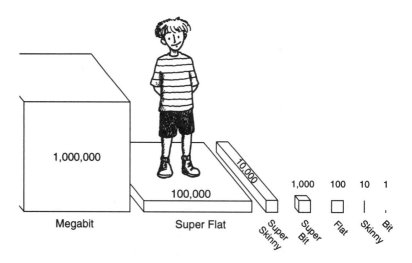

Figure 2: Base-ten pieces for small and large numbers

Once the basics of the base-ten place value system for whole numbers have been reviewed and established, the system is extended to include decimals. Decimals have been studied since grade 1, but as an alternative notation for writing certain fractions rather than as an extension of the place value system. In grade 4, the ten-for-one trading rules and other aspects of our number system are extended to the right of the decimal point for the first time.

In grade 5, the number system is extended to very large numbers. The story of Archimedes' attempt to calculate the number of grains of sand that would fill the observed universe introduces students to numbers far beyond what we encounter in everyday life. With the use of scientific calculators in grade 5, scientific notation for large numbers is needed and is introduced. Students also consider ideas of infinity, which open up new vistas of mathematical thought.

Basic Number Facts

The MATH TRAILBLAZERS approach to the basic facts differs from that in traditional textbooks. We seek a careful balance between strategies and drill, an approach based on research and advocated by the NCTM in the *Curriculum and Evaluation Standards for School Mathematics* (1989). Our approach is characterized by these elements:

- ***Early emphasis on problem solving.*** Students first approach the basic facts as problems to be solved rather than as facts to be memorized. They invent their own strategies to solve these problems or learn appropriate strategies from others through class discussion. Children's natural strategies, especially counting strategies, are explicitly encouraged.

- ***De-emphasis of rote work.*** We believe that children must indeed learn their math facts, but we de-emphasize rote memorization and the frequent administration of timed tests. Both of these can produce undesirable results. Instead, our primary goal is that students learn that they can find answers using strategies they understand.

- ***Ongoing practice.*** Work on the math facts is distributed throughout the curriculum, especially in the *Daily Practice and Problems* and in the games. This practice for facility, however, takes place only after students have a conceptual understanding of the operations and have achieved proficiency with strategies for solving basic fact problems. Delaying practice in this way means that less practice is required for facility with the number facts.

- *Gradual and systematic introduction of facts.* Students study the facts in small groups that can be solved by a single strategy. Early on, for example, they study facts that can be solved by counting on 1, 2, or 3. Students first work on simple strategies for easy facts, and then progress to more sophisticated strategies and harder facts.

- *Appropriate assessment.* Students are assessed on the facts through teacher observation as well as through the appropriate use of written tests and quizzes.

- *Facts are not gatekeepers.* Students are not prevented from learning more complex mathematics because they do not perform well on fact tests.

The MATH TRAILBLAZERS approach to the math facts is discussed more fully in the TIMS Tutor: *Math Facts.*

Concepts of Whole-Number Operations

Concepts and Skills

Over the past 150 years, numerous attempts have been made to teach mathematics meaningfully rather than by rote. Unfortunately, as Lauren Resnick points out in *Syntax and Semantics in Learning to Subtract,* "… the conceptual teaching methods of the past were inadequate to the extent that they taught concepts *instead of* procedures and left it entirely to students to discover how computational procedures could be derived from the basic structure of the number and numeration system." (1987, p. 136).

Many educators have long recognized, however, that there is no real conflict between skills and concepts. (Whitehead, 1929; Dewey, 1938; Brownell, 1956; May, 1995) New conceptual understandings are built on existing skills and concepts; these new understandings in turn support the further development of skills and concepts. Thomas Carpenter describes the relationship in this way: "… It is an iterative process. Procedures are taught that can be supported by existing conceptual knowledge, and the conceptual knowledge base is extended to provide a basis for developing more advanced concepts. At every point during instruction, procedures are taught that can be connected to existing conceptual knowledge." (1986, p. 130) This integration of concepts and skills underlies our work with arithmetic in MATH TRAILBLAZERS.

Subtraction in Grades K to 4

To illustrate how concepts and skills are balanced in MATH TRAILBLAZERS, we outline in this section how one operation—subtraction—is developed with whole numbers in grades K–4. Though the details may differ for the other operations, the same general approach described here with subtraction applies to all four arithmetic operations.

In kindergarten and grade 1 of MATH TRAILBLAZERS, students solve a variety of problems involving subtraction of numbers up to and even beyond 100. These problems are based on hands-on classroom activities and realistic situations from children's experiences. A wide variety of subtraction problem types is represented, including take-away, comparison, part-whole, and missing addend problems. (See the TIMS Tutor: *Word Problems* for a discussion of these and other problem types.)

Students in even the earliest grades are thus faced with problems for which they have no ready solution methods, problems that in the traditional view are beyond their ability. They do, however, have much prior knowledge that is relevant. They have their common sense—their conceptual knowledge of the problem situations. They know, for example, that if Grace begins with 50 troll dolls and loses 17, then she must end with fewer than 50 troll dolls. Young students also have considerable procedural knowledge of our number system, including especially their skills at various kinds of counting: ordinary counting, counting on, counting back, and skip counting by 2s, 5s, and 10s. In addition, the students have tools they can use in solving the problems. These might include connecting cubes and links in kindergarten; cubes, links, 100 charts, ten frames, other manipulatives, paper and pencil, calculators, number lines, and so on in first grade.

On one side, then, are hard problems involving many varieties of subtraction. On the other side are the kindergartners and first-graders, with their common sense, their counting skills, and various tools. As the students apply their resources to solve the problems, they build their conceptual and procedural understanding of subtraction. They devise methods for solving the problems; they make records of their work; they discuss their methods with their teacher and classmates. Their new knowledge about subtraction is closely linked to their prior knowledge, especially their out-of-school knowledge and their counting skills. (Baroody and Ginsburg, 1986)

The teacher comments on students' methods and may show students how to use conventional symbols to describe their work, but he or she makes no attempt to standardize students' methods. Any method that yields a correct result is acceptable—as long as it makes sense. The goal is to encourage students to apply their prior knowledge to problems they encounter and to let students know that their intuitive methods are valid.

In addition, first grade focuses on various strategies that can be used to solve single-digit subtraction problems. For example, a problem like $9 - 3$ can be solved by counting back 3 from 9: 8, 7, 6. This work aims not at achieving quick facility with the subtraction facts, but rather at building conceptual understanding of subtraction and procedural skill with various strategies. (See the TIMS Tutor: *Math Facts.*)

In the beginning of grade 2, the problem-solving approach to subtraction continues. Problems with numbers up to 1000 are introduced, but again no standard solution method is taught. Students devise their own ways to solve the problems, drawing on their prior knowledge of the problem situations and the number system, and share their thinking with the class.

The strategies approach to the subtraction facts also continues in grade 2. As students' facility with the addition facts and simple subtraction facts increases, more sophisticated strategies become feasible. For example, a child may solve $14 - 6$ by reasoning that "to take away 6 from 14, I first can take away 4, which leaves 10. Then I take away 2 more, which equals 8." These new strategies, sometimes called derived fact strategies, illustrate how new knowledge builds on prior skills.

Later in grade 2, systematic work begins on paper-and-pencil methods for subtracting two digit numbers. Students are asked to solve two-digit subtraction problems using their own methods and to record their solutions on paper. The class examines and discusses the various procedures that students devise. At this time, if no student introduces a standard subtraction algorithm, then the teacher does so, explaining that it is a subtraction method that many people use. The standard method is examined and discussed, just as the invented

As the students apply their resources to solve the problems, they build their conceptual and procedural understanding of subtraction. They devise methods for solving the problems; they make records of their work; they discuss their methods with their teacher and classmates.

Giving children only multidigit problems that do not involve borrowing encourages the development of a rote and faulty algorithm that may not carry over into problems that require borrowing.

Problems that require borrowing are included from the beginning. Though this differs markedly from traditional approaches, we view it as important in developing a sound conception of subtraction algorithms. Giving children only multidigit problems that do not involve borrowing encourages the development of a rote and faulty algorithm that may not carry over into problems that require borrowing.

By the beginning of grade 3, students have a strong conceptual understanding of subtraction and significant experience devising procedures to solve subtraction problems with numbers up to 1000. They also have some experience with standard and invented paper-and-pencil algorithms for solving two-digit subtraction problems. In grade 3, this prior knowledge is extended in a systematic examination of paper-and-pencil methods for multidigit subtraction.

This work begins with a series of multidigit subtraction problems that students solve in various ways. Many of these problems are set in a whimsical context, the TIMS Candy Company, a business that uses base-ten pieces to keep track of its production and sales. Other problems are based on student-collected data, such as a reading survey.

As in grade 2, the class discusses and compares the several methods students use to solve these problems. Again, any method that yields correct results is acceptable, but now a greater emphasis is given to methods that are efficient and compact. This work leads to a close examination of one particular subtraction algorithm. (See Figure 3.) Students solve several problems with base-ten pieces and with this standard algorithm, making connections between actions with the manipulatives and steps in the algorithm. After a thorough analysis of the algorithm, including a comparison of the standard algorithm and other methods, students are given opportunities to practice the algorithm. Practice in paper-and-pencil methods for multidigit subtraction is distributed throughout grades 3 and 4.

Grade 5

In grade 5 students continue to use subtraction in activities and labs. As in earlier grades, they are encouraged to decide when it is appropriate to use paper and pencil, calculators, or estimation. A review of subtraction modeled with base-ten pieces is included for students who have not used MATH TRAILBLAZERS in previous grades. Distributed practice is provided in the Daily Practice and Problems and the Home Practice. Facility with the subtraction facts is assessed in the first unit, and remediation is provided in the Addition and Subtraction Math Fact Review in the Unit Resource Guide File.

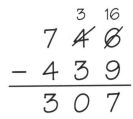

Figure 3: A standard subtraction algorithm

Students are also expected to achieve facility with basic subtraction facts in grade 3. Since by the end of grade 2, students have worked for two years on strategies for simple subtraction problems, and since by that time they should also have facility with the addition facts, the expectation of facility with subtraction facts by the end of grade 3 is reasonable. To make this expectation a reality for all students, a systematic program of assessment, review, and practice of basic subtraction facts is built into the Daily Practice and Problems for grade 3.

By the beginning of grade 4, basic work with whole number subtraction is complete. Students have a firm conceptual understanding of subtraction and they have a diverse repertoire of methods that they can use to solve subtraction problems. They also know their subtraction facts. Work in grade 4 is designed to maintain and extend these skills and understandings. Facility with the subtraction facts is verified and remediation is provided for students who need it. In the laboratory experiments and other work, students solve a wide variety of subtraction problems using methods of their own choosing. The *Daily Practice and Problems* and *Daily Home Practice* include distributed practice in paper-and-pencil subtraction so that those skills do not deteriorate.

Whole-Number Computation in *MATH TRAILBLAZERS*

Many other topics in *MATH TRAILBLAZERS*—addition, multiplication, division, fractions, and decimals—are treated in ways similar to that sketched for subtraction above. *In all these areas, we seek a balance between conceptual understanding and procedural skill.* For all operations, standard methods for solving problems are not introduced until students have developed good conceptual and procedural understandings—the too-early introduction of such procedures may short-circuit students' common sense, encouraging mechanical and uncritical behavior. (Brownell & Chazall, 1935; Resnick & Omanson, 1987; Rathmell & Huinker, 1989; Perry, 1991)

We seek a balance between conceptual understanding and procedural skill. For all operations, standard methods for solving problems are not introduced until students have developed good conceptual and procedural understandings—the too-early introduction of such procedures may short-circuit students' common sense, encouraging mechanical and uncritical behavior.

Grade	Addition	Subtraction	Multiplication	Division
K	• concepts of the operation	• concepts of the operation	• concepts of the operation	• concepts of the operation
1	• concepts of the operation • informal methods	• concepts of the operation • informal methods	• concepts of the operation	• concepts of the operation
2	• concepts of the operation • invented algorithms • standard methods for small numbers	• concepts of the operation • invented algorithms • standard methods for small numbers	• concepts of the operation • informal methods	• concepts of the operation • informal methods • strategies
3	• invented algorithms • standard methods for larger numbers	• invented algorithms • standard methods for larger numbers	• concepts of the operation • invented algorithms • standard methods for larger numbers	• concepts of the operation
4	• review, practice, apply, and extend	• review, practice, apply, and extend	• invented algorithms • standard methods for larger numbers	• invented algorithms • standard methods for larger numbers
5	• review, practice, apply, and extend	• review, practice, apply, and extend	• review, practice, apply, and extend	• standard methods for larger numbers

Table 1: Whole-number operations scope and sequence

In MATH TRAILBLAZERS, instruction in standard procedures is delayed slightly beyond the traditional time, but problems that would normally be solved by standard procedures are often introduced sooner than is customary. This forces students to use their prior knowledge to devise ways to solve the problems "from first principles," thus promoting students' construction of their own understandings.

Even after standard methods have been analyzed and practiced, students are still encouraged to solve problems in more than one way. Flexible thinking and mathematical power are our goals, not rote facility with a handful of standard algorithms.

Even after standard methods have been analyzed and practiced, students are still encouraged to solve problems in more than one way.

Varieties of Computation

There is much more to computation than the standard paper-and-pencil algorithms for adding, subtracting, multiplying, and dividing. These algorithms are good for obtaining exact answers with simple technology, but, depending on the resources available and the result desired, there are many other kinds of computation.

For example, if you are in a supermarket check-out line with several items and you find only $10 in your wallet, then a quick judgment whether you have sufficient funds is desirable. In this case, a rough mental estimate of the total cost of your purchases is what you want. If you are planning an addition to your house, however, different computational demands must be met. The situation is more complex than the supermarket check-out, and the penalty for making a mistake is more severe, so greater care must be taken. You will want more resources—paper and pencil, a calculator, time to work, perhaps a computer spreadsheet—and you will probably want rather precise estimates for the cost of various alternative designs for the addition.

A well-rounded mathematics program should prepare students to compute accurately, flexibly, and appropriately in all situations. Figure 4 shows a classification of computational situations using two criteria, the result desired and the resources available. Although you may want to move some of the questions to other cells or insert your own examples, these six categories of computation indicate the scope required of a modern mathematics curriculum (Coburn, 1989).

Resources Available

	Paper & Pencil	Machine	Mental
Exact	How many students are in the three third grades at my school?	How much will my monthly payment be on my car loan?	How much baking soda do I need if I am tripling a recipe that calls for 2 teaspoons?
Approximate	What is my share of the national debt?	House remodeling: Which design(s) can I afford?	Supermarket checkout: Do I have enough money for these items?

Figure 4: Six varieties of computation

The TIMS Philosophy: Meaning, Invention, Efficiency, Power

The treatment of computation in MATH TRAILBLAZERS proceeds in several stages. The grade levels for the stages vary with the operation—ideas of division, for example, develop long after addition—but the general pattern is similar for all the operations. Roughly speaking, the stages are:

- developing meaning for the operation,
- inventing procedures for solving problems, and
- becoming more efficient at carrying out procedures, all leading to
- developing mathematical power.

The goal of the first stage is to help students understand the meaning of the operation. Most of the work involves solving problems, writing or telling "stories" that involve operations, and sharing solution strategies. These methods typically involve a great deal of mental arithmetic and creative thinking. The use of manipulatives, pictures, and counting is encouraged at this stage. Discussing these informal methods helps develop students' understanding of the operation.

In the next stage, the focus shifts from developing the concept of the operation to devising and analyzing procedures to carry out the operation. At this stage, students "invent" methods for carrying out the operation, explaining, discussing, and comparing their procedures. Multiple solution strategies—mental, paper and pencil, manipulative, calculator—are encouraged, and parallels between various methods are explored. Evidence is accumulating that this "invented algorithms" approach enhances students' number and operation sense and problem-solving abilities (Madell, 1985; Sawada, 1985; Kamii, Lewis, & Jones, 1991; Burns, 1992; Kamii, Lewis, & Livingston, 1993; Porter & Carroll, 1995; Carroll & Porter, in press). Inventing their own methods helps make mathematics meaningful for children by connecting school mathematics to their own ways of thinking. The expectation that mathematics should make sense is reinforced.

In the third stage, a standard algorithm for the operation is introduced. This algorithm is not presented as the one, true, and official way to solve problems, but rather as yet another procedure to be examined. The algorithms used in MATH TRAILBLAZERS are not all identical to the traditional ones taught in school. The addition and subtraction algorithms are only a little different, but the procedures for multiplication and division are considerably different. (See Figures 5 and 6.)

$$
\begin{array}{r}
5\ 8 \\
\times\ 3\ 6 \\
\hline
4\ 8 \\
3\ 0\ 0 \\
2\ 4\ 0 \\
1\ 5\ 0\ 0 \\
\hline
2\ 0\ 8\ 8 \\
\end{array}
$$

Figure 5: All-partials multiplication

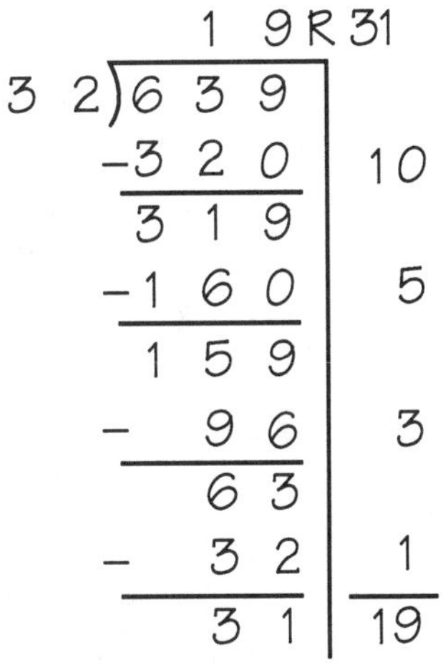

$$
\begin{array}{r}
1\ \ 9\ \text{R}\ 31 \\
3\ 2\overline{)6\ 3\ 9} \\
\underline{-3\ 2\ 0}\quad 10 \\
3\ 1\ 9 \\
\underline{-1\ 6\ 0}\quad 5 \\
1\ 5\ 9 \\
\underline{-\ \ 9\ 6}\quad 3 \\
6\ 3 \\
\underline{-\ \ 3\ 2}\quad 1 \\
3\ 1\quad 19
\end{array}
$$

Figure 6: A division algorithm

These alternative algorithms for multiplication and division have been chosen for several reasons. First, they are easier to learn than the traditional methods. Second, they are more transparent, revealing better what is actually happening. Third, they provide practice in multiplying by numbers ending in zero, an important skill for estimation. Finally, even though they are less efficient than the traditional algorithms, they are good enough for most purposes—any problem that is awkward to solve by these methods should probably be done by machine anyway.

Students who have no reliable method of their own are urged to adopt the standard algorithm. However, even after a standard algorithm for an operation has been introduced and analyzed, alternative methods are still accepted, even encouraged, for students who are comfortable with them. In particular, the standard algorithm is very inefficient with some problems. For example, students using MATH TRAILBLAZERS should be able to compute 40×30 mentally to get 1200. Using the standard algorithm here would be inefficient. Or consider $16,000 - 5$. Using a standard algorithm to solve this problem is tedious and often results in errors.

In the last stage, students achieve mathematical power through the mastery of procedures that solve entire classes of problems: efficient and reliable computational algorithms. This procedural facility, moreover, is based on solid conceptual understandings so that it can be applied flexibly to solve problems. These procedures become part of the students' base of prior knowledge— on which they can build more advanced conceptual and procedural understandings.

Fractions and Decimals

The approach to fractions and decimals in MATH TRAILBLAZERS parallels that for whole numbers. At first, the focus is on developing concepts and meanings for fractions and decimals. Next comes a period in which students invent procedures for solving problems, connecting school mathematics to their own informal methods and common sense. Finally, formal procedures are investigated, not as substitutes for common sense, but as more efficient methods for achieving desired results.

Fraction Meanings

One of the problems with fractions is that they are so useful. Consider some of the meanings for ½:

- half of a cookie
  (a part-whole fraction)

- 1 ÷ 2
  (division)

- one cup water to two cups flour
  (a ratio, sometimes written 1:2)

- ½ mile
  (a measurement)

- the point midway between 0 and 1
  (the name of a point on a number line)

- the square root of ¼
  (a pure number)

- the chance a fair coin will land heads up
  (a probability)

Because the same notation can mean so many different things, children and even adults sometimes become confused and may manipulate fraction symbols haphazardly, often with unfortunate results. A better approach develops sound meanings for the symbols before focusing on how to manipulate them (Mack, 1990).

Part-Whole Fractions

Beginning fraction work focuses on part-whole fractions. Many fractions in daily life are part-whole fractions, so even young children are familiar with terms like *one-half* and *three-fourths* in part-whole contexts. Also, many key ideas about fractions are well illustrated in part-whole situations.

There are two concepts that are fundamental in understanding part-whole fractions: knowing what the "whole" is and understanding what a part is in relation to the whole. For example, to understand the statement, "Last night I ate three-fourths of a carton of ice cream," requires knowing what the whole is: Just how big a carton of ice cream was it? One must also understand that the parts into which the whole is divided must be equal—they should have the same area or mass or number, etc. A way to make this clear to children is to talk about "fair shares."

The whole in a part-whole fraction can be either a single thing (e.g., a pizza) or a collection (e.g., a class of students). When the whole is a collection, then counting is generally used to make fair shares; when the unit is a single thing, the fairness of the shares depends on some measurable quantity. Half of one pizza is different from half of three pizzas. Often, area is the variable that must be equally allocated among the parts; such a situation may be called an area model for fractions.

Symbols and Referents

A key idea in the MATH TRAILBLAZERS approach to fractions is that fractions should be represented in several ways and that students should be able to make connections between those representations. The fraction two-thirds, for

Because the same notation can mean so many different things, children and even adults sometimes become confused and may manipulate fraction symbols haphazardly, often with unfortunate results. A better approach develops sound meanings for the symbols before focusing on how to manipulate them.

example, can be expressed in words, symbols, pictures, or real objects (Figure 7).

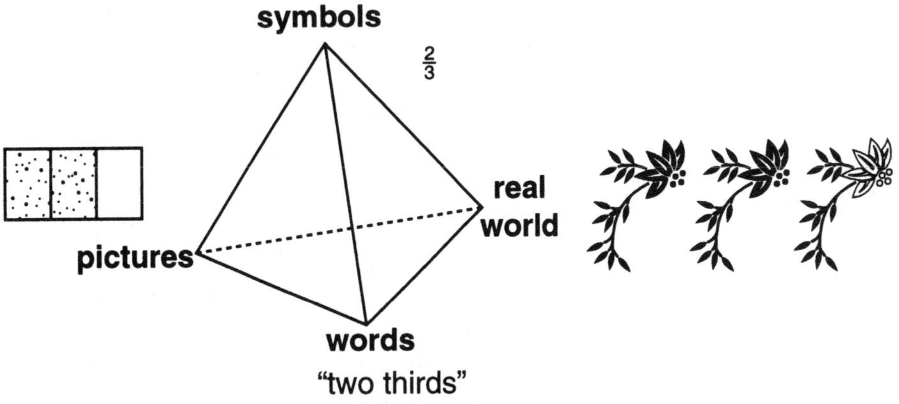

Figure 7: Representations of ⅔

The ability to move freely between these several representations is an essential component of the mathematical understanding of fractions. Especially important are connections between fraction symbols and the real-world situations to which those fractions refer. Given symbols for a fraction, can the student draw an illustrative picture or tell a story? Can students explain the relationship between a group of five girls and two boys and the fraction 5/7?

The ability to move freely between these several representations is an essential component of the mathematical understanding of fractions. Especially important are connections between fraction symbols and the real-world situations to which those fractions refer.

Decimals

Decimals are treated in two ways in *Math Trailblazers:* first, as another way to write certain common fractions—those with denominators that are powers of ten—and second, as an extension of the whole number place value system. Connections between fractions and decimals are stressed throughout.

A Developmental Approach

Fraction work in grades 1–3 of *Math Trailblazers* focuses primarily on establishing links between symbols and referents for part-whole fractions. Children learn to make connections between marks on paper and the real world. Concepts of the unit—identifying the unit, knowing how the size of the unit affects the value of the fraction, appreciating the importance of fair shares—are also explored (Figure 8). Decimals are treated primarily as an alternative notation for certain fractions, and some attention is given to the interpretation of decimals that appear on calculators. Real-world situations, especially fair sharing, and area models predominate.

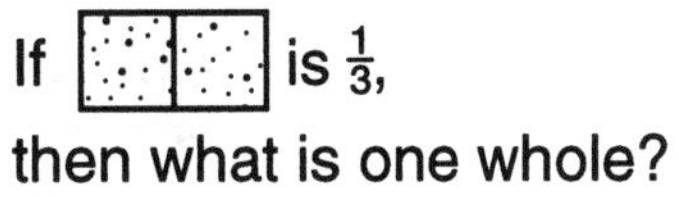

Figure 8: A concept-of-unit exercise

In grade 3, work continues with concepts of the unit, but more varied models begin to be used. Children explore the relative size of fractions, especially with respect to the landmark numbers 0, ½, and 1. Equivalent fractions are also studied in grade 3. Fractions are represented with a variety of manipulatives—paper folding, pattern blocks, geoboards. Collections of objects are divided to represent fractions.

Decimals are investigated more extensively in grade 3, again being treated as a kind of fraction. Decimals in metric length measurement and on number lines are investigated. Base-ten pieces are used to create concrete and visual representations of decimal fractions. Translating between common fractions and decimals is again stressed.

In grade 4, work on operations with fractions and decimals begins, but standard procedures are not taught. As discussed above, modeling concepts and procedures with manipulatives is intended to establish a basis for more algorithmic work in grade 5.

Operations with fractions and decimals include more than simply the four arithmetic operations. Putting fractions and decimals in order by size, renaming the same number in several equivalent forms, and estimating sums, differences, and so on, are all operations that can be carried out with fractions and decimals. Again, manipulatives, such as pattern blocks and base-ten pieces, are used to develop conceptual understanding and provide a concrete representation of the symbols.

In grade 5, paper-and-pencil procedures for addition, subtraction, and multiplication of fractions and decimals are explored, including use of common denominators and reducing. Repeating decimals are introduced. Students also use calculators to rename fractions as decimals for comparing and ordering common fractions.

Conclusion

Our goal in developing MATH TRAILBLAZERS has been to create a balanced program that will promote the coordinated development of both procedural skill and conceptual understanding. Moreover, by connecting school mathematics with intuitive knowledge and informal procedures and by using a variety of techniques and manipulatives for modeling the mathematical ideas, students will not only develop skills and concepts, but will be able to use those skills and concepts to solve problems.

References

Baroody, A. J., and Ginsburg, H. P. "The Relationship Between Initial Meaning and Mechanical Knowledge of Arithmetic." In J. Hiebert (ed.), *Conceptual and Procedural Knowledge: The Case of Mathematics.* Hillsdale, N.J.: Lawrence Erlbaum Associates, 1986.

Brown, J. S., and Burton, R. R. "Diagnostic Models for Procedural Bugs in Basic Mathematical Skills." *Cognitive Science,* 2, 1978, pp. 155–192.

Brownell, W. A., and Chazal, C. B. "The Effects of Premature Drill in Third-Grade Arithmetic." *Journal of Educational Research,* 29 (1), 1935.

Brownell, W. A. "Meaning and Skill—Maintaining the Balance." *Arithmetic Teacher,* 34 (8), 1987, pp. 18–25. (Original work published in 1956.)

Burns, M. "A Focus Issue—Arithmetic." *Math Solutions: The Newsletter for Math Solutions Participants,* 14, 1992, pp. 1–9.

Carpenter, T. P. "Conceptual Knowledge as a Foundation for Procedural Knowledge." In J. Hiebert (ed.), *Conceptual and Procedural Knowledge: The Case of Mathematics.* Hillsdale, N.J.: Lawrence Erlbaum Associates, 1986.

Carpenter, T. P., Fennema, E., and Franke, M. L. *Cognitively Guided Instruction: Building the Primary Mathematics Curriculum on Children's*

Informal Mathematical Knowledge. A paper presented at the annual meeting of the American Educational Research Association, April 1992, San Francisco.

Carroll, W., and Porter, D. (in press). "Invented Algorithms: Helping Students to Develop and Use Meaningful Mathematical Procedures." *Teaching Children Mathematics.*

Coburn, T. G. "The Role of Computation in the Changing Mathematics Curriculum." In P. R. Trafton (ed.), *New Directions for Elementary School Mathematics.* Reston, Va.: National Council of Teachers of Mathematics, 1989.

Dewey, J. *Experience and Education.* New York: Macmillan, 1938.

Finn, C. E., Jr. "What if those Math *Standards* are Wrong?" *Education Week,* 20 January 1993.

Good, T. L., Mulryan, C., and McCaslin, M. "Grouping for Instruction in Mathematics: A Call for Programmatic Research on Small-Group Processes." In D. A. Grouws (ed.), *Handbook of Research on Mathematics Teaching and Learning: A Project of the National Council of Teachers of Mathematics* (Chapter 9). New York: Macmillan, 1992.

Hiebert, J. "Children's Mathematical Learning: The Struggle to Link Form and Understanding." *Elementary School Journal,* 84 (5), 1984, pp. 497–513.

Hiebert, J. "A Theory of Developing Competence with Written Mathematical Symbols." *Educational Studies in Mathematics,* 19, 1988, pp. 333–355.

Kamii, C., Lewis, B. A., and Jones, S. "Reform in Primary Mathematics Education: A Constructivist View." *Educational Horizons,* 70 (1), 1991, pp. 19–26,

Kamii, C., Lewis, B. A., and Livingston, S. J. "Primary Arithmetic: Children Inventing Their Own Procedures." *Arithmetic Teacher,* 41 (4), 1993, pp. 200–203.

McKnight, C. C., Crosswhite, F. J., Dossey, J. A., Kifer, E., Swafford, J. O., Travers, K. J., and Cooney, T. J. *The Underachieving Curriculum: Assessing U.S. School Mathematics from an International Perspective.* Champaign, Ill.: Stipes, 1987.

Mack, N. K. "Learning Fractions with Understanding: Building on Informal Knowledge." *Journal for Research in Mathematics Education,* 21 (1), 1990, pp. 16–32.

Madell, R. "Children's Natural Processes." *Arithmetic Teacher,* 32 (7), 1985, pp. 20–22.

Mathews, J. "Psst, Kid, Wanna Buy a Used Math Book? They're Old-Fashioned and a Bit Tedious, but John Saxon's Books are Hot Stuff in the Education Underground." *Newsweek,* 121, 1 March 1993, pp. 62–63.

May, L. "Reflections on Teaching Mathematics Today." *Illinois Mathematics Teacher,* 46 (3), 1995, pp. 5–8.

National Council of Teachers of Mathematics. *Curriculum and Evaluation Standards for School Mathematics.* Reston, Va.: National Council of Teachers of Mathematics, 1989.

Perry, M. "Learning and Transfer: Instructional Conditions and Conceptual Change." *Cognitive Development,* 6, 1991, pp. 449–468.

Porter, D., and Carroll, W. "Invented Algorithms: Some Examples from Primary Classrooms." *Illinois Mathematics Teacher,* April 1995, pp. 6–12.

Press, M. "Drill and Practice Add Up." *San Jose Mercury News,* 27 February 1995.

Rathmell, E. C., and Huinker, D. M. "Using 'Part-Whole' Language to Help Children Represent and Solve Word Problems." In P. R. Trafton (ed.), *New Directions for Elementary School Mathematics* (pp. 99–110). Reston, Va.: National Council of Teachers of Mathematics, 1989.

Resnick, L. B. "Syntax and Semantics in Learning to Subtract." In R. Glaser (ed.), *Advances in Instructional Psychology* (Vol. 3). Hillsdale, N.J.: Lawrence Erlbaum Associates, 1987.

Resnick, L. B., and Omanson, S. F. "Learning to Understand Arithmetic." In *Advances in Instructional Psychology* (Vol. 3). Hillsdale, N.J.: Lawrence Erlbaum Associates, 1987.

Resnick, L. B., Lesgold, S., and Bill, V. *From Protoquantities to Number Sense.* A paper prepared for the Psychology of Mathematics Education Conference, Mexico, 1990.

Sawada, D. "Mathematical Symbols: Insight through Invention." *Arithmetic Teacher,* 32 (6), 1985, pp. 20–22.

Shuard, H. "CAN: Calculator Use in the Primary Grades in England and Wales." In J. T. Fey (ed.), *Calculators in Mathematics Education.* Reston, Va.: National Council of Teachers of Mathematics, 1992.

Skemp, R. R. "Relational Understanding and Instrumental Understanding." *Arithmetic Teacher,* 26 (3), 1978, pp. 9–15.

Swart, W. L. "Some Findings on Conceptual Development of Computational Skills." *Arithmetic Teacher* 32 (5), 1985, pp. 36–38.

Usiskin, Z. "Paper-and-Pencil Skills in a Calculator/Computer Age." *UCSMP Newsletter,* 16, 1994, pp. 7–14, 1994.

Van Lehn, K. "Arithmetic Procedures Are Induced from Examples." In J. Hiebert (ed.), *Conceptual and Procedural Knowledge: The Case of Mathematics.* Hillsdale, N.J.: Lawrence Erlbaum Associates, 1986.

Whitehead, A. N. "The Rhythmic Claims of Freedom and Discipline." In *The Aims of Education and Other Essays.* New York: Macmillan, 1929.

Averages

TIMS Tutor

Introduction

"Average" is one of those words that mean different things to different people. Baseball players talk about their batting averages. A teacher might confide to a colleague that "Jim is just an average student." At the university, students always want to know what the class average is on an exam. Sometimes you hear the statement that the temperature will be about average for this time of year. When someone asks you how you feel, you may reply, "Just average." In everyday usage, "average" is a word that can be anything from a synonym for "typical," "normal," or "usual," to a number derived according to some formula or rule. This TIMS Tutor attempts to lay out some of the different numerical meanings of "average" and to explain some of the importance of averages in mathematics and science.

The Mean—A Wage Dispute

In his wonderful little book, *How to Lie with Statistics*, Darrell Huff gives the example of a factory owner and his workers who are arguing over wages. There are 25 workers including the owner. The owner pays himself $45,000. The others make $15,000, $10,000, $10,000, $5700, $5000, $5000, $5000, $3700, $3700, $3700, $3700, $3000, $2000, $2000, $2000, $2000, $2000, $2000, $2000, $2000, $2000, $2000, $2000, and $2000. The owner says the average wage is $5700 but the workers claim the average wage is only $3000. Even though prices have gone way up since Huff wrote his book 40 years ago, the discrepancy is clear: there is a big disagreement over what people are being paid, let alone what they should be paid.

So, what's going on here? Who's right, the owner or the workers? Both! The factory owner's average is the (arithmetic) mean; the workers' average is the median. There are other averages too, such as the mode (the number or value that occurs most often in a data set). However, in MATH TRAILBLAZERS, we primarily use the mean and/or the median when finding average values. These two averages will be the focus of our discussion in this tutor.

Usually when people use the term "average," they are referring to the mean. This is the familiar add-up-all-the-numbers-and-divide average you learned in school. The mean has many useful properties that make it beloved by schoolteachers, statisticians, and scientists alike.

Consider finding the average height of all the children in a class. Data for 23 children from a third-grade class is shown in Figure 1.

The mean height of these 23 children is

$$\langle H \rangle = \frac{\text{sum of heights}}{\text{number of children}}$$

$$= \frac{(133 + 136 + \ldots + 129 + 134)\ \text{cm}}{23}$$

$$= \frac{3064\ \text{cm}}{23}$$

$$= 133.2\ \text{cm}$$

Name	H Height (in cm)
Karina	133
Federico	136
Ramon	135
Kiela	127
Aesha	126
Bravlia	128
Zuzia	133
Anthony	139
Iorta	146
Cordeli	135
Mary	137
Gennice	124

Name	H Height (in cm)
Curtis	139
Brian C	125
David	135
Anna	141
Brian M	131
Adriana	137
Boberto	134
Lucas	131
Gennifer	129
Amber	129
Nathan	134

Figure 1: Data from a third-grade class

For scientists, the mean is often the first number they calculate when looking at a data sample.

Although no child may have this mean height, it gives everyone a point of departure for making comparisons. For scientists, the mean is often the first number they calculate when looking at a data sample.

There is another way to interpret the mean height of this class. This may seem strange, but consider the following situation. Suppose you walk into another class and find 23 students all to be exactly the same height. The mean is clearly that height. If the mean height of this new class and the mean in our class are the same, then the sum of the heights of the children is the same. That is, imagine making two stacks of the children, one for our class and one for the new class. Stack the children one on top of another. Then the two stacks would be the same height. So, if two class means are the same and the number of children in each class is the same, then the sums of the heights in the classes are the same, even if the individual heights that make the sums are vastly different.

Statisticians like the mean because it is often the "best" estimate of an unknown quantity like a length, an area, or a mass. For example, suppose you are trying to measure the mass of a large steel sphere. You have an unbiased balance, and being well versed in TIMS you know that you need to take repeated readings to get an accurate measurement. So, suppose you make eleven measurements and find the sphere's mass to be 129 gm, 133 gm, 132 gm, 130 gm, 128 gm, 129 gm, 130 gm, 131 gm, 130 gm, 129 gm, and 131 gm. Then

$$\frac{(129 + 133 + \ldots + 130 + 129 + 131)\ \text{gm}}{11}$$

$$= \frac{1432\ \text{gm}}{11}$$

$$= 130\ \text{gm}$$

is the best estimate of the "true" mass of the sphere, given these measurements. (Notice that the quotient above is actually equal to 130.18181818... gm. However, since our original measurements are to the nearest gram, it makes sense to give the average only to the nearest gram.)

Similar situations arise all the time in everyday life. Our factory owner is using the mean; he computes the average wage by adding up everyone's salary (including his big fat one) and dividing by the total number of workers:

$$\frac{\$142,500}{25} = \$5,700$$

As one final example, suppose Marty scores 85, 84, 86, 87, 84, 87, 85, 85, 83, and 85 on 10 rounds of golf and Ellen scores 83, 83, 95, 97, 81, 83, 82, 84, 96, and 84. Then Marty's mean score is

$$= \frac{85 + 84 + 86 + 87 + 84 + 87 + 85 + 85 + 83 + 85}{10}$$

$$= 85.1$$

and Ellen's mean score is

$$= \frac{83 + 83 + 95 + 97 + 81 + 83 + 82 + 84 + 96 + 84}{10}$$

$$= 86.8$$

So, it would appear that Marty is a better golfer than Ellen.

But anyone who plays golf and bets will notice that if Marty and Ellen played 10 rounds against each other and scored as above, then Marty would win three times and Ellen would win seven times. And the workers in the factory still feel underpaid, despite that nice mean salary. So, to get some perspective on what's happening here, let's look at another average, the median.

The Median

The median is the number in the middle. That is, roughly speaking, the median splits a set of numbers into two halves: one half is less than the median; the other half is more than the median. So, to find the median, rank the numbers from smallest to largest and take the one in the middle.

Suppose, for example, you want to find the median selling price of homes in your town. You go to the town office and find that 15 homes have been sold in the last six months. The selling prices, in rank order, were $67,000, $78,000, $82,000, $85,000, $92,000, $97,000, $112,000, $118,000, $125,000, $132,000, $133,000, $139,000, $167,000, $175,000, and

The median is the number in the middle. That is, roughly speaking, the median splits a set of numbers into two halves: one half is less than the median; the other half is more than the median.

$186,000. The median price was $118,000: seven houses sold for less than $118,000 and seven houses sold for more than $118,000.

When there is an even number of values, then the median can be a little harder to find. Say only 14 of the homes above to have been sold. Suppose that the highest-priced house, the one costing $186,000, went unsold. What is the new median? Counting up seven from the $67,000 house, we end up at the $112,000. Counting down seven from the $175,000 house, we end up at $118,000. The 7th house from the bottom is *not* the 7th house from the top! What to do? Easy. Go halfway between the two numbers closest to the middle. Halfway between $112,000 and $118,000. That comes out to be $115,000. So the median price of the 14 homes that sold would be $115,000.

Going back to our factory workers' example, there were 25 employees including the owner. The thirteenth salary (from the top or from the bottom) is $3000: there are 12 employees who make less than $3000, and 12 who make more than $3000. So, the median salary is $3000.

Sometimes the median is a better average to use than the mean. One common situation where the median may be preferred is when there are extreme values. In such cases, the mean can give a distorted picture of the "average" because the extreme values tend to "pull" the mean away from where the typical values are. Statisticians say the median is more "robust" than the mean; that is, the median is less affected by extreme values than the mean. This is why the factory workers prefer the median: it gives a truer picture of what a typical worker earns than the mean, which is pulled up by the owner's big salary.

The median offers some insight into our golfing example, too. Marty's (ranked) golf scores were 83, 84, 84, 85, 85, 85, 85, 86, 87, and 87. The two numbers in the middle are 85 and 85, so Marty's median score is 85. Ellen's scores were 81, 82, 83, 83, 83, 84, 84, 95, 96, and 97. The two numbers in the middle are 83 and 84, so Ellen's median score is 83.5. Thus, using medians, Ellen is a slightly better golfer, on average. Every few rounds she has a high score, but her typical score is better than Marty's typical score, so she usually wins.

Obviously, the median has several advantages with respect to the mean: it is less affected by extreme values; it requires little computation; it can be a better indicator of what is typical. You will want to be flexible, sometimes using the mean, sometimes using the median.

One common situation where the median may be preferred is when there are extreme values. In such cases, the mean can give a distorted picture of the "average" because the extreme values tend to "pull" the mean away from where the typical values are.

Averaging in the *Math Trailblazers* Classroom

So how are averages used in *Math Trailblazers*? Suppose you have second-grade students who collected the data shown in Figure 2 for the TIMS Laboratory Experiment, *Rolling Along in Centimeters*. There are three experimental values for each car, and the students need some measure of the middle that fairly represents their data for each car. In this case, the median is a perfectly respectable average.

T Type of Car	*D* Distance (in $\frac{cm}{unit}$)			
	Trial 1	**Trial 2**	**Trial 3**	**Median**
Red	83	93	86	
Blue	44	44	43	
Orange	39	53	46	
Black	194	199	189	

Figure 2: Data from Rolling Along in Centimeters

Finding the median value of the three trials does not require young children to do any arithmetic and conceptually illustrates quite nicely the idea of an average representing a middle value.

One way to get a median from data like this is illustrated in Figure 3. The students cross out the largest and smallest numbers in each row and use the one that is left as their average value. Finding the median value of the three trials does not require young children to do any arithmetic and conceptually illustrates quite nicely the idea of an average representing a middle value.

T Type of Car	*D* Distance (in $\frac{cm}{unit}$)			
	Trial 1	**Trial 2**	**Trial 3**	**Median**
Red	~~83~~	~~93~~	(86)	86
Blue	~~44~~	(44)	~~43~~	44
Orange	~~39~~	~~53~~	(46)	46
Black	(194)	~~199~~	~~189~~	194

Figure 3: Finding the median

Finding the median can be illustrated more concretely by using links (or string, adding machine tape, etc.) to create "lengths" that match the actual distance that the cars roll each time. At the end of three rolls, the students will have three lengths of links that each represent the distance a car rolled in a trial.

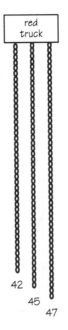

Figure 4: Finding the median
in Rolling Along with Links

42
45
47

This is illustrated in Figure 4. The median value can then be found by comparing the lengths and discarding the shortest and longest; the remaining length represents the median. A process somewhat like this is used in the first-grade experiment *Rolling Along with Links.*

In fourth grade, students begin finding the mean as well as the median. Again the concepts are introduced concretely. For example, students find the median value for several towers of cubes by lining them up from shortest to tallest and selecting the tower in the middle. This is illustrated in Figures 5a and 5b. Figure 6 illustrates the case when there is an even number of trials. To find the median here, students have to find the halfway point between the two middle towers.

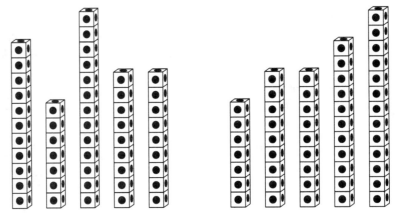

Figures 5a and 5b: Finding the median with cubes

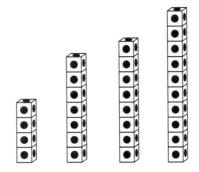

Figure 6: The median number of cubes is 7½.

Cubes are also used when introducing the mean. For example, suppose students begin with the same five towers that are illustrated in Figure 5a. They first estimate the mean by figuring out a way to "even out the towers," as illustrated in Figure 7. Then they calculate the mean using the numerical values. In this manner, the concept of the mean as a representative measure is stressed rather than focusing purely on the arithmetic procedure.

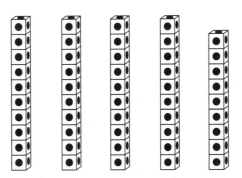

Figure 7: Estimating the mean by "evening out" towers of cubes

Students will often use calculators to calculate the mean of a data set. For example, the mean distance for the red car in Figure 2, when found by calculator, is:

$$\frac{(83 + 93 + 86) \text{ cm}}{3} = 87.333333 \text{ cm}$$

This is an example of too much of a good thing. In this case, the calculator gives many more digits than are meaningful. The students have to determine an appropriate level of significance. Keep in mind that our goal is to get a reasonable number to use as an average. Here, the original measurements were made to the nearest cm so it makes sense to also report the mean value to the nearest cm.

Why Average?

Finding the average is a critical step in a MATH TRAILBLAZERS experiment. It is an important step from raw data to understanding. Errors are inevitable when measurements are made, and averaging is one way to detect and control error. If a child makes the same measurement three times and gets 67 cm, 64 cm, and 84 cm, she should notice that the 84 cm is way off. She can detect her error and redo that measurement.

Even when all the measurements are close, the average minimizes error. If the measurements are 67 cm, 64 cm, and 67 cm, then the mean, 66 cm, is a more accurate prediction of future measurements than any of the actual measurements.

Another function of averaging is to aggregate raw data. Unlike computers, people cannot handle too many numbers at once. If I tell you the income of every child in a school, then you will be overwhelmed by numbers. If I tell you the *median* income of children in the school, you know less but probably understand more. The situation in a typical MATH TRAILBLAZERS experiment is similar. From 12 actual measurements in *Rolling Along in Centimeters,* we cut down to three averages which are plotted. Then we may even go further, to a single number, the slope of the best-fit line. But that's another story.

Estimation, Accuracy, and Error

TIMS Tutor

For many people, one of the most attractive aspects of mathematics is that it is exact. The story problems that we worked on in our youth were reassuring (or terrifying) in the certainty of their answers. If one potato weighs 2 pounds, then 100 potatoes weigh 200 pounds. The only problem is that the real world is not so exact. One potato does not weigh exactly 2 pounds and 100 potatoes probably do not weigh 200 pounds. In this tutor, we discuss ways we deal mathematically with situations where exactness is not called for (when we estimate) or impossible (when we measure within a certain degree of accuracy).

Virtually all mathematics educators agree that estimation should be an important part of any elementary curriculum. We can see evidence for this by noting that estimation is one of the nine content standards in the NCTM *Standards* and that the entire 1986 NCTM yearbook was devoted to estimation and mental computation. Unlike content areas such as number and operation and geometry, there is very little traditional curriculum on estimation as well as some disagreement about exactly what is meant by estimation. Some mathematicians and educators make a distinction between estimation and approximation, but there is no generally agreed definition of these terms. This tutor provides a general overview of the concept of estimation and discusses some of the more common strategies and applications. For a more exhaustive treatment of estimation, we recommend the NCTM yearbook (1986).

What Is Estimation?

According to *Webster's Ninth New Collegiate Dictionary,* **to estimate** means to judge tentatively or approximately the value, worth, or significance of something. Alternatively, it means to calculate approximately. **An estimate** is a general calculation of size, value, etc., especially an *approximate* computation of the probable cost of a piece of work. This leads one to ask for the definition of **approximate.** The dictionary states that approximate means located close together, or nearly correct or exact. Moreover, **an approximation** is an *estimate,* guess, or mathematical result that is close in value but not the same as a desired quantity.

Leaving aside the fact that these definitions appear to be circular (an estimate is an approximation and an approximation is an estimate), the dictionary does give us a general idea of what these words mean. As with most words, these words have several meanings and their exact meaning is determined by the particular context in which they are used. In particular, these words are used in a variety of ways in mathematics. You should first note that unlike most mathematical concepts, estimate and approximate do not have precise definitions. What does it mean for two numbers to be "near in position, close together?" Is 5 close to 10? Is 1250 close to 1300? Is 1000 close to 3000? It's hard to say. In spite of our inability to precisely define closeness, we shall see that the varied uses of estimation are an important ingredient in mathematical problem solving.

Pedagogical Aspects of Estimation

In her survey article, "Estimation and Number Sense," Judith Threadgill-Sowder (1992) points out that

Good estimators are flexible in their thinking, and they use a variety of strategies. They demonstrate a deep understanding of number and operations, and they continually draw upon that understanding.

> *Good estimators are flexible in their thinking, and they use a variety of strategies. They demonstrate a deep understanding of number and operations, and they continually draw upon that understanding. Poor estimators seem to be bound, with only slight variations, to one strategy—that of applying algorithms more suitable for finding an exact answer. Poor estimators have only a vague notion of the nature and purpose of estimation; they believe it to be inferior to exact calculation (Morgan, 1988) and equate it with guessing.*

It follows from this view of estimation that teaching estimation is a complex task. Rather than being a simple skill that follows a few basic rules, estimation requires a variety of strategies. Rather than being a separate subject, estimation is a habit of mind that is carried out in the course of many mathematical activities. Thus, there are few lessons in the MATH TRAILBLAZERS curriculum that are devoted solely to estimation, while there are many lessons that offer opportunities for estimation. While estimation is not a simple skill, there are a number of simple skills, such as "rounding" and mental multiplication, that are extremely useful when doing estimation.

Students often have difficulty with estimation because they are uncomfortable about having more than one correct answer. They want to know "the right answer" and dislike being told "that's a good estimate." So it is the task of the teacher to keep reminding students of the purpose of estimation and that different strategies can result in different correct answers. The laboratory experiments in MATH TRAILBLAZERS help students develop an appreciation of the approximate nature of measurement and the fact that problems can have more than one solution.

It is the task of the teacher to keep reminding students of the purpose of estimation and that different strategies can result in different correct answers.

To help organize our thoughts about estimation, we will break the uses of estimation in the elementary mathematics curriculum into four major categories:

1. Estimating the result of a calculation (in particular, addition, subtraction, multiplication, and division) to see if the answer is reasonable.

2. Measurement error, experimental error, and predictions.

3. Estimating the magnitude of a measurement; for example, the height of a building, the area of a wall, the volume of a jar, or the weight of a person.

4. Estimating how many; for example, the number of peanuts in a jar, the number of students in a school, the number of people at a concert.

Estimating the Results of a Calculation

Two of the primary reasons for estimating the results of a calculation are:

1. To check that the exact answer is (possibly) correct. The estimation can be done either before or after the calculation. Getting an answer that is far from your estimate indicates that the calculation is incorrect. On the other hand, an estimate that is close to the calculation does not guarantee that it is correct.

2. As a substitute for the exact answer. In many situations an exact answer is not needed and may not even make sense.

In the rest of this section, we will discuss a few of the more common strategies that are used to estimate the results of a calculation. Undoubtedly, you and your students will find other good strategies.

When estimating a sum or difference, one strategy that can usually be carried out mentally is to look at the first one or two place-value columns.

Addition and Subtraction

For the purposes of estimation, the most important digits in a number are the ones to the left, i.e., the leading digits. When estimating a sum or difference, one strategy that can usually be carried out mentally is to look at the first one or two *place-value columns*. For example, here are some statistics on the New England states from a 1987 almanac:

	Population (1984)	Area (sq mi)
Maine	1,164,000	33,215
New Hampshire	998,000	9304
Vermont	535,000	9609
Massachusetts	5,822,000	8257
Rhode Island	968,000	1214
Connecticut	3,174,000	5009

If we wanted to estimate the total population of New Hampshire and Vermont using "front end estimation," we could look at the first column on the left. In this case, it is the hundred thousands column. Adding the 9 and the 5 we get 14, which tells us that the sum is approximately 14 hundred thousands; in other words, one million, four hundred thousand. In fact, the first two digits of the sum must be either 14 or 15 (depending on whether or not there is any carrying when we do the addition algorithm). You can have your estimate be 1,400,000 or you can look at the next digits to see if there is likely to be any carrying. In this case, the digits in the ten thousands column are 9 and 3, so there will be carrying. Thus, 1,500,000 is an even better estimate. Of course, the whole point of estimation is to get a quick, approximate answer. If you start looking at too many digits, you might as well find the exact answer.

A second quick method for this estimate is to think that the population of New Hampshire is approximately 1 million and that of Vermont is about ½ million, so the total is about 1.5 million. Since the "exact" answer is 1,533,000, an estimate of 1.5 million is only off by about 2%. A more "rule-bound" approach that said, "round off the nearest million" would give us 1 million plus 1 million which is 2 million. This is not a very close estimate (it's about 30% off). In fact, there is no simple rule that gives a good estimate in all situations. A rule which often gives good results is "round each number to one significant digit and then add." (A whole number has one significant digit if all the digits after the first one are equal to zero.) That's what we did in this case, rounding 1,164,000 to 1,000,000 and 535,000 to 500,000.

The same strategies could be applied to estimate the results of subtraction calculations. For example, if we wanted to know how much larger the population of New Hampshire is than the population of Vermont, we could round each population to one significant digit, and subtract 500,000 from 1 million to get 500,000. Rounding to the nearest million definitely doesn't work in this problem, since both populations round to 1 million, and we would get the nonsensical estimate that there are no more people in New Hampshire than there are in Vermont! It should be noted that looking at the difference between two numbers is not always the best way of comparing them. If we wanted to compare the populations of New Hampshire and Vermont, it might be better to look at the ratio of their populations and say that New Hampshire has twice the population of Vermont.

The fact that the population figures are rounded off to the nearest thousand in the table is an acknowledgment that census figures themselves are estimates. In this case, there are two reasons that the data is not exact. Population data for the U.S. is based on census data. Since the population of the United States is so large and not everyone cooperates with the census takers, it is impossible to count everyone in the country. The population is also a moving target. Every day, tens of thousands of people are born or die. Finally, the figures for 1984 population are obtained by starting with the 1980 figures and extrapolating based on assumptions about the rate of population growth. Since many factors affecting population growth change, it is highly unlikely that predictions for population would be very accurate.

Rounding is also one effective strategy for mentally estimating the sum of a series of numbers. For example, to find the total population of New England from the individual state populations above, you might round the numbers in the population column to the nearest half million, namely 1, 1, ½, 6, 1, and 3 million. Adding these mentally gives 12½ million, which is pretty close to the actual total of 12,661,000 people. Try to estimate the total area of New England, mentally. The exact answer is 66,608 square miles.

Note that these are not the only strategies for estimating the sum or difference of several numbers. For example, if you wanted to purchase items that cost $3.79, $4.19, $2.23, and $6.49, you might want to add the dollars mentally (3 + 4 + 2 + 6 = 15) and then round the cents to the nearest quarter, i.e., 79 cents is about 75 cents, etc. This way, you see you need about $1.75 more (or 7 quarters). So, the total is pretty close to $16.75.

Multiplication: Rounding and Mental Math

The most basic technique for estimating the result of a multiplication problem is to replace (if necessary) the original numbers in the problem with other numbers which permit us to do the calculation mentally, or rapidly with paper and pencil. For example, if you wanted to know the number of minutes in a day, you would have to multiply 24 hours by 60 minutes per hour. Finding 24 × 60 is too hard for most people to do mentally, but 25 × 60 can be done by many fourth- and fifth-graders. Now, 25 × 60 is the same as 25 × 6 × 10, and 25 × 6 is 150. (Think of 6 quarters being a dollar-fifty. Most of us are pretty good at calculating with multiples of 5, 10, and 25, since we have had a lot of practice doing mental arithmetic with money.) Finally, if 6 × 25 is 150, then 6 × 25 × 10 is 1500. This is a pretty good estimate for 24 × 60. Note that we repeatedly used the commutative property of multiplication— i.e., the order in which we multiply several numbers does not affect the result. An alternative estimate for 24 × 60 can be obtained by rounding off 24 to 20 and multiplying 20 by 60 to get approximately 1200 minutes in a day. This estimate is not as close, but it may suffice for many purposes.

A basic skill that is fundamental to being able to estimate in multiplication and division situations is being able to multiply and divide by ten and powers of ten (100, 1000, etc.). Thus, as early as third grade in *MATH TRAILBLAZERS*, we observe the pattern that multiplying a whole number by 10 amounts to adding the digit 0 to the right of the number, i.e., 10 × 57 = 570, 10 × 365 = 3650, etc. Similarly, multiplying by 100 amounts to adding two 0 digits to the right, etc. When we start to work with decimals, we observe that multiplying a decimal by 10 amounts to moving the decimal point to the right one place. For

The most basic technique for estimating the result of a multiplication problem is to replace (if necessary) the original numbers in the problem with other numbers which permit us to do the calculation mentally...

example, $10 \times 45.76 = 457.6$. This is really the same pattern we see with whole numbers, since $10 \times 57.0 = 570$, etc.

Another fundamental process in the examples above was finding "convenient" numbers that were close to the numbers we started with. Here, "convenient" means numbers with which we can calculate mentally. For example, we rounded 24 to 25, since multiples of 25 are easy to figure out. Often, the "convenient" numbers are what we call round numbers, and the process of finding the nearest round number is called "rounding off." For example, when we used our second strategy to estimate 24×60, we rounded off 24 to the nearest 10, which gave us 20. All this means is that 20 is the multiple of 10 that is nearest to 24 (since 24 is between 20 and 30 but is closer to 20).

Rounding

Traditionally, students have been taught a lot of rules about rounding off, but they often are not able to apply them successfully since they did not understand the purpose of rounding off, nor did they have a good understanding of place value. When we are doing mental estimation, we frequently want to round off a number in the hundreds to the nearest hundred, a number in the thousands to the nearest thousand, etc. For example, 457 rounded to the nearest hundred is 500, while 447 rounded to the nearest hundred is 400. That's because both numbers are between 400 and 500, and 457 is closer to 500 and 447 is closer to 400. Now 450 is exactly halfway between 400 and 500, so it is not obvious how to round 450 to the nearest hundred. Strictly speaking, it does not make sense to talk about **the** nearest hundred in this situation, since 450 is 50 away from 400 and 50 away from 500. In the context of estimation, this means that you can use either 400 or 500 as an estimate for 450. For example, if we wanted to estimate 450×321, we could say $400 \times 300 = 120,000$ is an estimate for the answer. This estimate is certainly smaller than the actual answer, since 400 is less than 450 and 300 is less than 321. On the other hand, $500 \times 300 = 150,000$, which is probably bigger than the actual answer. So the answer is probably between 120,000 and 150,000 (it's actually 144,450).

It used to be taught that numbers halfway between should always be rounded up, but there is really no reason for doing so. In general, the type of rounding off to be done is determined by the context in which the rounding takes place and the reason you are rounding. For example, if you want to make sure you have enough money to purchase the items in your grocery cart, it is probably best to make a conservative estimate and round items that cost $12.50 up to $13. Banks have another solution to rounding off halves. They round 4.5 cents to 4 cents if they're calculating money they owe you and round 4.5 cents to 5 cents if they're calculating money you owe them.

Division

It may be surprising to realize that the operation we need to estimate most frequently in daily life is division! This results from the fact that many of the decisions we have to make are based on proportional reasoning. How many miles per gallon is your car getting? (Does it need a tune-up? A new brand of gas?) Which brand of cereal is the least expensive? (One costs $2.65 for 14 oz and the other costs $3.55 for 24 oz.) All these can be easily answered with a calculator, but we often have to make decisions when we do not have a calculator handy. More significantly, students often perform the wrong calculations on the calculator. Letting students first solve their problem using "convenient" numbers allows them to focus on the essential parts of the problem, without being distracted by a lot of digits and a lot of mechanical manipula-

It may be surprising to realize that the operation we need to estimate most frequently in daily life is division! This results from the fact that many of the decisions we have to make are based on proportional reasoning.

tions. Once they have found a reasonable solution strategy, they can return to solve the original "messy" problem.

The easiest problems to deal with are ones that can be turned into a problem that requires dividing by a power of 10. Dividing by 10 is the inverse of multiplying by 10. Thus, we can divide by 10 mentally by moving the decimal point one place to the left. For example, $\frac{27.9}{10} = 27.9$, $\frac{456.2}{10} = 45.62$, etc. Similarly, we can divide by 100 by moving the decimal point *two* places to the left. When dividing a whole number by 10, we get a fairly good estimate for the result by just dropping the one digit. For example, $\frac{279}{10}$ is approximately 27. Note that the estimate we get in this way is always smaller than the exact answer.

One method for estimating the results of a division problem is to replace each number by a suitable nearby "convenient" number and then carry out the first step in the division algorithm. The rounding is chosen in such a way as to make the division easy. For example, suppose we wanted to estimate the population density of Maine. The data in Table 1 tells us that the density is 1,164,000 people ÷ 33,215 square miles. We can round off the divisor to 30,000 square miles and round off the dividend to 1,000,000 people. To estimate 1,000,000 ÷ 30,000, we can ask what times 30,000 gives 1,000,000. Multiplying 30,000 by 10 gives 300,000 and multiplying this by 3.3 gets us near 1,000,000. So, our estimate is about 33. Another method would be to replace the divisor and dividend with nearby convenient numbers. For example, 33,215 is near 30,000 and 1,164,000 is close to 1,200,000. We chose this pair of numbers because 12 is divisible by 3. So, our estimate now amounts to 1,200,000 people ÷ 30,000 square miles. Again, we see we need to multiply 30,000 by 40 to get 1,200,000. So, 40 people per square mile is a reasonable estimate for the population density of Maine. Putting the numbers back into the context of the problem is important for checking any result.

A powerful technique for estimating the result of a division problem is to consider the division as a ratio.

A powerful technique for estimating the result of a division problem is to consider the division as a ratio. For example, suppose you had traveled 637 miles and used 22 gallons of gas. To find your miles per gallon, you would want to divide 22 into 637. Write the ratio 637 miles/22 gallons. Rounding 637 to 600 and 22 to 20 we get

$$\frac{637 \text{ mi}}{22 \text{ gal}} \approx \frac{600 \text{ mi}}{20 \text{ gal}}$$

Note that we have used the symbol ≈ instead of the equal sign. This symbol means "approximately equal." Now, we can simplify the ratio $\frac{600}{20}$ by dividing both numerator and denominator by 10. So

$$\frac{600 \text{ mi}}{20 \text{ gal}} = \frac{60 \text{ mi}}{2 \text{ gal}}$$

and dividing numerator and denominator by 2 gives us

$$\frac{60 \text{ mi}}{2 \text{ gal}} = \frac{30 \text{ mi}}{1 \text{ gal}}$$

Putting this all together, we get 637 mi/22 gal ≈ 30 mi/1 gal; in other words, our estimate is 30 miles per gallon.

A note on canceling. Many people learned to simplify ratios by "canceling" the same thing in the numerator and the denominator. You might be tempted to say that when we wrote 600 mi/20 gal = 60 mi/2 gal, we "canceled a 0" in the numerator and the denominator. Unfortunately, this can lead to some bad habits. For example, can you cancel the fives in $875/25$ to get $87/2$, or cancel the fives in $(X + 5)/(Y + 5)$ to get X/Y? You had better not, since this amounts to subtracting the 5 from the numerator and denominator and this results in a fraction that is not equal to the one we started with.

$$\frac{875}{25} \neq \frac{87}{2}$$

$$\frac{X + 5}{Y + 5} \neq \frac{X}{Y}$$

So, canceling does not always result in an equal ratio. For this reason, we always say exactly what we are doing, dividing numerator and denominator by the same number, rather than using the word "cancel."

Here are some examples of estimation in a division context:

Example 1: Estimate the quotient $80,000/30$. This is approximately $8000/3$, which is between $7500/3$ and $9000/3$, i.e., between 2500 and 3000. Note that if we estimated $80,000/30$ by replacing 30 with 40 (since 40 goes into 80,000 evenly) we get $80,000/40 = 8000/4 = 2000$, which is not as good as our previous estimate. This might be a little surprising, since we only made a change of 10 in replacing 30 by 40. But what is important here is not the size of the change (10), but the relative size of the change (10 out of 30 is 33%).

Here are some additional examples of estimation in a division context. See if you can follow the reasoning in these estimates. Can you make an estimate in a different way?

$$\frac{6206}{8271} \approx \frac{6000}{8000} = \frac{6}{8} = \frac{3}{4} = 0.75$$

$$\frac{78,221}{987} \approx \frac{80,000}{1000} = 80$$

$$\frac{77,921}{289} \approx \frac{75,000}{250} = \frac{7500}{25} = 300$$

$$\frac{828}{38,765} \approx \frac{800}{40,000} = \frac{8}{400} = \frac{2}{100} = .02$$

Measurement Error, Experimental Error, and Predictions

The theme of this tutor is the way in which "inexactness" is dealt with in real-world mathematics. One class of situations that involve "inexactness" is that which involves measurement error or experimental error. **Measurement error** is the unavoidable error that occurs due to the limitations inherent to any measurement instrument. Any measurement in the real world is an approximation. It is not really possible to guarantee that an object is exactly 1 meter long since any measuring instrument has a limit to its accuracy. For example, our centimeter ruler can only measure to the nearest tenth of a centimeter and the two-pan balance usually used in MATH TRAILBLAZERS can only measure mass to the nearest gram. **Experimental error** is the variation in measurement that results from the inability to control extraneous variables in an experiment.

Measurement error is the unavoidable error that occurs due to the limitations inherent to any measurement instrument.... Experimental error is the variation in measurement that results from the inability to control extraneous variables in an experiment.

These two types of error are closely related. Let's consider three examples of measurement in real-world contexts to get some idea of the meaning of measurement and experimental error:

Example 1: A student is selected from the class and every student measures the circumference of her head to the nearest tenth of a centimeter. Most students get between 47 and 49 centimeters. One student gets 37.4 centimeters.

Example 2: Students drop a ball from a height of 80 centimeters three times to see how high it bounces. They get 41 centimeters, 45 centimeters, and 44 centimeters.

Example 3: Students measure the volume of a marble using a graduated cylinder. Most students get either 7 or 8 cubic centimeters. Two students get 67 cubic centimeters.

Example 4: A student finds that the mass of one blue pattern block is 11 grams. She predicts that 2 blue pattern blocks will have a mass of 22 grams and 4 blue pattern blocks will have a mass of 44 grams. When she checks her results, she finds that 2 pattern blocks do have a mass of 22 grams, but 4 pattern blocks have a mass of 42 grams.

Errors vs. Mistakes

In Examples 1, 2, and 3, there were repeated measurements of the same thing that produced seemingly different answers. The fact that most students obtained slightly different answers in Example 1 is due to slight variations in how they performed the measurement—where they placed the tape measure, how tight they held it, etc. All these measurements are "close" to each other (see below for a discussion of "what's close?"). However, the student whose measurement was 37.4 centimeters probably made a *mistake* such as reading the tape measure incorrectly or placing the tape measure in the wrong position. In mathematics, we try to distinguish between the words "error" and "mistake." Of course, "mistake" is one of the common meanings of "error." *Webster's New World Dictionary of the American Language* gives as its first definition of the word "error," "the state of believing what is untrue, incorrect, or wrong." However, in the current context, "error" has a different meaning. This is the fifth definition given for "error" in that dictionary, namely "the difference between a computed or estimated result and the actual value as in mathematics." The dictionary goes on to explain that "error implies deviation from truth, accuracy, correctness, right, [while] mistake suggests an error resulting from carelessness, inattention, misunderstanding, etc." Most of the measurements in Example 1 involved some measurement error, but those measurements were correct. However, the student who measured 37.4 centimeters must have made a mistake. In this case, the teacher would help the student find the reason for the mistake and then repeat the measurement correctly.

In Example 2, it is not surprising that repeating the activity, i.e., dropping the ball from 80 centimeters, results in a different measurement. It's pretty hard to measure how high the ball bounces, since the ball does not stop at the height of its bounce and wait for you to measure its distance from the floor. Also, there can be slight variations caused by different parts of the ball being "bouncier" or different spots on the floor being "bouncier." This is a typical example of the experimental error that results from the inability to control all the "fixed" variables in an experiment. (See the TIMS Tutor: *The TIMS Laboratory Method.* Fixed Variables in Controlled Experiments.)

In mathematics, we try to distinguish between the words "error" and "mistake."

In Example 3, students used a graduated cylinder to measure the volume by displacement. Two students forgot to subtract the volume of the water in the cylinder, so they obtained measurements that were very different from the others. This is a clear example of a "mistake." The actual volume of the marble was between 7 and 8 cubic centimeters.

Reducing Experimental Error

In Examples 1 through 3, we have seen that repeating a measurement does not always give the same answer. To get more reliable and accurate results, scientists often repeat a measurement several times and then take the average of all the measurements. The "average" that we use in this situation can be either the mean or the median. (See the TIMS Tutor: *Averages.*) In Example 2, we can take the median of the three measurements and say that dropping the ball from 80 centimeters results in a bounce height of 44 centimeters. We could also use the mean, in which case the bounce height would be nearly the same—approximately 43 centimeters.

In many experiments, we have another way of minimizing experimental error. If the data points appear close to a straight line, we find a best-fit line that is close to all the data points. (See the TIMS Tutor: *The TIMS Laboratory Method.*) Using the best-fit line is a way of "averaging out" the experimental error. In *MATH TRAILBLAZERS*, we draw a best-fit line "by eye," using a transparent ruler. In addition to averaging out the error, these lines help scientists and mathematicians make predictions based upon the patterns in the data. Scientists, mathematicians, and statisticians use a variety of sophisticated methods to find best-fit lines for data, but the "eyeball" method is pretty good for making approximate predictions. One example of an activity where both averaging and best-fit lines are used to minimize experimental error is the *MATH TRAILBLAZERS* fourth-grade lab, *The Bouncing Ball.* In this lab, students drop a ball from heights of 40, 80, and 120 cm and record their data in a data table. (See Figure 1.) Note that the ball was dropped three times from each height. When the data is graphed, we can see that the data points lie close to a straight line. In Figure 2, we see an estimated best-fit line drawn by a student. For further information, see the TIMS Tutor: *The TIMS Laboratory Method,* Point Graphs: Fitting Lines and Curves.

To get more reliable and accurate results, scientists often repeat a measurement several times and then take the average of all the measurements.

Scientists, mathematicians, and statisticians use a variety of sophisticated methods to find best-fit lines for data, but the "eyeball" method is pretty good for making approximate predictions.

Tennis Ball

D Drop Height in cm	B Bounce Height in cm			
	Trial 1	Trial 2	Trial 3	Average
40	27	22	21	22
80	50	40	43	43
120	72	62	68	68

Figure 1: The Bouncing Ball *data table*

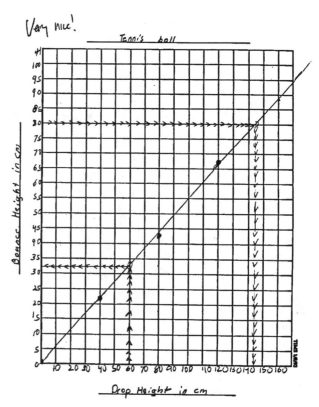

Very nice!

Figure 2: The Bouncing Ball *graph*

What's Close?

Recall that the notions of approximation and estimation involved the notion of finding a number that is close to a desired number. But how do we decide what's close? The most fundamental idea about closeness is that it is a **relative** idea. For example, suppose two merchants are selling the same item and the prices differ by $1. Are the prices close? If the merchant were selling cars that cost around $30,000, you would not make your decision based on a $1 difference in price. On the other hand, if you could buy a cup of coffee in one restaurant for $1 and it cost $2 at another restaurant, you might go out of your way for the $1 coffee (provided the quality was not vastly different). Why are these two choices for coffee significantly different? Because one brand costs **twice** as much as the other! This leads us to the fundamental idea for discussing closeness: when comparing closeness of numbers or measurements, we should look at the **ratio** of the two numbers, rather than the difference. The only problem with this approach is that the concept of ratio is difficult to understand fully. Developing this concept requires time and exposure to many experiences. We deal with this problem in two ways. First, instead of using ratios, we use a related concept—percent. Second, instead of calculating specific percentages (another difficult concept), we make comparisons to certain "benchmark" percentages, such as 10%. Using 10% as a benchmark for closeness, we see that $1 is not close to $2 since $2 is more than 10% bigger than $1 (in fact, it's 100% bigger). On the other hand, if we compare $30,000 and $30,001 we see that the difference, $1, is a lot less than 10% of $30,000.

In Example 1 above, the example in which many students measured the head circumference of one person, all the measurements fell between 47 and 49 centimeters. A rough estimate for 10% of these numbers is 4 cm. Now the difference between 47 cm and 49 cm is 2 cm, so there is clearly less than

*The most fundamental idea about closeness is that it is a **relative** idea.*

10% variation between the largest and smallest measurement. We can safely say that these measurements are "close." On the other hand, the student who got 37.5 cm was almost 10 cm less than 47 cm. This is nowhere close to being within 10% of the other measurements, so we should suspect that there is a mistake in that measurement. In Example 2, students took three measurements of the bounce height of a ball—41 cm, 45 cm, and 44 cm. Again, the variation is less than 10%. Finally, in Example 3, when students were measuring the volume of a marble, most obtained a value between 7 cc and 8 cc, while a few measured 67 cc. Now, 10% of 7 or 8 cc is less than 1 cc, so the students who measured 67 cc are nowhere close to the others. It should be pointed out that in situations such as Example 3, we do not decide who had the correct measurements by taking a majority vote. While the majority is usually right, it is not always right. The different results are a warning flag telling us to seek out the reasons for the discrepancies. Someone is making a mistake, but we can only find out who is making the mistake by looking more closely. Once the mistake is found, then we discard the incorrect information.

The 10 Percent Solution

It's natural to ask why we use 10% as a standard of closeness. We have a variety of reasons:

1. It's easy to find 10% of a number, or at least to estimate it. Just divide by 10. For whole numbers bigger than 10, the simplest estimate for 10% is obtained by dropping the last digit. Thus 10% of 187 is about 18 (it's between 18 and 19) and 10% of 5623 is about 562.

2. In many of the hands-on experiments we do in MATH TRAILBLAZERS, 10% is about the accuracy we can expect from students using the equipment they have, while 10% accuracy is still good enough for seeing the patterns in the data on graphs.

3. Psychologically, 10% is near the limit of our visual estimating ability. For example, if you show a person two drawings in sequence, one of which is an enlargement of the other, in most cases that person will have difficulty distinguishing pictures that are less than 10% different in size, but will be able to distinguish figures that are much more than 10% different in size. Of course, this 10% borderline is not exact, and the point at which different people will be able to make distinctions is different.

Estimating the Magnitude of a Measurement

The basic measurement variables in the MATH TRAILBLAZERS curriculum are length, area, volume, mass, and time. While much of the discussion that follows will apply to any type of measurement, it is a good idea to keep these few variables in mind. The examples given in this section will use these five variables.

There are two important types of knowledge that are used in many measurement estimation exercises. First, you need to know the measurements of some objects to use as a reference point. Second, you must know how to estimate unknown measurements by comparison with things you know. Very often this will involve some kind of proportional reasoning. The first type of knowledge is gained from experience. Therefore, students should have a wide variety of hands-on experiences as well as knowledge gained from external sources. For example, students should know the height of an average adult in English and metric systems (5½–6 feet, 160–185 cm), the length of their feet, and the width of their hands. We would hope that students have a general idea of the width of the continental U.S. from east to west (3000 miles) and from north to south (1000 miles). These facts can be used to make other estimates. For example, what is the area of the U.S.? The continental U.S. looks as though it would fit in a rectangle that is 3000 miles long and 1000 miles wide. This gives us an estimate of 3 million square miles. The actual area is close to 3.6 million square miles. To estimate the height of a three-story building (Figure 3), we could first estimate the height of one floor. Looking at an adult standing in the room, we might estimate that the distance from floor to ceiling is twice the height of the person. If the person is about 6 feet tall, then we get an estimate of 12 feet from floor to ceiling. If there are three floors, then the total height of the building is approximately 3 × 12 = 36 feet high.

Figure 3: Estimating the height of a three-story building

Accuracy and Precision

The accuracy required in a measurement depends on the use we are going to make of the measurement. By its very nature, any measurement we make in the real world is an estimation. What does it mean to say that a sheet of paper is 21.6 cm wide? How does one find this out? One way is to put the 0 cm mark on the ruler even with the left-hand edge of the paper and see that the right-hand edge of the paper is even with the 22.6 cm mark. If the paper is really 22.61 cm wide, we could not tell this with our ruler, which is only divided into tenths of a centimeter. So the measurements we make are really estimates that are accurate to the nearest tenth of a centimeter. Measuring the width of a piece of paper to an accuracy of more than a tenth of a centimeter would probably not make sense, since the sides cannot be perfectly even and measuring the width in different places would give different answers (like 22.613 cm and 22.615 cm). In any case, a measurement of 22.6 cm is probably more than sufficient for our purpose.

Dealing with Decimal Digits

One important fact to note is that in the course of solving a problem we can end up with a number that has many digits, most of which do not make sense in the real world (although they make mathematical sense). For example, suppose we wanted to share 16 ounces of orange juice among three students. When I divide 16 by 3 on my calculator, I get 5.3333333333. It makes no sense at all to say that we should give each student 5.3333333333 ounces of juice, since, with the tools we have, we cannot measure more accurately than

By its very nature, any measurement we make in the real world is an estimation.

to the nearest tenth of an ounce. In fact, when we say that we want to share 16 ounces of orange juice, we do not mean that we have exactly 16 ounces of juice. We might mean that we have measured the amount of juice to the limit of accuracy of our instrument, probably the nearest tenth (or eighth) of an ounce. Alternatively, we might mean that the juice came in a can that said 16 ounces on the label. Then, we have to wonder how accurately the manufacturer measured out the juice. What this finally boils down to is that unless we were using unusually sensitive measuring instruments, it would only make sense to say that we would give each student 5.3 ounces or 5⅓ ounces of juice. Although 5.3 and 5⅓ are not equal, they are approximately equal in this context.

Estimating "How Many"

In this type of estimation, we want to estimate the number of objects in some collection. It could be the number of trees in the United States, the number of students that will be in a school district next year, or the number of beans in a jar. This class of problems has a lot in common with the estimation problems we have already discussed. Many problems that require estimating "how many" are similar to estimating a measurement in that they involve knowing how many objects there are in some known set and then comparing the unknown with the known. Here are some examples:

Example 1: Students are asked to estimate the number of peanuts in a jar. If the students have not had any previous experience with peanuts or jars, this is not really an estimate, but rather a guess. The answers will vary widely because students do not have any idea of what the answer might be and no strategies to use to get a sensible answer. A more reasonable exercise is to give them a small jar and have them count how many peanuts can fit in the jar. If they are now given a larger jar, they should be able to make a sensible estimate by comparing the large jar to the small one. How many large jars would they think fit in the small jar? If the small jar holds 10 peanuts and it appears that 12 small jars fit in the large one, what is a reasonable estimate for the number of peanuts that fit in the large jar?

Example 2: How many students are in your school? The reference set here can be the number of students in a class. Students should know how many students are in their class. They should also be able to estimate the number of classes in the school. This gives an estimate for the number of students in the school (using multiplication).

Example 3: How many total hours of television were watched by all the children in the school? We can find the *exact* answer by asking every student how much they watched and then adding the number of hours. The answer can be *estimated* using a very important technique called sampling. Take a survey of some of the children in the school (say one class or two students in each class) and then "scale up."

Example 4: We have a picture of the crowd at a basketball game. How can we determine the number of people at the game? It would be tedious to count the number of people in the picture. We could draw a square on the picture and count the number of people in that square. The multiply that result by the number of such squares needed to cover the crowd. Figure 4 from the MATH TRAILBLAZERS fourth-grade curriculum shows a picture used to pose a similar problem.

Figure 4: Picture of a basketball game crowd

Example 5: Will more people vote for Fred or Amy in the next election? This is another example of a kind of problem that frequently occurs in the real world. The common technique for estimating the answer is to take a sample of the voters and use the sample to predict the results for the whole population. For example, if 40% of the sample says they will vote for Fred and 60% says they will vote for Amy, we might predict that Amy will win. We might even predict that Fred will get 40% of the vote and Amy 60%. We know from "real life" that predictions like this are not always accurate. Some things that affect the accuracy of such estimates are the size of the sample (compared to the whole population) and the "randomness" of the sample (how well the sample represents the whole population).

Example 6: How many households are there in the U.S.? We can only make this estimate if we know enough facts about the population of the U.S. We know that the population of the U.S. is about 250 million people and that the average family has 2.3 children. If we think that some households have only one person, while others have several generations living together, we might say that the average household size is about 4 or 5 people. Using a household size of 5 for our estimate (since 5 goes evenly into 25) we get a figure of 50 million households.

Conclusion

We hope that this tutor gives you an overview of the way estimation is treated in the *Math Trailblazers* curriculum. Naturally, it could not deal with all the types of estimation situations and all kinds of estimation strategies. The best way to become a good estimator is to estimate. The best way for children to learn to be good estimators is to be given meaningful situations that require estimation and to be given the opportunity to discuss their strategies with others. As with all mathematics instruction, the teacher plays a valuable role by moderating discourse and by adding new strategies when appropriate.

The best way to become a good estimator is to estimate.

References

Estimation and Mental Computation—1986 Yearbook. Schoen, Harold L., and Marilyn J. Zweng (eds.). Reston, Va.: National Council of Teachers of Mathematics, 1986.

Morgan, C. *A Study of Estimation by Secondary School Children.* Unpublished masters' dissertation. London: Institute of Education, 1988.

Sowder, J., "Estimation and Number Sense," in *Handbook of Research on Mathematics Teaching and Learning.* Grouws, Douglas A. (ed.). New York: Macmillan Publishing Co., 1992, pp. 371–389.

Threadgill-Sowder, J. "Computational Estimation Procedures of School Children." *Journal of Educational Research,* 77 (6), 1984, pp. 332–336.

Webster's Ninth New Collegiate Dictionary. Springfield, Mass.: Merriam-Webster, Inc., 1990.

Functions

TIMS Tutor

In mathematics and science, a function is a special and very important kind of relationship between variables. Discovering functional relationships between variables is what science is all about.

Introduction

Function is one of those words with a mathematical meaning that is not the same as the everyday meaning. In everyday life, a function can be an important celebration, a role someone or something has, or the purpose for something. In mathematics and science, a function is a special and very important kind of relationship between variables. Discovering functional relationships between variables is what science is all about.

Three Blind Men and an Elephant. There is a story about three blind men who encounter an elephant. The first comes up against one of the elephant's legs and says, "An elephant is like a tree." The second touches the side of the elephant and says, "No, no. An elephant is like a wall." The third blind man finds the elephant's trunk and claims, "You're both wrong. An elephant is like a big snake."

Each blind man has some notion of what an elephant is. The story doesn't tell whether they eventually resolve their differences and come to a proper understanding of elephants; we can only hope so. Our approach to functions will be similar: We will begin with three different views of functions. This, we hope, will lead to a fuller and more proper understanding of functions.

Tables

Many functions are displayed as tables. For example, consider this data table from the experiment *Mass vs. Number,* shown in Figure 1.

N **Number of Erasers**	M **Mass (in gm)**
1	39 gm
2	79 gm
4	158 gm

Figure 1: Mass vs. Number data table

This table displays a functional relationship between the variables *N* and *M.* For each value of *N* we have a value of *M;* we say that the mass is a function of the number of erasers. That is, if we know what *N* is, then we can find *M.* This is the essence of a function: knowing one variable's value enables us to find the corresponding value of the other variable. In this example, the data has a distinctive pattern: within experimental error, doubling one variable causes the other to double. *N* and *M* are said to be (directly) proportional.

Many of the functions we encounter in everyday life come to us as tables. Stock tables, for example, can be thought of as functions: one variable is the company, the other is the closing price. If you know the company, you can look up the price. Almanacs are filled with tables of information, most of which can be thought of as functions: one variable is the name of the country, the other is the population, and so on. The sports pages are filled with tabular functions of team standings and individual statistics.

Many functions come to us first as tables, and some, like batting averages or almanac information, are normally given only as tables. Tables of numbers, however, can be very difficult to understand. Patterns in the data can go undetected—patterns that might help us better understand the function. One of the best ways to get a handle on patterns is to make a visual image of the data in the form of a graph.

Graphs

If a picture is worth a thousand words, a graph is worth a billion numbers. The graph of the *Mass vs. Number* data, seen in Figure 2, is a good example.

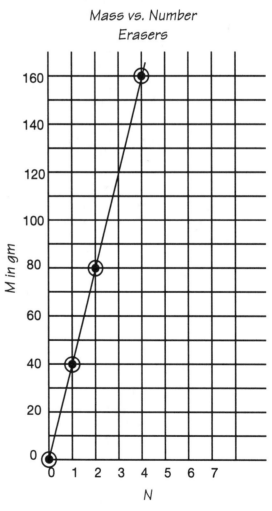

Figure 2: Graph of Mass *vs.* Number *data*

The key thing about this graph is that the data points lie on a straight line through (0,0). This confirms that *N* and *M* are proportional: we can fit a straight line through (0,0) if and only if the variables are proportional. Many other types of functions besides direct proportion are characterized by their graphs.

Often, experimental error obscures the nature of the relationship between the variables until the data is plotted. Like taking multiple measurements and averaging, graphing the data and fitting a curve can help control error. With error minimized, the true nature of the relationship between the variables may become clearer. Stock analysts graph their data to spot trends in order to make predictions (and money); such trends are unlikely to be noticed in the stock tables. Scientists graph their data almost as soon as they get it because the graph is so much more likely to be revealing than the raw data.

The graph is a crucial step on the road from the concrete apparatus to formal understanding. Sometimes, this formal understanding can be distilled in a few symbols, as in a formula.

Formulas

A more abstract way to consider a function is as a formula. In our *Mass vs. Number* example, we can exploit the fact that when variables are proportional, their ratio is constant. The value of this constant ratio is the slope of the best-fit line. So,

$$\frac{M}{N} = \frac{39.5 \text{ gm}}{1 \text{ eraser}}.$$

This can be rewritten to give a formula for *M* as a function of *N*:

$$M = \frac{39.5 \text{ gm}}{1 \text{ eraser}} \times N$$

Such formulas are very useful when they can be found. When we do manage to obtain a formula, it allows us to solve problems quickly and accurately. We can also use formulas to ascend to higher levels of abstraction. This movement to ever greater abstraction and generality is the driving force behind much of science and mathematics.

The graph is a crucial step on the road from the concrete apparatus to formal understanding.

G Number of Generations	A Number of Ancestors
1	2
2	4
3	8
4	16

Figure 3: Ancestors data table

Often students are not able to understand formulas, but they are, nevertheless, able to continue a pattern in a data table or devise a rule that works. For example, the pattern in the table shown in Figure 3 is easy to extend. Five generations back, you have 32 ancestors: each further generation doubles the number of ancestors (ignoring the inevitable overlap). Extending patterns like this is a first step towards formulas. Later, the students may be able to give a rule for a data table. For example, consider the table in Figure 4, the number of fence posts needed for a given length of fence.

L Length of Fence in _feet_	N Number of Fence Posts
10	2
20	3
30	4
40	5

Figure 4: Fence posts data table

The rule may be stated: the number of fence posts is just one more than $\frac{1}{10}$ the number of feet in the fence.

$$N = \frac{L}{10} + 1$$

It is not much harder for us to express this sentence as a formula, but this type of expression may be confusing to a third-grader. Often, a rule stated in ordinary language is more accessible.

Formulas are the most powerful way of looking at functions but are often not appropriate for elementary school students. The great temptation is to drive on to formulas as quickly as possible. This sometimes leads to quick gains, but over the long run it is usually disastrous. Pushing formulas at children is like building a house of cards: students need to build a conceptual foundation by handling apparatus, gathering data, and graphing and analyzing it. Only after the students have developed an understanding of the relationship of the variables is it proper to distill that understanding into a formula. Extending patterns and figuring out rules are excellent alternatives for younger students moving towards higher levels of abstraction.

What Is a Function?

A function is a special kind of relationship between variables that can often be expressed as a data table, graph, or formula. One of the variables is the manipulated (or independent) variable; the other is the responding (or dependent) variable.

But not every relationship is a function. The main requirement for a relationship to be a function is that for each value of the manipulated variable, there is only one value of the responding variable. For example, suppose the manipulated variable is the edge length of a cube and the responding variable is the surface area. Then, for each given edge length there is exactly one surface area: if the edge is 3 cm, then the surface area is 54 sq cm, and so on. Or consider the manipulated variable to be the company and the responding variable to be the closing price: each stock has exactly one closing price each day. Notice that many stocks may have the same closing price; that's okay. The requirement says only that each value of the manipulated variable must have exactly one value of the responding variable. Values of the responding variable may repeat, and often do.

…not every relationship is a function. The main requirement for a relationship to be a function is that for each value of the manipulated variable, there is only one value of the responding variable.

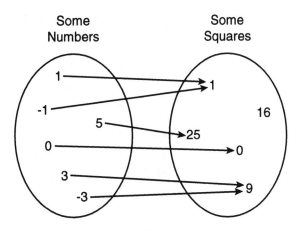

Figure 5: Map of a squaring function

One way to visualize this requirement is to think about functions as "mappings." Figure 5 shows a map of a squaring function.

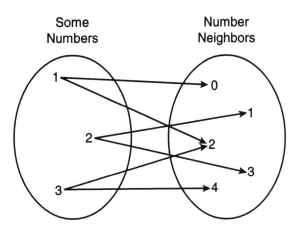

Figure 6: Map of a relationship that is not a function

Every number has exactly one square; this corresponds to the single arrow leaving each number on the left above. Notice that more than one arrow can end at a single number; the requirement is only that exactly one arrow leave each of the starting numbers. The mapping in Figure 6 is not a function because two arrows leave each number.

But you may object, saying that when we do experiments we often have several different values of the responding variable for each value of the manipulated variable. Isn't there a functional relationship between variables like the drop height and the bounce height in *The Bouncing Ball?* In a word, yes. But with real data, things get more complicated. Experimental error creeps in; there are other uncontrolled variables; there is uncertainty inherent in all our measurements. One useful way to think about the situation is to suppose there is some "true" value of the responding variable that we cannot measure exactly. So, instead we measure the responding variable several times and then take the average as our best estimate of the true value.[1] Then we have a function: for each value of the manipulated variable there is exactly one *true* value of the responding variable. The only trouble is, in most real-world situations, we usually don't know what that true value is.

[1]See the TIMS Tutor: *Averages.*

Mathematicians have precise and abstract definitions of function. We could go on and on describing more precisely the requirements a relationship must have to be a function. We could spell out the meanings of technical terms having to do with functions—terms like *domain, range, one-to-one, many-to-one,* and so on. For most purposes, however, thinking about functions in the terms outlined above is enough. To paraphrase Justice Potter Stewart, we may not know exactly what a function is, but we know one when we see it.

Functions in the Classroom

The concept of a function is a powerful one for organizing and extending mathematical ideas. From time to time, we have activities that deal with functions, for example, *Function Machines* in second grade. The best approach to functions, however, is just doing the MATH TRAILBLAZERS lessons. As your students do TIMS Laboratory Experiments and other activities, they will move naturally from the apparatus to the data table, graph, and questions. Much of the data analysis is designed to help the children see how changes in one of these correspond to changes in the others. Thus, in each experiment the students will deal with specific functions in several guises and will gain facility in moving between different representations of functions. This is the best possible preparation for the explicit study of functions later in high school and beyond.

As your students do TIMS Laboratory Experiments and other activities, they will move naturally from the apparatus to the data table, graph, and questions. Much of the data analysis is designed to help the children see how changes in one of these correspond to changes in the others....This is the best possible preparation for the explicit study of functions later in high school and beyond.

Journals

TIMS Tutor

Writing about mathematics and science helps students consolidate ideas, see connections between school and life, and think more abstractly.

We at TIMS embrace the idea of "writing across the curriculum"; we see helping students to write better as part of every teacher's job.

By writing in mathematics and science class, students improve their communication skills and develop their subject-matter understanding. Writing about mathematics and science helps students consolidate ideas, see connections between school and life, and think more abstractly.

Another reason to have students write about mathematics and science lessons is so that you can gain insight into how those lessons are being received and what the students are learning. Collecting and saving students' writing is also an excellent way to document long-term student progress.

We have tried several ways to incorporate writing into MATH TRAILBLAZERS. We often ask for students to write a short or extended answer to a question; we may also ask students to explain how they obtained their solutions. Students may be asked to write about problems they have solved in cooperative groups.

Journals can be another effective way to use writing in mathematics and science. Typically, a journal is a small, bound book in which students write regularly. The writing can be in response to various prompts, or it can be rather undirected. Because each student can respond at his or her own level and rate, journal writing is accessible to all students.

The teacher reads students' journals regularly, possibly responding in writing to what the students have written. Usually journal writing is not corrected for grammar, spelling, and punctuation—the focus is on the content of the writing rather than on the form.

The physical form of the journal is not important. A cloth-covered bound book, a spiral notebook, or even several sheets of paper stapled together will work just fine.

We urge you to have your students write regularly, every day or at least every week. Start with short periods and gradually extend the amount of time.

Journal Prompts

We urge you to have your students write regularly, every day or at least every week. Start with short periods and gradually extend the amount of time. When a student fills up one journal, give him or her another. Students will also enjoy reading their writing aloud and discussing it.

The writing your students do in their journals should take a variety of forms. Here are some suggestions for assignments ranging from highly structured to rather open-ended.

Sentence Completion

Give part of a sentence and ask students to complete it (Azzolino, 1990). For example, you might ask students to complete sentences like these:

"A shape is symmetric when…"
"Today we learned…"
"Before you use an equal-arm balance it's important to…"

A variation of this activity is to give one or more complete sentences and then to ask students to continue.

Explanations of Procedures

You might ask your students to explain how to measure the area of a leaf, how to use an equal-arm balance, how to add two three-digit numbers, or how to make a graph of some data. An explanation of an entire procedure or only of certain steps may be required.

Answers to Specific Questions

Sometimes you may want to pose a specific question about a lesson. For example, you might ask the students to describe the shape of the graph for a certain experiment and to explain why the graph has that shape. Many MATH TRAILBLAZERS lessons include questions that require some writing; these questions can be answered in the journals.

A question you might want to ask sometimes is, "How did working in your group turn out?" You may get valuable information that can help you improve the dynamics of your small groups.

Descriptions of Solutions

There are usually many ways to solve a mathematics problem; it is often worth exploring multiple solutions. To correct the common misconception that there is usually only one way to solve a problem, students need to learn that the process of problem solving is often as or more important than the answer. In MATH TRAILBLAZERS, they see connections by comparing different solutions. They learn that mathematics makes sense because their own ideas are validated. They are exposed to advanced ideas through other students' solutions, but without undue stress if they fail to understand those advanced ideas.

One way to encourage multiple solutions is to ask students to write about how they solved a problem. You can ask them to describe all the ways they were able to solve a problem or to describe a single way in depth. You might even ask them to write about failed solutions or what they did when they got stuck.

One way to encourage multiple solutions is to ask students to write about how they solved a problem. You can ask them to describe all the ways they were able to solve a problem or to describe a single way in depth. You might even ask them to write about failed solutions or what they did when they got stuck. Such assignments will encourage students to see such efforts not as failures but as periodic by-products of the problem-solving process.

Definitions

You might ask students to define a key concept like area or volume. You may be surprised at some of the answers you get.

Advice to Adventure Book Characters

Often the characters in our adventure books and other activities encounter problems that yield to the techniques the students have been learning in the labs and activities. You might stop part way through an adventure book and ask your students to write some advice, perhaps in the form of a letter, to the hero. When you finish the book, you can compare what the hero actually did with students' advice.

Reactions

You might ask your students what they liked or didn't like about a certain lab, activity, or adventure book. Or you might ask what they learned or what confused them.

Word Banks

You might supply a list of words or phrases and ask students to use those words in a piece of writing (Azzolino, 1990). For example, you might supply the following words, "ten, hundred, thousand, less than, seven, more than, nine."

Problems

Students enjoy writing their own problems. You can ask them to write another problem like a given problem; to write an addition, subtraction, or sharing problem; to write a number riddle; or to make up any problem that students in the class would find interesting to solve.

Free Writing

Other times you can leave it completely open, simply telling the students to write whatever they want about a certain lesson.

Some Tips for Getting Started

- Start with brief periods of writing and gradually extend the amount of time.

- Encourage pictures, data tables, graphs, number sentences, and other mathematical and scientific forms of communication.

- Vary the prompt. Sometimes be very specific; other times make the assignment more open-ended.

- Do not worry about grammar, spelling, and punctuation. Focus on content.

Conclusion

The name of our project—TIMS—expresses our conviction that the teaching of mathematics and science should be integrated. But we also feel strongly that integration should not stop there; language arts and social studies can and should be integrated with mathematics and science. Journals are one way to use writing in mathematics and science. Reading and writing are too important to be confined to language arts lessons.

Reference

Azzolino, A. "Writing as a Tool for Teaching Mathematics: The Silent Revolution." In *Teaching and Learning Mathematics in the 1990's: 1990 Yearbook.* T.J. Cooney, and C.R. Hirsch, Eds. Reston, Va.: National Council of Teachers of Mathematics, 1990.

Math Facts

TIMS Tutor

Students need to learn the math facts. Estimation, mental arithmetic, checking the reasonableness of results, and paper-and-pencil calculations require the ability to give quick, accurate responses when using basic facts. The question is not *if* students should learn the math facts, but *how*. Which teaching methods are most efficient and effective? To answer this question, the authors of MATH TRAILBLAZERS drew upon educational research and their own classroom experiences to develop a comprehensive plan for teaching the math facts. This tutor describes the teaching and learning of the math facts in the curriculum using the following outline:

Outline

This tutor is organized as follows:
 	
Philosophy
 	
Expectations by Grade Level
 	
Strategies for Learning the Facts
 	
    Addition
 	
    Subtraction
 	
    Multiplication
 	
    Division
 	
Math Fact Lessons
 	
Practice
 	
Assessment
 	
Conclusion
 	
References

Philosophy

The goal of the math facts strand in MATH TRAILBLAZERS is for students to learn the basic facts efficiently, gain facility with their use, and retain that facility over time. A large body of research supports an approach which is built on a foundation of work with strategies and concepts. This not only leads to more effective learning and better retention, it also leads to development of mental math skills which will be useful throughout life. Therefore, the teaching and assessment of the basic facts in MATH TRAILBLAZERS is characterized by the following elements:

- **Emphasis on problem solving.** Students learn the basic facts easily and naturally if they are encouraged to use a problem-solving approach to find answers to unknown facts. They first approach the math facts as problems to be solved rather than facts to be memorized. Many of the same thinking processes students develop to derive facts quickly are also useful for mental calculations and estimation. They can invent their own strategies or learn strategies through class discussions. If students are encouraged to use strategies and to share their thinking, they will continue to find math meaningful and related to what they already know.

- **Use of strategies.** Students should feel confident that they can think problems through to find answers they do not recall immediately. Therefore, we encourage the use of strategies to find facts and de-emphasize rote memorization.

- **Gradual introduction of the facts.** Students study small groups of facts which can be found using similar strategies. They first work on simple strategies for easy facts and practice these facts. Then, they can learn more sophisticated strategies to learn harder facts and more efficient strategies to gain facility with all the facts.

- **Ongoing practice.** Work on the math facts is distributed throughout the curriculum. Students find a need to learn the facts as they encounter them in the labs, activities, and games. Systematic practice of small groups of facts is provided in the *Daily Practice and Problems.* Students are also encouraged to practice groups of facts at home on a regular basis.

- **Appropriate assessment.** Students are assessed through teacher observation as well as through the appropriate use of written tests and quizzes. Beginning in third grade, periodic short quizzes naturally follow the study of small groups of facts organized around specific strategies. These short quizzes are less threatening and as effective as longer tests, so we strongly recommend against the use of weekly testing of 60 to 100 facts. As self-assessment in third, fourth, and fifth grades, each student can record his or her progress on Facts I Know charts and determine which facts he or she needs to study. The goal of the math facts assessment program is to determine the degree to which students can find answers to fact problems quickly and accurately and whether they can retain this skill over time.

- **Facts will not act as gatekeepers.** Students are not prevented from learning more complex mathematics because they cannot perform well on fact tests. Use of strategies, calculators, and printed multiplication tables allow students to continue to develop number sense and work on interesting problems and experiments while they are learning the facts.

Expectations by Grade Level

Since we are committed to increasing and diversifying the mathematical content in the curriculum, our treatment of the basic facts differs from that in traditional textbooks. Specifically, we have the following goals:

In kindergarten, students use manipulatives and invent their own strategies to solve addition and subtraction problems.

By the end of first grade, all students can solve all basic addition and subtraction problems using some strategy. Facility is not emphasized; strategies are.

In second grade, strategies for addition and especially subtraction continue to be emphasized. Some work with beginning concepts of multiplication takes place. By the end of the year, all students are expected to demonstrate facility with all the addition facts.

In third grade, strategies for subtraction are encouraged, leading to facility with all the subtraction facts by the end of the year. Development of the concept of division and strategies for the multiplication facts are included.

In fourth grade, we develop strategies for the multiplication and division facts. By the end of year, we expect facility with all the multiplication facts.

By the end of fifth grade, students are expected to demonstrate facility with all the division facts as well as the addition, subtraction, and multiplication facts.

These benchmarks are somewhat later than is traditional for a number of compelling reasons. First, concepts and skills are learned more easily and are retained better if they are meaningful. By first concentrating on concepts and strategies, we increase retention and reduce the amount of time necessary for rote memorization. Second, we spread the work on the facts over more years so that more time is made available at all grade levels for other topics such as measurement, probability, and statistics that have traditionally been neglected.

...concepts and skills are learned more easily and are retained better if they are meaningful. By first concentrating on concepts and strategies, we increase retention and reduce the amount of time necessary for rote memorization.

Studying more rigorous content provides practice using the facts in meaningful settings and furnishes intrinsic motivation for gaining facility with the facts. Third, the de-emphasis of paper-and-pencil computation in the elementary curriculum has reduced the need for early mastery of the facts. If long division, multidigit multiplication, and paper-and-pencil procedures in general receive less emphasis, then students do not need to learn the facts as early, even though their eventual importance is undiminished.

Grade	Addition	Subtraction	Multiplication	Division
K	• invented strategies	• invented strategies		
1	• strategies	• strategies		
2	• strategies • practice leading to facility	• strategies		
3	• review and practice	• strategies • practice leading to facility	• strategies	• strategies
4	• assessment and remediation as required	• assessment and remediation as required	• strategies • practice leading to facility	• strategies
5			• review and practice	• strategies • practice leading to facility

Table 1: Math Facts Scope and Sequence

Strategies for Learning the Facts

As stated in the previous sections, students are encouraged to learn the math facts by first employing a variety of strategies. Over time, students develop techniques that are increasingly sophisticated and efficient. In this section, we describe possible strategies for learning the addition, subtraction, multiplication, and division facts. The strategies for each operation are listed roughly in order of increasing sophistication.

Strategies for Addition Facts

Common strategies include counting all, counting on, doubles, making or using 10, and reasoning from known facts.

Counting all

This is a particularly straightforward strategy: to solve 7 + 8, for example, the student gets 7 of something and 8 of something and counts how many there are altogether. The "something" could be beans or chips, or marks on paper. In any case, the student counts all the objects to find the sum. This is perhaps not a very efficient method, but it is effective, especially for small numbers, and is usually well understood by the student.

Counting on

This is a natural strategy, particularly for adding 1, 2, or 3. Counters such as beans or chips may or may not be used. As an example with counters, consider 8 + 3. The student gets 8 beans, and then 3 more, but instead of counting the first 8 again, she simply counts the 3 "new" beans: "9, 10, 11."

Even if counters are not used, finger gestures can help keep track of how many more have been counted on. For example, to solve 8 + 3, the student counts "9, 10, 11," holding up a finger each time a number word is said; when three fingers are up, the last word said is the answer. There are efficient finger techniques you can teach your students if you wish, or you can let them use their own intuitive methods.

Doubles

Facts such as 4 + 4 = 8 are easier to remember than facts with two different addends. Some visual imagery can help, too: two hands for 5 + 5, a carton of eggs for 6 + 6, a calendar for 7 + 7, and so on.

Making a 10

Facts with sum 10, such as 7 + 3 and 6 + 4, are also easier to remember than other facts. A ten frame can be used to develop imagery to help even more. For example, 8 is shown in a ten frame like the one in Figure 1:

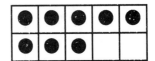

Figure 1: A ten frame

This sort of visual imagery helps the students remember, for example, that 8 + 2 = 10.

Using a 10

Students who are comfortable partitioning and combining small numbers can use that knowledge to find the sums of larger numbers. In particular, there are many strategies that involve using the number 10. For example, to find 9 + 7, we can decompose 7 into 1 + 6 and then 9 + 7 = 9 + 1 + 6 = 10 + 6 = 16. Similarly, 8 + 7 = 8 + 2 + 5 = 10 + 5 = 15.

Reasoning from known facts

If you know what 7 + 7 is, then 7 + 8 is not much harder: it's just 1 more. So, the "near doubles" can be derived from knowing the doubles. This is an example of reasoning from known facts.

Strategies for Subtraction Facts

Common strategies for subtraction include using counters, counting up, counting back, using 10, and reasoning from related addition and subtraction facts.

Using counters

This method consists of "acting out" the problem with counters like beans or chips. For example, to solve 8 – 3, the student gets 8 beans, removes 3 beans, and counts the remaining beans to find the difference. As with the addition strategy of "counting all," this is a relatively straightforward strategy that may not be efficient but has the great advantage of usually being well understood by the student.

Counting up

The student starts at the lower number and counts on to the higher number, perhaps using fingers to keep track of how many numbers are counted. For example, to solve 8 – 5, the student wants to know how to get from 5 to 8 and counts up 3 numbers: 6, 7, 8. So, 8 – 5 = 3. Special finger-counting techniques may be helpful, but this strategy seems to be a natural for most students.

Figure 2: Counting up

Counting back

Counting back works best for subtracting 1, 2, or 3; for larger numbers, it is probably best to count up. For example, to solve 9 – 2, the student counts back 2 numbers: 8, 7. So, 9 – 2 = 7.

$$9 - 2 = 7 \quad 9 \quad 8 \quad 7$$

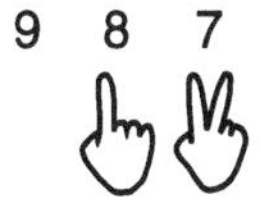

Figure 3: Counting back

Using a 10

Students follow the pattern they find when subtracting 10, e.g., 17 – 10 = 7 and 13 – 10 = 3, to learn "close facts," e.g., 17 – 9 = 8 and 13 – 9 = 4. Since 17 – 9 will be 1 more than 17 – 10, they can reason that the answer will be 8, or 7 + 1. In this strategy, 10 is a part in the whole-part-part scenario.

Making a 10

Knowing the addition facts which have a sum of 10, e.g., 6 + 4 = 10, can be helpful in finding differences from 10, e.g., 10 – 6 = 4 and 10 – 4 = 6. Students can use ten frames to visualize these problems as shown in Figure 4. These facts can then also be used to find close facts, such as 11 – 4 = 7. In this strategy, 10 is the whole in whole-part-part scenario.

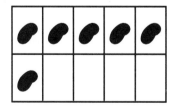

10 – 4 = 6

Figure 4: Using a ten frame

Using doubles

The addition doubles, e.g., 8 + 8 = 16 and 6 + 6 = 12, can be used to learn the subtraction "half-doubles" as well: 16 – 8 = 8 and 12 – 6 = 6. These facts can then be used to figure out close facts, such as 13 – 6 = 7 and 15 – 8 = 7.

Reasoning from related addition and subtraction facts

Knowing that 8 + 7 = 15 would seem to be of some help in solving 15 – 7. Unfortunately, however, knowing related addition facts may not be so helpful to younger or less mathematically mature students. Nevertheless, reasoning from known facts is a powerful strategy for those who can apply it and should be encouraged.

Strategies for Multiplication Facts

Common strategies for multiplication include skip counting, counting up or down from a known fact, doubling, breaking a product into the sum of known products, and using patterns.

Skip counting

Students begin skip counting and solving problems informally that involve multiplicative situations in first grade. By the time formal work with the multiplication facts is begun in third grade, they should be fairly proficient with skip counting. This strategy is particularly useful for facts such as the 2s, 3s, 5s, and 10s for which skip counting is easy.

Counting up or down from a known fact

This strategy involves skip counting forwards once or twice from a known fact. For example, if a child knows that 5 × 5 is 25, then this can be used to solve 6 × 5 (5 more) or 4 × 5 (5 less). Some children use this for harder facts. For 7 × 6, they can use the fact that 5 × 6 = 30 as a starting point and then count on by sixes to 42.

Doubling

Some children use doubling relationships to help them with multiplication facts involving 4, 6, and 8. For example, 4 × 7 is twice as much as 2 × 7. Since 2 × 7 = 14, it follows that 4 × 7 is 28. Since 3 × 8 is 24, it follows that 6 × 8 is 48.

Breaking a product into the sum of known products

A fact like 7 × 8 can be broken into the sum 5 × 8 + 2 × 8 since 7 = 5 + 2. (See Figure 5.) The previous two strategies are special cases of this more general strategy.

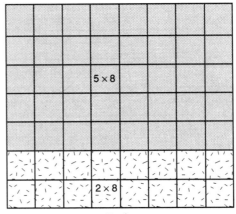

7 × 8 =
5 × 8 + 2 × 8 =
40 + 16 = 56

Figure 5: Breaking up 7 × 8

Patterns

A. Perhaps the best-known examples of patterns are the nines patterns:

1. When the nines products are listed in a column, as shown below, it is easy to see that the digits in the tens place count up by one (0, 1, 2, 3, ...) and that the digits in the ones place count down by one (9, 8, 7, ...).

   9
   18
   27
   36
   45
   54
   63
   72
   81

2. The sums of the two digits in each of the nines products above are all equal to nine. For example, the sum of the digits in 36 is 3 + 6 = 9; the sum of the digits in 72 is 7 + 2 = 9. Adding the digits of a number to see whether they add up to nine can be a strategy in remembering a nines fact. For example, a student might think, "Let me see, does 9 × 6 equal 54 or 56? It must be 54 since 5 + 4 is 9, but 5 + 6 is not 9."

3. The digit in the tens place in a nines fact is one less than the number being multiplied. For example, 4 × 9 = 36, and 3 is one less than 4. This can be combined with the previous pattern to derive nines facts. For example, 3 × 9 is in the twenties. Since 2 + 7 is 9, 3 × 9 must be 27.

4. Nines can easily be computed using the counting down strategy. Nine times a digit is the same as 10 times the digit, minus the digit. For example, 9 × 6 is 10 × 6 − 6 = 54. This works well because multiplying by 10 is so easy.

B. Other patterns: There are other patterns which can be useful in remembering other special facts:

1. 0 times a number equals 0.

2. 1 times a number equals the number.

3. 2 times a number is double the number.

4. 5 times a number ends in 0 or 5; even numbers times 5 end in 0 and odd numbers times five end in 5.

5. 10 times a number is the same number with a 0 on the end.

Sequencing the Study of Multiplication Facts

In kindergarten, children solve word problems involving multiplication situations. Beginning in first grade, the curriculum develops a conceptual foundation for multiplication through a variety of multiplication models, including the set model, array model, and number line model. Introduction of strategies to gain facility with the multiplication facts begins in Unit 13, *Multiplication Patterns,* of third grade. We do not introduce the multiplication facts in the order in which they are traditionally taught (first learning the 2s, then the 3s, then the 4s, etc.). Rather, we emphasize thinking strategies for the facts in the following order:

0s, 1s, 2s, 3s, 5s, and 10s. We call these the "Handy Facts." The 2s, 3s, 5s, and 10s are easily solved using skip counting (Third grade, Unit 13, Lesson 2).

Square numbers such as $3 \times 3 = 9$, $4 \times 4 = 16$, and $5 \times 5 = 25$. These are introduced by arranging tiles into square arrays (Third grade, Unit 13, Lesson 3).

Nines. Students explore patterns for nines in third grade. (Unit 13, Lesson 4)

Last six facts. After students have learned the facts listed above and their "turn around facts" ($9 \times 6 = 6 \times 9$), there are only six more facts to learn: 4×6, 4×7, 4×8, 6×7, 6×8, and 7×8.

Strategies for the Division Facts

The main strategy for learning the division facts is to think of the related multiplication fact. Therefore, mastery of division facts should be delayed until children have reasonable facility with the multiplication facts.

Using the "Right" Strategy

It is important to remember that different strategies appeal to different students. Students should not feel overburdened with the need to determine which is the "correct" strategy for a given fact. We do not intend to give them a new layer of things to learn. For example, when asked to explain a strategy for a fact, a student may say, "I've used it so much that now I just remember it." "Just remembering" is obviously an efficient strategy. The purpose of suggesting and discussing various strategies is to give students other, perhaps helpful, ways of learning the facts and to give them the confidence to think problems through when necessary. Students should have the opportunity to choose the strategies which work best for them or to invent their own.

Math Facts Lessons

Figure 6: Discussing fact strategies

Encouraging the everyday use of strategies such as those above is the most important part of our approach to the basic facts. Occasionally, however, we recommend special lessons that focus on particular strategies and explore how and why they work. Since our objective here is facility with all the facts, students are encouraged to choose strategies which they find effective in learning the facts.

Everyday work. As students work on problems in the labs and activities, they should be encouraged to use and to discuss various strategies for solving "math facts" problems. A number of important goals can best be reached through such discussions.

One goal is to legitimize all valid strategies, even those that may be "less efficient." When students see their intuitive methods recognized and validated, they tend to perceive mathematical knowledge as continuous with everyday knowledge and common sense. We thus hope to avoid the unfortunate tendency of many students to separate their knowledge of mathematics from their knowledge of the real world.

By discussing strategies as they arise in context, students and the teacher can explore how the strategies work and can verify that they are being used properly. Students should come to realize that a fast strategy that gives wrong answers is not very useful.

A second goal of our approach is to get the children used to communicating mathematics. There are several reasons to stress communication: Students can learn from one another; communicating a method requires higher orders of thinking than simply applying that method; and skill at communicating is important in itself. We are social creatures. Mathematics and science are social endeavors in which communication is crucial.

A third goal of encouraging discussions of various methods is to give the teacher opportunities to learn about how students think. Knowing more about students' thinking helps the teacher ask better questions and plan more effective lessons.

A final goal of discussing many strategies for solving problems is to emphasize that methods are often as important as answers. Too many students focus excessively on filling papers with correct answers. To paraphrase Thoreau, give a student an answer and you have fed her for a day; teach her a method and you have fed her for life.

Strategy lessons. We feel that occasionally it is appropriate for lessons to focus on certain strategies that are developmentally appropriate for most of your students. Our plan is to begin with simple strategies that should be accessible to all students and to progress gradually to more complex forms of reasoning. For example, in the fall of first grade, we have several lessons that stress counting on to solve certain addition problems. Later, we explicitly introduce making a 10 and other, more sophisticated, strategies.

In general, you should expect your students to come up with effective strategies on their own. Our "strategy lessons" are intended to explore how and why various strategies work and also to codify and organize the strategies the students invent. They are not meant to dictate the only appropriate strategy for a given problem or to discourage students from using strategies they understand and like. They should be seen as opportunities to discuss strategies that may be appropriate for many students and to encourage their wider use.

As students work on problems in the labs and activities, they should be encouraged to use and to discuss various strategies for solving "math facts" problems.

Our ultimate goal is to produce students who can think mathematically, who can solve problems and deal easily with quantified information, and who enjoy mathematics and are not afraid of it. It is easier to do all of the above if one has facility with the basic math facts.

Practice

Our ultimate goal is to produce students who can think mathematically, who can solve problems and deal easily with quantified information, and who enjoy mathematics and are not afraid of it. It is easier to do all of the above if one has facility with the basic math facts. We recommend, and have incorporated into the curriculum, the following practice to gain this facility.

Practice in Context

The primary practice of math facts will arise naturally for the students as they participate in the labs and other activities in the curriculum. These labs and activities offer many opportunities to practice addition, subtraction, multiplication, and division in a meaningful way. Our math facts lessons involve the student visually with drawings and patterns, auditorily through discussion, and tactually through the use of many tools such as manipulatives and calculators.

Pages of problems on the basic facts are not only unnecessary, they can be counterproductive. Students may come to regard mathematics as mostly memorization and may perceive it as meaningless and unconnected to their everyday lives.

Structured Practice

Student-friendly structured practice is built into the curriculum, especially in the *Daily Practice and Problems* and games. One small group of related math facts is presented to the students at a time. The practice of groups of facts is carefully distributed throughout the year. A small set of facts grouped in a meaningful way leads students to develop strategies such as *adding doubles, counting back,* or *using a 10* for dealing with that particular situation. Furthermore, a small set of facts is a manageable amount to learn and remember. Beginning in third grade, the learning of each small set of facts is assessed separately. Students are less stressed and more successful on the quizzes. They come to feel confident rather than overwhelmed about their abilities to remember the facts.

The *Daily Practice and Problems* is the place where much of the structured fact practice takes place. Beginning in third grade, a small group of facts to be studied in a unit is introduced here. Flash cards are presented, practice on the facts is given, and a quiz is provided. Facts are also practiced in many other problems of the DPP where the emphasis is on other interesting math. These problems allow students to focus on other interesting mathematical ideas as they are also getting more fact practice.

Games

A variety of games are included in the curriculum, both in the lessons and in the *Daily Practice and Problems* that are included in each unit. The games list can be found in the *Teacher Implementation Guide.* Once students learn the rules of the games, they should play them periodically, both in class and at home for homework. Games provide an opportunity to encourage family involvement in the math program. When a game is assigned for homework, a note can be sent home with a place for the family members to sign, affirming that they played the game with their student.

Figure 7: Playing a game

Use of Calculators

The relationship between knowing the math facts and the use of calculators is an interesting one. Using a multiplication table or a calculator when necessary to find a fact helps promote familiarity and reinforces the math facts. Students soon figure out that it is quicker and more efficient to know the basic facts than to have to use these tools. The use of calculators also requires excellent estimation skills so that one can easily check for errors in calculator computations. Rather than eliminating the need for facility with the facts, successful calculator use for solving complex problems depends on fact knowledge.

When to Practice

Practicing small groups of facts often (for short periods of time) is more effective than practicing many facts less often (for long periods of time). For example, practicing 8 to 10 subtraction facts for 5 minutes several times a week is better than practicing all the subtraction facts for half an hour once a week. Good times for practicing the facts for 5 or 10 minutes during the school day include the beginning of the day, the beginning of math class, when students have completed an assignment, when an impending activity is delayed, or when an activity ends earlier than expected. Practicing small groups of facts at home involves parents in the process and frees class time for more interesting mathematics.

Having a "math-literate" classroom will give your students many natural and meaningful chances to use mathematics and gain more practice with their math facts. We encourage you to look for opportunities to use mathematics with your students in the many occasions that arise in other subjects and throughout the day.

Assessment

The assessment of the math facts is closely aligned with the philosophy and organization of their instruction. Throughout the curriculum, teachers assess students' knowledge of the facts through observations as they work on activi-

Practicing small groups of facts often (for short periods of time) is more effective than practicing many facts less often (for long periods of time).

ties, labs, and games. In grades 3–5, students can use their Facts I Know charts to record their own progress in learning the facts. This type of self-assessment is very important in helping each student to become responsible for his or her own learning. Students are able to personalize their study of facts and not waste valuable time studying facts they already know.

At the third-grade level and above, a sequence of tests and quizzes is provided in the *Daily Practice and Problems.* The tests and quizzes assess facility of the facts appropriate at each grade level as outlined in the Expectations by Grade Level section of this tutor. As students develop strategies for a given group of facts, short quizzes accompany the practice. Students know which facts will be tested, focus practice in class and at home on those facts, then take the quiz. As they take the quiz, they use one color pencil to write answers before a given time limit, then use another color to complete the problems they need more time to answer. With the results of this type of quiz, students can use their Facts I Know charts to make a record of those facts they answered quickly, those facts they answered correctly but with less efficient strategies, and those facts they did not know at all. Using this information, students can concentrate their efforts on gaining facility with those facts they answered correctly, but not quickly. They also know to develop strategies for those facts they could not answer at all. In this way, the number of facts studied at any one time becomes more manageable, practice becomes more meaningful, and the process less intimidating.

The practice as well as the assessment of groups of facts is carefully distributed throughout the year. For example, in third grade, 72 subtraction facts are divided into eight groups of nine facts each. Each group is organized around a strategy such as *counting back* or *using a 10.* The fact groups are introduced and practiced (two groups at a time) in lessons and the *Daily Practice and Problems* for Units 2–5. These fact groups are reviewed, practiced, and then assessed through a series of quizzes in the DPP in Units 6–10. Unit 10 also includes a test of all 72 subtraction facts. The process is repeated in the second semester (Units 11–20) where each group of facts is reviewed and practiced two more times as part of the *Daily Practice and Problems* and assessed in a second series of quizzes. A second test of all 72 facts is given in the final unit.

The distribution of fact practice and assessment is similar in fourth and fifth grades. Such ongoing assessment is consistent with the goals of the math facts program. Students are evaluated on their abilities to use basic number facts quickly and accurately and to retain their skills over time. Tests of all the facts for any operation have a very limited role. They are used no more than two or three times a year to show growth over time and should not be given daily or weekly. Since we rarely, if ever, need to recall 100 facts at one time in the real world, overemphasizing tests of all the facts reinforces the notion that math is nothing more than rote memorization and has no connection to the real world. Quizzes of small numbers of facts are as effective and not as threatening. They give students, parents, and teachers the information needed to continue learning and practicing efficiently. With an assessment approach based on strategies and the use of small groups of facts, students can see mathematics as connected to their own thinking and gain confidence in their mathematical abilities.

Conclusion

Students enter school with considerable informal knowledge of mathematics. A challenge for teachers is to build on that knowledge, to make school mathematics continuous with what the students already know. One effective way to help students see connections between school mathematics and their lives outside of school is to encourage them to use their own informal strategies for solving simple addition and subtraction problems.

Recent research indicates that students learn the addition and subtraction facts easily and naturally if they are encouraged to use their own strategies. There are also indications of increased mathematical confidence in students who are encouraged to think problems through rather than rely on rote memorization. They will learn their facts as well if not better than with lots of drill, but more importantly, they will learn that mathematics is meaningful and that they can figure things out for themselves.

References

Ashlock, R.B., and Washbon, C.A. "Games: Practice Activities for the Basic Facts." In M.N. Suydam and R.E. Reys (eds.), *Developing Computational Skills: 1978 Yearbook.* Reston, Va.: National Council of Teachers of Mathematics, 1978.

Beattie, L.D. "Children's Strategies for Solving Subtraction-Fact Combinations." *Arithmetic Teacher,* 27 (1), 1979, pp. 14–15.

Brownell, W.A., and Chazal, C. B. "The Effects of Premature Drill in Third-Grade Arithmetic." *Journal of Educational Research,* 29 (1), 1935.

Carpenter, T.P., and Moser, J.M. "The Acquisition of Addition and Subtraction Concepts in Grades One through Three." *Journal for Research in Mathematics Education,* 15 (3), 1984, pp. 179–202.

Cook C.J., and Dossey, J.A. "Basic Fact Thinking Strategies for Multiplication—Revisited." *Journal for Research in Mathematics Education,* 13 (3), 1982, pp. 163–171.

Davis, E.J. "Suggestions for Teaching the Basic Facts of Arithmetic." In M.N. Suydam and R.E. Reys (eds.), *Developing Computational Skills: 1978 Yearbook.* Reston, Va.: National Council of Teachers of Mathematics, 1978.

Fuson, K.C. "Teaching Addition, Subtraction, and Place-Value Concepts." In L. Wirszup and R. Streit (eds.), *Proceedings of the UCSMP International Conference on Mathematics Education: Developments in School Mathematics Education Around the World: Applications-Oriented Curricula and Technology-Supported Learning for All Students.* Reston, Va.: National Council of Teachers of Mathematics, 1987.

Fuson, K.C., and Willis, G.B. "Subtracting by Counting Up: More Evidence." *Journal for Research in Mathematics Education,* 19 (5), 1988, pp. 402–420.

Fuson, K.C., Stigler, J.W., and Bartsch, K. "Grade Placement of Addition and Subtraction Topics in Japan, Mainland China, the Soviet Union, Taiwan, and the United States." *Journal for Research in Mathematics Education,* 19 (5), 1988, pp. 449–456.

Greer, B. "Multiplication and Division as Models of Situations." In D.A. Grouws (ed.), *Handbook of Research on Mathematics Teaching and Learning: A Project of the National Council of Teachers of Mathematics* (Chapter 13). New York: Macmillan, 1992.

Kouba, V.L., Brown, C.A., Carpenter, T.P., Lindquist, M.M., Silver, E.A., and Swafford, J.O. "Results of the Fourth NAEP Assessment of Mathematics: Number, Operations, and Word Problems." *Arithmetic Teacher,* 35 (8), 1988, pp. 14–19.

Myers, A.C., and Thornton, C.A. "The Learning-Disabled Child—Learning the Basic Facts." *Arithmetic Teacher,* 25 (3), 1977, pp. 46–50.

Rathmell, E.C. "Using Thinking Strategies to Teach the Basic Facts." In M.N. Suydam and R E. Reys (eds.), *Developing Computational Skills: 1978 Yearbook.* Reston, Va.: National Council of Teachers of Mathematics, 1978.

Rathmell, E.C., and Trafton, P.R. "Whole Number Computation." In J.N. Payne (ed.), *Mathematics for the Young Child.* Reston, Va.: National Council of Teachers of Mathematics, 1990.

Swart, W.L. "Some Findings on Conceptual Development of Computational Skills." *Arithmetic Teacher,* 32 (5), 1985, pp. 36–38.

Thornton, C.A. "Doubles Up—Easy!" *Arithmetic Teacher,* 29 (8), 1982, p. 20.

Thornton, C.A. "Emphasizing Thinking Strategies in Basic Fact Instruction." *Journal for Research in Mathematics Education,* 9 (3), 1978, pp. 214–227.

Thornton, C.A. "Solution Strategies: Subtraction Number Facts." *Educational Studies in Mathematics,* 21 (1), 1990, pp. 241–263.

Thornton, C.A. "Strategies for the Basic Facts." In J.N. Payne (ed.), *Mathematics for the Young Child.* Reston, Va.: National Council of Teachers of Mathematics, 1990.

Thornton, C.A., and Smith, P. J. "Action Research: Strategies for Learning Subtraction Facts." *Arithmetic Teacher,* 35 (8), 1988, pp. 8–12.

Portfolios
TIMS Tutor

A portfolio is a purposeful collection of a student's work that provides evidence of the student's skills, understandings, or attitudes. If the portfolio includes work collected over time, then it may also reflect the student's growth.

This tutor outlines reasons portfolios may be useful and provides some guidance for getting started and going further. A bibliography includes suggestions for additional reading.

Why Portfolios?

Portfolios can help teachers:

- better assess student learning;

- foster student autonomy;

- communicate the goals of instruction to students and parents; and

- improve their own teaching.

Student Assessment

Since a portfolio contains direct samples of student work, it may, for certain purposes, be superior to indirect indicators like grades. For example, an actual graph shows a student's skill at graphing better than a grade; and the juxtaposition of two graphs, one from September and the other from January, documents learning over time much more accurately than two grades could ever do.

Many outcomes that are hard to assess by more conventional methods—communication, reasoning, problem solving, confidence, perseverance, flexibility, and so on—can be assessed using portfolios. Portfolios can help teachers both to learn more about how students think and to track the development of that thinking.

Student Autonomy

Portfolios can encourage students to assess their own learning. Students become more self-directed and motivated by examining and reflecting on their own work and the work of their peers.

Many outcomes that are hard to assess by more conventional methods...can be assessed using portfolios. Portfolios can help teachers both to learn more about how students think and to track the development of that thinking.

Communication

Concrete examples of student work reveal much that cannot be easily conveyed in grades or comments. Parents and others can see for themselves progress and achievement.

The examples of student work in a portfolio also convey the content and goals of the curriculum in a specific way that complements the generalities of curriculum philosophies and scope and sequence charts. Portfolios focus on the work students actually do, not on ideology or wishful thinking. Communication between students and their parents, teachers, and peers can be enhanced by having particular examples to discuss.

Portfolios can help establish public norms for mathematics achievement. When assessment focuses on tests and grades, then a narrow conception of what is valuable in mathematics is communicated; when assessment is more broadly based, then a broader vision of mathematics is promoted.

Improvement of Instruction

Student portfolios can be useful both for making instructional decisions and for evaluating and improving instruction.

Certainly, better understanding of how students think and feel can help teachers make better decisions about directions for future instruction. But portfolios can also help teachers improve their teaching more generally. Portfolios can facilitate discussions with professional colleagues about different approaches to the same topic; they can reflect the range of instructional opportunities being offered; and they can indicate the use of manipulatives, group work, and technology in an implemented curriculum.

Student portfolios might be included in a Teaching Portfolio that a teacher can use for self-evaluation. One's own teaching can be refined by collecting and examining several years of student portfolios. Some of the benefits that portfolios promise for students—collegiality, establishment of public norms, improvement of higher-level skills—may thus become available to teachers.

Getting Started

The beginnings of all things are small.

–Cicero

There is no single right way to do portfolios. The suggestions offered below have worked for others and may work for you, but you should expect to learn by trial and error and to have to rely on your own judgment. If you have used portfolios for writing or some other subject, then your experience will be invaluable. If you possibly can, work with a colleague as you implement portfolios for the first time.

Starting small, with modest goals, is a good idea. For example, you may want to organize your portfolio program around one well-defined area that is hard to assess by more traditional methods. You might, for instance, choose one of the following areas as a theme for the portfolios:

- measurement

- graphing

- drawing pictures and diagrams

- communication of solution methods.

There is no single right way to do portfolios.

Besides starting small, you should also start early so that you have a baseline of student attitudes and achievement. Before and after comparisons are useful, but are impossible without early samples. All materials in a portfolio must be dated.

A box with a file folder for each child's work is a simple way to get started. If the box is easily accessible, then the portfolios are more likely to fit into classroom routines. Anticipate the need for more room as items are added to the portfolios.

What goes in the portfolios is a key question. Figure 1 shows some kinds of materials that might be included in a portfolio, although clearly no real portfolio will have such a wild collection. Figure 2 is a table of contents for a possible third-grade portfolio.

You might aim for balance in the selection of materials: group vs. individual assignments; short problems vs. longer projects; real life vs. purely mathematical problems; on-demand vs. no-deadline tasks; attitude vs. skill vs. concept-oriented work; and so on. The number of pieces should not be so few that there is not enough evidence about important outcomes, nor so many that there is no judgment about what is important or worthwhile. About eight to ten pieces might be enough for a semester.

How to pick what to put in the portfolios must also be decided. We suggest that the selection of items be made by the students subject to constraints imposed by the teacher. These constraints might range from compelling that particular items be included, to requiring that items be chosen to meet certain criteria, to allowing complete freedom of choice by the students. The amount of latitude allowed by the teacher will depend on his or her class and goals. Younger children, for example, usually need more direction. Putting fewer constraints on what goes in the portfolios may foster student autonomy, but may result in portfolios with few overlapping items so that comparisons between students are difficult, or may even yield useless collections of random scraps.

The number of pieces should not be so few that there is not enough evidence about important outcomes, nor so many that there is no judgment about what is important or worthwhile. About eight to ten pieces might be enough for a semester.

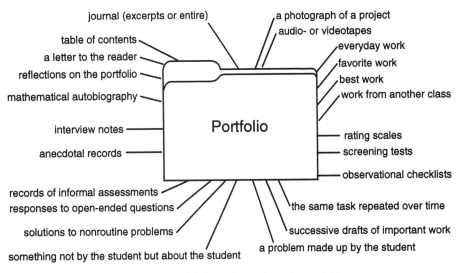

Figure 1: Possible items for mathematics portfolios

One way to organize the selection process is to have two folders for each child—a collection folder and the portfolio proper. Then, from time to time (once every several weeks or so), the collection folder can be harvested and a few select items added to the portfolio; the portfolio can also be weeded at the same time so that the total number of items does not become too large. This selection can be done by students in small groups or pairs subject to teacher constraints as described above. The items remaining in the collection folder can be kept there or sent home.

Eight to ten well-chosen and chronologically arranged pieces of work can be most useful. You will have specific examples that communicate at parent conference time what your curriculum is and how your students are progressing; you will have a sampling of the products of your instruction so that you can critically examine your teaching; and your students will be confronted with a cross section of their own work so that they can attain greater self-awareness and autonomy. You have accomplished much even if your portfolios are no more than this.

Going Further

There are, however, other things that you might want to try as you gain experience with portfolios, especially if you are working with older students. Periodic reviews of the portfolios, writing about the portfolios, and assessing the portfolios are worth considering.

	Jarrett's Portfolio • Table of Contents	
Item	Description	Date
Letter to Reader	My letter tells what my portfolio shows about my math work this semester.	1/22
Journal	A few times a week we write about math in our journals. Mine has 35 pages so far!	
Spinning Differences	I used a spinner to make subtraction problems and then graphed how many times I got each difference.	9/27
The Better "Picker Upper"	I used colored water to make spots on different kinds of paper towels. Then I counted square cm to find the areas of the spots.	10/25
Joe the Goldfish	Joe needed a raincoat and I figured out how much cloth he would need to make it.	11/1
Palindromes	A palindrome is a number that is the same frontwards and backwards. I used addition to make numbers into palindromes.	11/10
Lemonade Stand	This was the first line graph I ever made.	11/15
Mass vs. Number	I measured the mass of different numbers of marbles. Then I made a line graph and used it to make some predictions.	12/5
Stencilrama	This was my favorite. We made stencils out of index cards and then used the stencils to make designs. We had to figure out how many times we would have to move the stencil to make a border around the bulletin board.	1/15

Figure 2: Sample third-grade portfolio with an emphasis on graphing

Portfolio Review

Most teachers will be hard-pressed to find time to meet with individual students to review portfolios. Whole-class discussion and peer consultations, however, can accomplish many of the same goals.

For example, you might ask students to look through their collection folders for their best graphs to be added to their portfolios. First, through whole-class discussion, you can help students identify characteristics of a good graph. Then in small groups or pairs, students can examine their collections to pick out the best graphs. This opportunity for students to examine one another's work can help establish public norms for excellence.

Portfolio Writing

Asking students to write about the contents of their portfolios can encourage reflection and self-assessment. This writing can take a variety of forms.

The most basic writing is a table of contents with the name of each piece, a brief description, and the date it was completed. You may also want students to include who chose the piece and why, who worked on the piece, and what was learned or liked or hard about the piece.

You might ask students to write a letter to the reader of the portfolio. The letter can identify favorite pieces and explain why they are favorites, or best work, or work that shows the most progress. The letter might point out what the portfolio reveals about the student as a learner of mathematics.

Assessing the Portfolios

You should not feel that you must assess the portfolios. The work included in them, after all, has most likely been graded already, and the collection is itself a direct indicator of achievement and attitude, a direct indicator that may be sufficient for your purposes.

Assessing the portfolios, however, can have advantages, especially if you are working with older students. For one, it shows that you care about the portfolios and so communicates to the students that they should take them seriously. It can also model processes you want students to apply in peer- and self-assessment of the portfolios.

If you do intend to grade the portfolios, you should make your expectations known to the students in advance. The establishment of such public criteria for excellence, like the TIMS Student Rubrics for Grades 3–5, will help students know what they should aim for so that their work can be better focused. You might want to concentrate on how well the portfolios are organized—table of contents, correct chronological order, completeness, etc.—or on the quality of the reflective writing about the portfolio. You may want to encourage a balanced selection of items, documentation of improvement over time, clarity of communication, accuracy of self-assessment, neatness, or something else. As long as your criteria are known to the students and so long as you have the time to do it, such grading can be useful.

Conclusion

Portfolios will not solve all the problems of mathematics education. And there are some costs for using them. Using portfolios as part of an assessment program will certainly take extra time and can be difficult, especially at first. Getting students to reflect on their own learning is particularly hard. But despite such pitfalls, portfolios offer great promise for improving your teaching and your students' learning. The basic idea is simple: collect, select, reflect.

References

Crowley, Mary L. "Student Mathematics Portfolio: More Than a Display Case." *Mathematics Teacher,* 86:7, 1993, pp. 544–547.

Kuhs, Therese. "Portfolio Assessment: Making It Work for the First Time." *Mathematics Teacher,* 87:5, 1994, pp. 332–335.

Lambdin, Diana V., and Vicki L. Walker. "Planning for Classroom Portfolio Assessment." *Arithmetic Teacher,* 41:6, 1994, pp. 318–324.

Mumme, Judith. *Portfolio Assessment in Mathematics.* Santa Barbara, Calif.: University of California, 1990. (A publication of the California Mathematics Project.)

Stenmark, Jean Kerr, ed. *Mathematics Assessment: Myths, Models, Good Questions, and Practical Suggestions.* Reston, Va.: National Council of Teachers of Mathematics, 1991.

Vermont Mathematics Portfolio Project: Teacher's Guide. Montpelier, Vt.: Vermont Department of Education, 1991.

Word Problems

TIMS Tutor

In fact, word problems should not just be integrated into the mathematics curriculum; they should form the basis of the curriculum.

Carpenter, Fennema, and Peterson, 1987

Although word problems are not the *basis* of the MATH TRAILBLAZERS curriculum, we do agree that students should confront a wide variety of challenging word problems and exercises. Word problems can highlight applications of the mathematics students are learning, can be used to introduce, motivate, and develop new mathematics in a meaningful context, and, not least, can be fun.

This tutor provides a summary for teachers of recent research and background information about word problems. It is intended to outline the theoretical and practical frameworks that underlie the extensive use of word problems in MATH TRAILBLAZERS.

Problem Representations

Problems are presented to us in different ways. Sometimes a problem arises from a real situation; other times we have problems given in words, pictures, or symbols. These different ways are sometimes called modes of representation.

Real Situations

Consider this problem: "Jessica and Meri Joy baked 36 cookies. Then, Meri Joy dropped 12 cookies on the floor. How many were left?" Now this problem has a basis in reality: Jessica and Meri Joy are the daughters of two members of the MATH TRAILBLAZERS development team; they really did bake cookies; some cookies really were dropped and spoiled. Note that Meri Joy and Jessica could answer the question simply by counting the cookies that were not dropped.

Such real-life situations are the most concrete level of problem representation. People rarely go wrong when they solve such problems. (Resnick, 1987)

Concrete Model

If, however, some time has passed and the cookies are no longer at hand, we can still ask and answer the question. One way would be to get some beans and to pretend they are cookies. To solve the problem, we could count out 36 beans, separate 12, and count how many remain.

This use of beans to represent cookies is one step up the ladder of abstraction: a concrete model represents a real situation. Good evidence exists that even kindergarten students can handle complex problems that are represented by concrete models. (Carpenter, Ansell, Franke, Fennema, and Weisbeck, 1993)

Figure 1: Twelve of 36 cookies dropped

Pictures

Another way to approach the problem is via pictures. Each cookie could be represented by a circle. We could solve the problem by drawing 36 circles, crossing out 12, and counting those left.

This sort of pictorial representation is often useful in mathematics and science. Even when the picture does not lead immediately to a solution, it often helps us understand the problem situation and starts us on the road to a solution.

Verbal Representations

Most school problems are stated in words. This is often necessary (How else could our cookie problem have been presented in this essay?) and builds on a well-developed set of skills your students have—their language skills.

Language is the first and most powerful symbol system we learn. The recent emphasis on discourse and communication in learning is based at least in part on a recognition of the importance of language in human thought.

Symbols

We can also represent Jessica and Meri Joy's cookies in symbols:

$$36 - 12 = \square$$

Such symbolic representations are abstract and powerful. Much of the explosive growth of mathematics in the last 400 years is due to the invention of more efficient symbol systems.

Unfortunately, for too many students, mathematical symbolism is a code they never crack. Such students do not see the marks on paper as meaningful or related to the real world in any way. Instead, they see the marks as part of an arcane game.

When writing number sentences, it is important to use units. Of course, constantly writing the units can be tedious; one compromise is to omit the units in the middle of a sequence of symbolic representations, but to be sure to include them at the beginning and again at the end.

We want students to learn to write, read, and understand mathematical symbolism, especially number sentences. Here, word problems can be particularly useful. The situations in many word problems are straightforward enough that the corresponding number sentences are simple.

Usually, several number sentences are appropriate for each problem. Consider, for example, the following problem: "Janice had 9 stickers. Then her mother gave her some more. Then Janice had 16 stickers. How many stickers did Janice's mother give her?"

An adult might see this as a subtraction problem and write

$$16 - 9 = 7 \tag{a}$$

or

$$16 - 9 = \square \tag{b}$$

These number sentences are in the normal or "canonical" form. That is, the known quantities are on the left-hand side of the equals sign and the unknown or the answer is on the right-hand side.

Even when the picture does not lead immediately to a solution, it often helps us understand the problem situation and starts us on the road to a solution.

Many students, however, write something like

$9 + \square = 16$ (c)

or

$9 + 7 = 16$ (d)

These "non-canonical" forms reflect the students' way of thinking about the problem: Janice had 9 stickers, then she got some more, and then she had 16 stickers. Often a student who writes (c) or (d) will solve the problem by counting on from 9 to 16 rather than by subtracting 9 from 16. We consider these "non-canonical" number sentences to be as correct as the canonical forms. They can also be more understandable for the students.

Translations Between Representations

So we have a hierarchy of levels of representation: real objects, physical models, pictures, words, symbols.

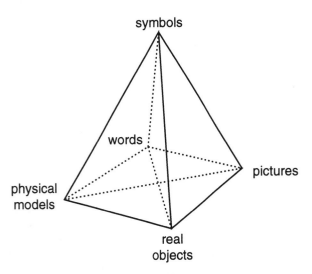

Figure 2: Modes of representation

But perhaps "hierarchy of levels" is not quite the right phrase; it may be better to consider that there are a number of different modes of representation, each of which has certain strengths and weaknesses. Recent cognitive theory indicates that the ability to translate from one representation to another is a crucial part of conceptual understanding and problem-solving skill. Being able to connect symbols with real referents, for example, permits one to understand symbolic manipulations and results in terms of real situations. Earlier, we saw how translating a problem from a real or verbal presentation to a concrete model could yield a solution by an elementary method.

Unfortunately, too much instruction in mathematics focuses exclusively on symbols. While symbolic representations are compact and powerful, they cannot stand alone. Our goal is to have students create mental "two-way streets" between symbols, words, concrete models, pictures, and real situations. Word problems are an excellent vehicle for reaching this goal.

Recent cognitive theory indicates that the ability to translate from one representation to another is a crucial part of conceptual understanding and problem-solving skill.... Our goal is to have students create mental "two-way streets" between symbols, words, concrete models, pictures, and real situations.

Solving Problems

One view of problem solving is that the most critical step is developing the right representation: when we see the problem in the correct light, then the solution is obvious. Of course, the right representation for me might not be right for you. Accordingly, just as multiple representations should be part of the mathematics curriculum, so should multiple solutions. Estimation and attention to the reasonableness of results must also be part of instruction in problem solving.

Multiple Solutions

Many students think the main thing in mathematics is to get the right answer. Incorrect or partial answers are seen as failures, and re-solving a problem in a different way is considered futile.

On the contrary, much can be learned by solving problems in several ways. When different methods yield the same answer, students gain confidence both in the answer and in the various methods. This can be particularly useful for students learning more abstract and powerful methods: if a more powerful method gives the same answer as a more familiar method, then the powerful method is more likely to be understood and trusted.

Students can also see connections within mathematics by comparing the points of view that generate different solutions to a problem. Making such connections is a key goal of the National Council of Teachers of Mathematics *Curriculum and Evaluation Standards* (NCTM, 1989). If students share their solution methods, then not only do they learn new methods from one another, but they also learn to communicate mathematically, another *Standards* goal.

Even incorrect or partial answers can be useful. Wrong answers are almost always the result of an honest attempt by the student to get the problem right. Examining and discussing wrong answers and the procedures that generated them can make students' thinking explicit so that misconceptions can be identified and cleared up.

Sometimes a partial answer is the best we can reasonably hope for. In fact, many practical problems are impossible or prohibitively expensive to solve exactly. In some real situations, a partial answer may be all that is required. A partial solution may be based on an idea that can be modified or extended to yield a complete solution. If a problem is hard, then making progress towards an answer is perfectly respectable, and certainly far better than giving up.

One way to get the most out of partial solutions is to encourage students to talk and write about the problem even if they cannot solve it. This will also help students stay with difficult problems longer.

Estimation

A common reason for estimating is that an exact answer is not necessary. If we have $5 and want to buy milk, bread, and eggs, a quick estimate will tell us if we have enough money. Sometimes an estimate must serve because an exact answer is impossible or impractical to obtain. The exact number of piano tuners who live in Chicago, for example, can only be estimated.

Another reason to estimate an answer is to verify the accuracy of a result obtained in some other way. This is especially important in our age of computing machines—if we do not have some idea what the answer should be, then we may be at a loss to know whether the answer the machine gives us is reasonable.

A less commonly recognized reason to make an estimate is as a step on the way to an exact answer. As one of our favorite teachers used to say, "Never solve a problem until you know the answer." We think he meant that finding an approximate answer can be helpful in the search for the exact answer. By estimating an answer, we come to understand the problem better.

Learning to estimate builds number sense and encourages students to rely on their common sense rather than on rote procedures. Making a good estimate requires a flexible combination of common sense, experience, rules of thumb, and specific knowledge. Estimation is a high-level skill that takes a long time to develop. Estimation is, accordingly, built into MATH TRAILBLAZERS from the beginning.

Reasonableness of Results

How often have you seen a student's paper with patently absurd answers? Such answers indicate that the student is not working at a meaningful level. Rather some procedures—half-understood, half-remembered—have been carried out and something has been produced, but the relationship of that product to the problem at hand is far from clear. No connection exists in the student's mind between the real situation and the symbolic manipulations.

Looking back when an answer is obtained, mapping the result of symbolic or other manipulations back onto the original problem statement, is a crucial part of the problem-solving process. George Polya, in his famous book *How to Solve It* (1957), included looking back as one of four basic steps in solving a problem. (Polya's other steps are to: understand the problem; to make a plan to solve the problem; and to carry out the plan.)

When students look back at a solution, they should assess whether it is reasonable and correct. They can also look for ways to improve the solution, simplify it, or generalize it. By comparing their solution to other solutions, they can obtain further evidence of correctness and they have an opportunity to make connections between different approaches.

Addition and Subtraction Problem Types

Children typically use many varied methods to solve word problems. This, in part, is related to the fact that there is an underlying variety of problem types. The different problem types have been explored extensively by educational researchers in the last 15 years or so. Several different examples are discussed here. Additional discussion about the methods children use to solve problems can be found in the TIMS Tutor: *Math Facts.*

Students should have experience solving many different types of word problems. It is important to note, however, that in discussing the different problem types, we are not suggesting a new level of material for children to learn, i.e., we do not expect nor want children to have to learn about the different types of problems as a study in and of itself. Rather, we discuss the diversity in problem types so that teachers recognize that this variety exists and subsequently are better prepared to present their students with a rich and varied collection of word problems.

Thomas Carpenter and his colleagues (Carpenter, Fennema, and Peterson, 1987; Carpenter, Carey, and Kouba, 1990) have devised a classification scheme for problems that most adults would solve by simple addition or subtraction. They identify four general types of situations which give rise to 11 different kinds of addition or subtraction problems. (Other researchers have devised similar schemes. See, for example, Riley, Greeno, and Heller, 1983, and Rathmell and Huinker, 1989.)

Join Situations

Carpenter begins with "join" situations. Here, something is joined to a beginning quantity so that a new quantity results. We think of these situations like this:

start + change = result

If the result is unknown, then we have an addition problem. Otherwise, we have a subtraction problem. Children often have more difficulty with problems in which the start is unknown than those in which the change is unknown.

Join/Result Unknown
Erick had 8 action figures. Then his father gave him 3 new ones. How many did he have then?

Join/Change Unknown
Janice had 9 stickers. Then her mother gave her some more. Then Janice had 16 stickers. How many stickers did Janice's mother give her?

Join/Start Unknown
Maria had some pennies. Then she found 3 more. Then she had 12 pennies. How many pennies did Maria have at first?

Take-Away Situations

We call Carpenter's second category "take-away." Here again, there is a beginning quantity, a change, and a result, but this time the change is negative. We think of these situations like this:

start – change = result

If the result or change is unknown, then we have a subtraction problem. Otherwise, we have an addition problem.

Take-Away/Result Unknown
Thomas had 8 cookies. Then he ate 6. How many cookies did he have left?

Take-Away/Change Unknown
Leah had 12 dolls. Then she gave some of her dolls away. Then she had 7 dolls left. How many dolls did Leah give away?

Take-Away/Start Unknown
Michael had some marbles. Then he lost 5 of his marbles. Then he had 7 marbles. How many marbles did Michael have at first?

Part-Whole Situations

Carpenter's third category is part-whole. Here, a single whole is broken into two parts:

part + part = whole

This is similar to the join situation. The difference is that part-whole situations are static, the two parts coexisting from the beginning, whereas in join situations, two things are put together to form a new whole.

If the whole is unknown in a part-whole situation, then we have an addition problem. Otherwise, we have a subtraction problem.

Part-Whole/Whole Unknown
Ian has some action figures. He has 8 good guys and 3 bad guys. How many action figures does Ian have altogether?

Part-Whole/Part Unknown
There are 14 children who live in Clayton's building. Five of the children are boys. How many girls live in Clayton's building?

Compare Situations

Carpenter's last category is "compare." Here, two independent quantities are being compared:

$$q1 - q2 = \text{difference}$$

If the difference or q2 is unknown, then we subtract. If q1 is unknown, we add.

Compare/Difference Unknown
Samantha has $14. Kristin has $5. How much more money does Samantha have?

Compare/Q2 Unknown
Jason has 13 crayons. Angela has 6 fewer than Jason. How many crayons does Angela have?

Compare/Q1 Unknown
Lamar has some markers. Robin has 15 markers. Robin has 7 fewer markers than Lamar has. How many markers does Lamar have?

Compare problems seem to be the hardest for children to solve. The other three types—join, take-away, and part-whole—all involve a whole with parts in situations that are either static or dynamic. In compare problems, on the other hand, there is no whole. Rather, there are two independent quantities and a difference between them.

Need for Diversity in Problem Types

Traditionally, just two of these 11 kinds of problems have dominated American elementary mathematics textbooks, a dominance that contrasts sharply with customary practice abroad (Stigler, Fuson, Ham, & Kim, 1986; Fuson, Stigler, & Bartsch, 1988). These favored problem types, moreover, are the easiest to solve: most of the subtraction problems are take-away/result unknown; most of the addition problems are join/result unknown. By presenting such a limited variety of problems, these texts give students a wrong impression about what addition and subtraction are. Carpenter's four situations—join, take-away, part-whole, and compare—and the various types of problems reflect a much wider conception of addition and subtraction. In MATH TRAILBLAZERS, we present this full range of addition and subtraction problems beginning in the earliest grades.

Types of Multiplication and Division Problems

Researchers who have studied multiplication and division have identified different types of multiplication and division problems. While students do not need to be able to identify these different types of problems by name, it is important that they encounter and solve them. The different types of multiplication and division problems are outlined below.

Problems Involving a Number of Equivalent Sets

These sets can be groups of objects, arrays, or jumps on the number line. An example might be: Ask a class of 20 students to stand in a group. Instruct them to break into teams of four.

Traditionally, just two of these 11 kinds of problems have dominated American elementary mathematics textbooks, a dominance that contrasts sharply with customary practice abroad.... These favored problem types, moreover, are the easiest to solve.

Using this situation, three different questions emerge. One question is interpreted as a multiplication problem, the other two as division problems.

The Unknown Is the Total Number in All the Groups

If there are 5 teams with 4 members on each team, how many players are there in all? There are two known factors and a missing product. Using established knowledge, students often interpret this correctly as a repeated addition problem $(4 + 4 + 4 + 4 + 4 = 20)$. Through classroom experiences with many such problems, they can connect the repeated addition sentence to a multiplication sentence $(5 \times 4 = 20)$.

The Unknown Is the Number of Groups

Twenty members of a class are divided into teams of four members each. How many teams are there? The problem gives the total number in all the groups and the measure or size of each group. This aspect of division is called *measurement division*.

The Unknown Is the Number in Each Group

Twenty members of a class are divided equally into five teams. How many students are on each team? The problem gives the total number of students and the number of partitions or groups. This aspect of division is known as *partitive division*.

Jumps on a number line and arrays provide additional experience with the multiplication and division of equivalent sets. Successive jumps of equal size on a number line provide a model for multiplication as repeated addition and division as repeated subtraction. In *MATH TRAILBLAZERS*, we model this situation using mythical creatures called "mathhoppers." For example, a +2 mathhopper starts at 0 and hops 4 times. On what number will it land?

An array is a group of objects arranged in rows and columns. For example, a candy box that contains 5 rows with 6 pieces in each row is a 5×6 array. One virtue of the array model is that it makes it very clear that $5 \times 6 = 6 \times 5$. The box can be rotated 90 degrees to form a 6×5 array. Another advantage is that it creates a visual image for both multiplication and division problems.

Problems Involving Scale Factors

This type of problem is often found in TIMS Laboratory Experiments. For example, after students have rolled three different cars down a ramp, they might be asked if one car rolled three times as far as another. Similarly, when finding the mass of objects, they may be asked if the mass of one object is one-half the mass of another object.

A Cartesian Product

This problem involves two sets of objects (such as shirts and pants) which must be joined into pairs (shirt-and-pant sets). The answer for this type of problem then becomes the number of unique pairs that can be formed from these two sets. While this type of problem is difficult for young children, they are able to solve it using manipulatives and diagrams.

Experiences with many types of problems should provide a strong conceptual foundation not only for multiplication and division, but for fractions, ratios, and proportional reasoning as well.

Problem Contexts

Most word problems in *MATH TRAILBLAZERS* are embedded in a larger context; this is often an advantage since situational problems are more meaningful to the students than abstract problems. Sometimes, however, providing a context is constraining or distracting. Also, problems may come to us without context; often, we have to provide extra information to make sense of a problem. Accordingly, in an attempt to provide a balance between problems embedded in situations and problems that are self-contained, we often provide free-standing word problems.

Teaching Word Problems

A variety of approaches to teaching word problem solving can be useful and stimulating. Here are several:

Whole Class, then Small Groups

First, present a sample problem to your whole class. Discuss the problem and ask students to estimate the answer. Also ask students to explain how they made their estimates. Neither the estimates nor the explanations are likely to be very good, but this is only the beginning.

Next, ask the students to solve the problem in groups of two or three students. Tell them you want (1) an answer for the problem, (2) an explanation of how the answer was obtained, and (3) a number sentence for the problem.

You might require that students who need help seek it first from other students in their groups. Clearly, this is beneficial for the students who need the help, but those who give the help also benefit since they must make explicit what they may understand only implicitly. You will also be freed up since your students will be helping one another instead of depending so much on you.

As the students work, you can move among them, listening to the strategies various groups are using. Use your judgment about what questions to ask and how much help to give, but try to restrain yourself: it will often be better if students struggle on their own as much as possible.

When the groups have answers, reconvene the whole class and ask students to explain their solutions and number sentences for the problem. Be sure they assess the reasonableness and correctness of their results. During these discussions, you should emphasize that every student is responsible for understanding his or her group's solution. One way to accomplish this is to call on random students to explain each group's work.

You can encourage students to solve problems in more than one way by accepting only novel solutions during class discussions. Thus, students will be motivated to search for multiple solutions in order to be able to contribute to the class discussion.

Small Groups, then Whole Class

As your students gain experience, you can abbreviate or eliminate the whole-class introduction to the problem. Again, a whole-class discussion of solutions is appropriate.

Individual Work, then Small Groups

One approach we like is for students to work individually first and then to come together in pairs or small groups to compare solutions. Then, the small-group solutions can be shared with other groups during a class discussion.

Other Suggestions

You might find some word problems appropriate for homework or for individual seatwork. Other problems may be so hard that no student is able to solve them; such problems can be used for whole-class investigations. You may want to use certain problems to introduce new mathematics like multiplication and division. An interesting problem can be used as an "opener" when students arrive or when math class begins.

TIMS Tips

- If students cannot solve a problem, ask them to describe the problem and to restate it in their own words or ask them to draw a picture. This may lead to a better understanding of the problem and then to a solution.

- Do only a few problems at a time. Distributed practice will be more effective than bunched practice.

- Vary the format: individual, small group, whole class, homework.

- Be sure to discuss multiple solution strategies. Compare and contrast strategies, and point out advantages of each, but accept all correct strategies.

- Discuss several number sentences for each problem. Ask students to explain how a given number sentence fits the problem situation.

- Ask students to explain why the answers they have are reasonable.

- Provide manipulatives and calculators to each group. Just having them available in the room may not be enough—these resources should be immediately at hand.

Conclusion

As your students work word problems and share solutions, they will be applying mathematics they already know, learning new mathematics, and having fun. Word problems deserve a prominent place in your mathematics and science lessons.

References

Carpenter, T.P., E. Fennema, and P. Peterson. "Cognitively Guided Instruction: The Application of Cognitive and Instructional Science to Mathematics Curriculum Development." In *Developments in School Mathematics Education Around the World,* I. Wirszup and R. Streit, eds. Reston, Va.: National Council of Teachers of Mathematics, 1987.

Carpenter, T. P., D. Carey, and V. Kouba. "A Problem-Solving Approach to the Operations." In *Mathematics for the Young Child,* J.N. Payne, ed. Reston, Va.: National Council of Teachers of Mathematics, 1990.

Carpenter, T. P., E. Ansell, M. L. Franke, E. Fennema, and L. Weisbeck. "Models of Problem Solving: A Study of Fourth Grade Children's Problem-Solving Processes." *Journal for Research in Mathematics Education,* 24 (5), 1993, pp. 428–441.

Fuson, K. C., J. W. Stigler, and K. Bartsch. "Grade Placement of Addition and Subtraction Topics in Japan, Mainland China, the Soviet Union, Taiwan, and the United States." *Journal for Research in Mathematics Education,* 19 (5), 1988, pp. 449–456.

National Council of Teachers of Mathematics. *Curriculum and Evaluation Standards for School Mathematics.* Reston, Va.: National Council of Teachers of Mathematics, 1989.

Polya, G. *How to Solve It.* Princeton, N.J.: Princeton University Press, 1957.

Rathmell, E. C. & D. M. Huinker. "Using Part-Whole Language to Help Children Represent and Solve Word Problems." In *New Directions for Elementary School Mathematics,* P. R. Trafton, ed. Reston, Va.: National Council of Teachers of Mathematics, 1989.

Resnick, L. B. "Presidential Address: Learning In School and Out." *Educational Researcher,* 16 (9), 1987, pp. 13–20.

Riley, M. S., J. G. Greeno, and J. I. Heller. "Development of Children's Problem-Solving Ability in Arithmetic." In *The Development of Mathematical Thinking,* H. P. Ginsburg, ed. New York: Academic Press, 1983.

Stigler, J. W., K. C. Fuson, M. Ham, and M. S. Kim. "An Analysis of Addition and Subtraction Word Problems in American and Soviet Elementary Mathematics Textbooks." *Cognition and Instruction,* 3 (3), 1986, pp. 153–171.

The TIMS Laboratory Method

TIMS Tutor

MATH TRAILBLAZERS is a comprehensive mathematics program that incorporates many important scientific ideas. Scientific concepts often provide contexts for developing and practicing math concepts and skills. The tools and processes of science are integral to mathematical problem solving throughout the curriculum.

This tutor expands upon the *MATH TRAILBLAZERS* connection with science. It outlines the TIMS view of science and describes the TIMS Laboratory Method, a version of the scientific method. This method forms a framework throughout the curriculum for students to explore science in much the way scientists work.

| Part I | The TIMS View of Science |

Outline

The tutor is organized as follows:

Part I: The TIMS View of Science

Part II: Variables in Scientific Experiments

Variables and Values

Manipulated and Responding Variables in Controlled Experiments

Fixed Variables in Controlled Experiments

Part III: The TIMS Laboratory Method

Phase 1: Beginning the Investigation/ Drawing the Picture

Phase 2: Collecting and Organizing the Data

Phase 3: Graphing the Data

Bar Graphs vs. Point Graphs

Labeling the Axes

Bar Graphs in *MATH TRAILBLAZERS*

Point Graphs: Fitting Lines and Curves

Predictions from Point Graphs: Interpolation and Extrapolation

Phase 4: Analyzing the Data

Picture, Table, Graph, and Questions: Putting It Together

Mathematics in Context

References

Traditionally, school science has focused on the results of science. Students learn about parts of the body, types of rocks, the solar system, evolution, and so on. Knowing basic facts of science is seen as part of being educated, today more than ever. However, the facts of science, important and interesting as they are, do not alone comprise a comprehensive and balanced science curriculum.

The great educator and philosopher John Dewey expressed this idea more than 85 years ago. In 1910, he wrote:

At times, it seems as if the educational availability of science were breaking down because of its sheer mass. There is at once so much of science and so many sciences that educators oscillate, helpless, between arbitrary selection and teaching a little of everything.

Visit schools where they have taken nature study conscientiously. This school moves with zealous bustle from leaves to flowers, from flowers to minerals, from minerals to stars, from stars to the raw materials of industry, thence back to leaves and stones.

Thus,... science teaching has suffered because science has been so frequently presented just as so much ready-made knowledge, so much subject-matter of fact and law, rather than as the effective method of inquiry into any subject-matter.

Surely if there is any knowledge which is of most worth it is knowledge of the ways by which anything is entitled to be called knowledge instead of being mere opinion or guess-work or dogma.

Such knowledge ... is not information, but a mode of intelligent practise, an habitual disposition of mind.

In 1996, the National Research Council (NRC) published the *National Science Education Standards* for K–12 science education. Among the many recommendations of the NRC document is a direction for decreased emphasis on teaching scientific facts and information, and increased emphasis on teaching for understanding of scientific concepts and developing abilities of inquiry. The NRC *Standards* state:

Emphasizing active science learning means shifting away from teachers presenting information and covering science topics. The perceived need to include all the topics, vocabulary, and information in textbooks is in direct conflict with the central goal of having students learn scientific knowledge with understanding.

If we were to describe the TIMS approach in the most concise way possible, we would choose two words, variable *and* experiment.

These points of view underlie the TIMS approach to science. If we were to describe the TIMS approach in the most concise way possible, we would choose two words, *variable* and *experiment*. The essence of modern science, as it is practiced by scientists, is to understand the relationships among variables. Out of the great sea of variables we have selected those that we feel are fundamental to the understanding of all areas of science, namely: length, area, volume, mass, and time. These variables might be considered the fundamental vocabulary of science. They are integral to the everyday work of biologists, chemists, physicists, astronomers, and earth scientists. The more that a child has explored these variables, the greater will be his or her command of scientific language and the more complete will be his or her ability to take up the adventure of science.

We have therefore made these variables the focus of experiments and activities in grades K through 5 of MATH TRAILBLAZERS. Explorations in kindergarten are conceptual in nature. As the curriculum progresses through the grades, students revisit the variables many times in increasingly more sophisticated ways. In grade 5, students are able to move on to compound variables such as density and velocity, which involve two of the basic variables. For example, density involves both mass and volume while velocity involves both length and time. To understand these compound variables, it is important that students are first familiar with the more basic variables. Through repeated investigation of the variables in different contexts, fundamental science concepts and skills become generalized.

Part II   ## Variables in Scientific Experiments

According to the dictionary, a variable is a quantity that may assume any one of a set of values. The variable is the heart and soul of science because the variable is to scientific investigation what the word is to language—its foundation and the basis of its structure. All experiments center around at least two variables, and the ability to measure these variables satisfactorily will determine the success or failure of the experiment.

Variables and Values

Variables fall into two broad categories: categorical and numerical. Would you say that the color of a person's hair is a categorical or a numerical variable? Would you say that the height of a person is a categorical or numerical variable? We shall define a numerical variable as one that may assume a numerical set of values. In contrast, a categorical variable is one which does not assume numerical values.

Color, then, which can take on values such as red, blue, or yellow, is a categorical variable. Other categorical variables are shape, kind of object, and type of material of which the object is made. In each case, you have the broad classification, the variable, and then the values the variable can assume.

The simplest kind of numerical variable is the number of objects in a set. For example, if we were studying the number of students who came to class each day, the variable would be "Number of Students," and the possible values of the variable would be 0 students, 1 student, 2 students, etc. A second category of numerical variable is those involving measurement. The basic measurement variables stressed in MATH TRAILBLAZERS are length, area, volume, mass, and time. The values for these variables are what we measure during the course of an experiment. For example, if we are investigating the variable length, the values might be the number of meters, centimeters, millimeters, or other appropriate unit of length. When the **variable** is area, the **values** might be the number of square centimeters. Or if volume is the variable, the value might be the number of cubic centimeters, and so on. The variable is the broad classification; the values for the variable describe what we are counting or measuring for that variable.

One point in studying variables that will take repeated practice for your students to master is the regular use of units of measure. In science, we never deal with numbers without understanding what their units are. For example, say that we tell you that Mary dropped a ball from a height of 30. A question your students will learn to ask is, "Thirty what?" Was it 30 centimeters, 30 feet, or 30 miles? The name after the number 30 is what we call the unit of measure, and every variable has a set of them. $5 + 4 = 9$ can be meaningless unless we know 5 of what. 5 apples + 4 apples = 9 apples, but 5 apples + 4 pears does not equal either 9 apples or 9 pears. The sum is equal to 9 pieces of fruit. Invariably, children will give you the numerical value of the variable and leave off its unit. Learning to use units is merely a matter of discipline; that is, using them correctly so often that you feel uncomfortable when you either forget them or use them incorrectly. Developing this discipline in your students will help them later in their schooling as they examine more complicated scientific concepts.

Manipulated and Responding Variables in Controlled Experiments

In an experiment, a scientist tries to find a relationship between two variables. Where possible, the experimenter chooses ahead of time the values of one of the variables. This variable is called the manipulated variable. The values of the second variable are determined by the results of the experiment—something that the experimenter does not know ahead of time. We shall call the variable whose values result from the experiment, the responding variable.

For example, consider the following situation from a fourth-grade experiment, *The Bouncing Ball*. In this experiment, children study how high a ball bounces. They drop a ball from various heights and measure how high it bounces. As the experimenters, they decide what drop heights they want to use in the experiment, say 40 cm, 80 cm, and 120 cm. The drop height is the manipulated variable. But the height to which the ball bounces can only be determined after you drop the ball. It is not known ahead of time. So, the bounce height is the responding variable.

Or, say that you fill a plastic jar with different-colored blocks and that you have chosen red, yellow, and blue as the colors of your blocks. You then ask a child to reach in and pull out as many pieces as he or she can in one grab, sort the blocks by color, and count them. Color is the manipulated variable in this experiment. The number of each color that he or she pulls out is the responding variable. You choose the values of the colors that go in but you have no choice over the number of each color that comes out.

Beginning in the first grade of MATH TRAILBLAZERS, the experimental variables are identified in all laboratory experiments. This is an essential part of conducting any scientific experiment. It is not until fourth grade, however, that we introduce the formal terms "manipulated" and "responding."

Note that in MATH TRAILBLAZERS, we have elected to use the terms "manipulated" and "responding" to describe experimental variables. We have found manipulated and responding to be less abstract for children (and adults) and easier to understand than the more commonly used terms for variables, "independent" and "dependent."

Fixed Variables in Controlled Experiments

Experiments often have more than two variables. In an ideal experiment, more easily realized in the laboratory than in the real world, a scientist focuses on only two variables—the ones we have called manipulated and responding—and strives to hold all others constant. If too many variables change simultaneously in an experiment, obtaining meaningful results can be difficult or impossible.

Consider a laboratory experiment done in second grade, *Rolling Along in Centimeters*. Students roll different kinds of cars down a ramp and use meter-sticks to measure the distance each car rolls. Here, the "type of car" is the manipulated variable and the distance each car rolls is the responding variable. The height of the ramp, the starting line, the floor onto which the cars roll, and the method for releasing the car are all held constant each time a car is rolled down the ramp. We refer to these as the "fixed variables" (or "controlled variables") in the experiment. Children intuitively understand this as "keeping things fair" while the data are collected during the course of the experiment.

In many situations, some of the variables in an experiment are "hidden"; that is, they are not immediately obvious, although changing them will greatly alter the results of your experiment. Consider an experiment in which you collect data on the kinds of pets owned by each child in the classroom. The kind of pet is the manipulated variable and the number of each kind of pet is the responding variable. If you think about it, you can see that your results depend upon where the pet owners live—in a high rise or a single-family house, in the city or a farm community, and even in which country. Thus the variable, "location," can drastically change the results.

One of the reasons cancer research is so difficult is because there are so many variables which are either difficult or impossible to control (such as environmental factors, personality traits, multitudinous viruses) that it is hard to pinpoint the variables that might be the cause of cancer. It is the complexity of

In an ideal experiment, more easily realized in the laboratory than in the real world, a scientist focuses on only two variables—the ones we have called manipulated and responding—and strives to hold all others constant. If too many variables change simultaneously in an experiment, obtaining meaningful results can be difficult or impossible.

biological and sociological systems that makes doing repeatable experiments in these areas very difficult.

Nonetheless, children can learn how to deal with simple physical systems where three or four variables are present. They should learn how to recognize the different variables involved and understand the importance of controlling all but two—the manipulated and the responding variable.

Part III

The TIMS Laboratory Method

Throughout MATH TRAILBLAZERS, children carry out quantitative investigations in which they explore the relationships between variables. Each investigation is carried out with the same general format, which we call the TIMS Laboratory Method. One may call this our version of the scientific method. There are four phases: beginning the investigation/drawing the picture, collecting and organizing the data, graphing the data, and analyzing the experimental results. We discuss these four phases below, illustrating our discussion with references to *The Bouncing Ball* experiment described above and to *Marshmallows and Containers,* a second-grade experiment in which children study the number of marshmallows that fit into different-sized jars.

Phase 1: Beginning the Investigation/Drawing the Picture

Most investigations begin with a question. The question does not have to be momentous, but it must be meaningful to children. If the question connects in some authentic way with their experience, children will need no flashy inducements to want to find the answer. This is illustrated in the following classroom anecdote involving *Marshmallows and Containers.*

> As class begins, students sit together in groups of three. Each group has three different containers: a margarine tub, a 100 cc graduated cylinder, and a small paper cup. The teacher shows the class a bag of miniature marshmallows and asks, "Which container will hold the most marshmallows? Why do you think so?"
>
> The teacher encourages the groups to discuss their predictions and explanations and to record their ideas in their journals. When the groups report to the class, many groups think that the graduated cylinder will hold the most because it is the tallest. One boy explains that he thinks the cylinder holds the most because even if he could stretch the plastic in the bowl so it was tall like the cylinder, it still would not be as tall and would not hold as much. Other groups choose the tub because it is fatter than the other containers.
>
> The teacher then asks, "How could you find out which container holds the most marshmallows?" This question leads naturally to an experiment: The students will fill each of the containers with marshmallows, count them, and record the numbers in a data table.

Once a suitable question has been posed—and posing such questions is far from trivial—then variables related to the question must be identified. *Marshmallows and Containers* examines the kind of container and the number of marshmallows. The size of the marshmallows and the method for packing the marshmallows into the jars is held fixed. In *The Bouncing Ball,* students measure the drop heights and bounce heights of a ball, while holding fixed the type of ball, the floor onto which the ball is dropped, and the method for dropping the ball.

Through class discussion, the original question has been refined into a precise query about the relationship between two variables. These variables become defined well enough so that the children know how to gather information about them. Drawing a picture is an excellent way to summarize and communicate this beginning phase, and also to plan what is to come.

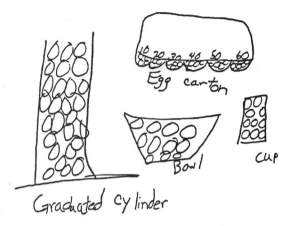

Figure 1: Picture for Marshmallows and Containers

Figure 2: Picture for The Bouncing Ball

Scientists often make sketches in experimental situations. In the TIMS Laboratory Method, drawing pictures helps children understand and organize what they are to do. A sketch gives the child time to think, to see relationships between variables, to place diverse relationships in a compact form, and to "explain" the experiment or problem to someone at a glance.

Scientists often make sketches in experimental situations. In the TIMS Laboratory Method, drawing pictures helps children understand and organize what they are to do. A sketch gives the child time to think, to see relationships between variables, to place diverse relationships in a compact form, and to "explain" the experiment or problem to someone at a glance. Pictures also help teachers assess whether students are ready to proceed. Figure 1 shows one student's picture for *Marshmallows and Containers*. The picture indicates the student's understanding of the experimental variables and the procedure. Note that the student is using an egg carton to make groups of 10 when counting marshmallows. Figure 2 shows a picture from *The Bouncing Ball*, indicating the manipulated and responding variables (the drop height and the bounce height) and the procedure for the experiment. The students who drew these pictures are ready to go on to the next step, gathering data.

Phase 2: Collecting and Organizing the Data

In Phase 2 of the TIMS Laboratory Method, children gather the data and organize it in a table. To illustrate, we return to our classroom anecdote involving *Marshmallows and Containers*:

> On the next day, the children use their pictures to review the experiment before beginning the data collection. Each group receives a two-column data table, fills in the column headings, and writes the names (or draws pictures) of the containers in the first column. The teacher emphasizes the need for accuracy in counting, and the children discuss various methods for grouping and counting the marshmallows. As the students begin to collect the data, the teacher circulates among the groups, coaching and assessing.

> After the children complete their data tables (Figure 3), the teacher leads a discussion in which the groups compare their results. This discussion centers on whether the groups' results are reasonable or not. Most groups report about 130 marshmallows in the graduated cylinder. Students agree that numbers close to 130, but not exactly 130, are acceptable. Based on this discussion, a group that had recorded only 110 marshmallows for the cylinder decides to refill the cylinder and count again.

Container	N Number of Marshmallows
Graduated cylinder	133
cup	121
bowl	181

Figure 3: Data table from Marshmallows and Containers

Tennis Ball

D Drop Height in cm	B Bounce Height in cm			
	Trial 1	Trial 2	Trial 3	Average
40	27	22	21	22
80	50	40	43	43
120	72	62	68	68

Figure 4: Data table from The Bouncing Ball

Figure 3 shows a student's data table for *Marshmallows and Containers.* Figure 4 is a student's data table from *The Bouncing Ball.* The name of a variable, including units if appropriate, heads each column.

When creating data tables, scientists and mathematicians generally place the manipulated variable in the left column and the responding variable in the right column. Since the values for the manipulated variable are chosen by the experimenter before the experiment begins, the first column of the data table can be filled out prior to the experiment. Values of the responding variable can only be filled in as the experiment is conducted.

When creating data tables, scientists and mathematicians generally place the manipulated variable in the left column and the responding variable in the right column. Since the values for the manipulated variable are chosen by the experimenter before the experiment begins, the first column of the data table can be filled out prior to the experiment. Values of the responding variable can only be filled in as the experiment is conducted.

Data tables are tools for organizing data. In a real laboratory experiment, scientists have to record the data clearly and correctly the first time, during the experiment. It has to be recorded in such a way that not only you can read it but also your colleagues and even a stranger. A story is told about the Nobel Prize-winner James Watson, who helped discover DNA. His teacher at Indiana University was asked if he suspected that Watson might go on to great things when he graduated. Yes, he answered. Watson would go far. Why? The teacher replied that although Watson did not take great care of his personal appearance, and his desk was a mess, he kept a neat notebook. That is a lesson that even young children can understand.

The data table is also useful in controlling error and identifying patterns. Children can detect blunders when a measurement deviates too much from established patterns (as in the *Marshmallows and Containers* anecdote above), and they can control inevitable measurement error by averaging several trials.

Note that in *The Bouncing Ball* lab, the students performed three trials for each measurement. In other words, to answer the question of how high does the ball bounce when dropped from 40 centimeters, they dropped the ball three times from 40 centimeters and recorded the bounce height, in this case (Figure 4), 27, 22, and 21 centimeters. The students then take the average (they used the median for the average) bounce height for their value of the bounce height. This is done to minimize the effect of measurement and experiential error on the experiment. (See the TIMS Tutor: *Estimation, Accuracy, and Error.*)

Phase 3: Graphing the Data

Graphing is the heart of scientific analysis. Graphs are powerful communication tools that create a picture of the data and "tell its story." They allow you to compare, predict, and infer. If there is a pattern in the relationship between the variables, you are more likely to see it clearly in a graph. Being able to read a graph and produce a graph from data should be a major goal of school science. Graphing cuts across many disciplines: biology, chemistry, sociology, and economics all use graphing. Students using MATH TRAILBLAZERS work extensively with graphs from kindergarten on.

Bar Graphs vs. Point Graphs

In MATH TRAILBLAZERS, data are mostly graphed as either a bar graph or a point graph; these two types of graphs will thus be the focus of our discussion in this section. Since a graph is a visual representation of the relationship between variables, the type of graph used depends upon the types of variables studied in the experiment.

When both variables are numerical, a point graph is often (though not always) appropriate. In *The Bouncing Ball,* for example, both variables—the drop height and the bounce height—are numerical. Since the values for these variables are numbers and are not discrete—that is, there are values between the data points that make sense, such as 52.5 cm—it is possible to use points and lines on the graph instead of bars to represent the data. Drawing a line or a curve makes sense only when the variables are numerical and there is a pattern in the data. Figure 5 shows a student's graph from *The Bouncing Ball.*

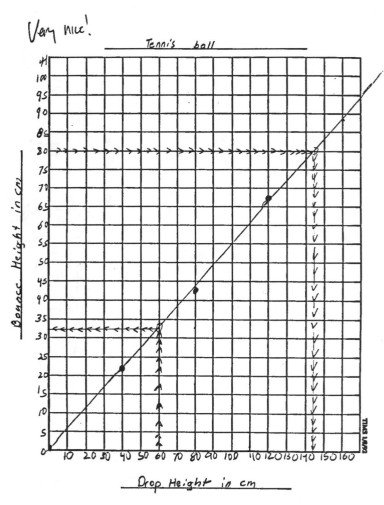

Figure 5: Point graph from The Bouncing Ball *showing best-fit lines, interpolation, and extrapolation*

Point graphs are introduced in MATH TRAILBLAZERS in third grade and are used to represent a variety of different mathematical situations as well as to display data from laboratory experiments.

A bar graph is usually best when one of the variables is categorical (qualitative). In *Marshmallows and Containers,* for example, the type of container is a categorical variable and the number of marshmallows is numerical. Figure 6 shows the graph for *Marshmallows and Containers.* There are no values that make sense between the types of containers. Thus it does not make sense to connect them on the graph with a line. A bar graph, therefore, is appropriate for these kinds of situations.

Although point graphs are most often used when both experimental variables are numerical, that is not always the case. For example, in the experiment *First Names* from third grade, students collect data about the number of letters in the first names of students in the class. The two primary variables in this experiment are the number of letters (the manipulated variable) and the

A bar graph is usually best when one of the variables is categorical (qualitative).

number of names (the responding variable). A graph for the experiment is shown in Figure 7. While both the variables in this experiment are numerical, they are also discrete—that is, it is not meaningful to speak of 6½ letters in a name or 3¼ people who have that number of letters in their names. Thus, we can see why a point graph, in which values between the data points are represented, would not be appropriate in this case. Instead, the data is best represented on a bar graph.

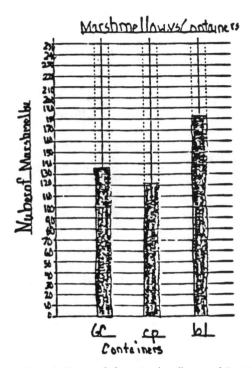

Figure 6: Bar graph from Marshmallows and Containers

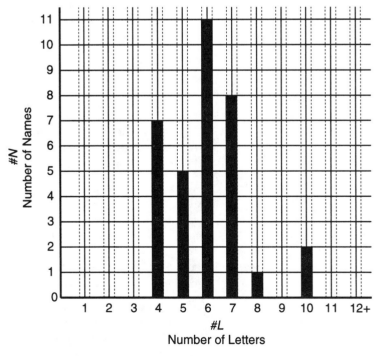

Figure 7: Graph from First Names

Labeling the Axes

All graphs contain a horizontal and vertical axis which are perpendicular to each other. With most types of data, it is conventional in science to place the manipulated variable along the horizontal axis and the responding variable along the vertical axis. The horizontal axis is labeled with a word or letter describing the manipulated variable and the vertical axis with a word or letter describing the responding variable. In Figure 7, for example, the horizontal axis—the manipulated variable—is labeled "#L, Number of Letters" and the vertical axis—the responding variable—is labeled #N, Number of Names."

Once the axes are in place, the children can label the axes with the values for each variable. In the case of the *Marshmallows and Containers* in Figure 6, the student wrote in labels to represent the different kinds of containers.

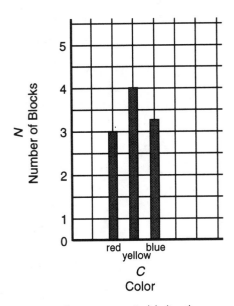

Figure 8: Common errors in labeling the axes

A common error in labeling axes is illustrated in Figure 8. This graph shows irregular spacing on both axes. The vertical axis in Figure 8 is incorrect with one space between 0 and 1 and two spaces between the other numbers. Technically, the categorical variables displayed on the horizontal axis do not have to be equally spaced, but it is a good idea to get your students into the habit of spacing their bars across the axis in regularly spaced intervals. This is because when dealing with numerical data, the values *must* be equally spaced.

Scaling the axes for numerical data requires an analysis of the range of the data and comparing it with the number of available intervals on your particular graph paper. Scaling by ones, two, fives, tens, or other numbers might be appropriate depending upon the data for a particular experiment. What is essential, however, is that the intervals are all equal along a given axis. Students will learn that it is best to determine the appropriate interval ahead of time. Otherwise they will end up plotting their initial data points and later discovering that other points will not fit on the graph.

In most cases, the scale on the horizontal axis is independent of the scale on the vertical axis. Students should number the axes in ways that make sense for the data. For example, the horizontal axis in *The Bouncing Ball* graph (Figure 5) is scaled by tens but the vertical axis is scaled by fives. One exception to this is when making scale maps. Here, using different scales for the different axes would create a distorted image and make it difficult to find distances on the map.

As scientists do, students using the TIMS Laboratory Experiments often use their graphs to make predictions about physical phenomena. When making point graphs, therefore, we often encourage students to scale their axes to allow room for extrapolation. (See the section below entitled *Predictions from Point Graphs: Interpolation and Extrapolation* for information about extrapolation.)

Bar Graphs in MATH TRAILBLAZERS

As early as kindergarten, students using MATH TRAILBLAZERS work on graphing concepts, including making and interpreting simple graphs. A quick way to make bar graphs of classroom data is to place self-adhesive notes on a labeled graph. An example of this with *First Names* is illustrated in Figure 9. In this graph, each student placed a self-adhesive note with the data for his or her name on the graph. The data are clearly represented. The one-to-one correspondence between data points and the number of students in the class is particularly apparent in this type of graph, which we use primarily in kindergarten, first, and second grades.

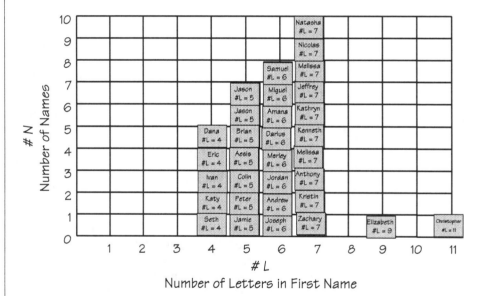

Figure 9: First Names *graph using self-adhesive notes*

In first grade, we introduce a graphing protocol that is different in MATH TRAILBLAZERS than in some other programs: when making bar graphs, we encourage students to create their bars along the vertical lines in the graph rather than in the spaces between the lines. (See Figures 6, 7, and 9.) This does not affect the data or the reading of the graph. Rather it prepares students for making point graphs, where data points are plotted at the intersection of lines extending from the horizontal and vertical axes.

To assist students with this, we have created a special graph paper for making bar graphs. A version of this graph paper is shown in Figure 10. The dark vertical grid lines across the page are where the data for the manipulated variable is plotted. These lines are surrounded on both sides by a pair of dashed guide lines. Students make bars by coloring in the space on either side of the dark vertical lines. The result is a straight bar that is centered along a vertical line. The values for the manipulated variable are indicated on the horizontal axis directly below each bar.

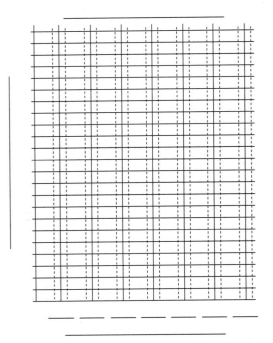

Figure 10: TIMS bar graph paper

The benefit of making bar graphs in this manner is most apparent in third grade as students make the transition to creating point graphs. To simplify students' initial attempt at creating a point graph, they first graph a data set as a bar graph and then convert the bar graph to a point graph. This is shown in Figure 11.

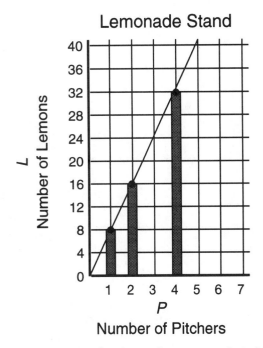

Figure 11: Transition from bar graphs to point graphs in third grade

Point Graphs: Fitting Lines and Curves

With point graphs, the data are plotted at the junction of the values of each variable. Once the data are plotted, we look for patterns. If the data points form a line or close to a line, we try to fit a line through the points. If the data form a curve, we try to fit a smooth curve through the points.

Figure 11 shows a graph in which the data points lie *exactly* on a straight line. Fitting a line to these data points is simply a matter of laying down a ruler and connecting the points.

For most experiments, we cannot expect the data to be so precise. In these experiments, the data may lie close to, but not exactly on a straight line. The "zigzags" in the data are due to experimental error. (See the TIMS Tutor: *Estimation, Accuracy, and Error.*) To average the error, one fits a line which comes as close to the data points as possible even though the line may not pass through any of these points. To assure a good fit, you would like as many points above the curve as below. You do not want to force the line through two points while missing the third by a mile. It is better to miss them all but come close to all than be too far from any one point.

As shown on *The Bouncing Ball* graph in Figure 5, a line can be fit to the data points, not by using some complicated statistical procedure, but simply "by eye." The student uses a clear ruler or a thread and moves it around until it fits the data points as closely as possible. This best-fit line is useful for minimizing error and making predictions.

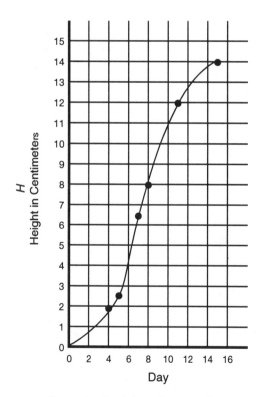

Figure 12: Graph from Plant Growth

Of course, not all experimental relationships result in data that yields straight lines on graphs. In MATH TRAILBLAZERS, we also explore data that exhibits other kinds of patterns. Figure 12 shows the graph from a fourth-grade experiment, *Plant Growth,* where the data shows a pattern, but not a straight line.

When you can fit a smooth curve through the data points, you have uncovered one of nature's secrets—that the variables are related, that there is a predictable pattern to the data. We are then not restricted only to our specific data points but can now use the pattern to predict what the value of the responding variable will be for any value of the manipulated variable.

Predictions from Point Graphs: Interpolation and Extrapolation

A major goal of mathematics and science is to find patterns in data and to use the patterns to make predictions. Interpolating and extrapolating on a point graph are two ways to do this.

Using the graph to find data points that lie between those in your data table is called interpolation. *Inter* means "between" or "among." The simplest situation is when the pattern of data points produces a straight line. In the graph in Figure 5, the student interpolated to predict that a ball dropped from 60 cm would bounce about 32 cm. Note that in Figure 5 the student showed how she made her interpolation by starting at 60 cm on the horizontal axis, drawing a line (with arrows) up to the best-fit line, and then drawing a horizontal line to find the corresponding value of the bounce height—about 32 cm.

Extrapolation is an attempt to predict information beyond the last data point. *Extra* means "outside" or "beyond." To extrapolate, we must extend the line into a region where there is no data. You can do this easily by laying a ruler on the straight line, extending the line, and reading off your prediction. In Figure 5, the student extrapolated to predict that a ball that bounced 80 cm was dropped from a height of about 144 cm. Here, the student began with values on the vertical axis (the bounce height) and predicted a value on the horizontal axis (the drop height). It is possible to interpolate and extrapolate in either of two directions: from values on the horizontal axis to values on the vertical axis or vice versa.

Having used these techniques to make predictions, it is important to have the children check their predictions experimentally and see how close their new data comes to the curve. This is one of the joys of science—to see that nature is often regular and predictable and that you can carry out predictions that come true! Checking predictions, though time-consuming, is worthwhile because it reinforces connections between mathematical abstractions and the real world.

Phase 4: Analyzing the Data

After making the graph, students have explored the relationship between the variables in four ways: with the physical materials, in the picture, in the data table, and in the graph. The last phase of the TIMS Laboratory Method is the analysis of the entire situation, where students explore the relationship quantitatively and represent it symbolically (i.e., with numbers).

One way to structure this analysis is to ask a series of questions. The questions usually begin on the literal level: *Did the tallest container hold the most marshmallows? How high did the tennis ball bounce when dropped from 60 cm?* More demanding questions require prediction: *How many marshmallows would two bowls hold? If a ball bounced to 45 cm, what height was it dropped from?* Asking what would happen if one of the fixed variables is changed can build a broader understanding of the situation: *What would happen if we used large instead of miniature marshmallows? What would happen if we used a super ball instead of a tennis ball?* This quantitative analysis of the data is one place in MATH TRAILBLAZERS where students regularly practice and reinforce arithmetic and other math skills.

A major goal of mathematics and science is to find patterns in data and to use the patterns to make predictions. Interpolating and extrapolating on a point graph are two ways to do this.

The end of the investigation may be a completely satisfying answer to the original question, but, more often than not, the end is another question that can lead to further investigations. *Marshmallows and Containers,* for example, might lead to an investigation of the liquid capacities of other short and tall containers. After an initial experiment with tennis balls in *The Bouncing Ball,* children carry out an investigation using another type of ball and compare the results from the two experiments.

Picture, Table, Graph, and Questions: Putting It Together

Each of the four phases described above may require one or more class periods. In addition, time may be spent becoming familiar with the equipment at the beginning and on further experiments at the end. Thus, a lab is an extended activity that may last a week or even longer. This is much longer than a typical mathematics or science lesson, but there are significant benefits.

First, the four phases simplify the scientific method enough for children to use, but not so much that it fails to resemble what scientists do. Identifying variables, drawing pictures, measuring, organizing data in tables, graphing data, and looking for patterns are part of many scientists' work. Students are thus inducted via this method into the authentic practice of science.

The method fosters children's sense-making. Children handle numbers they have generated themselves by counting or measuring, numbers that are thus meaningful to them. As they deal with experimental error, they develop number sense and estimation skills. As they look for patterns in their tables and graphs, they make sense of the numbers before them. Arithmetic in context is more understandable.

The approach is multimodal, which has benefits for both individual students and heterogeneous groups of students. The multiple representations of relationships between the variables permit problems to be solved in more than one way, allowing different students to approach the same content in ways they understand. The container that holds the most marshmallows, for example, can be found from the graph, from the data table, or from the marshmallows themselves. A prediction about a bounce height might be obtained by extrapolating on the graph or by extending patterns in the data table, and can then be verified using the apparatus. Students can compare these various approaches, thus helping them make connections within mathematics as well as between the informal mathematics of their everyday experience and more formal mathematics.

Mathematics in Context

Two principles underlie the TIMS Laboratory Method. First, an investigation should begin within the children's own experiences. Children use objects from their everyday lives to investigate a familiar situation. Children's everyday knowledge, like a scientist's theory, provides a framework for interpreting the results of the investigation. Without that framework, the investigation would remain hollow and meaningless.

The second principle is that an investigation should also transcend children's everyday experiences. The exploration must go somewhere; it must lead the children both to a better understanding of the immediate situation and to improved skills, understandings, habits, and attitudes. The concepts can then be extended and transferred to new contexts.

Balancing these principles requires teacher judgment. The key is to enable students to follow their own ideas, but with the intention that those ideas will

Identifying variables, drawing pictures, measuring, organizing data in tables, graphing data, and looking for patterns are part of many scientists' work. Students are thus inducted via this method into the authentic practice of science.

lead somewhere. How much scaffolding to provide, how much to guide students in directions that are fruitful rather than sterile, must be decided by the teacher in context. The goal is that students should advance not only in skill and understanding, but also in autonomy and perseverance. Just how much structure to provide along the way is perhaps a teacher's most important and difficult job.

The TIMS Laboratory Method helps children connect their everyday experiences with formal mathematics. As they investigate everyday situations quantitatively, children handle variables, explore relationships between variables, master a few powerful techniques for representing these relationships, and use these multiple representations to generate a wide variety of problem solutions. By beginning and ending in familiar situations, the abstractions of mathematics are linked to children's everyday knowledge. As students master this method, they become increasingly autonomous and flexible in its application. Then we can truly say they understand the fundamentals of *doing* science.

References

Archambault, Reginald D. (ed.), *John Dewey on Education: Selected Writings.* Modern Library, 1964.

Bruner, Jerome S. "The Course of Cognitive Growth." *American Psychologist* 19(1), 1964: pp. 1–15.

Dewey, John. "Science as Subject-Matter and as Method." *Science* 31(787), January 28, 1910: pp. 121–7.

Goldberg, Howard, and F. David Boulanger. "Science for Elementary School Teachers: A Quantitative Approach." *American Journal of Physics* 49 (2), 1981: pp. 120–124.

Goldberg, Howard, and Philip Wagreich. "Focus on Integrating Science and Math." *Science and Children* 2(5), 1989: pp. 22–24.

Goldberg, Howard, and Philip Wagreich. "A Model Integrated Mathematics and Science Program for the Elementary School." *International Journal of Educational Research* 14(2), 1990: pp. 193–214.

Hiebert, James. "A Theory of Developing Competence with Written Mathematical Symbols." *Educational Studies in Mathematics* 19, 1988: pp. 333–355.

Lesh, Richard, Thomas Post, and Merlyn Behr. "Representations and Translations among Representation in Mathematics Learning and Problem Solving." In C. Janvier (ed.), *Problems of Representation in the Teaching and Learning of Mathematics.* Hillsdale, N.J.: Lawrence Erlbaum Associates, 1987.

National Research Council. *National Science Education Standards.* Washington, D.C.: National Academy Press, 1996.

Silver, Edward. "Using Conceptual and Procedural Knowledge: A Focus on Relationships." In J. Hiebert (ed.), *Conceptual and Procedural Knowledge: The Case of Mathematics.* Hillsdale, N.J.: Lawrence Erlbaum Associates, 1986.

The Concept of Length

TIMS Tutor

Units

In dealing with scientific problems, we must often know such things as the location of an object, the distance between objects, how tall or wide an object is, or how fast it is moving. Central to all these ideas is the concept of length. In this tutor, we shall examine the various disguises in which length can appear.

First, however, we must note the messy problem of units. The kinds of units chosen for length were for a long time quite arbitrary. The cubit, used by several ancient civilizations, was the length of a forearm between the tip of the middle finger and the elbow. The fathom was the width of a Viking sailor's embrace. (Fathom that!)

The foot was a convenient length defined as the length of a person's foot. Of course, everyone has a different-sized foot, so if we want to use, say, the king's foot as a standard, we will have to mark it permanently; we cannot very well lug the king around! Since the king is the ruler of the land, it was both rational and proper to call this marker a ruler as well. To show students the chaos caused by not having a standard length, have them measure the length of their desks in cubits or the width of the room in feet with each child using his or her own body measurements. You will have as many different values as measurers.

The foot was a convenient length defined as the length of a person's foot. Of course, everyone has a different-sized foot, so if we want to use, say, the king's foot as a standard, we will have to mark it permanently...Since the king is the ruler of the land, it was both rational and proper to call this marker a ruler as well.

The Link System

At first, we have the children measure the length of objects in links. A link is shown in Figure 1 along with a chain of links. The measurement of the object shown is 4½ links. The reasons we go to links are: (1) to make counting the unit length easy and (2) to keep the numbers manageable. Rather than dealing with hundreds of cm, we can count 50 links. And to count a link is easy since they are so large.

By alternating link colors (2 reds, 2 whites, 2 reds, etc.), one can make the counting even easier by skip counting by 2s. If you want to have the children skip count by 5s, then have a chain with 5 blues, 5 yellows, 5 blues, etc.

With links, it is also easy to round off to ½ link as shown in Figure 1. If the edge we are measuring is near the middle, then the length is 4½ links. If shorter, then $L = 4$ links; if longer, $L = 5$ links.

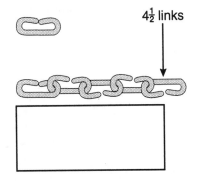

$4\frac{1}{2}$ links

Figure 1: Links

The Metric System

Of course, links are not a commonly used standard of measure. In the United States, it is feet. Unfortunately, many objects are smaller than a foot. This means one must subdivide the standard unit. For some miserable reason, the smaller unit, the inch, is $\frac{1}{12}$ of a foot. Who likes to divide by 12? So, the French scientific community at the time of the French Revolution (c. 1790) chose as the standard unit of length a distance which they called a meter. It was chosen so that 10^7 (10 million) metersticks laid end to end would just fit between the North Pole and the equator, as shown in Figure 2. A platinum-iridium rod was constructed with two marks a meter apart and stored in a vault near Paris. Every meterstick, albeit indirectly, comes from this standard. Having defined the meter, the French were smart enough to define all subsequent subdivisions of the meter as integral powers of ten. The foot is divided into $\frac{1}{12}$'s and $\frac{1}{48}$'s, and other equally horrible numbers; for the meter, the divisions are $\frac{1}{10}$'s, $\frac{1}{100}$'s, and $\frac{1}{1000}$'s. We shall now explore this point further.

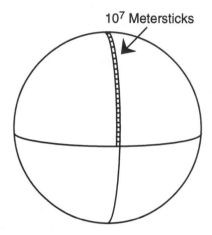

Figure 2: Metersticks from the North Pole to the equator

For measuring ordinary objects in the classroom, the meter is divided into three other units; the millimeter, the centimeter, and the decimeter (although the latter is rarely used). Without being specific as to the size of each unit, we can order them using the greater than (>) or less than (<) sign. Starting with the smallest, we have:

1 millimeter < 1 centimeter < 1 decimeter < 1 meter.

Reversing the order and starting with the largest, we have:

1 meter > 1 decimeter > 1 centimeter > 1 millimeter.

It is important that the child know at least this much before going on to more exact relations.

The key to the subdivision of the meter is the prefix *milli*. Milli is related to the word mile. Mile was the distance it took a Roman soldier to step off 1000 paces, a pace being two steps. Since an average pace is approximately 5 feet (try it and see), a mile would be approximately 5000 feet. The crucial point is the number 1000 as related to the word mile. Milli is the prefix for " $\frac{1}{1000}$ of." Thus, a millimeter is one-thousandth of a meter. There are 1000 millimeters in a meter just as there are 1000 paces in a mile. In each case, we have a subunit that is one-thousandth of the main unit. The word mile is to remind us that there are 1000 paces in a mile. The word millimeter is to remind us that there are 1000 millimeters in a meter. One should try to picture this in one's mind. Millimeters are tiny; it takes a lot of them to make up any macroscopic length. (By macroscopic, we are referring to something one can see unaided versus microscopic where one would need a magnifying glass or microscope to see it.) On the other hand, because a meter is large, a millimeter is usually a fraction of most lengths one would measure in the lab. Thus, it is reasonable that a third-grader knows how to measure the length of his thumb as 3 cm or 30 mm, but not as 0.03 m.

How are mm, cm, dm, and m related? Let's start with the smallest and see how many mm are in a cm, a dm, and a meter.

1 centimeter contains 10 mm;

1 decimeter contains 100 mm;

1 meter contains 1000 mm.

Based on these relationships, we should be able to figure out how many centimeters are in a decimeter or in a meter. Here, however, the French have made it easy for us; the prefix for each word gives the answer away. *Centi* stands for 100th and *deci* stands for one-tenth. Thus one centimeter is one-hundredth of a meter; there are 100 cm in a meter. A decimeter is one-tenth of a meter; there are 10 dm in a meter. What this boils down to then is the following:

1 decimeter contains 10 cm;

1 meter contains 100 cm;

1 meter contains 10 dm.

Everything depends upon the size of the meter. Once that is fixed (by our rod in Paris), the sizes of all other metric units are determined.

Measuring Length

The simplest way to get started in the metric system is to count, using a meterstick, the number of mm or cm (and if they do not equal fractions, dm or meters) in a given length. Say we measure the width of the sheet of paper in cm. Then depending upon the accuracy of the meterstick (a cheap one could be off a bit) and the judgment of the student, one can see that there are between 21 and 22 cm across the page. If you stick to cm, then for students who are not yet comfortable with fractions or decimals, this is all you can say. As they begin to learn decimals, the children can determine the width as 21.6 cm. However, you can get still better accuracy even without decimals by going to mm instead of cm. Here, all one has to be able to do is count beyond 100. Thus, the width is 216 mm. In fact, one of the neat things about the metric system is that you can always choose a set of units to obtain almost any accuracy you want without going to fractions or decimals. On the other hand, you can purposely choose units that will give decimal or fractional answers. As we just saw, in cm units, the width of the page is a decimal, 21.6 cm. We could have asked for the width in meters. Since the width is less than a meter, we are dealing with fractions. In this case, the width is 0.216 meters or roughly ⅕ of a meter. Clearly, there is great potential in the metric system for teaching math and linking this to scientific measurement.

With regard to addition, when adding numbers they must always have the same units. For example:

(a) 5 cm + 6 m = ? This is a "no-no"; the units are mixed.

(b) 5 cm + 600 cm = 605 cm. This is okay—we are adding the same units.

(c) 8 mm + 50 cm = ? We should convert the cm to mm and get:

(d) 8 mm + 500 mm = 508 mm.

Thus, if we ask a student to measure the length of his arm by separately measuring his hand (say in mm), his lower arm (say in cm), his upper arm (say in decimeters), and then adding them, he will first have to convert to a set of consistent units that he or she can handle. If you do not choose to have the students work with fractions, the students can change the units to millimeters as shown above. If you want to give the students a chance to work on decimal fractions, they can change the units to centimeters.

$$.8 + 50 \text{ cm} = 50.8 \text{ cm}$$

This brings us to another point—how to use a ruler. At first it seems quite apparent: just place the end of the ruler at the end of the object and read the length directly (Figure 3). However, a better test of whether students really understand how to use a ruler as well as a test of their ability to subtract is to place the object in the center of the ruler. Clearly, the length of the object should not depend upon its position vis-a-vis the ruler, but we have found that many young people (and even a few at our university) have trouble understanding how to find the length in the latter case.

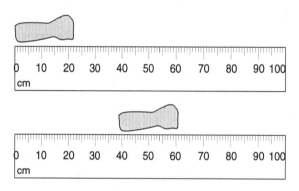

Figure 3: How to use a ruler

Since we do not always have a ruler handy, a few "natural" rulers might be fun to discuss and use. For example, say the length of a person's upper thumb from knuckle to tip is generally about 3 cm while his spread-out fingers span about 20 cm, as shown in Figure 4. Either can now be used to measure the length of an object. Of course, there is the foot, a convenient measure for stepping off distances. This person's foot, without his shoes, is 23 cm or about 9 inches. Anyway, you should have the children measure a few objects using natural rulers and have them compare their results with that of a meterstick.

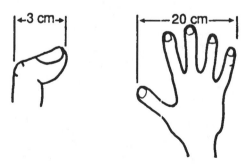

Figure 4: Natural rulers

The Concept of Area

TIMS Tutor

Defining Area

The area of a shape or object can be defined in everyday words as the "amount of stuff" needed to cover the shape. Common uses of the concept of area are finding the amount of tile needed to cover a floor, the amount of wallpaper needed to cover a wall, and the amount of paint needed to cover a ceiling. Areas of different objects can often be compared directly, without measurement. For example, if one piece of carpet completely covers another, we know the top piece has more area.

Just as with length, in order to measure area we need a unit of measure. Many different units have been used throughout history. The acre is still used as a measure of land area, along with square miles. The square inch, square foot, and square yard are area units in the English system. For example, square yards is the unit of area measure for carpeting in the United States. Most of the world and all scientists use the metric system. For the classroom, the most frequent metric unit of area is the square centimeter. It is defined as the amount of flat surface within a square that is 1 cm on a side. This is illustrated in Figure 1.

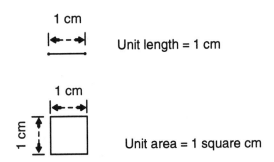

Figure 1: Units of length and area

A note on terminology: Scientists often use the term "centimeters squared" in place of "square centimeters." This may be due to the fact that one way of writing the symbol for square centimeters is cm^2. We prefer to use sq cm for square centimeters. On occasion, the use of cm^2 can confuse students. Since 7 squared is 49, they may reason that 7 centimeters squared is 49 square centimeters. Unfortunately, the symbols 7 cm^2 and $(7 cm)^2$ sound the same when spoken, if you say cm^2 as "centimeters squared." For that reason, we stick to "square centimeters" and sq cm.

Measuring Area by Counting Square Centimeters—Part I

3 cm
4 cm

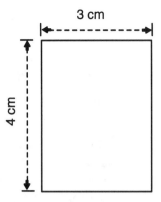

Figure 2: A rectangle

One way to find an area is to count the number of sq cm needed to cover a surface. To count the number of sq cm, you can construct unit squares within the desired area. For example, the rectangle in Figure 2 is 3 cm wide and 4 cm high. You can find its area by completing the following steps.

(1) Draw a grid of lines so that each square in the grid is 1 cm on a side. (Figure 3.)

1 cm
1 cm

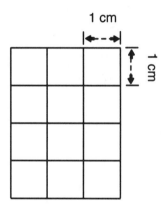

Figure 3: A rectangle tiled with centimeter squares

(2) Count the number of sq cm enclosed in the rectangle. (Figure 4.)

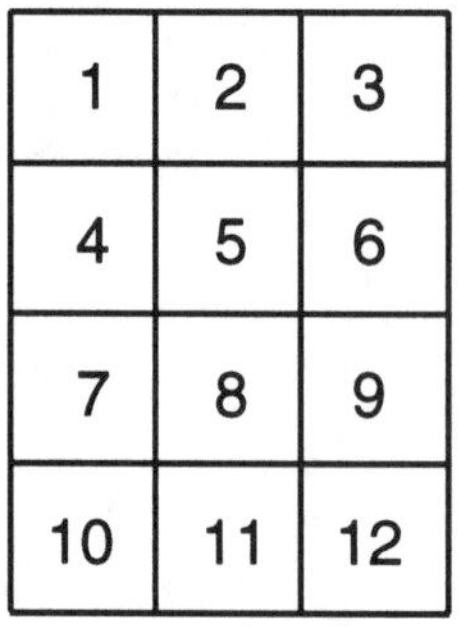

1
2
3
4
5
6
7
8
9
10
11
12

Figure 4: Counting square centimeters

There are 12 sq cm in a rectangle that is 3 cm wide and 4 cm high. So the area of the rectangle is 12 sq cm.

Why Not Use Length × Width?

You may be wondering why we did not use the formula *length × width* to find the area of the rectangle. After all, 4 × 3 = 12. The formula works. Indeed, the reason the formula works is precisely because the rectangle can be represented by an ordered array of squares, 3 squares in each row and 4 rows of 3 squares each.

In any ordered array, you can count the total number of elements by multiplying the number of rows by the number of columns. Figure 5 shows 24 apples arrayed in 6 rows. Instead of counting each apple, we take advantage of the array and multiply 4 × 6 to obtain 24 apples. You may use this trick often. For instance, when you buy stamps and want to check to see if the number you purchased was correct, you may multiply the rows by the columns. Using the length times width formula does give the area of a rectangle, but we delay teaching the formula for two reasons. First, we want students to build a mental image of the concept of area. Premature use of the formula for area of rectangles leads to rote use of the formula without understanding. In particular, many students are led to believe that the definition of area is length times width and that this formula works for any shape. While there are formulas for the areas of rectangles, circles, and other geometric shapes, there is no formula for the area of a leaf!

Figure 5: An array of apples

Furthermore, using the formula can be harder than counting square centimeters when the sides of the rectangle are not whole numbers.

For example, what is the area of the rectangle, 3½ cm wide and 2½ cm high, shown in Figure 6? We asked a group of sixth-graders to find the area of this rectangle. Even though the students knew the length × width formula, 80% could not find the area. They were not able to multiply fractions. It is likely that these students would have been able to find the area by counting sq cm, as we shall see in the next section.

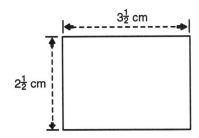

Figure 6: Another rectangle

Counting Square Centimeters—Part II

In Figure 7, we have set up the square cm grid. To keep track of the sq cm, we first number the whole square centimeters. There are six whole sq cm in the rectangle. Next, we turn to the fractions of sq cm. Students can manipulate sq cm pieces of paper to complete the task. The two half sq cm on the right make up the seventh sq cm and so both are numbered 7. The two half sq cm along the bottom make up the eighth sq cm and are numbered *8*. One half sq cm and one fourth square cm make up the remaining areas. The result is A = 8¾ sq cm.

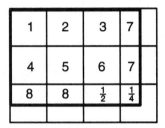

Figure 7: Whole and part centimeter squares

Most students can count squares to find area—no multiplication is necessary. But what if there is no "order" to the figure? The shape in Figure 8 has no unique length or width; the formula *length × width* does not apply. The only way to find the area is to count the number of sq cm contained within the boundary of the figure.

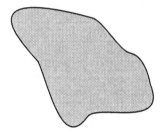

Figure 8: A blob

First, construct a sq cm grid to fit over the shape of Figure 8. It's often easier if the horizontal and vertical boundary of the grid each touch the figure at one point. The grid should extend beyond the figure. The completed grid would look similar to the grid in Figure 9.

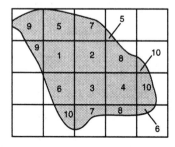

Figure 9: Finding area by counting centimeter squares

Next, count and number the whole sq cm. There are four. Now estimate which fractions of grid squares add together to form one square centimeter. For example, square centimeter number 5 is a big piece upper left and a little piece farther to the right. Number 6 is two pieces, a big piece on the left and a smaller piece in the lower right corner. Square centimeter number 7 is two pieces, each around a half square cm. Square centimeter 8 is made up of a ¾ and ¼ square cm piece. So is square centimeter 9. Three pieces make up square centimeter 10, two half square cm pieces and a smaller piece to the right.

Now, all of the shape is covered and counted in square centimeters. The shape has an area of about 10 square cm. While the method does not always give an exact area, the result is usually close. And, the primary benefit of this method is that students will have the opportunity to "see" area, aiding their understanding of this important mathematical concept.

Surface Area

Often, students who understand area quite well seem to have difficulty with the notion of surface area. One problem may be that they have been led to believe that area and surface area are two different things. This is not surprising, since we use two different words. However, area and surface area are identical; a measure of the number of sq cm (or square units) needed to cover an object. Customarily, the term "surface area" is usually used for three-dimensional shapes and "area" for two-dimensional shapes.

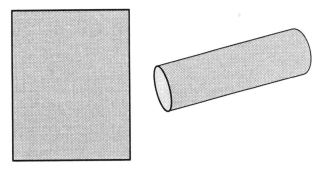

Figure 10: Paper flat and rolled

To measure the surface area of a 3-D object, we count the number of square centimeters needed to cover it, just as with flat shapes. In some cases, this is easy as in the case of a rectangular box (since it is made up of flat pieces). Another easy example can be made by taking a sheet of flat paper and rolling it to make a cylinder (Figure 10). As long as the edges do not overlap, the surface area of the outside of the cylinder will be the same as the flat piece of paper. Another way to find the area of a cylinder is to cover it with one square centimeter "stamps." As with flat shapes, you may need some fractional pieces. With more complex shapes, like a sphere, it is hard to get an exact measurement of the surface area, but we can approximate the surface area by covering the object with square centimeters or smaller squares.

The Concept of Volume

TIMS Tutor

Defining Volume

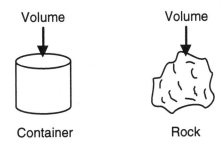

Figure 1: Two meanings of volume

Figure 1 shows a container and a rock. The space that the container sur-
rounds (and is occupied by air) and the space that the rock takes up (and is
occupied by elements such as oxygen, silicon, and aluminum) are both called
volume.[1] The concept of volume is tricky. Two objects (like our container
and rock) might occupy the same volume but might contain totally different
amounts of matter. Children often confuse the amount of matter, which we
call mass, with the space occupied, which we now know is volume. Thus
children tell us that a "heavy" object has more volume than a "light" object
even though the latter may actually occupy more space. Indeed, volume is
so oversimplified in the elementary schools that many eighth-graders we asked
thought of volume as length × width × height, no matter what the shape of the
object. Others told us that volume was length squared. Misconceptions such
as these are a result of a curriculum that emphasizes memorization of formulas
without attention to the conceptual foundations of volume.

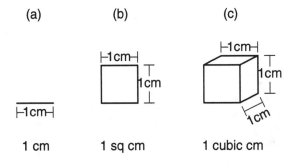

Figure 2: Units of length, area, and volume

Units

As with length and area, if we wish to measure volume, we need to decide on
a unit of measure. In the metric system, the metric unit of length is the centimeter (Figure 2a), and the unit of area is the square centimeter (the extent of
the plane surface that is bounded by a square 1 cm on a side) (Figure 2b), so it
is not unreasonable that we take as our unit of volume the space occupied
within a cube that is 1 cm on a side (Figure 2c). The volume occupied by

[1]Sometimes, the space inside a container is called the capacity of the container. For simplicity, we prefer to use
one term, volume, to denote both
"space inside" and "space occupied."

---

such a cube is defined as 1 cubic centimeter whether that volume is occupied by a solid object (Figure 3a) or by empty space (Figure 3b).

Figure 3: Full and empty cubic centimeter

Unlike area, it is very hard to divide an object up and count cubic cm. We can't trace the volume the way we trace areas on square cm paper. In theory we could slice it up into 1 cubic cm pieces, but this process will destroy the object. Therefore, learning to understand and measure volume can be more difficult than understanding and measuring area.

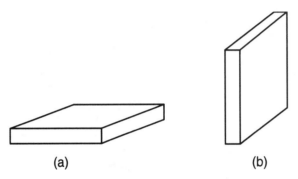

Figure 4: Flat vs. tall shapes

In everyday life, we are accustomed to a variety of other units of volume measure. Gallons, quarts, pints, and fluid ounces are one set of units, usually used to measure the capacity of a container. Cubic feet and cubic inches are also frequently used. For example, in the United States, air conditioners are often rated on the volume of space they can cool, measured in cubic feet. The remainder of this tutor uses metric units of measure, but many of the same underlying ideas apply to any system of measure.

Problem of Dimensionality

Another great difficulty in understanding volume is that the concept deals with three dimensions. As Piaget pointed out, it is much easier, and therefore usual, for a child to focus on one dimension. They will decide that a tall object has lots of volume because they only focus on the height and fail to take into account the other two dimensions to make a proper estimate of V. In Figure 4, the two objects have the same volume, but because (a) is flat and (b) is upright, young children will tell you that (b) has the greater volume.

Volume is an extremely important scientific variable. The way it is related to area and to mass and the manner in which it may change with time are all intrinsic to every area of scientific investigation. It is well worth our time to do a good job on volume.

Another great difficulty in understanding volume is that the concept deals with three dimensions. As Piaget pointed out, it is much easier, and therefore usual, for a child to focus on one dimension. They will decide that a tall object has lots of volume because they only focus on the height and fail to take into account the other two dimensions to make a proper estimate of V.

Measuring Volume—Early Activities

One way to begin to deal with volume in the primary grades is to have the children make figures out of a set of cubes. In first and second grade, we usually use connecting cubes that are about ¾-inch on a side. At the end of second grade, we start using standard centimeter linking cubes, usually called Cube-o-Grams. For example, you can give each child 10 cubes and ask him or her to make a figure whose volume is 10 cubic units. You will get a variety of shapes, all of which have the same volume. This will begin to impress upon the children the idea that many different shapes can have the same volume.

Another centimeter cube activity to build the children's understanding at this level involves building shapes with different volumes. Give each child a few (3–10) centimeter cubes. Have each child make a shape with his or her centimeter cubes. Then have the children sort themselves into groups according to the volume of their shapes.

You can bring in some simple solid shapes, like a piece of chalk, a match box, a pile of washers, etc., and have the children make figures out of cubic units that approximate the volume (size and shape) of these objects. In this way, they can estimate the volume of the original object by keeping track of the number of cubic cm they used. An example is given in Figure 5 of a marking pen and cubic cms linked together to make a shape of approximately the same volume.

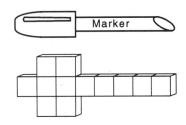

Figure 5: A marker and a cm cube model

The next step would be for you to make several cube models and have the children count the number of unit cubes in each one. Pictures of three typical models, each a bit more complex than the previous, are given in Figures 6a, b, and c. There are two potential problems here. The children may confuse surface area and volume and count the faces of the cubes calling each face a cubic cm. A subtle problem, exemplified by Figure 6c, is when there are one or more "hidden" cubic centimeters buried inside the figure.

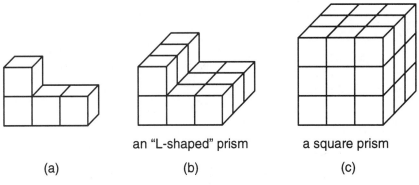

(a)   an "L-shaped" prism   a square prism
           (b)   (c)

Figure 6: Shapes made from centimeter cubes

We want the children to learn to be systematic, look for patterns, and use simple addition and multiplication to count the cubic cm.

A very basic problem is learning to count the cubic centimeters properly. It is relatively easy to pick up 12 cubic centimeters, make a figure, and say the volume is 12 cu cm. It is quite another to hold a centimeter cube figure like that in Figure 6b, turn it over, and keep track of all the cubic cm. We want the children to learn to be systematic, look for patterns, and use simple addition and multiplication to count the cubic cm. For example, Figure 6a is easy since it is only 4 cc. Figure 6b is made up of three layers, each of which is exactly like Figure 6a. Your students can then use addition to see that the volume is 4 cc + 4 cc + 4 cc, or use multiplication, 3 × 4 cc. Likewise in Figure 6c, it would be difficult to find and keep track of each cubic cm. A systematic approach allows the children to solve the problem easily. There are 9 cc in the top layer, and there are three layers; therefore the volume is

$$9 \text{ cc} + 9 \text{ cc} + 9 \text{ cc} = 27 \text{ cc}.$$

Note that Figures 6b and 6c are labeled as prisms. This means they are made of a number of identical layers. Figure 6b has three "L-shaped" layers and 6c has three "square-shaped" layers. It is important to know that these are prisms. Otherwise, there might be some hidden cubes behind the object that we cannot see, or there might be missing cubes "inside" the object.

A more difficult skill is finding the volume of an object directly from a perspective drawing, without actually building the object. This kind of spatial visualization skill can be developed by first having students build cube models from pictures. Students as early as first grade can build simple models from pictures. As the models get more complex, this task can become quite difficult. One important subtlety is that pictures such as 6b and 6c do not give enough information to reconstruct the model. For example, there might be some unexpected cubes hidden behind the model in Figure 6c (see Figure 7).

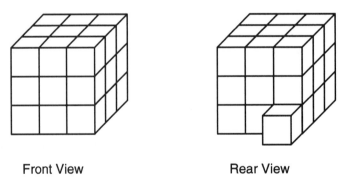

Front View   Rear View

Figure 7: Front and rear views of Figure 6c

For example, in Figure 7 we see what appears to be a 3 × 3 × 3 cm cube from the front, but when we view the model from the rear, we see there is an "extra" cube stuck on.

Finally, and hardest of all, you can ask the children to try to draw a figure with a given number of cubic cm. It is very hard for anyone to draw a cube, and a figure with several cubic cm is harder still. Nevertheless, it is worth a try since doing so will help them improve their spatial perception and will force them to "think" in three dimensions.

Let's review the four steps we have just described:

(1) Make figures out of a given number of centimeter cubes.

(2) Count cubic cm in a cube model.

(3) Count cubic cm in the drawing of a cube model—usually prisms.

(4) Draw a figure with a given number of cubic cm.

This discussion covers volumes of objects made from cubes. The most important tool, however, for determining volume will be the graduated cylinder which we will discuss in the section after next. But first we want to talk about how the volume of prisms can be calculated.

Calculating Volume—An Upper Grade Exercise

The volume of a rectangular prism made of cubic cm can be found using multiplication. The number of cubic cm in the top layer is just the product of 3 × 6 since there are 3 rows of 6 cubic cm (see Figure 8). Thus, in each layer there are 18 cubic cm. Because there are 5 layers, the total number of cubic cm is 5 × 18 cc = 90 cc. As often written in math books, this type of counting is expressed as

$$V = l \times w \times h.$$

You should interpret this as the number of cubic cm in the top layer (given by the value of $l \times w$) times the number of layers (given by the value of h).

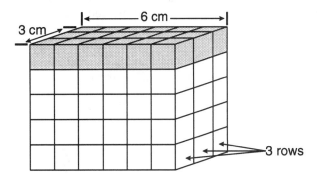

Figure 8: A rectangular prism

If the top layer is not rectangular but the figure is a right solid (sides perpendicular to top and bottom), then we can still find the volume by the above technique. The formula *length × width × height* will no longer work since the layers are not rectangular. However, since each horizontal slice has the same shape (see Figure 9), all we have to do is find the number of cubic cm in the top layer and multiply this by the number of layers. To find the number of cubic cm in the top layer, we have to find the number of square cm in the top surface, since each square cm of the surface is attached to a cubic cm in the top layer. Thus, if in Figure 9 by counting square cm we find that there are 22 sq cm on the top surface, then there must be 22 cubic cm in the top layer and in each subsequent layer. The total volume, then, is:

$$\frac{22 \text{ cubic cm}}{1 \text{ layer}} \times 5 \text{ layers} = 110 \text{ cubic cm}$$

for the object shown in Figure 9. As a general formula we have:

$$V = A \times h,$$

where the area A of the top tells us the number of cc in the top layer, and the value of h tells us the number of layers. The children should not just memorize each formula. They should understand what is behind the formulas.

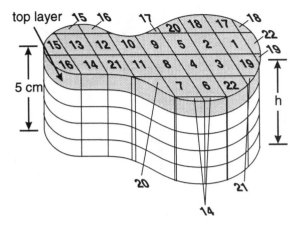

Figure 9: A right solid

When using a formula like $l \times w \times h$, the old bugaboo of units reappears. Since l, w, and h are all measured in cm, it is tempting to say that the units of volume are centimeters cubed written as $(cm)^3$. And indeed this is what is often done in scientific texts. Yes, it's technically correct to write $(cm)^3$ or cm^3, but again it can be misleading for children just as "centimeter squared" can be misleading for area. If we say a volume is 7 centimeters cubed, is that $(7\ cm)^3 = 343$ cc? We can avoid this confusion by writing what we mean; that the volume is 7 cubic centimeters or 7 cc.

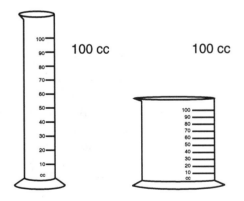

Figure 10: Graduated cylinders

Clearly, the ability to calculate volume is rather limited to certain special shapes. An irregularly shaped container or object will require a different approach.

A Volume Measurer: The Graduated Cylinder

We have seen that a ruler which is calibrated in cm can be used to measure length. There is no comparably simple device for measuring area, but there is one for measuring volume. It is the graduated cylinder calibrated in cubic cm.

Two graduated cylinders are shown in Figure 10. They can be made of glass or Pyrex, both of which are breakable, or plastic, which is not. The cylinder most suitable for classroom use would be calibrated in 1 cc, 5 cc, or 10 cc divisions and have a capacity of 100 to 150 cc. When filled with a liquid (usually water) or a fluid substance like sand or salt, one can read the volume of the material off the side of the graduated cylinder. One cannot use this device to directly measure the volume of a number of marbles since the marbles piled in the cylinder will leave an unknown volume of air spaces between them. This is illustrated in Figure 11b. As we shall see in the next section, we can find the volume of solid objects like marbles by the method of displacement. The rest of this section will discuss using the graduated cylinder for finding the volume of liquid, particularly water.

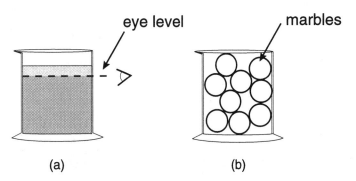

Figure 11: Liquid and marbles in graduated cylinder

To read the volume of water in a graduated cylinder, your eyes must be level with the liquid, as shown in Figure 11a. Since water is pulled up at the sides of the cylinder into a curved surface called a meniscus, one must measure the water level at the center of the cylinder. This is done by using the lower of the two lines that one sees (Figure 12) when looking at the water from the side. The top line is due to the pulled up water and should be ignored. (This phenomenon tends to be more pronounced when using glass rather than plastic graduated cylinders.)

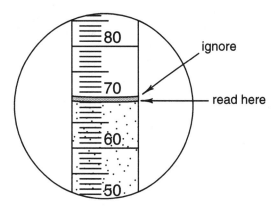

Figure 12: The meniscus

One must be careful about what one puts into a graduated cylinder. A tall, narrow one will generally have 1 cc divisions and thus can be used for accurate measurements. The trouble is, that because it is narrow, only small objects can be used. Many a time a student has misjudged the size of an object and found it stuck in the narrow cylinder never to come out again.

Chalk off one cylinder. A good general size that we like is one about 4 cm in diameter with a 150 cc capacity and made of plastic. The divisions are usually 5 or 10 cc. We shall discuss in the next section how to use a "big" graduated cylinder to measure the volume of small objects.

Many graduated cylinders that you purchase will have several different scales along the sides. This is due to the diversity of units for liquid measurements. Many cylinders will have a scale for fluid ounces and another for milliliters. The metric unit of volume is the milliliter, which is defined to be 1 cubic cm:

1 ml = 1 cc.

The liter is often encountered in daily life (for example, soda bottles are often 1 or 2 liters). It is exactly 1000 ml.

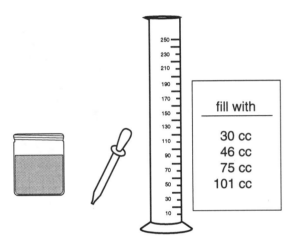

fill with

30 cc
46 cc
75 cc
101 cc

Figure 13: A graduated cylinder exercise

One of the first exercises the children can do with a graduated cylinder is simply to fill the cylinder to a specified level—10 cc, for example. An eyedropper is handy for getting the volume exactly right, since by pouring one usually overshoots or undershoots the mark. Whatever the divisions of the cylinder are, choose some volumes that fall right on a major division and some that fall between divisions, where the children will have to interpolate. An example is shown in Figure 13 for a cylinder with 10 cc divisions.

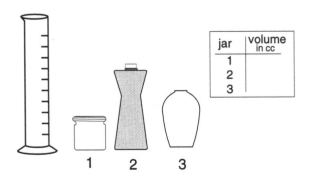

jar	volume in cc
1	
2	
3	

Figure 14: A capacity exercise

Once the second- or third-graders are good at reading the scale, they can use the graduated cylinder to find the capacity or volume of a set of three jars (Figure 14). You should build up a collection of jars of all shapes and volumes, from small baby food jars, through peanut butter containers, to large coffee jars. Exotic shapes are nice. To find the volume of a jar, one can either fill the jar to the brim and then keep pouring the water into the graduated cylinder, or one can keep filling the graduated cylinder and pour the water into the jar until it is filled. Either way, the children have to keep track of the number of times the graduated cylinder is filled and the total volume of water accumulated this way. This activity appears as a lesson called *Fill 'er Up* in third grade.

Volume Measurement by Displacement

How would you measure the volume of a small rock? This problem is dealt with in lessons on volume beginning in grade 2. The technique is illustrated in Figure 15. First, you fill the graduated cylinder with a convenient amount of water, for example, 40 cc rather than 43 cc. Then you place the rock in the graduated cylinder without losing any water (there must be enough water in the cylinder initially to cover the object). You then read the new volume V. Since the volume of water V_{water} stays constant, the volume V is due to the water plus the rock. The rock displaces, or pushes aside, its volume in water and the water level rises. Thus, we have:

$$V_{rock} = V - V_{water}.$$

For example, in Figure 15 the volume of the rock is 22 cc. Note that subtraction is easier if you start with a multiple of ten for the volume of water. The technique works for any solid object no matter what its shape. To start with, then, the children should be asked to find the volume of a wide variety of objects, some spheres, cubes, rocks, coins, washers, etc.

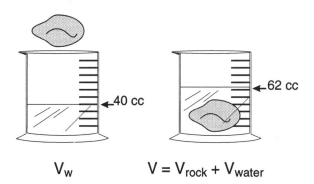

$$V_w \qquad\qquad V = V_{rock} + V_{water}$$

Figure 15: Volume by displacement

But what if the object is too big to fit into the graduated cylinder? If a bigger graduated cylinder isn't handy, then you can use your graduated cylinder to calibrate a large jar, and then away you go. One word of warning: When you place a large object in a graduated cylinder or jar, a considerable amount of water may splash out, even though you are very careful. You can get around this by placing the object in the graduated cylinder first and then pouring in a known amount of water V_w, and then read $V = V_{rock} + V_{water}$ off the scale. An alternative method is to find a large container and fill it with water to the brim. When the object is carefully placed in the container, it overflows, and the volume of the overflow liquid is equal to the volume of the object. If you catch all the overflow liquid in a second container, you can then use a graduated cylinder to find the volume of that liquid.

Finding the volume of small objects is also a problem: the object may be so small you can't see the water level rise. Of course, you can always use a smaller graduated cylinder, one with 1 cc divisions instead of 5 or 10 cc divisions. The trouble is that sometimes even 1 cc per division is too large. The only way out is to measure the volume of several of the small objects at once (Figure 16b). (The volume of the several objects are identical.) For example, suppose you have 10 identical objects. If V_{water} is the volume of the water initially, then the final volume in the graduated cylinder is $V = V_{water} + 10V_{object}$, where V_{object} is the volume of one of the small objects. To find the volume of one object, subtract the volume of the water and divide by 10. In this fashion, the children can find the volume of small washers, paper clips, pins, etc. Using 10 objects is a good idea since it is easy to divide by 10.

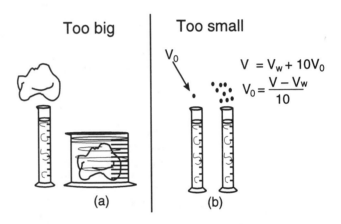

Figure 16: Finding volumes of large or small objects

Obtaining Accurate Results

A few words about accuracy are appropriate here. Most of the time you have to interpolate between divisions in order to read the volume. This usually leads to a reading error of about 20% of the value between the scale marks. Thus, if your graduated cylinder has 10 cc divisions, you might expect an error (i.e., children will get readings that differ) by up to 2 cc. This is illustrated in Figure 17a. If the object has raised the water level several divisions, then this 20% per division uncertainty is not a serious problem. For example, our rock changed the water level from 40 cc to 62 cc. If a reading error is up to 2 cc, then three children who read the same graduated cylinder might read 62 cc, but possibly 61 cc or 63 cc (if they are careful; maybe even more if they are not). But the volume of the rock is 62 cc – 40 cc = 22 cc for one child, but 23 cc for another, and 21 cc for the third. Thus we have a spread in reading of about 2 parts in 22 or 10%. A bigger rock, with a volume of, say, 46 cc would still have the same reading error of 2 cc, but its volume error would only be 2 parts in 46 or about 5%.

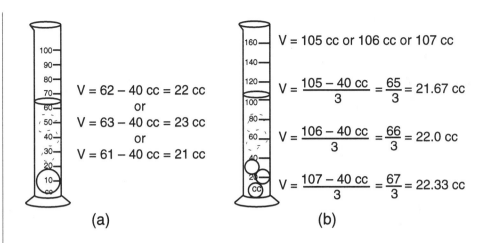

$$V = 62 - 40 \text{ cc} = 22 \text{ cc}$$
or
$$V = 63 - 40 \text{ cc} = 23 \text{ cc}$$
or
$$V = 61 - 40 \text{ cc} = 21 \text{ cc}$$

(a)

$$V = 105 \text{ cc or } 106 \text{ cc or } 107 \text{ cc}$$

$$V = \frac{105 - 40 \text{ cc}}{3} = \frac{65}{3} = 21.67 \text{ cc}$$

$$V = \frac{106 - 40 \text{ cc}}{3} = \frac{66}{3} = 22.0 \text{ cc}$$

$$V = \frac{107 - 40 \text{ cc}}{3} = \frac{67}{3} = 22.33 \text{ cc}$$

(b)

Figure 17: Measurement error

A good rule of thumb is that your reading will not be accurate unless the object raises the water level by more than one division. There are two ways to achieve this. One, use a narrow graduated cylinder, or two, use several identical objects if they are available. In the case of the latter, you find the volume of one object by dividing by the number of identical objects, as we did above for very small objects. For example, three objects would still produce a reading error of 2 cc but a volume error of only 2 cc/3 = 0.67 cc. This is illustrated in Figure 17b where three marbles give a volume spread of only 0.67 cc in 22 cc or 3%, compared to 10% for one marble. Of course, this would not work for finding the volume of a rock, since it would be difficult to find three identical rocks.

If the object floats, you have to push it under in order to measure its volume. In this situation, what is important is how you push it under. If you use your finger, then what you measure is the volume of the object plus the volume of your submerged finger. Since the volume of your finger may be comparable to the volume of the object, this is clearly not a good idea. What you need is a pusher whose volume is much less than the volume of the object. A straightened paper clip or a pin will do (Figure 18).

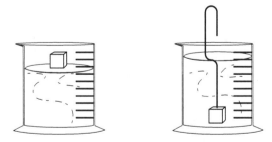

Figure 18: Finding the volume of something that floats

Two Misconceptions

Early on, the children should come to grips with two important ideas concerning volume:

(1) The volume of an object is independent of the material it is made of.

(2) The volume of an object does not change when its shape changes.[2]

²Usually. See later discussion.

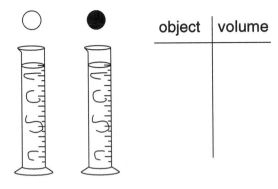

Figure 19: Volume vs. material

As to the first point, you can study spheres of the same volume but made of a wide variety of materials (steel, lucite, glass, even wood). The children should discover that their volumes are the same. As illustrated in Figure 19, students can fill two identical cylinders to the same level with water, carefully place both objects in, and see that the volume displaced is the same. Initially, many children will say that the heavier object has more volume and that the water will go up higher in its graduated cylinder. They are confusing mass and volume. If you take a clay cube and mash it into a thin disk, many children will say that the disk has less volume than the cube. Here they confuse one dimension, thinness, with volume: they mistakenly assume all thin objects have a small volume. Again, using the graduated cylinder the child can see that the volumes are the same (Figure 20). They can make all kinds of shapes out of a single piece of clay and determine that they all have the same volume. Indeed, the only way that they can change its volume is to tear off a piece.

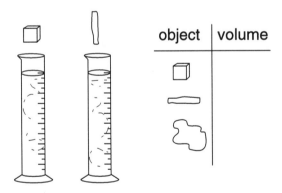

Figure 20: Volume vs. shape

The Concept of Mass

TIMS Tutor

Defining Mass

Mass is one of the most difficult variables to understand. It is also one of the most important. Length, area, and volume have straightforward definitions. The volume of an object, for example, was defined as a measure of the space it occupies. Does mass have a similar straightforward definition? In a sense it does and in a sense it does not. Basically, mass is a measure of the quantity of matter in an object. That is its simple definition. Unfortunately, that begs the question. One can ask, what is matter, and we are back to where we started. So we have to look more closely at mass. And that is where things get difficult. Mass is defined through what it *does*, and this sets it apart from length, area, and volume. Moreover, mass does two things which means, in a sense, it has two definitions.

One of the things that mass does is absolutely crucial for the existence of our universe. Mass is the cause of the force of gravity. Without mass, there would be no gravity, and without gravity, matter would not have clumped into galaxies and stars and us. Since mass causes gravity, we can define mass through the pull of gravity—the greater the pull, the greater the mass an object has.

The other thing that mass does has to do with the motion of an object. All other variables being equal, the mass of an object determines how much the velocity of an object will *change* when subject to a given force. In layman's terms, the larger the mass of an object, the harder you have to push to change its speed. Since we are not ready to study motion, we will not discuss the details of this aspect of mass. Nevertheless, we might note that it was Einstein's contemplation of both properties of mass (gravity and motion) that led him to his general theory of relativity.

One way, then, to determine which of two objects has more mass is to determine which one is pulled on more strongly by the Earth's gravitational force. One possible way to do this is to drop two objects, as shown in Figure 1, and see which reaches the ground first. You might suppose, since the more mass an object has, the bigger the force of gravity, that the more massive object would fall faster and reach the ground first. If you do this exercise, however (as Galileo did), you will find that both objects reach the ground at the same time! What went wrong? Well, we are breaking one of our cardinal rules, which is keeping variables fixed. When the objects fall, we not only have gravity pulling on them, but their velocity is changing as well. Therefore, both definitions of mass are involved and the overall effect is no longer obvious. It appears that in some way the effects cancel!

Basically, mass is a measure of the quantity of matter in an object.

Figure 1: Dropping two objects

So we need a way of measuring the pull of gravity (i.e., using definition 1) without having the object move (i.e., eliminating definition 2). As we shall see in the next section, we can do this with an equal arm balance.

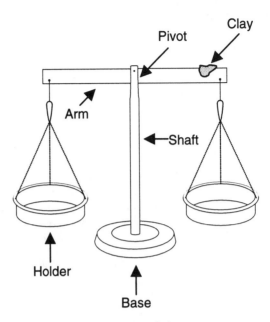

Figure 2: A balance

Equal Arm Balance

The equal arm balance is the key to our operational definition of mass for children. If two objects balance, they have the same mass. If the arm tilts to one side, the object in the lower of the two pans has more mass than the object in the other pan.

Basically, the equal arm balance is a stick that is pivoted at its center and has two holders that are mounted on at points which are equidistant from the pivot (hence the name equal arm balance). Figure 2 pictures a balance that we use in MATH TRAILBLAZERS. It is quite sturdy and accurate enough for use in the elementary classroom. The tall wooden shaft and long arms of the balance make it very useful in a wide variety of balancing experiments. If you would like to make your own, you can use a block of wood (Figure 3a) or a book to hold the pivot rod (Figure 3b). A ruler can act as the arm and the bottom of paper cups as pans. These latter pieces can be attached to the arm with string and paper clips.

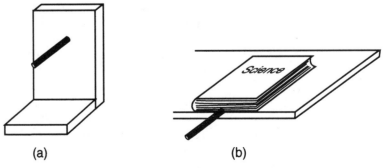

(a)   (b)

Figure 3: Making a balance

Once you have put your equal arm balance together, it must be zeroed; that is, the arm must be level before any masses are added. You can do this by adding small pieces of clay to one end of the arm, as shown in Figure 2, until it is level. We suggest that you do this once for each balance and then have the children check to see that it is level before and during each experiment.

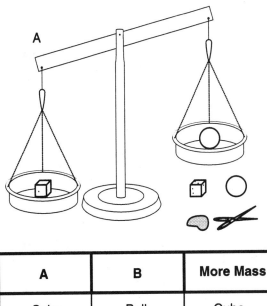

A	B	**More Mass**
Cube	Ball	Cube
Scissors	Ball	Scissors

Figure 4: Comparing masses

We are now ready to find out which of two objects, A or B, has greater mass. One is placed in each pan. Since the object with more mass will experience the bigger gravitational pull, the balance will tilt either one way or the other. If A has more mass it will tilt to the left, as shown in Figure 4, while if B has more mass it will tilt to the right. If $m_A = m_B$, the pull of gravity on both is the same and the balance will remain level. One word of caution, though: If the masses are the same and the arm is tilted when the masses are placed on the balance, then the ruler will often remain tilted. Thus, to be sure $m_A = m_B$, bring the arm back to level and see if it remains there. One of the first exercises you can do with children in kindergarten through second grade is to have them compare, two at a time, the masses of a wide variety of objects. Then they should order the objects from the most massive to the least massive (see *Putting Masses in Order* in grade 2, Unit 10). A washer, connecting cube, small scissors, steel ball, etc., can be used. Notice that the equal arm balance does away with the motion definition of mass since the balance is at rest when the measurement is made. Thus, the equal arm balance allows us to relate the object's mass directly to the pull of gravity.

Measuring Mass: The Mass Standard

The above is fine for comparing masses, but how do we measure *the* mass of an object? In other words, how do we assign a number to the mass of our object? Just as when we measure length, area, and volume, we need to decide on a unit. Say that we take as our standard masses a set of identical washers (paper clips would do as well). Let's call the mass of each washer 1 *ugh.* Then, if our object is balanced by 4 washers, its mass is 4 ughs, as shown in Figure 5. If the mass of the object is between 4 and 5 ughs, then the balance will not level out but tilt one way for 4 washers and the other way for 5. In this way, the child can assign unique masses to a wide range of objects. Clearly, the smaller the washer, the more accurately one can determine the mass of an object.

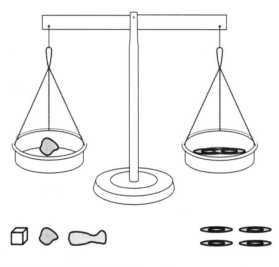

Object	Number of Washers	Mass in ughs
Ball	4	4
Cube	2	2

Figure 5: Measuring masses

The Paris Academy of Sciences submitted a report to the French National Assembly in which 1 cc of water was defined to have a mass of 1 gm, the gram being the name chosen for the unit of mass.

But washers are not a very satisfactory standard. The washers in your class may not have the same mass as those used in another school in your district, much less in another city or another country. What we need is a universal standard that is accepted by the entire scientific community. This problem was recognized by scientists a long time ago and was resolved when the Paris Academy of Sciences submitted a report to the French National Assembly in which 1 cc of water was defined to have a mass of 1 gm, the gram being the name chosen for the unit of mass. Then, using this definition, a platinum cylinder was made and declared to be the standard for 1000 grams. In 1875, an international treaty was signed by most "civilized" nations which established an International Bureau of Weights and Measures in Sevres, France, near Paris. The international prototype kilogram, made of platinum iridium alloy, is kept there. If you want your own kilogram, you have to go to Paris with an equal arm balance and some material and hack away at the material until it balances the platinum iridium standard. The National Bureau of Standards in Washington, D.C., has an accurately constructed copy as do other governments throughout the world.

For small measurements, one needs a mass that is smaller than a kilogram, just as one needs a length that is smaller than a meter. The gram, like the centimeter, is perfect for this. Most objects that you will deal with in the elementary school science program will have masses between 1 and 100 grams. Masses are commercially available, usually in 1-, 5-, 10-, 20-, 50-, 100-, 200-, 500-, and 1000-gram pieces. It might be a good idea to have one good set of very accurate standard masses for your school (locked in a closet marked "Paris," of course), but they are expensive. A complete set of brass or other metal masses can cost more than $80 (at 1994 prices). For general classroom use, there are less expensive sets of plastic masses available. A set of such masses is included in the MATH TRAILBLAZERS manipulatives kit. However, since the plastic masses may not be as accurate, you may wish to compare them to a good set of standard masses or find their mass using a triple beam balance or other accurate scales.

The cheapest standard mass is a nickel. It has a mass very close to 5 grams! But alas, a dime does not have a mass of 10 grams. There are two ways to get around having to buy sets of expensive standard masses. To determine the mass of a small object, you can measure the mass of several of the objects and then divide the total mass by the number of objects. For example, if it turns out that 10 small objects balance a 5-gram piece, then each object will have a mass of 0.5 grams. (5 grams ÷ 10 objects = 0.5 grams per object.)

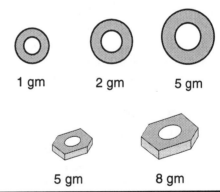

Object	Number of Standard Masses				Mass in gm
	1 gm	2 gm	5 gm	8 gm	
Plastic Cylinder	3	1	2	2	31

Figure 6: Using washers as standard masses

If you go to a hardware store and make a pest of yourself—bring your equal arm balance—you can usually find washers that have "nice" masses, like 1, 2, 5, 8 grams, etc. Figure 6 shows such a collection that can be used as standard masses. Once you have the washers, you can give each child several of each and a lot of objects whose mass you want them to determine. A good data table is a big help since you want to keep track of the number of different washers it takes to balance the object. Then, as shown in Figure 6, a little multiplication and addition is necessary to obtain the final mass in grams. In the example above, the total mass is:

$$m_{total} = 3 \times 1 \text{ gm} + 1 \times 2 \text{ gm} + 2 \times 5 \text{ gm} + 2 \times 8 \text{ gm} = 31 \text{ gm}.$$

Finding masses in grams is a great way to practice multiplication, addition, and mental math.

A second way to get around using expensive standards is again to use washers but place them in packages of sets of 1, 5, 10, 20 grams, etc. The package can be composed of several washers wrapped in masking tape with enough tape or small washers to make an even 5 gm or 10 gm, etc. Either way, the cost of a washer is at most 7 or 8 cents. The children, therefore, can have a set of masses for a few dollars.

Mass vs. Weight

In everyday language, we talk about the weight of an object rather than its mass. Are these two words for the same thing? Technically, weight and mass are distinct concepts. In scientific terms, the **mass** of an object is the amount of matter in the object. Mass is measured in kilograms and grams in the metric system and in pounds and ounces in the English system. The **weight** of an object is the measure of the pull of gravity on that object. Sir Isaac Newton first explained the importance of gravity for the motions of the planets and for the fall of an object more than 300 years ago.

Because of the awareness of space travel, most children know that the pull of gravity is different on different planets and that there is essentially no gravity in outer space. Many museums and planetariums have exhibits that show your weight on the moon and various planets. For example, since the moon's gravity is weaker than the Earth's, the pull on an individual object would be less. Thus, a human being would weigh less on the moon than on the Earth.

How is the mass of an object affected by gravity? The mass of an object remains constant regardless of space travel since gravity does not influence mass. Since we use a two-pan balance to measure mass, both sides of the balance are equally affected by gravity. If an 11-gram pencil balances one 1-gram and two 5-gram standard masses on Earth, it will balance those same masses on the moon.

However, since most of us are likely to spend our lives on Earth, the distinction between mass and weight may be lost on many students.

We suggest two pedagogical alternatives with regard to the distinction between mass and weight:

1. Ignore it. This point is fairly subtle and eludes many adults.

2. Provide a simple explanation, but don't worry about it too much.

Manipulatives List

The *Manipulatives List* outlines all manufactured manipulatives and other materials needed to implement *MATH TRAILBLAZERS* successfully.

Students explore shapes using geoboards.

Manipulatives List

Following are the manipulatives for fifth grade. There are several categories of manipulatives listed here:

Manufactured Manipulatives: a list of each of the manipulatives needed to implement fully the MATH TRAILBLAZERS curriculum. Many of these manipulatives may be available already in your classroom or school.

Manipulatives which you need can be purchased:

- in kit form from Kendall/Hunt Publishing Company;

- in a kit configuration which allows sharing between classrooms from Kendall/Hunt;

- or as individual items from your manipulatives supplier.

Please contact Kendall/Hunt directly for additional information.

Other materials are needed for the successful implementation of the MATH TRAILBLAZERS curriculum for the entire year. These materials are listed in three categories to aid in planning for the year:

- **Consumables** (edible or one-use items such as beans, paper towels, etc.)

- **Collectibles** (throwaway items such as magazines, egg cartons, jars, etc.)

- **School Supplies** (items usually available in classrooms such as tape, glue, markers, etc.)

Manipulatives for MATH TRAILBLAZERS Fifth Grade

Manufactured Manipulative, classroom	Number per Group	TOTAL per Classroom of 30 Students
base-ten pieces, set consists of: 2 packs (10 cm × 10 cm × 10 cm), 14 flats (10 cm × 10 cm × 1 cm), 30 skinnies (10 cm × 1 cm × 1 cm), 50 bits (1 cm × 1 cm × 1 cm)	1 set per student pair	15 sets
bubble solution	1 per student group of 3	10
bubble wands	1 per student group of 3	10
calculator, TI-30 Challenger	1 per student	30
compasses	1 per student	30
connecting cubes	40 per student	1200
eyedroppers	1 per student group of 3	10–15
geoboards	1 per student pair	15
graduated cylinder, 250 cc	1 per student group of 3	10–15
metersticks	1–2 per student group of 3	10–15
Mr. O	1 per classroom	1
overhead base-ten pieces		1 set
overhead geoboard	1 per classroom	1
overhead pattern blocks		1 set

Manufactured Manipulative, classroom	Number per Group	TOTAL per Classroom of 30 Students
pattern blocks, fraction (1 cm or $\frac{1}{2}$ cm to match size of standard pattern blocks used)	3 brown trapezoids, 6 purple triangles per student	270
pattern blocks, standard	6 green triangles, 5 blue rhombuses, 1–2 yellow hexagons, and 3 red trapezoids per student	480
protractors	1 per student	30
ruler, cm/inch, transparent	1 per student	30
spheres, small steel ($\frac{1}{2}$-inch diameter)	5 per student group of 3	50
spheres, medium steel (1-inch diameter)	1 per student group of 3	10–15
spheres, large steel ($1\frac{1}{4}$-inch diameter)	1 per student group of 3	10–15
spinners, clear plastic	1 per student pair	15
square-inch tiles, colored	25 per student	750
standard masses	1 set per student pair (10 5-gram masses, 5 10-gram masses, 2 20-gram masses, 10 1-gram masses)	15 sets
stopwatches	24 per classroom	24
two-pan balances	1 per student group of 3	10–15
*wall chart, laminated: data tables & graph	1 set per classroom	1 set

*The wall chart is available through Kendall/Hunt Publishing Company ISBN 0-7872-0762-4.

Collectibles, Consumables, and School Supplies Needed for MATH TRAILBLAZERS Fifth Grade

Collectible Materials	Number Required
bags, paper lunch	1 per group of 3
bags, plastic self-closing	1 per group of 3
beans, baby lima	1 lb bag per group of 3–4
cardboard, 14 cm by 24 cm	1 per student
cans and lids of various sizes	2–3 per student pair

Collectibles, Consumables, and School Supplies Needed for *MATH TRAILBLAZERS* Fifth Grade (Con't.)

Collectible Materials	Number Required
one of the following:	
large grassy area,	
piece of sod,	
nylon netting,	
window screen, or	
large beach towel	1 per classroom
clay	1 handful per group of 3
cups/pans for holding/pouring water	1 per group of 3
small objects to measure mass/volume	
cork	
wood	
paraffin block	1–2 per group of 3
string	1 ball (at least 200 ft)
pennies	20 per group of 3
nickels	1 per group of 3
playing cards	1 deck per group of 3
pony beads or ditali noodles	77 per student
scoops, three sizes	
small, 2 tablespoons	
medium, 4 tablespoons	
large, 6 tablespoons	1 of each per group of 3–4

Consumable Materials	Number Required
chenille sticks	4 per group of 3
straws	10 per group of 3

School Supplies	Number Required
easel paper	41 sheets
letter-size envelopes	1 per group of 3
manila folders	2 per student
file rack	1 per classroom
paper towels	3 brands, 1 roll each
rubber bands	2 boxes per classroom
3- by 5-inch index cards	2 packages

The following supplies are used throughout the year:

masking tape

scissors

scotch tape

chalk

crayons or markers

overhead markers

glue

Literature List

The *Literature List* provides suggested titles and recommended reading of commercially available trade books, which are used in many *MATH TRAILBLAZERS* lessons.

Students connect math and literature by reading a trade book.

Literature List

Many lesson guides in MATH TRAILBLAZERS suggest the use of commercially available trade books. A listing of these trade books is provided here. These books can be used to extend or enhance a particular lesson.

Unit 1

Populations and Samples

Bash, Barbara. *Ancient Ones.* Sierra Club, San Francisco, CA, 1994.

George, Jean Craighead. *One Day in the Tropical Rain Forest.* HarperCollins, New York, 1990.

Kipling, Rudyard. *The Jungle Books.* Dell, New York, 1964.

Yolen, Jane. *Welcome to the Green House.* Scholastic, New York, 1994.

Unit 2

Big Numbers

Asimov, Isaac. *Our Solar System.* Garth Stevens Publishing, Milwaukee, WI, 1988.

Cole, Joanna. *The Magic School Bus: Lost in the Solar System.* Scholastic, New York, 1990.

Heymann, Thomas. *On An Average Day.* Fawcett Columbine, New York, 1989.

Sandburg, Carl. *Complete Poems.* Harcourt, Brace, Jovanovich, New York, 1950.

Schwartz, David M. *If You Made a Million.* Scholastic, New York, 1989.

Simon, Seymour. *Our Solar System.* Morrow Junior Books, New York, 1992.

The World Almanac and Book of Facts. Funk and Wagnalls, Mahwah, NJ, 1995.

Unit 3

Fractions and Ratios

Xiong, Blip. *Nine in One, Grr! Grr!* Children's Book Press, San Francisco, CA, 1989.

Unit 4

Division and Data

Adair, Gene. *George Washington Carver: Botanist.* Chelsea House Publishers, New York, 1989.

Mitchel, Barbara. *A Pocketful of Goobers.* Carolhoda Books, Inc., Minneapolis, MN, 1986.

Moore, Eva. *The Story of George Washington Carver.* Scholastic, New York, 1971.

Unit 6	**Geometry**

Hopkinson, Deborah. *Sweet Clara and the Freedom Quilt.* Paintings by James Ransome. Alfred A. Knopf, New York, 1993.

Kinsey-Warnock, Natalie. *The Canada Geese Quilt.* Illustrated by Leslie W. Bowman. Cobblehill Books/Dutton, New York, 1989.

Paul, Ann Whitford. *Eight Hands Round A Patchwork Alphabet.* Illustrated by Jeanette Winter. Harper Collins, New York, 1991.

Unit 7	**Decimals and Probability**

Lowry, Lois. *Number the Stars.* Houghton Mifflin Co., Boston, MA, 1989.

Unit 8	**Applications: An Assessment Unit**

Appelhoff, Mary; Fenton, Mary Frances; and Harris, Barbara Loss. *Worms Eat Our Garbage.* Flower Press, Kalamazoo, MI, 1993.

Bowdin, Joan. *Where Does Our Garbage Go?* Delacorte Press, New York, 1992.

Cole, Joanna. *The Magic School Bus: Lost in Space.* Scholastic, New York, 1990.

Schwartz, David M. *If You Made a Million.* Scholastic, New York, 1989.

The EarthWorks Group. *50 Simple Things Kids Can Do to Save the Earth.* Andrews and McMeel, Kansas City, MO, 1990.

Too Much Trash? Kids Handbook. National Geographic Society, Washington, D.C., 1991.

Wilder, Laura Ingalls. *Little House in the Big Woods.* Harper and Row, New York, 1932.

Unit 9	**Connections to Division**

Wilder, Laura Ingalls. *Little House in the Big Woods.* Scholastic, New York, 1992.

Unit 11	**Number Patterns, Primes, and Fractions**

Hulme, Joy N. *Sea Squares.* Hyperion Books for Children, New York, 1991.

Unit 14	**Using Circles**

Few, Robert. *Children's Guide to Endangered Animals.* Macmillan Publishing Company, New York, 1993.

Lasky, Kathryn. *The Librarian Who Measured the Earth.* Little, Brown, and Company, New York, 1994.

Levy, Judith (ed.). *The World Almanac for Kids, 1996.* Funk and Wagnalls, Mahwah, NJ, 1995.

Unit 16	**Bringing It All Together: An Assessment Unit**

Cannon, Janell. *Stellaluna.* Harcourt Brace & Company, Orlando, FL, 1993.

Levy, Judith (ed.). *The World Almanac For Kids, 1996.* Funk and Wagnalls, Mahwah, NJ, 1995.

Games List

The *Games List* section includes descriptions of games used in MATH TRAILBLAZERS.

A student uses counting strategies while playing a math game.

Games List

Games are often used in MATH TRAILBLAZERS to engage students in practicing basic arithmetic and other math concepts. A complete listing of the games for your grade and a description of the games are provided below.

Once introduced, these games can be used throughout the year for ongoing practice. We suggest that after the games have been introduced and played in class, they be added to a "Games Menu," with necessary materials placed in a math center somewhere in the classroom so that students can replay the games during indoor recess, when they have completed other assignments, and at other times during the day.

Unit 2 | Big Numbers

Spin and Read Number Game in Unit 2, Lesson 1

A player spins a spinner and draws that number of cards from a deck. The player then lines up the cards and says the number the cards create aloud. If he or she says the number correctly, then it is recorded on a place value chart. Play continues for four rounds. At the end of the fourth round, players find the sum of the numbers on their place value chart. The highest sum wins.

Unit 5 | Investigating Fractions

Fraction Cover-All in Unit 5, Lesson 3

Students draw a 3 by 4 centimeter rectangle on dot paper. One player draws a card from the game deck and reads the fraction on the card aloud. Players represent the fraction called on their rectangles. Play continues as students represent fractions from cards drawn on their rectangles. When one player fills his or her rectangle completely, the game ends. Players then write number sentences for the fractions represented on their rectangles. The winner is the player who writes the most correct number sentences.

Unit 7 | Decimals and Probability

Digits Game in Unit 7, DPP Item F

To begin the game, students draw the set of boxes on their paper as shown:

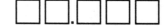

The teacher chooses a digit at random from a set of *Digit Cards (0–9).* Students place the digit in a box in such a way as to try to get the largest number. Once a digit is placed, it cannot be moved. Then, the teacher chooses a second digit without replacing the first to the deck. Play continues until the teacher has read enough digits to fill the boxes. The player with the largest number wins. Play again; however, this time students try to make the smallest number.

Score One in Unit 7, Lesson 2

This game is played in pairs. Each player makes a list of 20 decimals between 0–1 that have values in the hundredths. Each player then selects a number from his or her list and challenges his or her opponent to find it on the

Number Line. The player marks the position of the number on the Number Line with a toothpick and uses the Decimal Scale to verify the position of the number. If the number is within one-tenth of its actual location on the Number Line, that player earns 0.10 point. The first player to get 1 point in all, wins.

How Many Heads? in Unit 7, Lesson 8

Students flip two pennies. If 0 heads show, then the 0-Heads player gets a point. If 1 head shows, then the 1-Head player gets a point. If 2 heads show, then the 2-Heads Player gets a point. The first player to score 10 points wins. As students play the game several times, they record data in a table in order to determine if the game is mathematically fair.

Matching Two Pennies in Unit 7, Lesson 8

Students flip two pennies. If the two pennies match (HH or TT), then Player 1 gets a point. If the two pennies don't match (HT or TH), then Player 2 gets a point. The first player to score 10 points is the winner. As students play the game several times, they record data in a table in order to determine if the game is mathematically fair.

Unit 8   Applications: An Assessment Unit

Three in a Row in Unit 8, Lesson 2

A player chooses two factors from the factor frame and finds the product using a calculator. He or she then places a game marker on the product on the game board that is closest to their product. The first player to cover three squares in a row is the winner.

Unit 9   Connections to Division

Digits Game: Addition and Subtraction with Decimals in Unit 9, DPP Items L and P

To begin the game, students draw the set of boxes on their papers as shown:

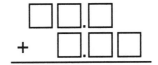

The teacher chooses a digit at random from a set of *Digit Cards (0–9).* Students place the digit in a box in such a way as to try to get the largest sum. Once a digit is placed, it cannot be moved. Then, the teacher chooses a second digit without replacing the first to the deck. Play continues until the teacher has read enough digits to fill the boxes. The player with the largest sum wins. Play again; however, this time students try to make the smallest sum. The game can also be played with subtraction. Students fill the boxes following the same rules, but try to get the largest (or smallest) difference. Different configurations of boxes can also be used for addition, subtraction, multiplication, and division of whole numbers.

Unit 10   Maps and Coordinates

The Great Barrier Reef in Unit 10, Lesson 2

On graph paper, each player hides a pod of whales (5 coordinate points), a shipwreck (4 coordinate points), migrating turtles (3 coordinate points), and a flock of birds (2 coordinate points). Players make a table to record their guesses and sightings. Player 1 names an ordered pair and records it in the table. Player 2 says "sighting" or "miss." If Player 1 gets a sighting, his or her turn continues. If not, it becomes Player 2's turn. The first player to identify correctly all the coordinates of all of the opponent's objects wins the game.

Unit 11 Number Patterns, Primes, and Fractions

Factor 40 in Unit 11, Lesson 1

Player A chooses a number on the Factor 40 Game Board and marks the square containing that number with his or her symbol (X or O). Player A records this number as his or her score for this turn. Player B finds and marks all of the remaining factors of Player A's number. Then, Player B selects another number as his or her turn. Player B adds up all of the numbers he or she has marked and records a score. (Note: Each player gets points two ways: points for the factors of the other player's number and points for the number he or she chooses.) A number can be used only once. If a player chooses a number that has no available factors, this is considered an illegal move. He or she earns no points. The game resumes with the opponent choosing a number. Play continues until there are no more legal moves. Players add up their points. The player with the most points wins the game.

Unit 12 Using Fractions

Hexagon Duets in Unit 12, Lesson 1

One yellow hexagon is one whole. Each player spins the spinner twice. Each time they spin, they place the pattern blocks on the outline of the two hexagons and add the two fractions together. Players may need to trade the pattern blocks for other pattern blocks to find the sum. They write a number sentence for the sum of the two fractions. Then, each player adds his or her sum to their partner's sum to find a grand total. The team with the largest total wins the round and earns $\frac{1}{3}$ of a point. Continue to play more rounds. The first team to earn one whole point is the winner.

Software List

The *Software List* outlines recommended computer software used to enhance *MATH TRAILBLAZERS* lessons.

Students use software to practice math facts and solve problems.

Software List

Software Titles by Topic

Applying Mathematics to Other Disciplines

The Amazon Trail   A Field Trip to the Rain Forest
The Second Voyage of the Mimi   The Voyage of the Mimi
Wood Car Rally

Data Collection/Reading and Interpreting Graphs

The Amazon Trail   Cricket Graph
A Field Trip to the Rain Forest   Graphers
The Mystery of the Hotel Victoria   Outnumbered
The Second Voyage of the Mimi   The Voyage of the Mimi
Wood Car Rally

Fractions/Decimals/Percents

Fraction Concepts, Inc   Fraction Munchers
Math Football: Decimals   Math Football: Fractions
Math Football: Percents
More Teasers from Tobbs: Decimals and Fractions
New Math Blaster Plus

Geometry

Building Perspective
Elastic Lines: The Electronic Geoboard
The Factory   The Geometer's Sketchpad
The Geometric PreSupposer   Logo
Quadrominoes   The Super Factory
TesselMania   Tetris

Integers

How the West Was One + Three x Four
Teasers By Tobbs with Integers

Logical Thinking/Problem Solving

The Amazon Trail   Building Perspective
The Factory   A Field Trip to the Rain Forest
The King's Rule   Math Blaster Mystery
The Mystery of the Hotel Victoria   Puzzle Tanks
Quadrominoes   Safari Search
Super Factory
What Do You Do with a Broken Calculator
Wood Car Rally

Number Theory (Factors and Primes)

Math Blaster Mystery   Number Munchers

Practice with Basic Operations

Divide with Balancing Bear
How the West Was One + Three x Four
Math Football: Rounding   Multiply with Balancing Bear
The Mystery of the Hotel Victoria New Math Blaster Plus
Number Maze   Outnumbered
Puzzle Tanks
Teasers by Tobbs with Whole Numbers
Wasatch Math Construction Tools: Number Blocks
What Do You Do with a Broken Calculator

Probability

Prob Sim
Taking Chances

Programs for Illustrating Problems

Kid Pix

Understanding of Basic Operations

Divide with Balancing Bear
How the West Was One + Three x Four
Multiply with Balancing Bear   New Math Blaster Plus
Puzzle Tanks   Teasers by Tobbs with Integers
Teasers by Tobbs with Whole Numbers
Wasatch Math Construction Tools: Number Blocks
What Do You Do with a Broken Calculator

Unit 1 | Populations and Samples

Voyage of the Mimi is a multimedia product that has sections relating to the rain forest.

A Field Trip to the Rain Forest integrates mathematics with science.

The *Amazon Trail* takes students on an adventure to the Amazon basin.

Unit 2 | Big Numbers

Divide with Balancing Bear provides practice and develops understanding of division.

Math Football: Rounding provides practice in rounding.

Number Maze provides practice in multiplication and division facts.

Teasers by Tobbs with Whole Numbers provides practice with multiplication and problem solving.

Wasatch Education System Math Tools allows students to model problems with graphics of base-ten pieces.

Unit 3 | Fractions and Ratios

Students can organize and graph their data using *Cricket Graph* or another spreadsheet and graphing program.

Unit 4 | Division and Data

Cricket Graph provides spreadsheet and graphing capabilities.

Divide with Balancing Bear develops understanding of division and provides practice.

Teasers by Tobbs with Whole Numbers develops understanding of multiplication and division and provides practice.

Number Maze provides practice in multiplication and division.

Number Munchers provides practice in facts.

Outnumbered provides practice in basic operations and interpreting graphs in a game format.

The Mystery of Hotel Victoria provides practice in basic operations while solving a mystery.

New Math Blaster Plus provides practice with the basic operations.

How the West was One + Three x Four provides practice in the order of operations.

Unit 5	**Investigating Fractions**

Fraction Munchers provides practice in identifying fractions and finding equivalent fractions.

Elastic Lines: The Electronic Geoboard develops area and perimeter constructs using the geoboard.

Unit 6	**Geometry**

Tesselmania provides opportunities to design tessellations and develop an understanding of the geometry involved in tessellations.

Quadrominoes provides students the opportunity to develop visual thinking and improve their understanding of geometric concepts by placing domino-like shapes, "quadros," on a board.

The Geometric preSupposer is an interactive program that gives students the opportunity to draw geometric shapes and explore geometric concepts.

Elastic Lines: The Electronic Geoboard is an interactive program that gives students the opportunity to explore geometric concepts by making shapes on a geoboard.

Tetris develops spatial visualization in a game setting.

Building Perspective develops spatial reasoning and visual thinking in three dimensions.

The Super Factory develops spatial visualization as children construct cubes with various designs.

Unit 7	**Decimals and Probability**

Prob Sim provides an opportunity for children to recreate Kerrich's experiments.

Taking Chances explores probability.

Unit 9	**Connections to Division**

Divide with Balancing Bear develops understanding of division and provides practice.

Fraction Concepts, Inc. provides practice with equivalent fractions, adding fractions, and basic fraction concepts.

Fraction Munchers provides practice with ordering fractions and equivalent fractions.

How the West was One + Three x Four provides practice with the order of operations.

Math Football: Fractions provides practice with fraction operations.

More Teasers by Tobbs: Decimals and Fractions develops understanding of computations with decimals and fractions.

New Math Blaster Plus provides practice with the basic operations.

Number Maze provides practice with multiplication and division.

Number Munchers provides practice with the facts.

Outnumbered provides practice in basic operations and interpreting graphs in a game format.

Teasers by Tobbs with Whole Numbers develops understanding of multiplication and division and provides practice.

The Mystery of Hotel Victoria provides practice in basic operations while solving a mystery.

What Do You Do With a Broken Calculator develops understanding of the basic operations as students do computations on a calculator with disabled keys.

Unit 10 · Maps and Coordinates

Building Perspective develops spatial reasoning and visual thinking in three dimensions.

Elastic Lines: The Electronic Geoboard is an interactive program that gives students the opportunity to explore geometric concepts by moving shapes on a geoboard.

National Geographic on the World Wide Web has the children use coordinates to locate other Web sites with which they are sharing information. A map is provided within the program.

Teasers by Tobbs with Integers provides practice in working with integers.

Tetris is an interactive program that provides opportunity for the development of spatial perception.

Tesselmania provides students with the opportunity to tessellate the plane by using slides and other transformations.

The Geometric preSupposer is an interactive program that gives students the opportunity to draw geometric shapes and explore geometric concepts.

The Super Factory develops spatial visualization as children construct cubes with various designs.

Quadrominoes provides students the opportunity to develop visual thinking and improve their understanding of geometric concepts by placing domino-like shapes, "quadros," on a board.

Unit 11 · Number Patterns, Primes, and Fractions

Number Munchers provides practice in identifying multiples, factors, primes, equivalent and nonequivalent expressions, and the basic operations.

Math Blaster Mystery provides skill development and problem solving in the context of a mystery.

Fraction Munchers provides practice with ordering fractions and equivalent fractions.

New Math Blaster Plus provides practice with the basic operations and fractions, decimals, and percents.

Fraction Concepts, Inc. provides practice with equivalent fractions, adding fractions, and basic fraction concepts.

Math Football: Fractions provides practice with fractions and operations.

More Teasers from Tobbs: Decimals and Fractions provides practice in adding and multiplying fractions and decimals.

Unit 12 **Using Fractions**

Fraction Concepts, Inc. provides practice with fractions and operations.

Fraction Munchers provides practice with ordering fractions and equivalent fractions.

Math Football: Fractions provides practice with fractions and operations.

More Teasers from Tobbs: Decimals and Fractions provides practice in adding and multiplying fractions and decimals.

New Math Blaster Plus provides practice with the basic operations and fractions, decimals, and percents.

Unit 13 **Ratio and Proportion**

Cricket Graph provides spreadsheet and graphing capabilities.

Unit 14 **Using Circles**

Logo helps students develop spatial reasoning and an understanding of geometry.

The Geometer's Sketchpad gives students the opportunity to create their own geometric drawings.

Geometric preSupposer is an interactive program that gives students the opportunity to draw geometric shapes and explore geometric concepts.

Unit 15 **Developing Formulas with Geometry**

Elastic Lines: The Electronic Geoboard develops the concepts of area and perimeter using the geoboard.

The Geometric preSupposer is an interactive program that gives students the opportunity to draw geometric shapes and explore geometric concepts.

Logo helps students develop spatial reasoning and an understanding of geometry by constructing shapes on the computer.

Unit 16 **Bringing It All Together: An Assessment Unit**

Bandelier National Monument World Wide Web site (http://www.nps.gov/band/) provides information about the monument.

Bat Conservation International World Wide Web site (http://www.batcon.org/) provides information about bats as well as links to other information sources.

The Amazon Trail by MECC

Students explore the Amazon rain forest as they search for a medicinal plant. Students practice problem solving and learn about the ecosystem and South American history as they try to save the ancient Incas. The program is recommended for grades 3 and up.

Bandelier National Monument
World Wide Web site (http://www.nps.gov/band/)

This web site provides information for visitors to Bandelier National Monument, including location, hours, and fees. There is also information about climate, activities, and accessibility.

Bat Conservation International World Wide Web site (http://www.batcon.org/)

This comprehensive web site is dedicated to the conservation of bats. It includes bat activities and facts as well as links to other bat sites. There is information about bat workshops and museum exhibits.

Building Perspective by Sunburst Communications

This program develops students' problem-solving skills, spatial perception, and visual thinking skills. Students are presented with ground-level views of an array of buildings. The task is to predict how the buildings will look when viewed from above. This program is recommended for grades 4–adult.

Cricket Graph (CA-Cricket Graph 1.3.2) by Computer Associates, Inc.

Cricket Graph is a graphing program in which students can organize data in a table and make either a bar graph or a point graph. The program will fit a line or a curve to the points. This program was not specifically designed with children in mind.

Divide with Balancing Bear by Sunburst Communications

This program helps students gain a conceptual understanding of division in the context of a jellybean factory. Students sort jellybeans into equal sets, determine the cost per jellybean in prepackaged sets, and determine which sets have an equal price per jellybean. The difficulty level for each of the activities can be changed. This program is recommended for grades 3–6.

Elastic Lines: the Electronic Geoboard by Sunburst Communications

This program enables students to work on an electronic geoboard. Students stretch "rubber bands" around "pegs" to construct shapes. This program develops concepts such as area, perimeter, reflections, slides, and turns. The program is recommended for grades 2–8.

The Factory by Sunburst Communications

Students are asked to produce or duplicate products in a simulated assembly line. Students direct the machines to punch, rotate, and stripe a variety of geometric shapes. Students explore sequences, patterns, and spatial relationships. The program is recommended for grades 4 and up.

A Field Trip to the Rain Forest by Sunburst Communications

This program integrates mathematics with science. Children explore plants and animals indigenous to a rain forest. In the activities, children use data tables to gather information and explore various aspects of the rain forest. The program allows children to create their own tables. It is recommended for grades 2 and up.

Fraction Concepts, Inc. by MECC

Students learn about fractions in the context of a "fraction factory." The program helps students understand the role of the numerator and denominator. Students practice working with fractions and finding equivalent fractions. This program is recommended for grades 3–5.

Fraction Munchers by MECC

In a game-like format, children identify numerators, denominators, and proper, improper, mixed, and whole-number fractions. The program also asks children to identify fractions in lowest terms, find equivalent fractions, and evaluate simple expressions. Teachers can set the level of difficulty. The program is recommended for grade 3–adult.

The Geometric preSupposer by Sunburst Communications

This program allows students to draw shapes and do other geometric constructions such as make perpendicular and parallel lines. Students can also measure lengths, angles, and areas. There is a grid with Cartesian coordinates. The program is recommended for grade 4 and above.

The Geometer's Sketchpad by Key Curriculum Press

The Geometer's Sketchpad is an interactive program that allows students to construct geometric shapes and then transform them. Shapes can be colored, labeled, and measured. The program also allows the user to record the steps of the construction. This program is recommended for upper elementary and above, but can be successfully used with younger children.

Graphers by Sunburst Communications

This program provides a data graphing tool for young students. The program allows even very young students to create pictographs, bar graphs, circle graphs, and data tables from data they have collected. It can also be used to provide practice in reading and interpreting different types of graphs. Students can write their interpretation of the graphs directly into an on-screen notebook to be printed out with the graph. The program is recommended for grades K–4.

How the West Was One + Three x Four by Sunburst Communications

Students learn about order of operations as they race their stagecoach or locomotive along the number line trail. The computer generates three numbers. The players make combinations of these numbers using the four basic operations and parentheses to be the first to reach Red Gulch. Teachers can customize the program. The program is recommended for grades 4-8.

Kid Pix by Broderbund Software Inc.

This program allows students to create their own illustrations for many different applications throughout the curriculum. In mathematics, students can use this program to illustrate problems they have been given to solve or they can create and illustrate their own patterns or problems. The program is recommended for grades K–4.

The King's Rule by Sunburst Communications

Students develop logical thinking as they explore number patterns. The players are given three numbers that fit a rule. The players try to discover the rule by hypothesizing and testing their hypotheses. Once the players think they know the rule, they tell the computer to quiz them. There are six levels of difficulty. The program is recommended for grades 4–12.

Logo

Logo is an interactive program that allows users to create geometric shapes by issuing commands. As students construct figures, they learn about the geometric properties of shapes. There are many commercially available Logo programs. One recent version is **MicroWorlds 1.0** by LCSI. In this version of *Logo,* students can add text, animation, and sound. This program is recommended for grades 2 to adult.

Math Blaster Mystery by Davidson & Associates, Inc.

This program combines skill development with problem solving in the context of solving a mystery. There are various levels which include problems with whole numbers as well as fractions, decimals, percents, and ratios and proportions. Students can also practice finding factors and multiples. The program is recommended for ages 10 to adult.

Math Football: Decimals by Gamco Industries, Inc.

The program provides practice in working with decimals in the context of a football game. Students play against another student or the computer. There are 4 games corresponding to increasing difficulty levels. Problems include adding, subtracting, multiplying, and dividing decimals. The game allows the user to choose the operations they wish to use. The program is recommended for grades 5 and above.

Math Football: Fractions by Gamco Industries, Inc.

This program provides practice in addition, subtraction, multiplication, and division of fractions. Students can play against each other or the computer. There are 4 games corresponding to increasing difficulty levels. At the first level, students practice adding and subtracting fractions with like and unlike denominators. At the next level, students add and subtract mixed numbers. The third level provides practice in multiplying and dividing fractions and mixed numbers while the last level combines all types of problems. The program is recommended for grades 4 and above.

Math Football: Percent by Gamco Industries, Inc.

The program provides practice in working with percents in the context of a football game. Students play against another student or the computer. There are 4 games corresponding to increasing difficulty levels. Problems include finding equivalences between percents and simple fractions, finding the percent of a number, finding a number when the percent is known, and finding unknown percents. The program is recommended for grades 6 and above but can be used by younger children as well.

Math Football: Rounding by Gamco Industries, Inc.

This program provides practice in rounding in the context of a football game. Students play against another student or the computer. There are four games corresponding to increasing difficulty levels. The games range from rounding two-, three-, and four-digit whole numbers to the nearest 10, 100, and 1000 to rounding whole numbers to the nearest 10 million and decimals to the nearest hundred-thousandth. The program is recommended for grades 5 and up.

More Teasers from Tobbs: Decimals and Fractions by Sunburst Communications

This program is very similar to *Teasers by Tobbs with Whole Numbers,* but children gain practice in adding and multiplying fractions and decimals. The teacher can determine whether fractions or decimals are used and the range of the numbers. The number of decimal places can be set as well as what denominators are used. Decimal games have an estimation option. The more difficult levels are not straightforward practice but involve problem solving. The program is recommended for grades 5 and up.

Multiply with Balancing Bear by Sunburst Communications

This program develops conceptual understanding and practice with multiplication. Children are asked to balance balloons that have varying costs so that the bear has the same total cost in both hands. There are three levels of the program. The program is recommended for grades 3–6.

The Mystery of the Hotel Victoria by Tom Snyder Productions

Students gather clues by answering various problems to discover why things are disappearing at the hotel. Students must gather enough information to decide how to solve the problems. A notepad is available to carry out calculations. Problems involve the basic operations and reading charts and graphs. The program is recommended for grade 5.

National Geographic
World Wide Web site (http://www.nationalgeographic.com)

This web site provides a link to scientific and educational information and resources. Students can exchange ideas and questions with leading professionals and scientists. Comprehensive atlas and maps of countries of the world are provided.

New Math Blaster Plus by Davidson & Associates, Inc.

This program is now called *Math Blaster 1—In Search of Spot* for grades 1–6 and *Math Blaster 2—Secret of The Lost City* for grades 3–8. The program provides practice with the basic operations and fractions, decimals, and percents in a game format. It is recommended for ages 6–12.

Number Maze by Great Wave Software

The object of the game is to guide a horse through a maze. In order to pass various obstacles, the child must answer questions. These questions include numerical problems and word problems presented in different formats. The problems involve counting and the basic operations. The teacher can control the types of problems given and their difficulty. It is recommended for children 5–12 years of age.

Number Munchers by MECC

Number Munchers provides practice in identifying multiples, factors, primes, equivalent and nonequivalent expressions, and the basic operations. Children must identify all the numbers in a grid which match the given criteria before they are eaten by the troggles. The graphics are excellent, and the teacher can control the difficulty level. It is recommended for grades 3 and up.

Outnumbered by The Learning Company

Outnumbered provides practice in the basic operations. It also provides practice in reading and interpreting graphs, charts, and maps. Practice is set in a game format. The user must stop the Master of Mischief from taking over a TV studio. In order to do this, the user must answer questions and collect clues. The program can be customized and there are other complementary activities on blackline masters provided for the teacher. The program is recommended for grades 3–6.

Prob Sim by Intellimation

Prob Sim is a probability simulator. Students can estimate the probability of real-world events by building a model, generating and analyzing data. It is generally recommended for older students, but can be used with middle grade students with teacher guidance.

Puzzle Tanks by Sunburst Communications

Students use problem-solving strategies to solve spatial and number puzzles as they transfer volumes from different tanks to arrive at a target amount. The problems reinforce concepts of basic operations as students test and revise solutions. The program is recommended for grades 3 and up.

Quadrominoes by Sunburst Communications

The program contains five games which develop spatial visualization and logical thinking. There are three levels of difficulty and three board sizes. In each game, students manipulate 40 playing pieces called quadros. A quadro is a square made of four smaller squares. Each of the smaller squares may be divided in half to form two triangles. The small squares and the triangles may be white or tan, thus creating different patterned tiles. The program is recommended for grades 4–8.

Safari Search by Sunburst Communications

Safari Search develops problem-solving skills and logical inference. The 12 games involve finding one or two hidden animals in a 5 by 5 grid. The players must deduce by collecting and organizing information where the animal is hidden. The types of clues vary from game to game. One game responds with "hot" if the player chooses a cell adjacent to where the animal is hidden, "warm" if they are diagonally adjacent, and "cold" otherwise. Another game gives the "taxicab" distance to the hidden animal. This program is recommended for grades 2 and up.

The Second Voyage of the Mimi by Sunburst (video or videodisc, computer, and print materials)

Like the first *Voyage of the Mimi,* this series of videos captures the adventures of a scientific expedition to explore science, mathematics, and social studies. This voyage takes the crew to the coast of Mexico where archeologists are studying ancient Maya sites. As in the first voyage, there is a vast amount of print and computer materials to develop the concepts explored in the story. The program is recommended for grades 4–8.

Super Factory by Sunburst Communications

This program develops spatial visualization and reasoning about orientation and symmetry. Students analyze cubes with different figures drawn on the faces and try to duplicate the cube. The program allows the pictures to be changed and the level of difficulty to be varied. The program is recommended for grade 6–adult but can be used successfully with younger students.

Taking Chances by Sunburst Communications

Taking Chances helps build an intuitive understanding of probability. There are six activities centered around a machine that dispenses balls in two colors. The computer randomly picks balls to dispense. In some activities, students predict what color ball will be ejected; in others, they predict how many balls out of 10 balls will be a given color. Other activities ask children to decide from which machine a given sample was more likely to come from. The activities explore sampling with replacement and without replacement. The program brings across the notion that sometimes events do not occur as predicted. The program does not use fractions or decimals and so is suitable for young children. It is recommended for grades 3 and up.

Teasers by Tobbs with Integers by Sunburst Communications

The format of the program is similar to *Teasers by Tobbs with Whole Numbers*. This program provides practice with adding and multiplying negative numbers. The range of numbers can be set, and there are several difficulty levels. The game is recommended for grades 2 and up.

Teasers by Tobbs with Whole Numbers by Sunburst Communications

Teasers by Tobbs with Whole Numbers provides practice in addition, subtraction, multiplication, and division in a problem-solving environment. Children must use logic and number facts to discover missing numbers in a grid. There are six levels of difficulty. The size of the numbers varies as well as the missing pieces of the grid. In the easiest problems, students practice addition and subtraction with one-digit numbers. The harder levels include problems in which students must examine the constraints of the problem, and multiple solutions are possible. The program is recommended for grades 3 and up.

TesselMania by MECC

TesselMania is a very versatile program that allows students to create their own tessellations. Children explore the geometry of tessellations while learning about rotations, translations, and glide reflections. Symmetry and patterns in art can be explored. There is an extensive teacher's guide. The program is recommended for grades 3 and up.

Tetris by Spectrum HoloByte

Students improve spatial visualization skills and their understanding of geometric transformations as they play this game. All the game pieces consist of four squares arranged in different configurations. As the four-square pieces tumble from the top of the screen into an empty pit, the player must rotate them into a position which leaves no gaps at the bottom. There are ten levels to this game.

The Voyage of the Mimi by Sunburst (video or videodisc, computer, and print materials)

This program of 13 videos tells the story of a research expedition that studies whales off the coast of New England. Each episode concludes with an interview with a scientist. The materials integrate science, mathematics, social studies, and language arts in a fascinating story. The vast amounts of computer programs and print materials focus on the concepts introduced in the story. The materials are recommended for grades 4–8.

Wasatch Math Construction Tools: Number Blocks by Wasatch Educational Systems

This is an interactive program that allows students to work with base-ten pieces. Children can move, group, and regroup pieces. The program also provides problems with the basic operations. It is recommended for grades 1 and up.

What Do You Do with a Broken Calculator by Sunburst Communications

Players must get to a goal number using a calculator that has one or more disabled keys. This program promotes logical thinking and deepens students' understanding of the basic operations as they search for innovative ways to do a computation. The program provides problems, or users can generate their own. The goal numbers can be whole numbers or decimals. This program is recommended for grades 3 to adult.

Wood Car Rally by MECC

Wood Car Rally is a computer simulation program which models experiments that are similar to *Downhill Racer* (Fourth Grade, Unit 6). Students can design experiments to see the effects of five different variables (shape of the car, weight, lubrication, angle of the ramp, and length of the ramp) on the distance a wood car will travel. *Wood Car Rally* is recommended for grades 3–8.

Software Companies | Addresses and Telephone Numbers

Broderbund Software Inc.   1-800-521-6263
500 Redwood Blvd.
Novato, CA 94947

Computer Associates International, Inc.   1-408-432-1727
1240 McKay Drive
San Jose, CA 95131

Davidson & Associates, Inc.   1-800-545-7677
P.O. Box 2961
Torrance, CA 90509

Gamco Industries, Inc.   1-800-351-1404
P.O. Box 1911
Big Spring, TX 79721

Great Wave Software   1-408-438-1990
5353 Scotts Valley Dr.
Scotts Valley, CA 95066

Intellimation   1-800-346-8355
P.O. Box 1922
Santa Barbara, CA 93116

Key Curriculum Press   1-510-548-2304
2512 Martin Luther King Jr. Way
Berkeley, CA 94704

The Learning Company   1-800-852-2255
6493 Kaiser Drive
Fremont, CA 94555

LCSI   1-800-321-5646
P.O. Box 162
Highgate Springs, VT 05460

MECC   1-612-569-1500
6160 Summit Dr. North
Minneapolis, MN 55430

Spectrum Holobyte   1-510-522-3584
Division of Sphere, Inc.
2061 Challenger Drive
Alameda, CA 94501

Sunburst Communications   1-800-321-7511
101 Castleton Street
P.O. Box 100
Pleasantville, NY 10570

Tom Snyder Productions   1-800-342-0236
80 Coolidge Hill Road
Watertown, MA 02172-2817

Wasatch Educational Systems   1-800-877-2848
5250 S. 300 West
Suite 101
Salt Lake City, UT 84107

Parents and *MATH TRAILBLAZERS*™

The *Parents and MATH TRAILBLAZERS* section provides suggestions and tips to help parents participate in their child's understanding of *MATH TRAILBLAZERS* and to enhance its benefits for their children.

A teacher, student, and parent work together to solve a problem.

Working with Parents

Parents and *Math Trailblazers*™

As you begin to use the *Math Trailblazers* curriculum in your classroom, it is important that you give thought to how you will help parents understand the curriculum and how it works. Parents want assurances that the content and approaches of the school's mathematics program will not only educate and interest their children now, but also benefit them later in their educational careers when test scores and school admissions become serious realities. Parents' understanding and support of the curriculum can be a key factor in their children's success with mathematics. This understanding and support also play an important role in the successful implementation of this curriculum.

As a *Standards*-based curriculum, *Math Trailblazers* is very different from the mathematics parents grew up with. If parents are going to provide effective support for their child at home, they need to have a clear understanding of what *Math Trailblazers* includes and what your school hopes to achieve by using it. Most adults experienced in their own schooling a mathematics curriculum that focused on teaching facts and procedures for computing. In contrast, *Math Trailblazers* maintains a careful balance between developing skills, underlying mathematical concepts, and problem solving. Parents need to understand this balance. It has many implications for the kind of work their children will be doing in class and bringing home.

You may want to communicate to parents:

- how the varied contexts for solving problems in *Math Trailblazers* help children learn to use mathematics in meaningful ways;

- that current research supports the approaches used in *Math Trailblazers* for teaching math facts and procedures and that these approaches allow students to gain facility with less drill and memorization than former methods and that retention will be enhanced;

- how practice with skills and procedures is distributed between homework, *Daily Practice and Problems,* and within most problem-solving activities in the program;

- how mathematical ideas are represented with manipulatives, pictures, tables, graphs, and numbers—and how these representations allow children to access the mathematics in varied ways;

- that *Math Trailblazers* encourages students to develop varied ways to solve problems—not just the solutions that adults might select; and

- that the types of activities in *Math Trailblazers* are designed precisely to provide their children with the varied skills that they will need in the workplace of the 21st century.

Most importantly, parents will also want to learn specific ways they can work with their children at home.

None of these things is likely to occur without a concerted effort on the part of teachers and the school to educate parents. Furthermore, getting parents on board early will save effort in the long term. We recommend that you antici-

---

Grades 4 & 5

Grades 4 and 5 include an information sheet for parents, called Math Facts Philosophy: Information For Parents, that outlines the Math Trailblazers philosophy for presenting math facts. This letter is located in the Unit 3 Unit Resource Guide (p. 189) in fourth grade; in fifth grade it is in the Unit 2 Unit Resource Guide (p. 101).

---

pate potential parental concerns about a new math program and address them proactively through an ongoing parent education effort.

Built-in Tools for Communicating with Parents

MATH TRAILBLAZERS provides several tools to help you communicate with parents about the curriculum.

Parent Brochure

A parent brochure in Spanish and English provides an introduction to the program for parents. The masters of these brochures are located at the end of this section. They have been created for you to copy and fold, thus creating a two-sided brochure that can be sent home at the beginning of the year or used as a handout at a fall parent meeting.

Parent Letters

Parent letters are included at the beginning of each unit to give parents specific information about what their children will be studying. These letters describe the concepts presented in each unit and how parents or family members can provide follow-up and encouragement to their children at home. A sample parent letter is shown in Figure 1.

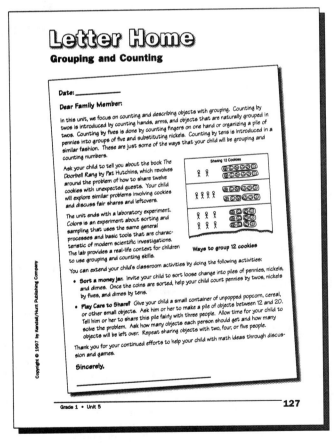

Figure 1: Sample parent letter from Grade 1

Homework Notes

Some homework assignments, especially in grades 1–3, include a separate explanation for family members, outlining the purpose of the activity and providing hints for assisting the child. An example of such a note is shown in Figure 2. Our experience is that these kinds of explanations help parents feel comfortable with the content and goals of the curriculum. We encourage you to supplement the parent instructions with additional short notes of your own.

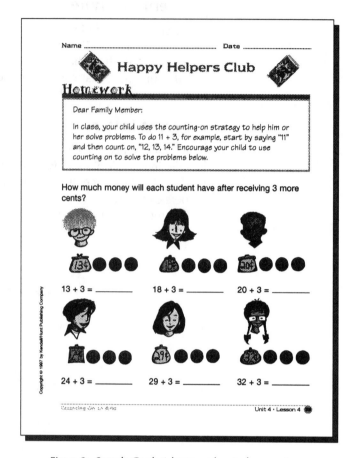

Figure 2: Sample Grade 1 homework note for parents

Special Programs for Parents

Math Nights

One way to help parents further understand the goals and philosophy of MATH TRAILBLAZERS is to organize special math-related events or presentations, such as a "Math Night," that focus on the topics and format from the MATH TRAILBLAZERS curriculum. A Math Night program typically includes two or more problem-solving activities or math games for parents to try. These activities can be coupled with a short presentation by the teacher and/or other school personnel.

The following illustrate the types of activities in MATH TRAILBLAZERS that have worked well in Math Night programs:

- sorting apples from *How Many? How Much? How Far?* in kindergarten;

- parts of the *Pockets* activity in Unit 2 of Grade 1;

- a portion of *High, Wide, and Handsome* in Unit 4 of Grade 2;

- the *First Names* activity from Unit 1 of Grade 3;
- a portion of *Arm Span vs. Height* in Unit 1 of Grade 4;
- the game *Three in a Row* from Unit 8 of Grade 5.

These activities can be adapted to involve parents in active problem solving. They also illustrate key ideas of the curriculum, such as the use of multiple representations of math concepts, the focus on problem solving, the broad range of mathematical content, and the strong connection with science. The use of one or more games as part of Math Night illustrates one way to engage students in practicing math facts. A videotape on the goals and philosophy of MATH TRAILBLAZERS, available from Kendall/Hunt Publishing Company, can be an effective component of a "Math Night."

It is usually helpful to complement the activities with a short presentation. This presentation might, for example, discuss the underlying philosophy of the MATH TRAILBLAZERS program (see Section 1), discuss some of the key NCTM recommendations (see Section 5), discuss plans for future lessons, or provide practical suggestions for parents to work with their children, such as how to encourage children to explain their math thinking about how manipulatives can be used to model math concepts.

Another way to bring home an understanding of a problem-solving mathematics classroom is to videotape a class session in which you can capture students engaged in some way: working collaboratively, collecting data, explaining their thinking. This tape could be used in conjunction with Math Nights or checked out for home viewing.

Family Math

Another good way to generate parent understanding of and support for a reform mathematics program is to organize a *Family Math* program at your school. *Family Math,* developed by Project Equals at the Lawrence Hall of Science, involves a series of classes in which parents and children come together to enjoy stimulating math games and activities. The program introduces families to key mathematical principles, involves parents as active partners in their children's education, develops students' critical and logical thinking skills, and connects mathematics to everyday life. These goals, of course, complement the goals of MATH TRAILBLAZERS. As a result, parents who participate in a *Family Math* program are likely to have a good understanding of the approaches used in MATH TRAILBLAZERS and will feel comfortable working with their children on mathematics. The *Family Math* book of activities can be ordered through various math publishers or supply houses, your local bookstore, or directly from the Lawrence Hall of Science. For more information about the program, including training for *Family Math* workshop leaders, contact:

Family Math
Lawrence Hall of Science
University of California at Berkeley
Berkeley, CA 94720-5200

(510) 642-1823

Roles for Parent Volunteers

Parent volunteers can be used in a variety of capacities to support the implementation of *Math Trailblazers*.

Hands-on programs, by their very nature, involve many manipulatives and other materials. *Math Trailblazers* is no exception. In addition to the commercially purchased manipulatives, many activities call for collectible materials, such as jars, container lids, paper towel cores, etc. The job of gathering and managing these materials can be eased with the assistance of a parent volunteer.

Many teachers use parent volunteers to assist with classroom activities. The parents can be assigned to work with particular groups of students or with individual students who need extra assistance. They can work on special projects or lesson extensions with small groups. Some teachers periodically invite several parents to assist with "station activities," where student groups rotate from station to station. In many cases, it is simply just helpful to have an extra set of hands and eyes in the classrooms to assist as needed.

The roles parents play in providing support will obviously need to be tailored to your needs and the interests and capabilities of individual parents. There is little doubt, however, that cooperative parents are a valuable asset as you work with *Math Trailblazers*.

MATH TRAILBLAZERS™

A Mathematical Journey Using Science and Language Arts

An Introduction for Families

A TIMS® Curriculum from the University of Illinois at Chicago

Published by Kendall/Hunt Publishing Company

How can parents talk with their children about math?

Your child will have a lot to share with you about mathematics. Here are some conversation starters to help your child communicate what he or she is doing in mathematics:

☞ What problems did you solve in math today? How did you solve the problems? Are there other ways to solve that same problem?

☞ Did you use any special materials in math today? What were they? How did you use them?

☞ Did you measure anything in school today? What did you measure?

☞ Did you collect data in math today? How did you record the data?

☞ Did you hear a math story today? Please tell me the story.

> **"One of the things I've noticed … is that when he [my child] brings home an activity and he brings a measuring tape or something kind of special, he's excited about doing it. The fact that we're involved in the games—he loves that—and he's proud of what he's doing."**
>
> **Parent**

You can contact the developers of *MATH TRAILBLAZERS* at the following address:

UIC The University of Illinois at Chicago
TIMS Project
Institute for Mathematics and Science Education (M/C 250)
950 South Halsted Street, Room 2075 SEL
Chicago, IL 60607-7019

 KENDALL/HUNT PUBLISHING COMPANY
4050 Westmark Drive   Dubuque,   Iowa   52002

 Development of *MATH TRAILBLAZERS* was supported in part by the National Science Foundation.

What connections does MATH TRAILBLAZERS make with other school subjects?

> "It seems a lot of this carries over to different subject areas. It's not just isolated to math."
>
> **Teacher**

In *MATH TRAILBLAZERS*, children learn mathematics, in part, by applying it in many different contexts. This makes mathematics meaningful for students and models the way mathematics is used outside of school.

Science investigations are used often in *MATH TRAILBLAZERS* to provide a context for learning and applying mathematics. Children design experiments; collect, organize, and graph data; and analyze experimental results in much the same way scientists do. Measurement of length, area, volume, mass, and time is done repeatedly within the context of scientific experiments. This strong connection with science engages students in rich problem-solving activities and introduces students to the tools and methods scientists use.

MATH TRAILBLAZERS also has many connections with language arts—communication of math ideas in writing and orally are an integral part of every lesson. Children write journal entries, record data, and share ideas. They also read children's books and TIMS Adventure Books that connect with many class lessons. As children communicate their methods for solving problems and justify their answers, they better understand important math concepts. Their writing and other communication skills also improve.

Why is my child using calculators with MATH TRAILBLAZERS?

The calculator is a tool used in appropriate situations to help your child explore number ideas and relationships, solve more complex problems, and explore mathematics on his or her own. The use of calculators is supported by the National Council of Teachers of Mathematics.

A curriculum for your children

The mathematics curriculum being taught in many schools today is very similar to the curriculum that was taught when the parents, grandparents, and even great-grandparents of today's school children attended school. Many of the math skills in that curriculum remain important today. But the world has changed considerably since the time of our grandparents. Advances in technology have created many other essential math skills that your children will need when they complete their formal schooling and enter tomorrow's work force. The National Council of Teachers of Mathematics recognized these needs when, in 1989, it made a series of recommendations for updating math instruction in U.S. schools. *MATH TRAILBLAZERS* was developed to reflect these national recommendations.

MATH TRAILBLAZERS will prepare students to:

★ know and apply basic math skills;

★ solve problems using many different strategies;

★ be independent thinkers;

★ reason skillfully in diverse situations;

★ effectively communicate solutions to problems and methods for solving them;

★ work alone and in groups to solve problems.

MATH TRAILBLAZERS was developed and tested over a six-year period by a team from the Teaching Integrated Mathematics and Science (TIMS) Project at the University of Illinois at Chicago. Using the results of educational research and over 15 years of previous experience in curriculum development, the TIMS Project has written an innovative program that will prepare your children with math skills needed for the 21st century.

What is in the *MATH TRAILBLAZERS* curriculum?

MATH TRAILBLAZERS is a comprehensive curriculum that maintains a balance between the development of math concepts and basic skills. Students apply basic math skills while working on meaningful and challenging tasks. The math content of the traditional math curriculum is studied; but other topics—estimation, geometry, measurement, patterns and relationships, algebra concepts, and statistics and probability—are investigated at an appropriate level in each grade.

The curriculum includes different types of lessons:

Activities—explorations of math concepts and skills that use a variety of tools and methods.

Labs—extended investigations that use a simplified version of the method scientists use.

Daily Practice and Problems—items that provide practice in math skills and concepts.

Games—math games that build familiarity with math skills and concepts.

Adventure Books—illustrated stories that deal with math and science ideas.

Assessments—activities that allow the teacher and student to assess progress.

What is a *MATH TRAILBLAZERS* classroom like?

When you walk into your child's *MATH TRAILBLAZERS* class, you will probably notice that it does not look like the mathematics classroom you experienced when you were your child's age. Children might be working in groups, rolling cars down ramps, dropping water onto paper towels, or pulling jellybean samples from bags. As they work, children discuss different ways to solve problems. The room is filled with a feeling of excitement and discovery.

In a *MATH TRAILBLAZERS* classroom, children are:

☆ learning mathematics by using it to solve many different kinds of problems;

☆ drawing on their own experiences and working with real-world problems;

☆ using concrete objects to understand abstract mathematical concepts;

☆ communicating mathematical ideas to their peers and teacher;

☆ gaining confidence in mathematics and developing an "I can do it" feeling.

MATH TRAILBLAZERS™*

Una Aventura en Matemáticas usando Ciencias y el Arte de Lenguaje

Una Introducción para Familias

Desarrollado por el Proyecto de TIMS—Teaching Integrated Mathematics and Science— (Integrando la Enseñanza de las Matemáticas y de las Ciencias) de la Universidad de Illinois en Chicago

Publicado por Kendall/Hunt Publishing Company

*Abriendo un camino de matemáticas

¿Qué es lo que los padres de familia pueden hacer?

Su hijo/a tendrá mucho que compartir con usted acerca de matemáticas. Aquí hay algunos temas para iniciar conversaciones que ayudarán a su hijo/a a que él o ella comunique lo que usted esté haciendo en matemáticas.

☞ ¿Qué problema resolviste el día de hoy en tu clase de matemáticas? ¿Cómo lo resolviste? ¿Hay alguna otra forma de resolver ese mismo problema?

☞ ¿Utilizaste algúnos materiales especiales en tu clase de matemáticas? ¿Qué eran? ¿Cómo los usaste?

☞ ¿Mediste hoy algo en la escuela? ¿Qué fue lo que mediste?

☞ ¿Acumulaste algunos datos en matemáticas? ¿Cómo registraste esos datos?

☞ ¿Escuchaste alguna historia en matemáticas? Por favor cuéntame la historia.

> "Una de las cosas que he notado… es que cuando él [mi hijo] trae una actividad a la casa y trae una cinta métrica o algo especial, está emocionado para hacerlo. El hecho que nosotros estamos enredados en los juegos—le encanta—y está orgulloso de lo que está haciendo."
>
> Un padre de familia

Se puede comunicar con los diseñadores de *MATH TRAILBLAZERS* a la siguiente dirección:

UIC The University of Illinois at Chicago
TIMS Project
Institute for Mathematics and Science Education (M/C 250)
950 South Halsted Street, Room 2075 SEL
Chicago, IL 60607-7019

KENDALL/HUNT PUBLISHING COMPANY
4050 Westmark Drive   Dubuque, Iowa 52002

El desarrollo de *MATH TRAILBLAZERS* fue ayudado en parte por la National Science Foundation.

¿Qué conexiones hace *MATH TRAILBLAZERS* con otras materias escolares?

En Math Trailblazers, los estudiantes aprenden matemáticas, en parte, aplicandolo a diversas situaciones. De esta manera las matemáticas se hacen interesantes y adquieren sentido.

Investigaciones científicas en *MATH TRAILBLAZERS* proveen la oportunidad frecuente de la aplicación de las matemáticas. Los estudiantes diseñan experimentos; acumulan y organizan datos; hacen gráficas de datos; y analizan los resultados de los experimentos en una manera semejante a lo que hacen los científicos. Se hacen mediciónes de longitud, area, volumen, masa, y tiempo como parte de experimentos científicos. Esta fuerte conexión con la ciencia hace que los estudiantes resuelvan problemas como "científicos," usando métodos y herramientas de la ciencias.

MATH TRAILBLAZERS también tiene muchas conexiones con el arte de lenguaje. La comunicación de ideas en matemáticas—a través de escribir, hablar, y dibujar—es una parte integral de cada lección. Los estudiantes escriben en sus diarios, registran datos, y comparten ideas. Ellos también leen libros infantiles y "libros de aventuras" que se conectan con muchas lecciónes. Los estudiantes mejoran en su entendimiento de conceptos matemáticos al comunicar sus métodos de resolver problemas y explicar sus respuestas. Sus habilidades en escribir y comunicar también mejoran.

¿Por qué mi hijo/a está usando calculadoras en *MATH TRAILBLAZERS*?

Las calculadoras son instrumentos usados para ayudar a su hijo/a a investigar ideas con números y sus relaciones, resolver problemas complejos, y explorar la matemática. El uso de estas herramientas es recomendado por el Concejo Nacional de Maestros de Matemáticas.

Un programa para sus hijos

Los programas de matemáticas que se encuentran hoy día en muchas escuelas son muy semejantes a las classes que tenían los padres, abuelos, y aún bisabuelos de los estudiantes de hoy. Mucha del material de esos programas antiguos todavía se necesita hoy. Pero el mundo ha cambiado desde el tiempo de nuestros abuelos. Avances en tecnología han creado la necesidad de desarrollar otras técnicas especiales que sus hijos necesitarán en el mundo de trabajo del futuro. El Concejo Nacional de Maestros de Matemáticas reconoció estas necesidades cuando hizo una serie de recomendaciones para mejorar la enseñanza de matemáticas en las escuelas de los Estados Unidos. Hemos desarrollado el programa *MATH TRAILBLAZERS* para incorporar esas recomendaciones nacionales.

MATH TRAILBLAZERS preparará estudiantes para:

★ aprender y usar técnicas básicas en matemáticas;

★ resolver problemas usando varias estrategias diferentes;

★ pensar independientemente;

★ razonar con habilidad en diversas situaciones;

★ comunicar efectivamente tanto las soluciones como los métodos;

★ resolver problemas trabajando solos y en grupos.

El programa *MATH TRAILBLAZERS* fue desarrollado y ensayado por un equipo del Proyecto de TIMS—Teaching Integrated Mathematics and Science—(Integrando la Enseñanza de las Matemáticas y de las Ciencias) de la Universidad de Illinois en Chicago. Han creado un programa innovativo que proveerá a sus hijos con las bases matemáticos necesarios para poder competir en el campo del trabajo en el Siglo XXI.

¿Qué hay en el programa *MATH TRAILBLAZERS*?

El programa *MATH TRAILBLAZERS* es un programa integral que mantiene un balance entre el desarrollo de los conceptos y las técnicas básicas de matemáticas. Los estudiantes usan las técnicas básicas mientras están trabajando con problemas interesantes y estimulantes. Se estudian los tópicos matemáticos de un programa tradicional; pero también se investigan otras materias—estimación, geometría, medición, patrones y relaciones, conceptos de álgebra, estadística y probabilidad—en un nivel apropiado para los niños.

El programa contiene varios tipos de lecciones:

Actividades—exploraciones de conceptos matemáticos y técnicas usando diferentes herramientas y métodos.

Laboratorios—investigaciones que usan una versión simplificada del método que los científicos usan.

Prácticas y Problemas Diarios—problemas breves que proveen práctica con técnicas y conceptos matemáticos.

Juegos—juegos matemáticos que estimulan familiaridad con técnicas y conceptos matemáticos.

Libros de Aventuras—historietas ilustradas que tratan con conceptos de las ciencias y matemáticas.

Evaluaciones—actividades que permiten al maestro y a los estudiantes evaluar el progreso.

> "Cuando mi hija mayor comenzó, no tenía confianza con las matemáticas. Y ahora que ha tenido *MATH TRAILBLAZERS*, dice que es buena en las matemáticas. Eso me hace sentir bien."
>
> **Un padre de familia**

¿Cómo es una clase de *MATH TRAILBLAZERS*?

Si usted entra a un salón de clases *MATH TRAILBLAZERS*, probablemente notará que no se parece al que usted asistía cuando tenía esa edad. En ese salón, los niños puedan estar trabajando en grupos, poniendo gotas de agua a toallas de papel, o analizando muestras de confites. Mientras los estudiantes trabajan, ellos discuten diferentes formas para resolver los problemas matemáticos. Se percieve en clases *MATH TRAILBLAZERS* los sentimientos y la emoción de descubrimiento matemático.

En un salón de estas clases los alumnos están:

☆ aprendiendo matemáticas en la resolución de problemas;

☆ usando experiencias propias y trabajando con problemas verdaderas;

☆ usando objetos concretos para entender conceptos matemáticos abstractos;

☆ comunicando sus ideas de matemáticas a sus compañeros y maestros;

☆ adquiriendo confianza en las matemáticas y desarrollando un sentimiento de, "Yo sí lo puedo hacer."

> "Me encanta llegar a una clase donde los estudiantes están recolectando datos. Algunos están en el piso midiendo esto o trabajando con aquello o haciendo preguntas. Es tan emocionante ver los niños enredados en este tipo de descubrimiento de matemáticas."
>
> **Director de escuela primaria**